The Journals of

ANDRÉ GIDE

The Journals of

A N D R É   G I D E

1889–1949

EDITED, TRANSLATED, ABRIDGED, AND
WITH AN INTRODUCTION BY

Justin O'Brien

VOLUME I: 1889–1924

NORTHWESTERN UNIVERSITY PRESS
Evanston, Illinois

NORTHWESTERN UNIVERSITY PRESS PAPERBACK EDITION
Published 1987
Northwestern University Press, Evanston, Illinois 60201

THE JOURNALS OF ANDRÉ GIDE *were originally*
published in English as follows:
VOLUME I, 1889-1913: *September 15, 1947;*
VOLUME II, 1914-1927: *May 24, 1948;*
VOLUME III, 1928-1939: *March 21, 1949;*
VOLUME IV, 1939-1949: *April 16, 1951;*

PUBLISHED IN THE UNITED STATES OF AMERICA

INTRODUCTION

BY

JUSTIN O'BRIEN

Wɪᴛʜ the death of André Gide in February 1951 he who had so long been one of the most present forces in modern letters suddenly became a part of the past. And as that past recedes, he takes his place definitively in the great tradition—related to La Fontaine and Racine by his essential conciseness and crystalline style, to Montaigne and Goethe by his inquiring mind which reconciled unrest and serenity, to Baudelaire by his lucid, prophetic criticism. To be sure, his individual works—not one of which fails to raise, over and above the particular destinies it unfolds, considerations of the most general and most basic kind—will continue to provide subject for dispute. But this only bears witness to the living force that he continues to be and helps to establish his stature among modern writers.

To many today it becomes increasingly apparent that he deserves to live at least for those gems of discreet narration (*L'Immoraliste, La Porte étroite, La Symphonie pastorale*), for his highly ingenious and fruitful experiments in the novel (*Les Caves du Vatican* and *Les Faux-Monnayeurs*), and for his vivid exteriorization of subtle psychological problems in the drama (*Saül, Le Roi Candaule, Œdipe*). Such a conviction has grown simply because many have actually reread this scrupulous author who aimed to write for posterity and clearly stated: "My writings can be compared to Achilles' spear, with which a second contact cured those it had first wounded. If one of my books disconcerts you, reread it; under the obvious poison, I took care to hide the antidote; each one of them aims less to disturb than to warn."

As with the west wind which Shelley calls "destroyer and preserver," so it is with those vigorous, iconoclastic minds which shape our vision of the world. At first we are

aware only of the negative achievement, the havoc wrought
to our intellectual comfort, the shattering of our illusions
and upsetting of our habits. But as time passes we feel
grateful for the positive preservation of true values that
accompanies such destruction.

Like any original thinker and artist, Gide early began
to scandalize. His contemporaries were shocked when he
returned in 1895 from Africa and mocked them in the
first of his ironic works, *Paludes* (*Marshlands*), that brilliant satire on banality and stagnation which showed them
to what an extent they were prisoners of their habits,
their ideas, and their emotions. Two years later, the urgent
call to freedom of *Les Nourritures terrestres* (*The Fruits
of the Earth*) provided another shock. Breaking forth from
the cloistered walls within which French literature was
becoming ever more hermetic, André Gide instinctively
voiced in it the message of Nietzsche and Walt Whitman
and expressed more emphatically than had Pater or Wilde
the doctrine of supreme individualism. While the very
popular Maurice Barrès was teaching the need of rooting
oneself firmly in one's native soil and clinging to tradition,
Gide exhorted his reader: ". . . and when you have read
me, throw this book away—and go out. I should like it
to have made you want to get away—away from anywhere, from your town, from your family, from your room,
from your thought."

Gide always claimed that the true writer must swim
against the current of his time, and the scant admiration
this handbook of revolt originally aroused suggests that he
was already practicing his doctrine. Yet it struck the note
of the future, for twenty years later the little book preach-
ing the cult of unrest and ardor with the attendant glorifi-
cation of desire and spontaneity came to be the chief agent
of that Gidian influence which to conservative critics has
seemed nothing less than diabolical.

"To free oneself is nothing; it's being free that is hard,"
says Michel in *L'Immoraliste*, and this is the problem that
André Gide examined from all sides during the next thirty
years. The over-generous Candaules and the too receptive
Saul (heroes of two early dramas), together with the
protagonist of *L'Immoraliste*, end tragically because of
breaking with conventional morality in their search for

self-realization and thus offer a commentary on the doctrine of *Les Nourritures terrestres*. The heroine of the tale *La Porte étroite* (*Strait Is the Gate*, counterpart of *The Immoralist*) illustrates the dangers of the other extreme, renunciation, and her very different form of selfishness leads to just as tragic a conclusion. In *Le Retour de l'enfant prodigue* (*The Prodigal's Return*) the prodigal son, while admitting his own errors, yet helps his younger brother to escape as he had done. And the attractive hero of *Les Caves du Vatican* (*Lafcadio's Adventures*), born and educated without any reference to tradition, still finds himself the prisoner of a free, unmotivated act he has committed simply to prove his own liberty.

During his period of full maturity between the two wars, André Gide constantly returned to the problem of personal freedom: in his daring memoirs entitled *Si le grain ne meurt . . .* (*If It Die . . .*); in his dialogues on the subject of homosexuality (*Corydon*); in his various studies of criminology; in his tragedy of *Œdipe*, which enacts the struggle of the individualist against religious authority; and in the one work he consented to classify as a novel, *Les Faux-Monnayeurs* of 1926. However fascinating the composition of that rather Dostoyevskian novel may be and however complicated the interweaving of multiple themes in a counterpoint inspired by Bach's *Art of the Fugue, The Counterfeiters* (as this work is known in America) strikes the reader most forcibly as a study of the free individual in opposition to the institution of the family. Once again Gide's long preoccupation with self-realization fused with his equally permanent concern with the nature of virtue. As we watch the evolution of the numerous characters, particularly the adolescents Bernard and Olivier, we are reminded of the author's own early search for a rule of conduct that should combine expression and restraint. His admirable form of equilibrium and his advice: "It is good to follow one's inclination, provided one go upward" have nothing static about them.

The definition of virtue and the problem of self-integration are so fundamental in Gide's work as to make of him a *moraliste* or moral philosopher in the best French tradition. "The only drama that really interests me," he wrote in his *Journals* in 1930, "and that I should always be willing to depict anew, is the debate of the individual with whatever keeps him from being authentic, with whatever is opposed to his integrity, to his integration. Most often the obstacle is within him. And all the rest is merely accidental." This is a capital text for the understanding of all his literary work. Bernard Profitendieu is not the only Gidian hero to wrestle with the angel, nor the early Prometheus the only one upon whom an eagle feeds. In his last great work, the *Thésée* of 1946, Theseus finds himself while venturing into the unknown to slay a baneful monster, never forgetting, however, to unwind his Ariadne's thread which links him to the past and tradition.

But this text is also—since the obstacle is not always within the individual—a key to André Gide's social preoccupations. Having from his earliest years enjoyed an enviable economic independence permitting a life devoted wholly to disinterested art, he could have ignored such concerns. Had he remained faithful to the doctrines of pure art current during the nineties, he would have done so. But with his discovery of life beyond the *cénacles* came also a sense of responsibility and solidarity. His keenly sympathetic nature and anxiety for freedom caused him to become increasingly a champion of the oppressed. As mayor of a small Commune in Normandy (1896), later as a juror in Rouen (1912), and finally as a special envoy of the Colonial Ministry in the Congo (1925–26), he had ample opportunity to observe social injustice. His *Travels in the Congo,* in fact, led to legal reform and eventually to curbing of the industrial concessions in the colonies.

He thus did for the exploited Negroes of central Africa what he had earlier done for the homosexual instinct in his *Corydon.* Indeed, in a public debate that took place in 1935, Gide emphasized the essential relationship of such literary "campaigns" when he said: "Enthusiastically and almost systematically I become the advocate of whatever voice society ordinarily seeks to stifle (oppressed peoples or races, human instincts), of whatever has hitherto been prevented from or incapable of speech, of anything to which the world has been, either intentionally or unintentionally, deaf."

When he made this statement, he was trying to explain his admiration for Soviet Russia and his sympathy toward

Communism, which in the early thirties had shocked even his most faithful admirers and raised another barrier between himself and official honors. For a time, on the other hand, he became the darling of the Communist world—until in 1936 he made a trip through Russia to observe the realization of Utopia at close hand. Appalled by the lack of personal liberty, the intellectual regimentation, the continued existence of poverty he found there, and the reconstitution of social classes that he had hoped were forever abolished, he did not hesitate to speak out in his *Return from the U.S.S.R.* and *Afterthoughts* at the risk of another scandal, this time in other quarters. Once again Gide was ahead of his time. In Soviet Russia, as in the new Germany and Fascist Italy, he now discerned a dangerous current that he instinctively resisted and he once more resolutely took an independent attitude.

Almost every one of André Gide's books constituted a major risk resulting from an inner necessity to speak the truth, no matter how painful. Despite his constantly growing prestige, some of his outspoken writings and the unpopular stand he took on various issues effectively kept his name off the honors-lists which are so much a part of French literary life, while throughout his long career he was to see younger writers, often those formed by his influence, crowned by prize-juries, decorated by the State, and admitted to the supreme honor of membership in the French Academy. By the time he received the international recognition of the Nobel Prize at the age of seventy-eight, he must have been aware himself of the rare distinction of his unadorned lapel and the lack of honors in his biographical listing. Even then, when a journalist asked him if he regretted any of his works, he replied that he would have "bade farewell to the Nobel Prize" if he had had to disown anything to obtain it. But far from having to disavow any of his "subversive" writings, he had the pleasure of hearing them officially praised by the Swedish Academy as "a form of the passionate love of truth that, since Montaigne and Rousseau, has become a necessity in French literature."

The same love of truth is apparent from one end to the other of André Gide's monumental *Journals*. From the age of twenty in 1889 until the last entry of 1949 written in his eightieth year he carefully set down his reflections about men, ideas, events, and himself. Nowhere in his writings did he more consistently practice the cult of sincerity so intimately identified with his name. Originally begun as a literary exercise, the *Journals* little by little assumed more importance in his own eyes until, as André Malraux says, they became almost an obsession with their author, gradually drawing him from art to life, away from Racine toward Stendhal. In their complete form they record sixty years of full and varied life—and not only that of André Gide. The period covered includes the Dreyfus case, the first World War, the spread of Fascism and Communism, and the second World War. Though in each case a noncombatant, André Gide had significant things to say about these and other historical moments. In literature and art, on the other hand, he occupied a position on the front line during the whole of that changing period.

To a growing number of readers the *Journals* appear as Gide's greatest and most enduring work, simply because they reveal the man behind the writer. Like Montaigne's *Essays* and Rousseau's *Confessions,* they display their subject in undress. And his strong personality emerges as that of a moral philosopher at grips with the fundamental problems of humanity. Each of the finished masterpieces that Gide produced—from *The Immoralist* through *The Counterfeiters* to *Theseus*—offers but a partial image of its author through the voluntary simplification dictated by æsthetic reasons. By themselves they would suffice to assure Gide a position among the great, but as a friend once told him, "In order to have a somewhat lifelike portrait of you, one would have to be able to read them all at once. As soon as one knows you well, one understands that all of the states which, out of regard for art, you depict as successive can be simultaneous in you . . ." And he complained that even *Si le grain ne meurt . . .* was disappointing in this regard. The same complaint, however, cannot be made of the *Journals,* whose very informality allows them to reproduce the Protean multivalence of their creator. Only here can we grasp the real personality of André Gide, his *"esprit ondoyant et divers,"* for never has a writer seemed to hesitate, to contradict himself, and to complicate his thought as he did—not even the great

Montaigne, who first used these words about his own mind.

In the *Journals* we see Gide as naturalist, musician, teacher, individualist, moral philosopher, critic, and artist —as an infinitely inquiring spirit ever loath to commit himself to this or that of his many potentialities. And we finally understand here the many temperamental conflicts that produced those antinomies on which his dynamic equilibrium rests—the soul and the flesh, life and art, expression and restraint, the individual and society, ethics and æsthetics, classicism and romanticism, Christ and Christianity, God and the devil. Nor can we fail to note, through all his transformation and growth, an unusual fidelity to his youth.

Obviously the present edition cannot include everything that was contained in the definitive American edition of the *Journals* published between 1947 and 1951. It is hardly desirable that it should, for no private diary of that scope can be uniformly interesting and valuable from beginning to end. Many years ago, Gide himself defined journalism as "everything that will be less interesting tomorrow than today." Our today is already the tomorrow to which he was then referring, and the principle upon which the deletions have been made for this edition is simply that of omitting all that, with the same perspective we enjoy, the author himself would agree to call "journalism."

Among modern writers, André Gide already occupies a very high rank both as thinker and as stylist. For his style he has always been admired even by those of his countrymen who are least sympathetic to his "message." The apparent paradox of his basing his æsthetics on the very classical austerity that he had fled on the ethical plane has been pointed out by commentators. One even suggests that his original puritanism, inculcated by his widowed mother and rigorous upbringing, merely deviated into literary purism, for if the puritan is a purist in morals, the purist is also a puritan in taste.

It might seem that the thought would strike the reader of the *Journals* more obviously than the concern for style. Yet even here can be seen Gide's deliberate forging of a style at once classical and personal until the slightest thing he wrote bore a peculiar mark. From 1889 to 1949 there is a steady progression toward naturalness and assurance and, despite the often apparent artifice, the paragraph becomes more supple. Frequently in these pages the author also discusses his stylistic problems. He tells why he purified his language of metaphors in his first book and then longed for an even poorer, nuder style, for which he sought inspiration in Stendhal. Later, he confesses his desire to achieve inimitability by dint of the secret perfection of his sentences. On the other hand, he often sees the *Journals* themselves as an exercise in spontaneous rapid composition, since, disliking to write rapidly, he must force himself to do so here. Nothing could be more characteristically Gidian, as his adolescence and African experience abundantly illustrate, than this need of constraining himself to cast off constraint.

Perhaps it is above all his literary artistry, as Gide thought himself, that will most contribute to assuring his immortality. For over sixty years André Gide worked to emancipate the minds of men. Some of his ideas have already gained acceptance, and in the future others among them will gradually lose their shocking quality and become part of the common heritage. At such time, his priority as the first to expound them will seem less important, doubtless, than the fact that he expressed those ideas better than anyone else.

The Journals of

ANDRÉ GIDE

Dates in brackets have been supplied by the editor.

1889

Autumn

With Pierre.[1] We climb to the sixth floor of a house in rue Monsieur-le-Prince, looking for a place where our group can meet. Up there we find a huge room seeming even larger because of the lack of furniture. To the left of the door the ceiling slopes downward as in a mansard. Near the floor a small door opens into an attic extending the whole length of the house under the roof. In the opposite wall a window, just waist-high, provides a view over the roofs of the Medical School, over the Latin Quarter, of an expanse of gray houses as far as the eye can see, the Seine and Notre-Dame in the setting sun, and, in the far distance, Montmartre barely visible in the evening mist.

And together we dream of the impecunious student's life in such a room, with an unfettered pen as the only means of earning a living. And at your feet, on the other side of your writing-table, all Paris. And take refuge there with the dream of your masterpiece, and not come out until it is finished.

Rastignac's famous cry as he looks down on the City from the heights of Père Lachaise: "And now . . . you and I come to grips!" [2]

[1] Pierre Louis (who later signed his name: Pierre Louÿs). [Note supplied by the author in the French edition. Such notes will hereafter be indicated by an A. in brackets.]

[2] At the end of Balzac's *Père Goriot.*

1890

I had always felt vaguely that I communicated my zeal to others, but that they lacked the divine spark. I make an exception of Pierre, of course. When I excited them, I used to feel that they were almost on my level of enthusiasm and boldness.

Then it was that J. wanted to come in and that I saw the mediocrity of their writings.

André Walckenaër, if he wrote, would write too well; but he does not feel the need of writing; the work of others is enough for him. Léon Blum does not know; he is still seeking; he is groping; has too much intelligence and not enough personality. Fazy imitates Mendès too subtly; one can't make out what belongs to the pupil and what to the master. Drouin deserts charmingly, with a modesty that sounds so frank I like him for it. And I am left alone with my bankrupt hopes.

Nevertheless, so powerful is my enthusiasm, so naïve my faith, that all this amuses me and I cannot believe in my defeat. If I had more wit, more talent, and above all a more supple personality, less interested in asserting itself —I could have launched the review[1] alone with Louis, or almost alone, playing the parts of several people without anyone's suspecting it. . . . But such a feat is repellent to me; I could not keep it up.

My pride is constantly being irritated by a thousand minute slights. I suffer absurdly from the fact that everybody does not already know what I hope some day to be, what I shall be; that people cannot foretell the work to come just from the look in my eyes.

· · · · · · · · · · · · · · · ·

18 March
I live in expectation. I no longer dare begin anything. My courage is all on edge from repeating over and over

---

[1] Louÿs and Gide dreamed of founding a literary review to add to those which were burgeoning under the influence of the symbolist movement. *La Conque*, edited by Louÿs, finally appeared in March 1891 and ran for eleven numbers, limited to 100 copies each. Several fragments by Gide and many of Valéry's early poems appeared in it.

again: how I shall be working in two weeks, when I give all my time to *Allain!* [2] Oh, those long days of struggling with the work! The thought of them clings to me and keeps me from concentrating on other things now.

My head is cluttered with my work; it tosses about in my head; I can no more read than write; it always gets between the book and my eyes. This is an intolerable mental restlessness. At times I am seized by a mad desire to drop everything, at once, to cancel my lessons, to send everyone packing and ignore the necessity of paying visits, to take refuge in myself "as in a tower," and to develop my vision. . . . But I can do this only in a new, unknown environment. Unless my senses are disoriented I shall fall back into the familiar ruts, into day-dreams built on recollections. Life must be utterly new, and nothing in the surroundings must remind me that, outside, there are other things. The illusion of working in the absolute.

But where? The dream-cell; in the Causses, in the Dauphiné? I thought once of the room I had discovered in Paris; but active life is too close; besides, a real incognito would be impossible; my mind would be too restless. . . . Meanwhile, perhaps a week at Mortefontaine.

One thing is certain, and that is that I drop all lessons, all shackles, in twelve days, or fourteen.

My mind is so taut now that I am afraid it may relapse, may relax at the moment when . . .

10 November

I am still clumsy; I should aim to be clumsy only when I wish to be. *I must learn to keep silent.* Merely from having talked to Albert yesterday about this projected book, my will to see it through was weakened. I must learn to take myself seriously; and not to hold any smug opinion of myself. To have more mobile eyes and a less mobile face. To keep a straight face when I make a joke. Not to applaud every joke made by others. Not to show the same colorless geniality toward everyone. To disconcert at the right moment by keeping a poker face. Especially never to praise two people in the same way, but rather to keep toward each individual a distinct manner from which I would never deviate without intending to.

[2] A part of Gide's first published work, the anonymous *Cahiers d'André Walter* (*André Walter's Notebooks*) (1891).

End of November

Whenever I get ready again to write really sincere notes in this notebook, I shall have to undertake such a disentangling in my cluttered brain that, to stir up all that dust, I am waiting for a series of vast empty hours, a long cold, a convalescence, during which my constantly reawakened curiosities will lie at rest; during which my sole care will be to rediscover myself.

For the last two months I have not enjoyed a single moment of monologue. I am not even egotistical any longer. I am not even any longer. Lost, on the day when I began my book. . . .

RULE OF CONDUCT

First point: Necessity for a rule.

2. Morals consist in establishing a hierarchy among things and in using the lesser to obtain the greater. This is an ideal strategy.

3. Never lose sight of the end. Never prefer the means.

4. Look upon oneself as a means; hence never prefer oneself to the chosen end, to the work.

(At this point a blank space in which the question arises as to the choice of the work, and the free choice of that work. To manifest. And yet . . . Can one choose?)

Thinking of one's salvation: egotism.

The hero must not even think of his salvation. He has *voluntarily* and *fatally* consecrated himself, unto damnation, for the sake of others; in order to manifest.

RULE OF CONDUCT

Pay no attention to *appearing*. *Being* is alone important.

And do not long, through vanity, for a too hasty manifestation of one's essence.

Whence: do not seek to *be* through the vain desire to *appear;* but rather because it is *fitting* to be so.

1891

10 *June*

An impression worth noting (but I shall remember it anyway) is the sound of a piano in a closed-up house (the de Flaux house in Uzès). You open the shutters; the sounds reverberate. Above all the smell; of cretonne and mouse dung. And also the flat notes of the piano; a puny, almost tremulous sound; for playing Bach it is perfect.

One thing that is indisputable is that Pierre Louis is thoroughly practical while I am hardly at all. But I don't want to be. I take pride in not being. Then it is pointless to long for the advantages of something I abhor. *There are certain things that I shall never have.* Oh, if only I could really convince myself of that! But it is very hard. At least I shall not compromise myself by showing that I do desire them. Essential to remain tightly buttoned up in one's attitude like Barbey d'Aurevilly in his frock-coat.

But, in practical matters, I always flounder absurdly. I am bold in taking the first steps, but I stop after the first effort; and you never get returns before the second effort. I make many acquaintances and then neglect to go back and see them because they bore me.

I can never succeed in entirely convincing myself that certain things really exist. It has always seemed to me that they ceased to exist when I stopped thinking about them; or at least that they are no longer interested in me when I cease to be interested in them. To me the world is a mirror, and I am amazed when it gives a bad reflection of me.

One should want *only one thing* and want it constantly. Then one is sure of getting it. But I desire everything and consequently get nothing. Each time I discover, and too late, that one thing had come to me while I was running after another.

One of Louis's dodges, which has always worked, is imagining that he instinctively and passionately desires everything that serves his purpose.

. . .

I must stop puffing up my pride (in this notebook) just for the sake of doing as Stendhal did. The spirit of imitation; watch out for it. It is useless to do something simply because another has done it. One must remember the rule of conduct of the great after having isolated it from the contingent facts of their lives, rather than imitating the little facts.

Dare to be yourself. I must underline that in my head too.

Don't ever do anything through affectation or to make people like you or through imitation or for the pleasure of contradicting.

No compromise (either ethical or artistic). Perhaps it is very dangerous for me to see other people; I always have too great a desire to please; perhaps I need solitude. I might as well admit it frankly: my solitary and sullen childhood made me what I am. Perhaps it would be better to exaggerate that aspect. Perhaps I would find great strength in doing so. (But there should not be any "perhaps" in matters of conduct. There's no use creating question marks. Answer everything in advance. What a ridiculous undertaking! How rash!)

Brunetière talks of the men of the seventeenth century (at least most of them; not Pascal) who never indulged in profound thoughts on life (like Shakespeare's, for instance) or who never dared to express them because society had accustomed those writers to make their thought accessible to women.

I read in Taine (*English Literature*) his description of the celebrations and customs of the Renaissance. Perhaps that was real beauty; utterly physical. Some time ago all that luxurious display would have left me cold. I am reading it at the right moment, when it can most effectively intoxicate me. My mind is becoming voluptuously impious and pagan. I must stress that tendency. I can see the readings I should indulge in: Stendhal, the eighteenth-century *Encyclopedia*, Swift, Condillac . . . to dry up my heart (sear is a better word; everything is mildewed in my heart). Then the vigorous writers and especially the most virile: Aristophanes, Shakespeare, Rabelais . . . these are the ones I must read. . . . And don't worry about the rest. There is enough possibility of tears in my soul to irrigate thirty books.

22 July

Maeterlinck reads me his *Sept Princesses*.[1]

Yesterday saw Bruges and Ostend. Such boredom, such a lugubrious fatigue strikes me as soon as I am in a new town that I can think of nothing but the desire to get away again. I dragged myself through the streets with a real anguish. Even when these things are most worthy of admiration, the idea of seeing them alone appalls me. It seems to me that I am taking from Em.[2] a bit of that delight that we ought to enjoy together. I sleep every afternoon to be able at least to dream a little. Or else I read. The "landscape," instead of distracting me from myself, always assumes desperately the color of my lamentable soul.

At Ostend the sky and the sea were gray; dire desperations rained down on the sea. I wanted to lose myself in a sensual emotion and, while watching the downpour, I absorbed ices. I had a fever. My nose bled all day long.

[early August]

My mind was quibbling just now as to whether one must first be before appearing, or first appear and then be what one appears. (Like the people who first buy on credit and later worry about their debt; appearing before being amounts to getting in debt toward the physical world.)

Perhaps, my mind said, we *are* only in so far as we *appear*.

Moreover the two propositions are false when separated:

1. We *are* for the sake of appearing.

2. We *appear* because we are.

The two must be joined in a mutual dependence. Then you get the desired imperative: *One must be to appear.*

The appearing must not be distinguished from the being; the being asserts itself in the appearing; the appearing is the immediate manifestation of the being.

[1] *The Seven Princesses*, a play (1891).

[2] "Em." stands for Madeleine Rondeaux, André Gide's cousin, whom he married in 1895.

But, after all, what does all this matter!!?

8 October

More than a month of blanks. Talking of myself bores me. A diary is useful during conscious, intentional, and painful spiritual evolutions. Then you want to know where you stand. But anything I should say now would be harpings on myself. An intimate diary is interesting especially when it records the awakening of ideas; or the awakening of the senses at puberty; or else when you feel yourself to be dying.

There is no longer any drama taking place in me; there is now nothing but a lot of ideas stirred up. There is no need to write myself down on paper.

Uzès, 29 December

O Lord, I come back to thee because I believe that all is vanity save knowing thee. Guide me in thy paths of light. I have followed tortuous ways and have thought to enrich myself with false goods. O Lord, have pity on me: the only real good is the good thou givest. I wanted to enrich myself and I impoverished myself. After all that turmoil I am poorer than ever. I remember my former days and my prayers. O Lord, lead me as thou didst in thy paths of light. O Lord, keep me from evil. May my soul again be proud; my soul was becoming ordinary. Oh, may those early struggles and my prayers not be in vain. . . .

I have lost real possessions in the pursuit of vanities that I took to be serious because I saw others believe in them. I must recover the real possessions. "Hold fast to what thou hast." . . . Yet I knew all these things.

31 December

When one has begun to write, the hardest thing is to be sincere. Essential to mull over that idea and to define artistic sincerity. Meanwhile, I hit upon this: the word must never precede the idea. Or else: the word must always be necessitated by the idea. It must be irresistible and inevitable; and the same is true of the sentence, of the whole work of art. And for the artist's whole life, since his vocation must be irresistible. He must be incapable of not writing (I should prefer him to resist himself in the beginning and to suffer therefore).

The fear of not being sincere has been tormenting me for several months and preventing me from writing. Oh, to be utterly and perfectly sincere. . . .

1892

1 January

Wilde, I believe, did me nothing but harm. In his company I had lost the habit of thinking. I had more varied emotions, but had forgotten how to bring order into them. Above all, I could no longer follow the deductions of others. A few thoughts from time to time, but my clumsiness in handling them made me give them up. I return now, with difficulty but also with great delight, to my history of philosophy, where I am studying the problem of language (which I shall take up with Müller and Renan).

3 January

A man's life is his image. At the hour of death we shall be reflected in the past, and, leaning over the mirror of our acts, our souls will recognize *what we are*. Our whole life is spent in sketching an ineradicable portrait of ourselves. The terrible thing is that we don't know this; we do not think of beautifying ourselves. We think of it in speaking of ourselves; we flatter ourselves; but later our terrible portrait will not flatter us. We recount our lives and lie to ourselves, but our life will not lie; it will recount our soul, which will stand before God in its usual posture.

This can therefore be said, which strikes me as a kind of reverse sincerity (on the part of the artist):

Rather than recounting his life as he has lived it, he must live his life as he will recount it. In other words, the portrait of him formed by his life must identify itself with the ideal portrait he desires. And, in still simpler terms, he must be as he wishes to be.

11 January

I am torn by a conflict between the rules of morality and the rules of sincerity.

Morality consists in substituting for the natural creature (the old Adam) a fiction that you prefer. But then you are no longer sincere. The old Adam is the sincere man.

This occurs to me: the old Adam is the poet. The new man, whom you prefer, is the artist. The artist must take

the place of the poet. From the struggle between the two
is born the work of art.

Munich (second day), 12 May

If I do not write any longer in this diary, if I shudder
at the thought of letters to write, this is because I have no
more personal emotions. In fact, I have no more emotions
except those I want to have, or those of other people. On
my good days, and they are becoming frequent again, I
enjoy an intellectual and nervous exaltation that can be
converted, as if at will, into joy or sorrow, without either
one being more pleasant than the other. I am like a well-
tuned harp, which sings, according to the poet's whim, a
gay scherzo or a melancholy andante.

This mental and emotional mood seems to me excellent
for writing. I am myself *ad libitum;* doesn't this amount
to saying that I can take on the emotions of my characters?
The important thing is being capable of emotions, but to
experience only *one's own* would be a sorry limitation.

In any event, egoism is hateful. I am less and less interested in myself and more and more in my work and my
thoughts. I no longer wonder every day and every hour if
I am worthy of my God. But that is a great error; one
must be capable of reflecting even the purest things.

Moreover, the judgments of others do not interest m
any more than my own. But yes, they do, in so far as they
are the statement of a relation between the object and
the person who judges it, which permits me to know them
both better. But it is enough for me if that other person
asserts his judgment; when he tries to explain it, to prove
that he is right, he becomes a bore; one can never prove
anything. "Judge not." Every judgment bears within it the
testimony of our weakness. In my case, the judgments I
have to make sometimes about things are as irresolute as
the emotions that those things arouse. This explains that
boundless uncertainty which upsets my acts when they
must be based on a judgment.

I always see, almost simultaneously, the two sides of
each idea, and the emotion is always polarized in me. But
even though I understand the two poles, I also am keenly
aware, between them, of the point beyond which the
understanding of a mind which takes the strictly personal
view, which can see only one side of truth, which chooses

once and for all one or the other of the two poles, cannot extend.

And when I am talking with a friend, I generally am concerned only with telling him what he thinks, and I myself share his opinion, paying attention only to establishing and measuring the relations between him and things. (This is particularly true with Walckenaër.)

But when I am with two friends and they disagree, I remain on edge between them, not knowing what to say, not daring to take sides with one or the other, accepting every affirmation and rejecting every negation.

After all, these questions of psychology are absurd and petty.

1893

Montpellier, March

. . . which gave to my sorry joys, to each one of them, all the bitterness of sin.

. . . and my greatest joys have been solitary and laden with care.

I lived until the age of twenty-three completely virgin and utterly depraved; crazed to such a point that eventually I came to seek everywhere some bit of flesh on which to press my lips.

Paris, end of April

And now my prayer (for it still is a prayer): O my Lord, let this too narrow ethic burst and let me live, oh, fully; and give me the strength to do so, oh, without fear, and without always thinking that I am about to sin!

It now takes as great an effort to let myself go as it used to take to resist.

That ethic of privation had so thoroughly established itself as my natural rule of conduct that the other is now very painful and difficult for me. I have to urge myself to pleasure. It is painful for me to be happy.

La Roque, 14 July

I shall remember that then, as last year, I read Tacitus as I walked along the avenue of pines and distant landscape (that admirable thirteenth book in which Nero gradually loses his softness and his inborn fears). Nature, all around, seemed imbued with a horrible and dull sadness.

The cultivation of my emotions was bad; the Stendhalian upbringing is unfortunate and dangerous. I have lost the habit of lofty thought; this is a *most regrettable* thing. I live in a facile manner, and this must not go on. Everything in life must be intentional, and the will constantly taut like a muscle.

Yet I do not regret having changed my method for a year; but one must always come back to oneself. No, I do not regret it; I know that everything can be turned to advantage, provided one is conscious about it. *And I*

*have lived much. But one must certainly pull oneself to-
gether.*

[August]

Before leaving I reread all of my journal; I did so with
inexpressible disgust. I find nothing in it but pride; pride
even in the manner of expressing myself. Always some
form of pretentiousness, claiming either to be profound
or to be witty. My pretensions to metaphysics are absurd;
that constant analysis of one's thoughts, that lack of
action, those rules of conduct are the most tiresome, insipid, and almost incomprehensible things in the world
when one has got beyond them. I could never get back
into certain of those moods, which nevertheless I know to
have been sincere. To me this is all over, a closed book,
an emotion that has cooled off forever.

Reacting against all this, I have come to wish not to be
concerned with myself at all, not to worry, when I want to
do something, whether I am doing good or evil, but
simply to do it, and the devil take the consequences! I no
longer want strange or complicated things at all; as for
complicated things, I don't even understand them any
more. I should like to be normal and strong, merely not
to have to think of these things any more.

The desire to compose the pages of this journal deprives them of all worth, even that of sincerity. They do
not really mean anything, never being well enough written
to have a literary value. In short, all of them take for
granted a future fame or celebrity that will confer an
interest upon them. And that is utterly base. Only a few
pious and pure pages satisfy me now. What I dislike the
least in my former self are the moments of prayer.

I almost tore it all up; at least I suppressed many
pages.[1]

La Roque

I wanted to suggest, in the *Tentative amoureuse*, the
influence of the book upon the one who is writing it, and
during that very writing. As the book issues from us it
changes us, modifying the course of our life, just as in
physics those free-hanging vases, full of liquid, are seen,
as they empty, to receive an impulse in the opposite direc-

---

[1] Since then I have almost entirely burned the first journal (1902).
[A.]

tion from that of the liquid's flow. Our acts exercise a retroaction upon us. "Our deeds act upon us as much as we act upon them," said George Eliot.

In my case I was sad because a dream of irrealizable joy was tormenting me. I relate that dream and, isolating the joy from the dream, I make it mine; my dream has broken the spell and I am full of joy.

No action upon an object without retroaction of that object upon the subject. I wanted to indicate that reciprocity, not in one's relations with others, but with oneself. The subject that acts is oneself; the object that retroacts is a literary subject arising in the imagination. This is consequently an indirect method of acting upon oneself that I have outlined; and it is also, more directly, a tale.

Luc and Rachel [2] also want to realize their desire, but while, by writing mine down, I realized it in an ideal way, they, dreaming of the park that they saw only from the outside, want to go in materially; when they do, they experience no joy. In a work of art I rather like to find transposed, on the scale of the characters, the very subject of that work. Nothing throws a clearer light upon it or more surely establishes the proportions of the whole. Thus, in certain paintings of Memling or Quentin Metzys a small convex and dark mirror reflects the interior of the room in which the scene of the painting is taking place. Likewise in Velázquez's painting of the *Meniñas* (but somewhat differently). Finally, in literature, in the play scene in *Hamlet,* and elsewhere in many other plays. In *Wilhelm Meister* the scenes of the puppets or the celebration at the castle. In *The Fall of the House of Usher* the story that is read to Roderick, etc. None of these examples is altogether exact. What would be much more so, and would explain much better what I strove for in my *Cahiers,* in my *Narcisse,* and in the *Tentative,* is a comparison with the device of heraldry that consists in setting in the escutcheon a smaller one "*en abyme,*" at the heart-point.

That retroaction of the subject on itself has always tempted me. It is the very model of the psychological

[2] The protagonists of *La Tentative amoureuse* (*The Attempt at Love*) of 1893.

novel. An angry man tells a story; there is the subject of a book. A man telling a story is not enough; it must be an angry man and there must be a constant connection between his anger and the story he tells.

13 September

RULE OF CONDUCT

Originality; first degree.

I omit the lower degree, which is mere banality; in which man is merely gregarious (he constitutes the crowd).

Therefore: originality consists in depriving oneself of certain things. Personality asserts itself by its limitations.

But, above this, there is a still higher state, to which Goethe achieves, the Olympian. He understands that originality limits, that by being personal he is simply anyone. And by letting himself live in things, like Pan, everywhere, he thrusts aside all limits until he no longer has any but those of the world itself. He becomes banal, but in a superior way.

It is dangerous to try to achieve too early that superior banality. If one does not absorb everything, one loses oneself completely. The mind must be greater than the world and contain it, or else it is pitifully dissolved and is no longer even original.

Whence the two states: first the state of struggle, in which the world is a temptation; one must not yield to things. Then the superior state, to which Proserpine, who always remembered having taken the pomegranate seeds, did not attain; which Goethe entered at once and hence, refusing himself nothing, could write: I felt myself god enough to descend to the daughters of men.

Montpellier, 10 October

Christianity, above all, consoles; but there are naturally happy souls who do not need consolation. Consequently Christianity begins by making such souls unhappy, for otherwise it would have no power over them.

Whereupon, ceasing to call my desires temptations, ceasing to resist them, I strove on the contrary to follow them. Pride seemed to me a less desirable thing. In that splendid egoism full of religion, I now saw, perhaps wrongly, only restrictions and limitations. Self-abandon struck me as a superior wisdom; it seemed to me that I would find in it greater profit for my soul. This was, I am well aware, still a form of egoism, but a newer, more curious form and one that satisfied in me more potential powers. I maintain that expression: satisfy potential powers; this had now become my rule of conduct; I wanted to live powerfully. O beauty! O desires! How skillfully you distracted my soul! That was the time when every smile diverted it; I used to smile myself and was never serious; I abhorred sorrow and protested against my inclinations toward sympathy. What more need I say? What I had begun with effort a charm or habit made me continue without restraint. Yet the habit of asceticism was such that in the beginning I had to force myself toward joy and it was with difficulty that I smiled; but how short a time those efforts lasted! Was I not following, mean-while, perfectly natural laws? This occurred to me from the fact that, to live happily, I had perhaps only to let myself go. I say "perhaps" because I am not quite sure; yet I had the naïveté to be amazed at first; wasn't this exactly what I had wanted: simply to let myself go? . . . I was like a sailor who drops his oars and lets himself drift; at last he takes the time to look at the shores; while he was rowing he saw nothing. My will, so constantly stretched taut, relaxed at present without any function. At first I experienced a mild discomfort; then even that dis-appeared, melting into the infinite charm of living, and of living carelessly. This was the great rest after the long fever; my former anxieties became incomprehensible to me. I was amazed that nature was so beautiful, and I called everything nature.

DETACHED PAGES

"Do you see that wrinkle?" I asked him; "it comes from a horrible fatigue. And the fatigue is the result of my free-dom. Freedom of action is all right when a powerful de-sire, a great passion, or an unflagging will directs it. But not this: having given an equal freedom of the city to all my desires, having welcomed them all with open arms, I now find that all of them at the same time claim the place of honor. I now firmly believe that man is incapable of

choice and that he invariably yields to the strongest temptation. Even renunciation is a temptation of pride, or else
it's the passion of love. A little less understanding of all
the other things (which I am not doing), a little less
attraction toward them, makes action easier; and even the
most voluntary act is merely a concealed surrender to an
inclination. Etc.

Oh, if only my thought could simplify itself! . . . I sit
here, sometimes all morning, *unable* to do anything, tormented by the desire to do everything. The yearning to
educate myself is the greatest temptation for me. I have
twenty books before me, every one of them begun. You
will laugh when I tell you that I cannot read a single one
of them simply because I want so much to read them all.
I read three lines and think of everything else . . . (in
an hour I shall have to go and see Paul and Pierre; good
Lord, I almost forgot Étienne, and he might have been
hurt; on the way I ought to buy some cuffs; and Laure is
expecting me to take her some flowers . . .). Oh, my
time! my time will be frittered away like this until death.
If only I could live on some foreign shore where, the moment I stepped outdoors, I could delight in the sun, the
wind and the infinite horizon of the sea! . . . Perhaps I
ought to go out. My head is tired; a short walk will cure
me. . . . But I had promised myself to spend an hour
at the piano. . . .

Ah, a knock on the door! Someone is coming to see me.
Good Lord! . . . (Saved; this is at least an hour lost!)
Happy, I exclaimed, are those whose every hour is filled
in advance and who are obliged to go *somewhere.* Oh
for a pair of blinders!

Let us beware, Nathanael,[3] of all the instruments of
happiness. And above all let us not choose them. To begin
with, you cannot choose, but it is dangerous even to think
you are choosing, since in order to choose you must judge,
and judging always presupposes . . . ; besides, etc., etc.

FOR THE USE OF M. D.[4]

[3] The character whom Gide addresses in his *Nourritures terrestres*
(*The Fruits of the Earth*), which appeared in 1897.
[4] Marcel Drouin (1870–1946), classmate of André Gide who was
to become his brother-in-law and a distinguished professor of philosophy in Alençon, Bordeaux, and Paris.

Means of enticement and instigation to work.

1. Intellectual means:

(a) The idea of imminent death.

(b) Emulation; precise consciousness of one's period and of the production of others.

(c) Artificial sense of one's age; emulation through comparison with the biographies of great men.

(d) Contemplation of the hard work of the poor; only intense work can excuse my wealth in my own eyes. Wealth considered solely as a permission to work freely.

(e) Comparison of today's work with yesterday's. Then take as a standard the day on which you worked the most and convince yourself by this false reasoning: nothing prevents me from working as much today.

(f) Reading of second-rate or definitely bad works; recognize the enemy and exaggerate the danger. Let your hatred of them urge you to work. (Powerful means, but more dangerous than emulation.)

2. Physical means (all doubtful):

(a) Eat little.

(b) Keep your extremities very warm.

(c) Do not sleep too much (seven hours are enough).

(d) Never try to urge yourself on at the moment of writing by either reading or music; or else choose an ancient author and read, with the proper attitude of piety, only a few lines. The ones I choose in such a case are always the same: Virgil, Molière, and Bach (read without the aid of the piano); Voltaire's *Candide;* or, for quite different reasons, the first volumes of Flaubert's *Correspondance* or Balzac's *Lettres à sa sœur.*

In my room a low bed, a little space, a wooden upright with a broad horizontal board elbow-high, a small square table, a hard straight chair. I create lying down, compose walking up and down, write standing up, copy out sitting down. These four positions have become almost indispensable to me.

I should not cite myself as an example if I did not find it very difficult getting to work. I readily imagine that anyone else works more easily than I and tell myself that, consequently, anyone else could have done just as well what I have done; this allows me the better to scorn. I have never been fundamentally convinced of my superiority over anyone else; this is how I succeed in reconciling a great deal of modesty with a great deal of pride.

(e) Be well. Have been ill.

In the workroom no works of art or very few and very serious ones: (no Botticelli) Masaccio, Michelangelo, Raphael's *School of Athens;* but preferably a few portraits or death-masks: Dante, Pascal, Leopardi, the photograph of Balzac, of . . .

No books other than dictionaries. Nothing must distract or charm. Nothing must rescue you from boredom except your work.

Never indulge in politics and almost never read the newspapers, but never lose an opportunity to talk politics with anyone whatsoever. This will not teach you anything about the *res publica,* but it will inform you admirably as to the character of the people you talk with.

Imagination (in my case) rarely precedes the idea; it is the latter, and never the former, that excites me. But the latter without the former produces nothing but a useless exaltation. The idea of a work is its composition. Because of imagining too rapidly so many writers of today create ephemeral, poorly composed works. With me the idea of a work precedes often by several years its *imagination.*

As soon as the idea of a work takes on consistency— that is, as soon as the work organizes itself—the elaboration consists in little more than suppressing everything that is useless to its *organism.*

I am aware that everything that constitutes the originality of the writer is added unto this; but woe to him who thinks of his personality while writing. It always comes through sufficiently if it is sincere, and Christ's saying is just as true in art: "Whosoever will save his life (his personality) shall lose it."

This preliminary work, then, I perform while walking. Then it is that the outside world has the greatest hold over me and that distraction is most dangerous. For since work must always be natural, you must develop your idea without tension or violence. And sometimes it does not come at once. You have to wait. This requires infinite patience. It's no good to seize hold of the idea against its will; it then seems so surly that you wonder what attracted you in it. The preferred idea comes only when there is no other idea in its place. Hence you can evoke it only by thinking of nothing else. At times I have spent more than an hour waiting for it. If you have the misfortune, feeling nothing coming, to think: "I am wasting my time," it's all over and you *have* wasted your time.

1894

Neuchâtel, *end of September*

The most beautiful things are those that madness prompts and reason writes. Essential to remain between the two, close to madness when you dream and close to reason when you write.

It seems to me that *Paludes*[1] was the work of an invalid, judging from the difficulty I have in getting back to it now. This is a proof, in the reverse, that I have now recovered; lyric enthusiasm does not leave me an instant and the hardest thing to write is this work, so voluntarily narrow. In short, I no longer suffer from the state of mind that forced me to write it; it has become a sort of disinterment.

I am unwilling to understand a rule of conduct which does not permit and even teach the greatest, the finest, and the freest use and development of all our powers.

13 October

O Lord, I must hide this from everyone else, but there are minutes, hours even, when everything in the world strikes me as without order and lost, when every harmony that my mind has invented disintegrates, when the very thought of the pursuit of a higher order is a bore to me, when the sight of poverty upsets me, when my old prayers and my former pious melancholy rise into my heart, when the passive virtue of the humble man again seems to me the most beautiful.

O Lord, give me the strength to reveal my thought to others only as serene, admirable, and mature.

At certain moments I tell myself: I shall never find my way out. One cannot get out. O Lord, teach me!

But this outcry springs from a temporary rule of conduct.

Religious doubts: mediocrity. The description that others have given me of their doubts has always bored

---

[1] *Marshlands*, Gide's first *sotie*, or satirical work, published in 1895.

and embarrassed me. Such doubts are born of a diffident
mind that thinks one can lose sight of God as soon as one
ceases looking in the direction of Mecca.

To create an antagonism between two parts of your
nature, to make of yourself an enemy of nature, can perhaps flatter pride and contribute to poetry, but it is not
reasonable. A clear understanding of God makes one want
to follow the direction of things, the direction of oneself.
That is much more difficult than resisting the current and
at least calls for more wisdom. It presupposes intelligence, which is in no wise necessary to resistance. And
serving God without intelligence (when you have intelligence) amounts to serving him with only a part of yourself.

Laws and rules of conduct are essentially educative and
hence provisional. All well-understood education tends to
the point where it can do without them. All education
tends to negate itself. Laws and rules of conduct are for
the state of childhood; education is an emancipation. A
perfectly wise city or state would live and judge without
laws, the norms being in the minds of its Areopagus. The
wise man lives without a rule of conduct, according to
his wisdom. We must try to reach a higher immorality.

In every relationship lies a possibility of influence.

The history of the past is the story of all the truths that
man has released.

Take upon oneself as much humanity as possible. There
is the correct formula.

1895–1896

LEAVES GATHERED
BY THE WAYSIDE

I

16 December

Race through the corridors joining the Uffizi to the Palazzo Pitti; the wonderful Palatine Gallery. The head of the young man on the left in Giorgione's *Concert* is made of a marvelous substance. All the tones are melted and fused to form a single, new, hitherto unknown color at any given spot on the canvas—and all so closely linked together that you could not take anything away or add a single touch. Your eyes follow the forehead, the temple, the soft approach to the hair, without finding any trace of a joining; it all seems a melted enamel that had been poured in still liquid form onto the canvas.

In front of this painting you think of nothing else, and that is characteristic of a masterpiece: be exclusive; make any other form of beauty seem inferior.

Last year I didn't fully understand Fra Angelico; I seemed to find in him only a wholly pious, moral beauty, and his painting seemed merely a sort of means, the most efficacious possible, of praying. The story of Savonarola, which concerned me at that moment, struck me as the story of the "iconoclast" in its most fearful aspects and I was unwilling to admit that a work of art could have issued from the convent of San Marco. I must confess now that certain works of Fra Angelico are delightful. To be sure, he oversubordinated line to the form. The form was a means of expressing the soul, and the soul a praise of his God—and color a mere addition, a filling-in of the forms—but he colors minutely and smoothly every space and fortunately did not consider too pagan the joy he evidently took in the childlike arrangement of his colors.[1]

---

[1] Absurd judgment. I blush as I reread it today. Fra Angelico is not only a "delightful" painter; he is a great painter. (1902.) [A.]

Looked at the Raphaels of the Tribuna; shadows consist too often for him in a simple darkening of the lighted parts and have no special quality. The pleasure of modeling comes above all from a horror of sharpness, from a need to round the contours without hiding them, and perfection consists in achieving a gradual shading off from the light to the less light to the dark. It has nothing in common with the perfection sought by the colorist—Venetian or Spanish, Dutch or English—always more restless, more difficult, and more debatable. Giorgione, often even more than Titian, painted each passage with a color that seems peculiar, *unique*, though always of a homogeneous quality and participating at once in the adjacent color.

28 December

Saw this morning Roberto Gatteschi, who tells me of his desire to establish an international review, of his volume of poetry, of still another, of his novel.

He would like a preface by Coppée; but he is intelligent and if he talks of Coppée this is because he is ill informed. In Paris he would certainly belong to the *Mercure. . . .*[2]

When you talk to him of the French writers he knows, he cites Daudet, Coppée, Bourget, Zola.

After dinner I joined Roberto Gatteschi at the Arena, where we were to find d'Annunzio. The latter arrives around ten o'clock, and an hour later we leave the circus with Orvieto, who introduces me to his friend. Together we go to the Gambrinus; d'Annunzio indulges with obvious greediness in little vanilla ices served in small cardboard boxes. He sits beside me and talks gracefully and charmingly without, it seems to me, paying any special attention to the role he is playing. He is short; from a distance his face would seem ordinary or already familiar, so devoid is he of any exterior sign of literature or genius. He wears a little pointed beard which is pale blond and talks with a clearly articulated voice, somewhat cold, but

---

[2] *Le Mercure de France,* a literary review (at first monthly, then fortnightly) founded in 1890 and edited by Alfred Vallette. It published all the vigorous young writers and introduced many foreign writers to France. The whole symbolist school rallied around this eclectic periodical, which soon became one of the leading influences in French letters. In 1893 it founded a publishing house by the same name, which was for many years to issue Gide's books.

supple and almost caressing. His eyes are rather cold; he is perhaps rather cruel, but perhaps it is simply the appearance of his delicate sensuality that makes him seem so. He is wearing a black derby, quite unaffectedly.

He asks questions about French writers; talks of Mauclair, Régnier, Paul Adam—and as I say to him laughingly: "But you have read everything!" "Everything," he replies gracefully. "I believe one has to have read everything." "We read everything," he continues, "in the constantly renewed hope of finally finding the masterpiece that we are all awaiting so eagerly." He does not much like Maeterlinck, whose language strikes him as too simple. Ibsen displeases him by "his lack of beauty." "What do you expect?" he says as if to excuse himself; "I am a Latin."

He is preparing a modern drama of classical form and observing the "three unities.". . . With Herelle, last summer, he followed the coast of Greece in a yacht and "read Sophocles under the ruined gates of Mycenæ.". . .

. . . And when I express my amazement that his great erudition allows him so sustained and so perfect a literary production—or that his work as a writer leaves him the time to read so much: "Oh," he says, "I have my own method for reading quickly. I am a terrible worker; nine or ten months in the year without stopping I work twelve hours a day. I have already produced about twenty books."

Moreover, he says this without boasting at all and quite simply. In this way the evening is prolonged without difficulty.

31 December

Em. somewhat tired. Bad overcast weather. I go out a bit toward evening and shadow a couple of fellows who intrigue me. In *Valentin Knox*[3] I shall speak at length of that mania for following people.

In the evening we play parlor games. Em., too ill to take part, went to bed after dinner. And all evening long I suffer because of not having remained with her and think, each time that the door is opened or that someone shouts too loudly, that the noise will waken her and increase her sick headache. At the end of the evening, around midnight, an almost irresistible melancholy takes

[3] A book that Gide projected but never wrote.

hold of me because of the lack of seriousness of all this and because Em. is not with me. I should have liked to leave and never did I so long to return to her. I thought also, amidst the laughter, of Paul's and my so calm and solemn vigil two years ago at Biskra. I wondered how I had formed such a definite decision not to have any personal melancholy and if it really was so definite. Instead of these dances and shouts, at this approach of the New Year, which we like to treat as especially impressive, I longed rather for communal prayers, for a service of divine worship, or merely for a serious vigil. Horror of everything that is not serious—I have always had it. What was Em. thinking of all alone, during this same time? . . .

Rome, January (1896)

This afternoon visited the horrible bulk of St. Peter's. I see Rome through Stendhal, despite myself. I have found the secret of my boredom in Rome: I do not find myself interesting here.

In Rome, saw especially the Palatine, the baths of Caracalla, the Sistine Chapel—but decidedly I do not like Rome.

The small bronze *Boy with a Thorn in His Foot* at the Capitoline Museum (the one on the right) near a statue of the *Diana of Ephesus* is a wonder beyond compare. I do not believe I prefer any ancient work to it—not even the *Niobe* of the Beaux-Arts or the *Sleeping Faun* in Munich. (I have since seen the extraordinary *Mercury as a Fisherman* of Naples.)

The very substance of bronze, smooth and polished like jasper, almost black, seems to lend to the contours a more intentional and durable decisiveness; no flabbiness in spite of so much grace; and the amazing slimness of this body which has not yet reached the age of puberty does not make one regret that the forms are neither more childish nor more fully developed.

Syracuse

See Syracuse in the summer. Then the papyrus of the two banks of the Cyane join together, say our sailor guides, to form above your boat a filigreed vault. The flat boat bumps the shores, tears up the weeds in the shallow water, drags the roots along with a rustling sound. The very low sky pulls the clouds down to earth. The boat goes slowly back upstream.

The spring is surrounded by papyrus formerly planted by the Arabs; I imagine the approaches to the great African lakes as differing very little from this. This spring is at the bottom of a deep basin. Rather thick, the water seems strangely blue. Great azure fish are swimming in it; I should like to throw in a ring. . . . I think of the swimming-pools of Gafsa, those pools of warm water where huge blind fish, supposedly left by the great Tanit, brush against the swimmers and one can see blue snakes wriggling over the tiles on the bottom.

Latomie; closed gardens; caves; orchards in a deep quarry; delicate trickling of the fountain of Venus; liana. This is where prisoners were locked up, in these abandoned quarries. The thick, heavy, moist air was horribly loaded with the scent of orange-flowers. We bit into not quite ripe lemons; the first unbearably acid taste gradually disappeared, leaving only an unbelievably delicate perfume in the mouth. This is a scene of rape, of murder, of abominable passion, one of those subterranean gardens of which Arabian tales speak, in which Aladdin seeks fruits that are precious stones, where the Calender's cousin shuts himself up with his sister and mistress, where the wife of the King of the Islands joins at night the wounded black slave whom her enchantments keep from dying.

Greek theater seen at night at the hour when the moon rises. Above it is the avenue of tombs leading to fields of asphodels. I have never seen anything more silent.

II

[Tunis, February–March]

Now sidewalks have been laid in the souks. In one of the finest alleyways the base of the little columns that support the vault is buried. Twisted, green and red colonnettes with a massive and figured capital. The vault is whitewashed, but barely lighted. Even on the most radiant days these souks are always half-dark. The entrance to the souks is marvelous; I am not speaking of the portico of the mosque, but of that other narrow, withdrawn entrance shaded by a leaning jujube tree which makes a sort of prefatory shade for the dark little alleyway that turns sharply and is lost to view. But the jujube tree, covered with leaves in the autumn, hasn't any yet this spring. This is the beginning of the saddlers' souk; the alley turns, then continues indefinitely.

In the perfumery souk Sadouk-Anoun still sits cross-legged in his little shop, a mere recess in the wall, with its floor elbow-high and cluttered with flasks; but the perfumes he sells today are diluted. On my return to Paris I gave to Valéry the last two authentic bottles, which I saw Sadouk-Anoun fill, using a pipette, with essence of apples and, drop by drop, precious amber. He no longer wraps them up today, now that they are half-filled with a commoner merchandise, so minutely with virgin wax and white thread and doesn't make me pay so dearly for them.

Two years ago, with Laurens, his meticulousness had amused us; it seemed to give their proper value to things. With each added wrapping the perfume became rarer. Finally we stopped him, for our purse would not have sufficed.

I also sought in vain that dark café where the only habitués were tall Negroes from the Sudan. Some of them had their big toe cut as a sign of slavery. Most of them wore, stuck in their turban, a little sprig of white flowers, of fragrant jasmine, which intoxicates them; it falls along the cheek like a curl of the romantic epoch and gives their face an expression of voluptuous languor.

They like the odor of flowers to such an extent that often, not able to smell them strongly enough, they insert the crushed petals in their nostrils. In that café one of them would sing, another would tell stories, and tame doves would fly about and perch on their shoulders.

CARACOUS. A small oblong room, street-stall in the daytime, which collapses at night; a small stage is set up with a curtain of transparent linen as a background for the shadows. Perpendicular to the stage are two benches along the walls. They are for the distinguished members of the audience.

The middle of the room fills up with very young children who sit on the ground and jostle one another. Everyone eats a quantity of melon seeds dried in salt, such a provocative delicacy that my pocket is emptied of them every evening, but I refill it in the morning for two cents. It is true that I give many of them to children.

The oddest thing here is the recesses in the wall, or very uncomfortable bunks like terns' nests, to which you pull yourself up and from which you fall out rather than get down. They are rented only for the whole evening to young habitués. I came back here many evenings; there was almost always the same public, in the same seats, listening to the same plays, and laughing at the same places—like me.

The actor who provides the voice for these shadows is excellent.

CARACOUS. Another shop. Here the play is merely a pretense for assignations. Always the same habitués, from one evening to another, under the benevolent eye of the proprietor. A strangely beautiful child plays the bagpipes; everyone gathers around him; because of him; the others are his gallants. One of them plays that odd drum in the shape of a vase, the bottom of which must be of donkey's skin. The piper makes the café what it is. He seems to smile at everyone without favoring anyone. Some of them recite verses to him or sing them; he replies, approaches, but most often, I think, it does not go beyond a few caresses in front of everyone. This shop is not a brothel, but rather a court of love. At times one of the children gets up and dances; at times two of them together, and then the dance becomes a sort of broad mimicry.

The play itself is almost always obscene. I should like to know the history of Caracous. He must be very ancient. I have been told that he came from Constantinople and that everywhere except Constantinople and Tunis the police would have forbidden his appearance on the stage; he appears only at the time of Ramadan. For forty days everyone fasts from sunrise to sundown; a complete fast —no food, or drink, or tobacco, or perfumes, or women. All the senses held in check all day take their revenge at night and everyone has as good a time as possible. There are certainly other, very religious Arabs who spend the night, after a very frugal meal, in meditations and prayers, just as there are others who continue to have a good time even by day. But that is frequent only in the big cities contaminated by the French; the Arabs ordinarily practice their religion very scrupulously.

El Kantara

We arrived here at the end of the day, a radiant day. Athman had arrived in the morning, had slept a bit in the middle of the day, but had been waiting for us at the station for an hour. That hour seemed long to him. "And yet," he told me, "I thought to myself: now it is only an hour; before it was a whole year."

Three burnooses; a white silk gandurah lined with blue silk and edged with pink; his coat of blue cloth, the enormous brown cord turban clasping the fine white cloth that falls from it, brushes his cheek and floats loose under his chin. This headdress metamorphoses him; last year he was still wearing the child's simple chéchia; at the age of seventeen he wanted the man's complicated turban.

Athman has spent all he had for his "costume," dressing himself up for this reunion. Without his greeting I should hardly have recognized him.

Evening fell slowly; we went through the pass, and the fabulous Orient calmly appeared to us gilded by the sun. We went down under the palm trees, leaving Athman on the road to wait for the carriage that was to follow us. I recognized all the sounds—of the running water and the birds. Everything was just as before, calm, and our arrival changed nothing. In the carriage we followed the edge of the oasis for some distance. On our return the sun was setting; we stopped before the door of a Moorish café, the hour of Ramadan being past. In the courtyard, near us, some camels in heat were fighting. A keeper was shouting at them. The flocks of goats were returning; their hasty feet still made, as last year, the sound of a sterile shower.

From all the houses of gray earth a slender vapor arose, a blue smoke that soon enveloped the whole oasis and made it seem remote. The sky to the west was a very pure blue, so deep that it seemed still saturated with light. The silence became wonderful. You could not even imagine any song breaking it. I felt that I liked this landscape better than any other, perhaps; here more than anywhere else nature encourages contemplation.

Biskra

Yesterday we were in the gardens; we followed the paths that first led us to N'Msid then to Bab-el-Derb. We reached the old fort and returned by way of Sidi-Barkat. The walk was a long one and Em. was tired out by it. Athman was with us and Fedor Rosenberg; and Larbi accompanied us. We had coffee at the entrance to N'Msid in front of the bed of the Oued and the mountains of the Aurès.

I do not like this landscape so much as, on the other side, the vague expanse of the desert. Playing dominoes with us, Larbi constantly cheated and was charming. I am expecting Jammes with a delightful impatience. The earth here speaks a different language, but one that I understand now.

My room last year, on the ground floor of the hotel; with my window open, I was separated from the outside only by the balustrade; with a jump one could be over it. Sadek, Athman's big brother, and several others from the old Biskra would come and rest in my room, during Ramadan, before returning to their village. I had dates, cakes, syrups, and jellies. It was night; Sadek played the flute and it was easy to remain silent for a long time. At night I closed only the blinds. All the sounds from outside came in, and each morning they would waken me before dawn and I would go to the edge of the desert to see the sunrise. At that moment would pass Lascif's flock, made up of the poor people's goats; since they had no garden, they would entrust their goats to him every morning and Lascif would lead them out to graze in the desert. He would go knocking from door to door before dawn; each door would open and let pass a few goats. As he left the village he had more than sixty.

He would go off very far with them, toward the Hot Fountain, where the chokeweeds are and the euphorbiaceæ. There was also a huge ram on which he sometimes rode, he told me, when the way was difficult, or else to pass the time, for he did not know how to play the flute. One morning when he had left without passing under my window, I went to the desert to meet him. I like the desert enormously. The first year I feared it somewhat because

of its wind and sand; moreover, having no destination, I
didn't know when to stop and tired myself quickly. I
preferred the shady paths under the palms, the gardens of
Ouardi, the villages. But last year I went for long walks.
I had no other aim than to lose sight of the oasis. I
walked; I walked until I felt infinitely alone in the plain.
Then I began to look about me. The sands had velvety
patches in the shadow on the slope of their hillocks, where
insects' footprints could be seen; colocynths were wilting,
tiger-beetles were running over the sand; there were marvelous rustlings in each breath of wind and, because of
the intense silence, the most delicate sound could be
heard. At times an eagle would fly up from the direction
of the big dune. This monotonous expanse seemed to me
each day to contain a more apparent diversity.

I knew the keepers of nomadic flocks; I used to go to
meet them; I talked with them; some of them played the
flute. Occasionally I would sit for a long time near them
without doing anything; I always took along a book, but
almost never opened it. Often I did not return until evening. But Athman, to whom I spoke of these excursions,
told me that they were unwise since prowling Arabs frequent the approaches to the oases and rob foreigners
whom they know to be incapable of defending themselves;
it would have been normal for them to attack me. Thereafter he wanted to accompany me, but since he did not
like walking, my expeditions became shorter, then ceased
altogether.

Touggourt, 7 April

Athman tells me the story of Uriah's wife.

According to the Arab tradition, it was while pursuing
a golden dove from hall to hall in his palace that David,
whom he calls Daoud, finally reached that upper terrace
from which he could see Bath-sheba.

Athman relates: ". . . the Jew told him that Moses was
right and that God would receive first the Jews, then the
Arabs, and perhaps even the Christians. The Christian
told him that Christ was right and that God would take
unto himself the Christians, but also the Arabs and even
the Jews. The Arab told him that Mohammed was right
and that God would admit the Arabs into his paradise,

but that he would close the door on the unconverted Jews
and Christians. And when he had heard all three, he
hastened to become a Mussulman."

The Christians have seniority over the Mussulmans, who
say (and enjoy telling me) that if a Christian pronounces
before death the credo of Islam: "God is God and Mohammed is his prophet," he enters paradise before an
Arab.

"The Roumis," [4] they also say, "are superior to us in
many ways, but they are always afraid of death."

Biskra

The sounds of the Negro drum draw us. Negro music!
How often I heard it last year! How often I got up from
my work to hear it! No tones, just rhythm; no melodic
instrument, just long drums, tom-toms, and castanets. . . .
"*Florentes ferulas et grandia lilia quassans,*" [5] castanets that
in their hands make almost the sound of a downpour. In
a trio they execute real compositions; uneven rhythm
oddly cut by syncopated notes, which drives one mad and
sets every muscle in motion. They are the musicians of
funereal, gay, and religious ceremonies; I have seen them
in cemeteries feed the frenzy of the professional mourners;
in a Kairouan mosque exacerbate the mystic rapture of
the Aïssaouas. I have seen them beat out the rhythm for
the club dance and the sacred dances in the little mosque
of Sidi-Maleck. And I was always the only Frenchman to
see them. I don't know where the tourists go; I fancy the
paid guides show them a trashy Africa in order to protect
the Arabs, who like calm and secrecy, from intruders. For
I have never met a single one of them in the neighborhood of anything interesting; nor even, and fortunately,
but rarely in the old villages of the oasis where I used to
return daily until I no longer startled anyone. Yet the
hotels are full of travelers, but they fall into the trap set
by the quack guides and pay dearly for the falsified ceremonies tricked up for them.

There wasn't a Frenchman last year, either, at that extraordinary nocturnal celebration which I witnessed almost
by chance, attracted merely by the sound of the drum and

---

[4] Arab name for Christians.
[5] "Shaking flowering branches and tall lilies." (Virgil: *Bucolics*, X,
line 25.)

the ululation of the women. The celebration was in the Negro village: a dancing procession of women and musicians was going up the main street preceding torch-bearers and a group of laughing children who were leading by the horns a huge black he-goat covered with jewels and stuffs. He had bracelets on his horns, an enormous silver ring in his nostrils; he had necklaces around his neck; he was clothed in a piece of crimson satin. In the crowd that was following I recognized the tall Ashour; he explained to me that the ram was going to be slaughtered during the night to bring luck to the village, but first he was walked through the streets so that the evil spirits of the houses, which remain on the doorsteps, could enter into him and disappear.

Negro music! How many times, far from Africa, I have thought I heard you and suddenly there was re-created around you the whole south. In Rome for instance, Via Gregoriana, when the heavy wagons, going down in the very early morning, used to wake me. Their dull bounces on the paving blocks would deceive me a moment in my half-sleep and then leave me distressed for some time afterward.

We heard the Negro music this morning, but it was not for an ordinary celebration. They were playing in the inner courtyard of a private house, and the men at the entrance wanted at first to keep us out until some Arabs recognized me and protected our entrance. I was amazed at first by the large number of Jewish women gathered there, all very beautiful and richly dressed. The courtyard was full; there barely remained place enough in the middle for the dance. The dust and heat were stifling. A great ray of sunlight fell from the upper opening, whence, as from a balcony, were leaning clusters of children.

The staircase rising to the terrace was also covered with people, all attentive, as we too immediately became; what they were watching was terrible. In the center of the courtyard a large copper basin full of water. Three women got up, three Arab women; they took off their outer garments for the dance, undid their hair in front of the basin, then, bending forward, spread it on the water. The music, already very loud, swelled. Letting their wet hair fall over their shoulders, they danced awhile; it was a

savage dance involving the whole body. If you have not
seen it, nothing could give an idea of it. An old Negress
presided, who kept jumping around the basin and, holding a stick in one hand, occasionally struck the rim. We
were later told, as we were beginning to understand, that
all the women who danced on this day (and sometimes,
so numerous are they, on these two days) were, whether
Jewesses or Arabs, possessed of the demon. Each one in
turn paid to have her right to dance, and the old Negress
with the stick was a famous sorceress who knew the exor-
cisms and was able to make the demons pass from the
bodies of the women into the frequently renewed water.
As soon as it was impure it was thrown into the street.
She who told us all this was the beautiful Jewess Gou-
marr'ha, who did not like to talk about it, because of a
remainder of belief and something like shame to confess
that last year she too, her body horribly knotted with
hysteria, had taken part in the dance "hoping to find some
relief for her suffering." But afterward she had been much
more seriously ill, and her husband, learning that she had
danced at this gathering of witches, had beaten her steadily for three days to cure her.

The dance became animated; the women, haggard,
wild-eyed, seeking to lose consciousness of their flesh, or
better to lose all feeling, were reaching the crisis in which,
their bodies escaping all control of the mind, the exorcism
can operate effectively. After that instant exhaustion,
sweating, dying, in the prostration that follows the crisis,
they were to find the calm of deliverance.

Just now they are kneeling before the basin; their hands
clutching the rim, and their bodies beating from right to
left and forward and backward, swiftly, like a furious
pendulum; their hair whips the water, then spatters their
shoulders; each time they jerk forward they utter a low
cry like that of woodsmen chopping; then suddenly tumble
backward as if they had an epileptic fit, frothing at the
mouth, and their hands twisted.

The evil spirit has left them. The sorceress takes them,
lays them out, dries them, rubs them, stretches them, and,
just as in a treatment for hysteria, seizing them by the
wrists and half raising them up, presses with her foot or
her knee on their abdomen.

There took part today, we are told, more than sixty. The first ones were still twisting about when others rushed forward. One was short and humpbacked, wearing a yellow and green gandurah, unforgettable; her hair, black as ink, covered her completely.

Some Jewesses danced too. They sprang in disorder like delirious teetotums. They made only one leap and fell back immediately, dazed. Others held out longer. . . . Their madness communicated itself to us; we fled, unable to stand it any longer.

LITERATURE AND ETHICS

What in relation to fields we call rotation of crops we call the "cyclic phase of the manic-depressive psychosis" in a man.

Doctrine of sin: being capable of all evil and committing none; that is the definition of good. I do not like this merely negative exercise of the will. I prefer that blindness to evil should result from being dazzled by the good; otherwise virtue is ignorance—poverty.

I can no more be grateful to God for having created me than I could hold it against him for my not existing—if I did not exist.

One ought never to buy anything except with love. Anyone whatever, anything whatsoever, ought always to belong to the person who loves it best. Bread to the most hungry man; the sweet to the one who prefers it or who has already supped. You can explain the drunkenness of the masses on these grounds: they drink to forget that they haven't what they desire; moreover, the drunkenness of the upper classes can be explained in the same way. Drunkenness is never anything but a substitute for happiness. It amounts to buying the dream of a thing when you haven't money enough to buy the dreamed-of thing materially. The bottle that gave drunkenness is worth the Wild Ass's Skin as long as you are drunk. The terrible thing is that one can never get sufficiently drunk.

He thought: the world could have had a different history. The surface of the earth might have been covered otherwise. If the world had never had any other inhabitants than creatures like me, it would have had no history.

I hate all careers that owe their existence only to the spitefulness of men.

In this whole comedy the important acts stand at the two extremities: birth and death. Of one we are not yet aware; of the other we are no longer aware. And it is even likely that as soon as you are buried, you do not remember dying. We are aware only of the death of others—because it makes our life easier.

Individual characteristics are more general (I mean more human) than ethnical characteristics. To restate this: the individual man tries to escape the race. And as soon as he ceases to represent the race, he represents man; the idiosyncrasy is a pretext for generalities.

"The ego is hateful," you say. Not mine. I should have liked it in another; should I be hard to please simply because it is mine? On what worse ego might I not have fallen? (To begin with, I am alive, and that is magnificent.)

I pity you if you find something to hate in yourself. I hate only such sorry ethics. If I like my ego, do not think for a moment that I like yours any the less, or that this is because of my more or less happiness.

But you are alive too, I believe, and that is magnificent.

Social question? Yes indeed. But the ethical question is antecedent.

Man is more interesting than men. God made *him* and not them in his image. Each one is more precious than all.

It is easy to consider the soul as that particle of soil in which many different plants grow and so many insects live. There is superabundance, there is struggle; there will therefore be suppression. It's too much; it's too much! If you do not tear out this one, it will stifle that one. If you tear nothing out, nature will take care of the struggle.

In studying the question of the *raison d'être* of the work of art, one is brought to the conclusion that the justification, the symbol of the work, is its composition.

A well-composed work is necessarily symbolical. Around what could the parts group themselves? What could guide their arrangement except the idea of the work, which creates that symbolic arrangement?

The work of art is the exaggeration of an idea.

I will maintain that an artist needs this: a special world of which he alone has the key. It is not enough that he should bring *one* new thing, although that is already an achievement; but rather that everything in him should be or seem new, seen through a powerfully coloring idiosyncrasy.

He must have a personal philosophy, æsthetics, and ethics; his entire work tends only to reveal it. And that is what makes his style. I have discovered too, and this is very important, that he must have a personal manner of joking, his own sense of humor.

DETACHED PAGES

MEDITATION I (*outline*)

I reread Pascal's admirable passage: "The example of Alexander's chastity has not made so many continent men as that of his drunkenness has made intemperate ones." Etc. . . .

This is the thought that has inspired the frequent attempts to hide the feet of great men. But why should I care on what level their feet rest? Their feet are beautiful. And, indeed, that is not even the question; head and feet belong to the same man; there are secret relationships between them. Who can say whether I may not lose everything by trying to abstract the greatness alone—that is to say, by considering only the emotion or the thought and not the organ that produced them, the fruit without the tree that bore it? The great man's greatness does not lie solely in his head; if he carries his head higher, this is because his whole body is taller.

Moreover, this metaphor is deceptive. There are so many ways of being great; there are so many ways of being beautiful. There are so many ways of deserving men's interest.

*

Sorrento, Villa Arlotta; at Vollmœller's

Who could describe the vividness, the somber magnificence, the order, the rhythmic beauty, the softness of this garden-orchard. . . . I went in under the shade of the orange trees, half weeping, half laughing, and fully intoxicated; through the dense branches one could hardly see the sky. It had rained; the sky was still gray; it seemed that the light came entirely from the profusion of oranges. Their weight bent the branches. The lemon trees, frailer, more gracefully shaped, had less ostentation and greater elegance. At times protective mats above them made an almost dark shelter for them. On the ground, among the trunks whose number, modest height, and oily and polished surface reminded me of the rich pillars in the Córdoba mosque, a thick, unbroken carpet of wood-sorrel of a paler green than lawns, more on the bluish side, more subtle, more fragile. And on the paths of hard black earth, straight, regular, and narrow, where the shade, warmth, and humidity had allowed mosses to creep, one would have liked to walk barefoot.

The garden ended in a terrace, or a cliff rather, dropping straight into the sea. On the extreme edge the orange grove yielded to ilex and pines. A much wider path followed the brink, but in such a way that a fringe of trees rose between the walk and the sea. At intervals, where the rock jutted out, the bold terrace offered a circular bench, a table, a charming spot to rest. On one of these marble benches the diligent gardener had placed some oranges for our pleasure. They were of four kinds: to the largest, almost tasteless, sweet as watermelons, I much preferred the egg-shaped ones with a thick skin; they had an ethereal taste such as I fancy Oriental oranges to have; but I especially delighted in the very small tangerines, hard as lady-apples, with an orangey-green skin of delicate texture that looks like a glove leather. I can't say how many we ate, nor yet, alas, with what (rapture). . . . They satisfied at once both hunger and thirst. From the bench on which we were seated talking, when we threw the skins over the railing, they fell, a few hundred yards below, straight into the sea.

✻

And do not seek to welcome everything; repulse rather. Remember that the Hebrews killed but did not convert. It is always the enemy that one welcomes. The Mussulmans know this too; they do not listen to the thought of others; they resist it. What allows mules to be obstinate is their blinders. And what will you gain by understanding that all the rest has just as much reason to exist as you? Understanding is the beginning of approving. To negate with conviction one must never have looked at what one negates.

✻

(Recollections of the *Affair*.[1]) What constituted Rousseau's strength in his time was that, being the only one in his party, he was able to believe that his party was right. A party is always compromised by *the others;* there are always too many of them; and if there were fewer, the *party* would be too weak.

Yes, Rousseau's strength came from his solitude; for, since there is stupidity everywhere, the danger comes from the fact that one's partisans may exaggerate it; you see that stupidity too clearly and you cease to be convinced. So long as you remain alone on your side, you triumph; the stupidity seems to be all on the other side, and this helps you to get yourself in deeper.

And people think that it is for the sake of meditation that the most convinced theorists need solitude!

No matter: at that time they seemed to lack experience; the Roman experience had become merely historical; it was easy to reason about it. That of the French Revolution is superb. We are still crushed by it.

[1] The *affaire Dreyfus,* the fierce controversy that split France into two camps between the condemnation of Captain Alfred Dreyfus for treason in 1895 and his rehabilitation in 1906.

1902

Each one of us has his own way of deceiving himself. The important thing is to believe in one's own importance. In front of Henri Albert, Léon Blum, Charles Chanvin, Marcel Drouin (whom I had brought together for lunch), out of vanity I launched a few bloomers. Nothing humiliates me more profoundly, causes me to reproach myself more, or is easier for me to do again. I am no good except when alone. In a group it's not so much the others that bore and annoy me; it's myself.

After lunch the conversation becomes animated; that is to say that several talk at one time. Chanvin, Blum, and Albert do not use the same vocabulary; and not one of them is aware of this. The best thing for the one who is listening then is to be silent, if he doesn't want to have the three others jump on him at once.

The question is to what extent Stendhal loved women, what he wanted of them, and what he actually did with them. Chanvin confused everything by calling "sensuality" what I should call the risqué spirit. One ought to begin by defining one's terms.

In my opinion,[1] Stendhal felt much more interest in than love for women. I can readily conceive of him as proving to himself, at the brothel, that he is not so impotent as his subtlety makes him seem in the company of ladies and actresses.

He makes one recognize his mind to be more beautiful than his body. If I had been a woman, no one would have seemed to me less pleasing to satisfy and more pleasing to put off than Stendhal. To refuse oneself was to "stand up to him"; and in doing so one had the best of him.

Then, abruptly, and as if we already knew it, Henri Albert begins talking to us of Stendhal's syphilis! Then of Flaubert's!! We protest; he insists. . . . Marcel Drouin and I have just read Duclaux's lecture in which it is

[1] I transcribe this passage although today, 25 March, it strikes me as rather false. I must admit finding in the *Souvenirs d'égotisme* (p. 23): "In ten years I have not gone to the brothel three times." [A.]

stated that in any human gathering you can count one syphilitic out of six; and Drouin thinks: "What luck that there are only five of us!"

8 January

Why do I limit *L'Immoraliste*[2] to three hundred copies? . . . To hide from myself as much as possible the bad sale I know I shall have. If twelve hundred were printed, its sale would seem to me four times as bad; I should suffer four times as much.

Besides, everyone ought to risk a new adventure. I alone can risk this one; everything inclines me toward it; it amuses me; its results will educate me the more because they are unforeseen, and that is the real consideration.

Quietly spent yesterday evening finishing *Lamiel*[3] and meditating. I foresaw that it would be *indispensable* for me to go out. I did not go out, and I am not any the worse off (I even spent a rather good night). Two years ago I should have had to stay out until three in the morning, after having prowled the boulevards from ten o'clock on. I seem wiser; I am older.

10 January

Stendhal's need to write. . . . The need that makes me write these notes has nothing spontaneous, nothing irresistible about it. I have never enjoyed *writing rapidly.* That's why I want to force myself to do so.

10 p.m.

Alexandre S. met on the boulevards. At nineteen he is hardly any less beautiful than at fifteen. Yet he has perhaps lost some of that paleness, of that delicacy of features, which at first made us take him for Spanish.

I am with Ghéon. Alexandre says as he accosts us: "I have just lost my wife." (The little Aline with whom he had been living for a year.) "We quarreled too much," he adds. And he tells how, on New Year's Eve, when he had been even more brutal than usual, the poor girl, unable to stand it any longer, had fled to a friend's. The other girl, a morphine addict, advised her to take an injection. Did Aline make a mistake in measuring the dose?

[2] His tale *The Immoralist*, published by the *Mercure de France* in 1902.

[3] A novel by Stendhal, published posthumously in 1889.

or did she deliberately increase it? . . . She took so much that an hour later she was dead.

"You must have read it in the papers," says Alexandre by way of conclusion.

I ask him rather stupidly if this saddened him greatly.

"Of course!" he says; "we were very much in love. . . . And besides, now I don't know how to get along."

She used to bring in considerable money since the time when he gave up his original craft as a diamond-cutter. While waiting to make up his mind on a new trade, he dabbles in them all; and God only knows how many there are! Ah, if he only didn't lie, how much one would learn just to hear him talk! . . .

He claims to be completely secure from the police (they almost all say that); and he relates his tricks endlessly. We go into a little café on the boulevard Montmartre and, on the marble-topped table, where he orders a hot milk, I a kirsch, and Ghéon a sort of syrup, he spreads out his papers. His wallet is full of excellent recommendations, letters from jewelers for whom he used to work, etc. . . .

"And look! Search me if you wish; I never keep a paper that might compromise me."

Yet here is a letter from a state engineer, on a mission in Tonkin; a photograph of the engineer surrounded by Tonkinese men and women. Then another letter from the same, which he reads us and for which an anti-administration newspaper would pay dearly. . . . The engineer tells everything they are doing over there and especially what they are not doing; all they are costing the state and the little return they are giving. If I could only have made a copy! . . . In short, Alexandre would like to go and join his friend, whose constant companion he was for over two years. They lived, ate, and slept together. The engineer rarely went out, but he almost never went anywhere without Alexandre, whom he passed off as his cousin. He has been gone six months now.

Then Alexandre tells about last summer, his season at Trouville and Havre. Two women, one in Trouville and the other in Havre, kept him. He spent his days with one, and with the other his nights. Every morning he took the Trouville boat and went to play the races or the casino. Every evening he took the Havre boat back again.

"Ah!" he says, "I had a good time! I led the life of a prince. I had a hotel room, a fifty-franc room. . . ."

One evening, returning to Havre, he found an empty bed; his mistress, tired of waiting for him, had run off with an Englishman.

I ask him what has become of little Auguste, whom, some time ago, he used to introduce as his brother. But he never sees him any more and doesn't seem to enjoy talking about him. "He is in Madagascar," he says. The last time that I saw Auguste myself, he had just got out of the Petite Roquette prison.

Last night Ducoté's last Thursday reception. (He is leaving for Italy.) I get there about ten o'clock, having first stopped in at the Charles Gides'.

Leaving Ducoté's, Charles-Louis Philippe accompanies me. We walk for a long time on the boulevards.

"The thing that embarrasses me when I talk with you," he says, "is that I haven't yet discovered when you find me interesting."

"But precisely when you say such things as that, my dear Philippe."

12 January

Spent yesterday evening with Jules Iehl. It is the first time I have talked with him alone. Wonderful figure of Iehl, perhaps the most remarkable of this whole "generation" (I mean of this whole group) and I was about to write: of all of us.

Since he works in his office until eight o'clock, I wait for him at the door and together we go to dine in a little restaurant opposite the Café Voltaire.

During the whole dinner, forgetting to eat, he talks. (I have noted elsewhere the tale of his relations with Mme Audoux's niece.)

"But," I say when he has finished, "why don't you write all this down? Just as you have told it to me. . . . It's just as beautiful as *Krotkaïa*.[4]

"Oh!" he replies, "what will you say when I tell you the story of Madame Audoux? Yes, I shall write that one up, because I played no part in it. It's odd, but I have

---

[4] A fragment of Dostoyevsky's *Journal* for November 1876, translated by C. Garnett as "A Gentle Spirit."

no desire to write, or more exactly, I *cannot* write a story except when I am out of it altogether."

We talk of death. He says he does not fear it. I tell him of my continual "expectation of the worst."

"I understand that very well," he continues; "but . . . no, I know nothing of that feeling. . . ." He is silent a moment; then softly: "And that's because I have always lived the worst. Yes, the only surprising thing that could happen to me is happiness."

He says this without any pose whatever, just as naturally as he said all the rest.

I have a sort of respect for Iehl. That is to say that I need his esteem.

18 January

Émile X. used to work in his father's tailoring shop. But for the last two months the fact that they are working on half-time leaves him free almost every day. And every day he spends his whole afternoon at the baths. He gets there at one and stays until seven. Is that why he is as beautiful as a Greek statue? He swims remarkably well; and nothing so much as swimming imposes a rhythm, a harmony on one's muscles, or so hardens and lengthens them. Naked he is perfectly at ease; it is when clothed that he seems awkward. In his workman's clothes I hardly recognized him. Most likely he also owes to the habit of nudity the dull and even luster of his flesh. Everywhere his skin is blond and downy; on the hollows of his sacrum, exactly on the spot where ancient statuary puts the little tuft on fauns, this slight down becomes darker. And indeed yesterday afternoon, in the Praxiteles pose, his shoulder leaning against the wall of the pool, firmly and most naturally planted like the Apollo Saurochtonus, with his slightly snub-nosed and mocking face, he looked like a latter-day faun.

He is fifteen; one sister and one brother; all that remains of eleven children.

Sunday

We talk of the Goncourts:

"According to what I have been able to verify," says Jacques Blanche, "nothing is less true than their journals. Of certain conversations in which I took part, which I remembered perfectly, I was sure of finding in their journals only the least noteworthy bits, and even then often completely falsified. I assure you, Gide, that they didn't know how to listen. There is a paragraph in which they speak of my father and me—why, it's ridiculous; they misunderstood everything. . . . Listen: I remember a wonderful dinner I enjoyed with my father, Edmond de Goncourt, and Sardou. Sardou was in such good form that he was staggering, dazzling; he talked, during almost the whole dinner, about the French Revolution; Goncourt didn't say anything, but kept making indignant gestures at my father; he seemed to be saying: 'Just listen to him! Just listen to him!' That evening we took Goncourt home in our carriage as we often did. As soon as we had left Sardou, Goncourt began: 'No! But did you hear him? . . . And he dares to relate, in front of *me*, Goncourt, the historian of the Revolution, me who— But it was teeming with errors. . . .' And I am certain," added Blanche, "that Goncourt was the one who was wrong; that Sardou was just as well informed as he about the period; and that Goncourt's annoyance came from the fact that Sardou eclipsed him. For at one moment in the dinner, Goncourt having attempted to contradict, Sardou had immediately 'nailed' him like an unprepared pupil. He didn't know how to listen. He didn't understand what was interesting. For instance, I have seen him with Princess Mathilde. The Princess was an astonishing woman; one of the most remarkable dramas I have ever witnessed was going on within and around her. That woman was in love with Popelin, wildly in love; she dreamed, as a way of avoiding a misalliance, of a sort of legitimate concubinage, with all the obligations and all the fidelities of marriage. My father and Goncourt were the only ones she took into her confidence. . . . Well, Goncourt saw nothing, felt nothing, understood nothing in all this; and despite the fact that everything was told him! He was not at all intelligent."

"But," I say, "the words that he puts into the mouths of various people, however false they may be according to you, are almost never uninteresting. Watch out, for the more you reduce his stature as a stenographer, the greater you make him as a writer, as a creator. . . ."

Then we talk of Hugo and, at Blanche's urging, I recite to him several passages from the *Contemplations* and the

Légende des siècles; but I recite very badly and with a choking voice because he repeated to me a few minutes before the remark of (?—Henri de Régnier I suppose): "Gide does not like poetry." And I couldn't have proved this more conclusively if I had aimed to do so.

Dinner at the Charles Gides'. Returning home from dinner, irritated and dejected at not having been able to work almost all day, I calm myself by writing these notes.

20 January

Théo Van Rysselberghe is worn out and irritated by his painting (*Three Little Girls on a Sofa*).

"But—suppose you let it drop for a while?"

"Impossible! I can't stop thinking about it."

"Well then, work on it madly for a while."

"Impossible! . . . As soon as I touch it now, I spoil it. . . ."

His face is haggard with anxiety.

After dinner Philippe reads us the last two chapters of his *Père Perdrix*.[5] The next to the last especially seems to us excellent; and Philippe reads it very well.

21 January

This morning, letter from Marcel Drouin protesting against Philippe's last two articles. He is right. But each one of us, even without knowing it, works on the pedestal for his bust almost as much as on the bust itself. It's a question of placing oneself "in a good light."

Every morning I go to the Louvre, and I am at loose ends every Monday, when it's closed.

Spent an hour or two at J. C. Mardrus's. Mme Mardrus, charming, plays with her rings on the divan where I am half stretched out. J. C. Mardrus, in an old-fashioned dark-blue waistcoat speckled with white, under a vast camel's-hair dressing-gown, wide open, and which makes X. say as he comes in: "What! Are you ill?"

Mardrus relates: "Leaving the café, I meet Henri de Régnier. He *adds himself to me* for a time. . . ."

Mardrus cannot forgive Henri de Régnier for the fact that he is still writing "Schéhérazade."

Paul Valéry's affection; it is childlike and charming. No one understands friendship so nicely or has so much delicacy. I have the greatest affection for him; it takes

[5] *Papa Partridge*, published in 1902.

everything he says to diminish it. He is one of my best
friends; if he were deaf and dumb I could not want a
better one.

1 February

Yesterday, with Em. to the Anatomical Museum and
the Museum of Paleontology; pursued by the remark of
the Goncourts: "At the Jardin des Plantes . . . very little
outlay of imagination on the part of the Creator. Far too
many repetitions of forms among the animals." (*Journal,*
I, p. 231.)

The pettiness of a mind can be measured by the pettiness of its adoration or its blasphemy. Truly, those minds
understood nothing about God. This ceases to be atheism
and becomes sheer stupidity. Fancy being disappointed
at not finding more absurdity! Seeking, and regretting not
finding, a greater number of forms where those that exist
suffice; where adaptation tends toward simplification, toward an ever greater partial standardization; this is the
way beauty is slowly acquired. To be unable to admire
economy, the suppression of the useless, as much as one
would have admired fantasy, the inappropriate, and the
gratuitous. . . . Sure indication of a limited intelligence
that perceives only details, does not go beyond them,
and, thinking it is composing, merely juxtaposes.

There is nothing more *illuminating* than to go from the
hall of paleontology to the hall of comparative anatomy.
Why do species disappear? . . . There is always a reason
for their doing so. How many odd, irrational, monstrous
forms nature originally proposes and later is obliged to
drop!

5 February

Ghéon, after having wandered aimlessly for some time
around the central markets last Tuesday, ended up between three and four in the morning (his train was to
leave at six) in a wretched little café near the Pont-Neuf.
Inside there were many pimps and tarts; and this wouldn't
have been very odd were it not for the presence in such a
group of an elderly gentleman, who would have seemed
very respectable if he had not been decidedly in his cups.
Very much the center of things because he was buying
drinks; talking a great deal, footing the bill, acting as
everyone's tool. The others amuse themselves by making

him rage, laugh, or cry, according to their whim. At moments he seems to reach a decision, says: "I must be going," gets up, then sits down again, without any more effort of will to remain than to go. He lets them laugh at him, make fun of him, rob him; he protests a minute, then grovels. Around him, as part of the game, one pretends to pity him, another to treat him contemptuously; a prostitute pretends to be in love with him; they take off his hat; they pull his hair. . . . (Ghéon gives a spirited mimicry of the whole scene; at one and the same time he becomes the elderly gentleman, the procurers, the tarts; and since everything is in the way he does it, there is not much to write about it.)

Beside Ghéon a pimp had sat down who showed a great scorn for the others:

"It's disgusting; it's shameful," he said after they had just pinched a few more coins. "And would you believe it, sir, every evening the same scene takes place? Yes, the same scene. That gentleman comes here every evening. And every morning he doesn't get home until about six o'clock, and with sixty francs less in his pocket. It's disgusting!"

"Do you know who your elderly gentleman is?" I asked Ghéon. "He is THE WIDOWER."

Saturday, 8 February

At old Papa La Pérouse's.[6] His joy to see me again. He sadly reproaches me for not having come sooner. . . . He comes out onto the stairway with me, awkwardly holds my hand tightly clasped in his, then suddenly, not able to resist any longer, makes me go back up three steps and falls sobbing into my arms.

For not having gone to Petersburg I feel, not so much regret, as remorse. Giving yourself your word to do something ought to be no less sacred than giving your word to others.

9 February

There is plenty of claptrap in this. And that's what seems to me abominable. Racine is good enough to get

---

[6] Pseudonym for Marc de La Nux (1830–1914), André Gide's revered piano teacher. The same pseudonym appears in *Si le grain ne meurt . . .* and in *Les Faux-Monnayeurs*.

along without being played up to the audience. Sardou isn't. The habit of playing mediocre dramatists makes the actor see his contribution as too important. He therefore uses the same artifice in presenting Racine's pure gold as in foisting upon us Sardou's tin-plate.

During the first two acts I was sobbing; I didn't think I could see it through, so great was my emotion. I thought I was admiring Sarah;[7] but I was especially admiring Racine; and there was no mistake about it in the following acts. I couldn't see it through, in fact, but because of my annoyance. As long as she remained in the tone of the first two acts, I was aware only of Racine. But with the beginning of the third there was nothing but Sarah. At the fourth I left. Plastically she was marvelous. And just as she is, despite all her shortcomings, she remains unique, incomparable. What she should have had is a Sardou with the qualities of a Racine; and an intelligent public that would not applaud her when she is at her worst.

Sunday

. . . I have in my body and mind all I need to be, and to keep from being, a "great man." If I only knew how to deceive myself. . . . But I am still looking for maxims. What shall I become at Cuverville?

. . . And with that self-esteem which I had painfully acquired through pride, I was fed up and disgusted. I strained my ingenuity to lose it, and this was not hard. Acquisitions are worth amassing only for the sake of spending them easily later on. I gave myself up therefore to debauch; and indeed it did not displease me to introduce a bit of system into it; I mean to work hard at it. I envied ———, who got nothing but pleasure from it; I also gave myself a lot of trouble.

[Cuverville,] 23 March

The weather continues to be rainy, cold, and forbidding. But I am much better and, again, feel very fit for work.

Study of Schubert's Fantasie in C and Impromptus. I am reading Renan's *Souvenirs* and Stendhal's.

Since we have been here—that is, since the 2nd of March—without even excepting the two days in Paris, I have got up at six o'clock at the latest; almost every day I

[7] Sarah Bernhardt.

am at work at five thirty; and sometimes even at five o'clock. The day, according to the weather, is devoted, without a regular schedule, to gardening, reading, and piano-practice. The garden takes (and especially took in the beginning) an enormous amount of time. The drawing-room not being ready yet, Em. remains in the dining-room and I in my study; a fire is lighted in the two rooms and the big stove heats the rest of the house. Then dinner comes; in the evening we bring our lamps together.

25 March

Hellebores, lilies, and tiger-lilies have come from Holland. From seven in the morning until six in the evening I work in the garden without stopping.

27 March

Than that some day a young man of my age and my *worth* should be stirred as he reads me and *made over,* as I still am at thirty on reading Stendhal's *Souvenirs d'égotisme,* I have no other ambition. At least so it seems to me as I read this book.

Of my trip to Paris, too much to be said. Of my return here, not enough. Read a rather long speech by Brunetière on Calvin. We continue reading aloud Tolstoy's *Cossacks.*

Francis Jammes. He feels the need of constantly persuading you (or trying to persuade you) that he is much poorer, simpler, more modest, etc., than he is.

1903

Cuverville, April

These letters to write exhaust me, wear out my patience; they won't let me work. . . . No friendship matters in such a case; I would throw out the best friend. . . . But I don't. I always write eventually; to have peace, peace with myself; for, so long as I don't write, I reproach myself for not writing. The trouble is that when you write immediately, the one on the other end answers; and yet, until he has answered, I wait for his letter.

May

Georges reminded me of Mlle Siller's shocked amazement, two years ago, when she heard me say (to startle her, but in an offhand way): "And to think that if I didn't like literature so much I should already be in the Academy!"

Weimar

Blond hair; pure blue eyes like a *Vergissmeinnicht*. Though Mme Förster-Nietzsche was expecting me at five o'clock for tea, I tarried with the child, and a still younger child came to join him. We climbed up on a haystack; I hoisted them up onto the top and my clothes were soon full of bits of straw.

Mme Förster-Nietzsche, getting tired meanwhile of waiting for me, had started out in a carriage to look for me. In turn I started with the child to look for her. He accompanied me in the streets; he gave me his hand and talked constantly, in a full and transparent voice, although I understood but very little. When I went into Count Kessler's to pack my luggage (since I was to leave that evening), the child stationed himself, with two little comrades, on the steps of the house opposite; he was waiting; occasionally, from the window, I would wave to him, and he would reply laughing. He refused to believe in my departure, and when I spoke of it, he said: "*Es ist nicht wahr!*" Finally Mme Förster-Nietzsche's big landau called for me; I went down. Mme Förster-Nietzsche was in the

carriage. I almost made the children get in. The tall foot-
man covered with braid who helped me into my coat
dazzled them; I was aware that they took me for a prince;
and when I turned around for a last farewell, I saw my
little friend weeping.

Sunday, back in Paris.

1904

Wednesday, 17 March (?)

At the banquet for Edmund Gosse, Verhaeren is seated between Maeterlinck and Henri de Régnier; Verhaeren to Maeterlinck (in a whisper):

". . . Besides, in my case . . . I can confess this to you . . . in reality, the only writing that interests me is my own."

And Maeterlinck: "That's just like me . . . moreover, even what I write doesn't interest me much any more."

Whereupon Verhaeren, giving a jump: "Oh, just a minute! That's not the same thing at all. What I write interests me passionately—passionately, you understand . . . and that's the very reason why I am no longer much interested in the writings of others."

It is Verhaeren himself who tells this, the next day, in Théo Van Rysselberghe's studio. He adds:

"And a little later Maeterlinck told me also: 'What's more, I now work only out of habit.'"

At the offices of the *Revue des idées*,[1] where I had gone to inquire about the fate of Marcel Drouin's articles. Dujardin and Gourmont are there, whom I have not seen since . . . (?) Long before meeting Gourmont, I knew, I had a premonition that in his presence I should feel this discomfort, or rather this hostility. He has always been very considerate with me. But what can I do about it? I have read things by him that reveal a keen mind, a solid intelligence. . . . I collect my thoughts, reason with myself, stiffen myself. This time too I wanted to see him again and I approached him beaming with smiles. But I cannot: he is too ugly. I am not speaking of his superficial misfortune; no, but of a deeper ugliness. I declare that I already knew him to be ugly simply from reading him.

And I try to understand a little better the reason for my suffering in his presence. It comes, I think, even upon

---

[1] A monthly review (1904–13), edited by Edouard Dujardin and Remy de Gourmont, which was more concerned with philosophy and the sciences than with literature.

reading him, from the fact that with him thought is never a living, suffering thing; he always remains somewhere beyond it and handles it like an instrument. His reasonings, for he does reason and very well, are never involuntary. His thought never bleeds when he touches it; and this is what allows him to operate on it so easily. He brutalizes. What a heartless surgeon! And how I suffer in his presence! That abstract matter that he seizes remains so alive in me! I made great efforts to talk calmly with him. Quinton arrived . . . and I left.

The discomfort, the suffering that I experience on hearing them talk does not come only from my mind's difficulty in following them, but also, and especially, from a more subtle cause. There is, for thought too, an appropriate beauty, a grace, the lack of which always causes me a certain uneasiness. In their company I think irresistibly of men who, when lifting weights, exercise only their biceps. I do not like big strong arms, I like a harmony of the whole body. Likewise a certain harmony of the mind. As I grow older I can less easily get along without it.

". . . since no luminous body has ever seen the shadow of the body that it lights . . ." (Leonardo da Vinci: *Treatise on Painting*, Ch. cccxxviii.)

3 May

Met Blanche in the Luxembourg; I was with Jaloux, who had just arrived from Marseille. Blanche was with I don't know whom.

Every time I meet Blanche, I feel immediately that I am not wearing the proper necktie, that my hat has not been brushed, and that my cuffs are soiled. This bothers me much more than what I am about to say to him.

Have I already noted somewhere the conversation he had with Régnier? I was there and I heard this:

"Oh, my friend, what stunning trousers you have on! Where did you get them?"

And Régnier, considerably irritated, replied with dignity and roguishness:

"From the cleaner's."

De Groux could not swallow (following other grievances) the fact that Léon Bloy should say and repeat to him:

"You must, you see—you must vomit yourself—on others."

November

Since 25 October 1901, the day on which I finished *L'Immoraliste*, I have not seriously worked. My article on Wilde,[2] my lecture in Germany,[3] the recent one in Brussels (which did not amuse me and which I gave very badly)[4] don't count. A dull torpor of the mind has made me vegetate for the last three years. Perhaps, busy in my garden, in daily contact with the plants, I have taken on their habits. The least sentence costs me an effort; talking, moreover, is almost as painful as writing. And I must admit too that I was becoming difficult: at the least suspicion of a thought, some cantankerous critic, always hiding deep in my mind, would rise up to ask: "Are you sure that it's worth the trouble to . . . ?" And, since the trouble was enormous, the thought immediately withdrew.

The trip to Germany last summer shook off my apathy somewhat; but as soon as I got back here, it took a deeper hold on me. I accused the weather (it rained incessantly that year); I accused the air of Cuverville (and I still fear that it exerts a soporific influence over me); I accused my routine (indeed, it was very bad; I never left the garden, where, for hours on end, I would *contemplate* the plants one after another); I indicted my morals (and how could my utterly stagnant mind have triumphed over my body?). The fact is that I was becoming stultified; no enthusiasm, no joy. Eventually, seriously worried, intent on shaking off that torpor to which was added an unhealthy restlessness, I convinced myself and convinced Em. that nothing but the diversion of travel could save me from myself. To tell the truth, I did not convince Em. I was well aware of this, but what could I do? Go ahead anyway. I therefore resolved to go. I almost killed myself in efforts to justify my conduct; going was not enough for me; in addition Em. had to approve of my going. I hurled myself against a disheartening wall of indifference. No, I did not hurl myself; I sank in; I lost my footing; I was engulfed.

[2] Written in December 1901 for the first anniversary of Wilde's death.
[3] *On the Importance of the Public*, given at Weimar on 5 August 1903.
[4] *The Evolution of the Theater*, given 25 March 1904.

I know well enough today and already suspected then the
lamentable misunderstanding caused by Em.'s voluntary
(and yet almost unconscious)—abnegation (I can think
of no other word to describe it). It contributed not a little
to demoralizing me. Nothing more painful than the exaggeration of my restlessness, of my feelings, etc., to overcome that indifference. Fortunately, the memory of all
that is fading now. . . . But if I had to relive my life, I
could not see that period approach without anguish. . . .

And all the same, I started out (leaving behind minutely
detailed instructions for the setting out of fruit trees that
Croux was to send somewhat later). I started out, then
(as well as I can remember, the 10th of October), and
first took Dominique back to his parents in Bordeaux. I
planned to reach Africa by way of Spain; the ships' sail-
ings did not permit this. My horror of ocean-crossings
almost made me hesitate; but in Marseille, where I arrived around six in the morning, the radiant weather and
the lack of wind made up my mind for me and I reserved
my berth for the afternoon of the same day.

I was planning a book on Africa; I had not been able
to write it at Cuverville from the very insufficient notes I
had brought back from the trip with Em. and Ghéon. I
had to see the country again. I set out with the intention
of writing from day to day. Considerations, reflections, all
that can be added later; what cannot be recaptured or
invented is the sensation.

It is from this trip that I brought back the notes that I
put together (almost without changing a word) on my
return to Cuverville.[5] Em. joined me in Algiers more than
a month after my departure. That month of solitude put
me back on my feet; then the calm life that we lived together left nothing but good memories. In Algiers, and
during the rest of the trip, I was able to read the first
volume of Nietzsche's *Correspondence*, and that book
contributed not a little to my equilibrium. In Algiers also
I read *Les Vacances d'un jeune homme sage*,[6] a rather ordinary book that had just appeared, and the delightful

[5] *Le Renoncement au voyage* (Renouncing Travel), published in
1906.
[6] *A Nice Young Man's Holidays*, by Henri de Régnier (1904).

Enfant à la balustrade,[7] which I immediately reread to Em. Then, as soon as we reached Biskra, we began *Der Geheimnissvoll* by Tieck, which I found in the hotel library. Each of us separately read the dialogue "*Vom Tragischen*," which Bahr had just sent me.[8] In Rome we bravely launched into *Michael Kohlhaas*, which we did not finish until Paris, when we immediately took up *Die Marquise von O. . . .*[9]

We had frightful weather for crossing Sicily and did not see the sun again until Rome. In Naples, or rather at Sorrento, I went to see the mysterious Vollmœller (I have described that visit at some length in a letter to Drouin). In Rome I found Maurice Denis, but Mithouard was always at his elbow and I did not see him as much as I should have wished. On the other hand, I saw Jean Schlumberger every day and, as we treated each other with ever greater confidence, he came to be one of my inner circle of friends.

[7] *The Child at the Banister*, by René Boylesve (1903).
[8] An essay "On the Tragic" by Hermann Bahr.
[9] These are both stories by Heinrich von Kleist.

1905

Eighteen years ago de Max told me: "You smile with your eyes; you will wear out your face."

"What should I smile with?" I asked him, somewhat surprised.

"Merely with your lips," he went on; "just look at me."

"Theatrical smile," I read today in Stendhal's *Journal* (14 July 1804), speaking of Napoleon's smile, "in which the teeth are shown, but the eyes do not smile."

22 April

I realize that my health is better from the fact that the desire and the need to write have seized me again. Not a need to work, which, indeed, has never left me, but that sort of immediate and involuntary transposition of sensation and emotion into words. If I had been alone today, I think I should not have ceased writing all day.

I can barely scribble these few words this evening in bed. On my night-table, Stendhal's *Journal.*

Hendaye

In beach sandals I almost ran all the way to Urrugne. I was holding M.'s letter in my hand. The sun was dazzling. The hour went by and I was still alive. On the heights, along the slopes, asphodels grew abundantly; not that many-branched asphodel of the moors in the Gard region or of the sacred purlieus of Syracuse, but rather bearing its flowers on a single stem like tritomas.

The day before yesterday on the rocks, near Vera, we had gathered some heather with globular blossoms the color of digitalis, almost each one alone on its stem and so large that it seemed to bend the stem down.

On these rocks and on the embankments along the road a vigorous creeping plant with blue flowers (of that deep blue that I had never seen except in gentians, and which Jammes says is a gentian in fact) dots the grass with tiny gulfs of night. One's eye plunges voluptuously into them.

At San Sebastián, on the square, we ordered Spanish

chocolate, thick and strongly flavored with cinnamon; it is served in little cups, much too small to my way of thinking. Jeanne claims she cannot endure Spanish chocolate, so she asks for a French chocolate. Almost at once she is brought some of this chocolate; yes, the same. But the cup is much bigger and Jeanne declares it to be excellent. Em. is willing to try the Spanish chocolate, but shudders at the thought of the cakes made of eggs. And since I am irritated to see them both so resigned (or decided) to enjoy this country only through their eyes or, at most, to taste it with the tip of their tongues, I thought as I sank my teeth into that oily, curdled, saffron-flavored paste that I was biting right into Spain itself; it was terrible.

After thirty-five you are easily tempted to ascribe to age the least effect of fatigue, and even to prolong it by refusing to consider it at first as a passing discomfort.

My low physical condition of late (it had lasted for almost three weeks). I seriously began to think that I should never get over it.

Already I had accepted the inevitable, resigned to a half-life; writing had become a chore to which my will alone forced me; life had lost its savor.

Monday

Copeau tells me he is greatly disappointed by Claudel's "*Ode*";[1] so far I have not been able to read it attentively. Jammes's enthusiasm got in my way.

Copeau, with a subtle mind like that of a Jew (at first I thought he was a Jew): "I haven't any great fear for you," I told him; "I feel that you are well armed." He smiled. "Yes, I think so too," he replied; "and yet I don't get anywhere. Do you know what I need? A milieu. Yes, I have no milieu."

Read in Stendhal's *Journal*, that remark would be considered very discerning. Yes, of course you are right. But, in a few months, how the "milieu" can stand in your way! At twenty my youth, my long hair, my sentimental manner, and a frock-coat that my tailor had turned out beautifully made me acceptable in the drawing-rooms of Mme Beulé and the Countess de Janzé. If I had continued to

[1] Claudel's first ode, "The Muses," was published in 1905.

frequent them, I should be writing today for the *Revue des deux mondes*,[2] but I should not have written the *Nourritures*. I escaped early from that world, in which, to appear proper, I had to watch myself too closely.

Auteuil, Wednesday

I expect from this house whatever energy I put into my work, my genius. Already it houses all my hope.

I saw Gérard only for a minute. He is to see Ventura again this evening. Already he feels better. His whole health hangs on the outcome of this adventure. He already talks less of getting me mixed up in it.

I am resuming the habit of sleeping an hour in the middle of the day.

Before going to meet Ghéon and M. at the Place Saint-Sulpice, I stop at the office of the *Occident* to get Claudel's *Les Muses*.[3] The few lines that I read while walking seize hold of my thought at once. It is a shock to my whole being and, as it were, the *warning* that I have been awaiting for almost a month now.

Hofmannsthal came again this morning; I greatly enjoy seeing him. He speaks rather loudly and lacks hidden qualities, but the words with which he somewhat stuns you are not at all stupid. Suit and necktie in very good taste. He sits down only for a minute, gets up immediately, walks vigorously up and down, stops, starts out again, bumps into chairs and table, smiles, and plays the overgrown child.

Returning home, I stop at the Charles Gides'. I pick up Gérard, who accompanies me home. Ventura is the sole topic of conversation. He is regaining the ground that he had too quickly thought lost.

On my arrival Paul Laurens appears, then his brother. Impossible to talk pleasantly with the two of them together! Pierre's extremism forces me to defend what otherwise I shouldn't care about at all. I have always repented being sincere with him; that's a failing into which I fall almost every time; neither he nor I shall correct ourselves.

---

[2] A very conservative literary review, generally considered a stepping stone to the French Academy.

[3] Claudel's ode "The Muses" was published by *L'Occident*, a literary review and publishing house.

This evening I strive to work, but my thoughts have been dreadfully upset; I do not find any one of them in its place.

Read with great interest the chapters on the habits of scorpions in J.-H. Fabre. I should be glad to write a preface for this (*Souvenirs entomologiques*[4]—a rather badly written book however).

Count Kessler takes me to lunch at Armenonville with the Hofmannsthals.

The culture of these Germans astonishes me. I cannot find it at fault on any point of our literature.

This evening I feel nothing but discouragement and sleep. A reading aloud of Wilde's *De Profundis*, both in German and in English, comforts me somewhat.

Monday

I should like to take in hand all these causes of sterility that I discern so clearly, and strangle them all. I have conscientiously cultivated every negation in me. Just now I am struggling against them. Each one taken alone is easy enough to subdue, but, rich in relationships, it is skillfully tied to another. It forms a network from which I cannot free myself. What good is this journal? I cling to these pages as to something fixed among so many fugitive things. I oblige myself to write anything whatever in them just so I do it regularly every day. . . . Even here I seek my words, I grope, and I set down your name, Loxias!

Friday

"That," he said, "is the portrait of a society woman. But do you notice the vulgar hand? Do you know why? It is because it projects forward. Look at a photograph. *I* have noticed it: when a woman puts her hand in front of her, well, just look: the hand appears too big. At once. Manet saw that at once. No, you see, you don't set yourself *in front of* nature but rather *in* nature. Manet *is* Nature.

"And look! That woman in an evening gown—it's living,

---

[4] *Recollections of an Entomologist: Instinct and Customs among the Insects.* These volumes began appearing in 1883; the last one came out in 1907.

it's breathing! That breast—you desire that breast—if you love breasts."

These few remarks are uttered, among many others, in front of some wonderful Manets and some Cézannes, by M. Pellerin, whose collection I go to see with Count Kessler.

Thursday

The first really hot evening, after a stifling and radiant day. If I had some book under way, I should write this evening its most beautiful pages. My brain is lucid, not too gay, my flesh is at rest, my spirit staunch. This evening I should be a wonderful lover, and I cannot think of Gérard without pity. I should like not to have met M. before yesterday and not to have spoken to him until today. . . .

If I threw myself from my balcony tonight, I should do so saying: "It's simpler."

Wednesday

At my age and after the experiences of G., of R., and of so many others, I am still unable to defend myself against the temptation of a *noble gesture*. Immediately after doing it, I should like to take it back. That's all.

I have just lunched with Félix-Paul Grève; a fatiguing lunch and without any great interest. I come away drunk, having let myself drink and smoke too much during the too prolonged silences. I write these lines while waiting for Bourgerie in the lawyer's office. I have to consult him on behalf of poor dear old La Pérouse, who is worried and would like to add a codicil to his will in favor of his grandson. With all the lucidity of my best days I could not succeed in untangling anything in all this. In the confusion of mind in which I am today, these complicated matters give me an almost physical discomfort; I am sweating; I have a headache; I should like to bathe in the Eurotas.

Francis Jammes, who had entrusted to me his manuscript (*Le Poète et sa femme*) with the understanding that I was free to publish it in this number or the following one, in one or several installments, wrote me, as soon as I was back, that he intended to be published all at one time and right away.[5] Boylesve's article (on Rebell) having arrived, the number goes twenty pages beyond the limit. Verrier, Ducoté's secretary, writes to Francis Jammes that, to their great regret, they will be obliged to cut his piece. Jammes will not hear of it. Let them send the manuscript back to him or else let it appear all together; moreover, he adds, he is fed up with "such higglings." They are forced to make up a number of eighty pages instead of sixty, and this "higgling" costs Ducoté a hundred and fifty francs.

Wednesday

Tuesday, right after lunch, Em. and I go to the Champs-Élysées, where the King of Spain is to pass. Certainly if the King had been less young and less handsome, sobs would not have choked me when I saw him salute the crowd as he passed. His face was drawn; he saluted with a stiff little military salute.

When, two hours later, we saw him return from the Élysée, his smile was very different; his features, now amused rather than contracted, expressed only an amazed and still almost childish joy. Between the two parades we went to see the two Salons. Nothing so demoralizing as those exhibits.

In the evening we drive out in a carriage to see the boulevards and the squares lighted up. Em. returns home; I go back alone toward the Champs-Élysées, then to the Opéra. No very noteworthy encounter. The air is dusty and full of flames. On the avenue del'Opéra (which the King is to descend on his way back to the Palace of Foreign Affairs after the gala performance) the crowd becomes thicker and thicker. Finally, with my heart in my mouth, I get away and by a circuitous route reach the Place du Théâtre-Français. Here the crowd is not so thick. It is almost midnight. People come out of the

[5] *L'Ermitage*, founded in 1890 by Henri Mazel, took a new lease on life in 1897 when Edouard Ducoté became editor. Until its demise in 1906, it was a leading monthly review of symbolist flavor although its contributors (Gide, Gourmont, Copeau, Ghéon, Claudel, Vielé-Griffin, etc.) and illustrators (Maurice Denis, J.-É. Blanche, etc.) considered themselves above literary coteries. Jammes's *The Poet and His Wife*, verse play in three acts, appeared in the issue for June 1905.

Théâtre-Français. The procession cannot be very slow in coming. I climb up on one of the columns of the theater portico and wait among a group of children. From that spot I heard the bomb very clearly; it made less noise than people said. Several persons near me insisted that it was a firecracker. *I* thought it was a revolver-shot. Again I noticed in me that disinclination to *take the event seriously*. I was highly amused, and even fear of the crowd, which hardly left me a minute, kept all my senses keyed up and made my heart beat joyfully. The next day the papers spoke of an "indescribable tumult" following the report. But I was struck by the complete immobility that followed the detonation. The crowd, for about four minutes, remained as if rooted to the spot with stupor. Then there was a wonderful wave stirred up by a movement of the police. A little later a charge of the mounted police filled me with fear, horror, and a sort of wild enthusiasm. Yet I was completely master of myself, merely embarrassed by the tears that rose to my eyes. But impossible to *take seriously* what I saw; it didn't seem to be real life. As soon as the act was over, the actors would come back and take a bow.

Thursday, 14 June

Visit to La Pérouse. He asks rapidly for news of me and of others, but doesn't listen to my replies, and abruptly:

"You have to admit that there is something diabolic in the human race. Especially in women. I have just had a frightful scene with my wife. Please excuse me, Sir, if I am still all upset by it. Something that I was reproaching her with (in the midst of a discussion), something she did six years ago, she now says no, she never did it. And with the greatest assurance, without blushing, with such a complete absence of embarrassment that I am absolutely flabbergasted. It was all a question of a subscription to a box at the Théâtre-Français."

"Yes," I say, "you have already spoken to me about that incident."

"Well, she denies it now."

"What! She denies having had that box at the theater?"

"No. She denies having asked me to help her pay for it. Really if it were to her interest to say that this armchair, this one here, is a pair of slippers, she would do so; she would maintain it. If God is to judge us according to our intentions— Suddenly I left the room; my hands were clenched: I was on the point of strangling her. Do you know what she said to me? . . . She told me: 'Your grandchildren despise you.' "

"She had lost all self-control and was only aiming to hurt you."

"To hurt me, yes. I am crazy to attach any importance to it. . . . She told me: 'Moreover, Sir, everybody makes fun of you and despises you.' "

Touching his arm, I say:

"You know, don't you, that that is untrue?"

"I know; I know; I am even embarrassed by the affection and respect that some people show me."

"No one," I say, "has greater affection and respect for you than I have."

There followed a long silence. He held my hand in his. We didn't dare look at each other, for neither one of us had been able to check his tears. Finally I risk asking him:

"You were very young when you married her?"

"Yes . . . I was young."

Written a few notes on Bloy. Worked on *La Route étroite,* the correction of *Paludes.*[6] Went back to Baudelaire with the greatest pleasure.

Irony considered as a form of maceration. Very important.

10 *July*

The Jacques Copeaus left us at eleven o'clock. It is now three. In two hours I myself leave. Tomorrow I lunch at the Van Rysselberghes', go to visit the house again with them, etc. . . . Gérard takes his first law examinations in two days.

The pleasure I derived from talking with Jacques Copeau was very great, until the day before their departure. Perhaps I began to suffer a bit then from not daring to talk to him more freely, from the fact that he

[6] Gide had not yet decided on the definitive title for his novel, *La Porte étroite* (*Strait Is the Gate*), first published in 1909. *Paludes* (*Marshlands*) of 1895 was translated into German by Félix-Paul Grève and it was on Grève's manuscript that Gide was then working.

did not, or could not, invite me to. He excited me to work instead of distracting me. Yesterday I read him what I had written of *La Porte étroite*. I didn't like it a bit: farther on I shall write down the things I noticed. I am almost ready to chuck it all into the fire. Copeau, a very good adviser, is able to see, in what I read him, only the preparation of something better. A few years ago I should have been utterly demoralized to have read, amorphous as they still are, these pages that I thought to be already perfect (or almost). Nothing is created without a divine patience.

Copeau, at twenty-seven, seems ten years older; his overexpressive face is already worn by sufferings. His shoulders are high and hard like those of someone who takes a great deal upon himself. The softness of his voice is at times almost disturbing; he would charm naturally if occasionally he did not try too hard to charm. He expresses himself so well that one is suspicious; his voice takes on just the inflection he wants; his gestures are never involuntary; it took me some time, I confess, to admit that it could all be genuine. One gets to the point of suspecting the sincerity of too impeccable expressions. Everything in him improves when better known, when explained—even if by himself.

31 July

I have gone back to work with a certain regularity, but I make very slow progress. I spend hours on a group of sentences that I shall completely rewrite the next day. The scene in Geneviève's room, in particular, when he finds her kneeling, gave me great difficulty. But I admire now all the things I succeeded *in not saying*, in KEEPING BACK. (I think for some time of the virtue that "reserve" can become in a writer. But who, today, can appreciate it?) I try to consider patience as my greatest quality; in any case it is the one I must above all encourage in me. I write "patience"; I ought to say "obstinacy"; but what is really needed is a *supple obstinacy*.

I have again begun my piano-practice two hours a day (Beethoven's sonatas). Every evening, before going to bed, I read a few pages of Hebbel's correspondence. Interesting indeed, and written in a rather palpitating language, but I have not yet felt him speak to me *directly*.

Read several articles in the recent *Revue des deux mondes*, in the latest *Mercure*, etc. In spite of all the good I heard of it, I got very little pleasure from Georges de La Salle's book on the Manchurian war. Just now I am finishing (in translation) Hugo Ganz's *Russia, Land of Riddles*.

In small doses, for the good of my health, Stendhal's *Journal*.

In the train, 8 August

Left Cuverville this morning.

Gérard asks me if my patience is not taxed by so many people. (We are twelve at table every day.)—No, but only on condition that I can be "polite" only when I want to be. A few dips into solitude are as essential to me every day as my sleep at night. That is the way I smooth out my ruffled nerves. What joy I felt the other evening at my work, in the small room beside the linen-room, after I had left them all together in the drawing-room! My greatest advantage between the ages of eighteen and twenty-three was that I preferred that kind of pleasure to those of society.

My work is hardly getting ahead at all, and will not progress any better so long as I am not convinced that I am writing a masterpiece.

My Aunt Charles Gide has just been very ill; a very bad heart attack; less painful, however, than the one I saw her have one evening in Paris. Gérard, since he has begun emancipating himself, worries her. One must admit that he was not very reassuring. What a look he had the first evening! Apart from the other children, he was pacing up and down the garden; I was giving him the *indifferent* treatment, but eventually I took pity on him; in the darkness I sought him out on the path where I could see the light of his cigarette.

"I ought to be in Paris," he said right away. "Yes, Ventura was waiting for me. For the last hour I have been telling myself that I could be with her. . . . Well, too bad! Tomorrow she leaves for America and I shan't be able to see her for six months." A few steps more in silence; then he continues in a more muffled voice:

"This evening, without any doubt, I would have had her."

"You mean that she was giving up."

"Yes, more than a week ago she had ceased defending herself against me."

"Then you, for fear of not—being up to it, you abruptly side-stepped?"

Gérard (taken aback, sheepish and furious, after a pause):

"All right, yes! . . ."

But right now he is sick at having left just as he was sick at staying.

Paris, 8 August

Copeau, with whom I was dining, repeated a certain sentence that I supposedly said to him at Cuverville: "Even if the drama were to end in bloodshed, I do not know a single sentiment whose sincerity cannot be questioned."

I did not *acknowledge* that sentence (in the sense of "acknowledging a child"), yet did not disavow it; and yesterday, returning to the subject, I emphasized this: "The sensation is always sincere; it is the only guarantee of the authenticity of our sentiments; our sentiments are guaranteed by their physiological repercussions. Literature and fine arts (in modern times) have, for their own convenience, made man a much more emotional creature than he is, or than he *was* at least, for very soon man began to conform to the image that he was offered of himself."

It is odd how the stock of *Humanity* has risen on the market since the Greeks, or even since Shakespeare. Nothing does more harm to drama than this excessive evaluation. This is quite properly the very subject of my *Sylla*.[7]

14 August

Gourmont has published in the *Ermitage* of 15 July some new "*Pas sur le sable.*"[8] He certainly hasn't very beautiful feet!

"There are certain things one must have the courage *not* to write," says the first of his aphorisms; this first one

---

[7] If Gide ever wrote this work, it has not been published.

[8] "Footprints in the Sand."

ought to spare us many others; we should like him to be more "courageous."

"Rise above yourself to contemplate yourself," he writes immediately afterward. This is because he doesn't seem handsome to himself seen full-face; he hopes to be better in a bird's-eye view. From sentence to sentence he remains ugly; when he talks of women he does so as a repulsive man who has been repulsed and who is taking his revenge.

                                                24 August

Nothing is consistent, nothing is fixed or certain, in my life. By turns I resemble and differ; there is no living creature so foreign to me that I cannot be sure of approaching. I do not yet know, at the age of thirty-six, whether I am miserly or prodigal, temperate or greedy . . . or rather, being suddenly carried from one to the other extreme, in this very balancing I feel that my fate is being carried out. Why should I attempt to form, by artificially imitating myself, the artificial unity of my life? Only in movement can I find my equilibrium.

Through my heredity, which interbreeds in me two very different systems of life, can be explained this complexity and these contradictions from which I suffer.

                                                25 August

Too much novelty dazzles us; we can appreciate in others only what we are able to recognize (just as the Barbarians could make out in the words we spoke only the letters they were accustomed to pronouncing); as for the rest, we do not even hear it. The artists with the most genius are understood only after their savor has ceased to be rare; the new values they brought, not being in circulation, were not quoted on the market. If you praise so much my article on Wilde (I mean the last one), this is just because I say nothing new in it. My second regular chronicle (of this year) on the other hand awoke no echoes anywhere; the unaccustomed truths I put into it could have been assimilated only if they had been watered down with pages of common-places.[9]

[9] The article on Wilde is the one on *De Profundis* that appeared in the *Ermitage* for 15 August 1905. The "chronicle" is the second of Gide's regular articles in the form of imaginary interviews, which appeared in the *Ermitage* for February 1905. Both are collected in the fourth volume of the *Œuvres complètes*.

Would it not be possible to write a whole volume (and a successful one) on this subject, historically developing this argument that I merely suggested there:

A race as mixed as ours recognizes through their expression the elements that make it up. By an easy imitation, what it first expresses is what has already been expressed in a preceding period. Who dares to assert that the Latin elements are the strongest in our race—and not simply the most articulate, for very obvious reasons? What has not yet been expressed is no less important because it is less precocious. It is merely harder to invent than to imitate. We strengthen ourselves with the past; but where does that get us? Barrès is one such: leaning heavily as against a wall; motionless.

You cannot imagine an author so great that his most banal qualities are not the first to be appreciated. The crowd always enters by way of the "commons"—and most often never gets beyond them.

1 September

I am again losing my footing; I am letting myself be carried along by the monotonous current. A great drowsiness benumbs me from my awakening until evening; games occasionally shake it off, but I am gradually losing the habit of effort. I compare what I am to what I once was, to what I should have liked to be. If only . . . but no, everything becomes soft in such an easy existence. Sensual pleasure permeates everything; my finest virtues are dissipated and even the expression of my despair is blunted.

How can I call absurd a rule of conduct that would have protected me against this? At one and the same time my reason condemns it and calls out for it in vain. If I had a father confessor, I should go to him and say: Impose upon me the most arbitrary discipline and today I shall say it is wisdom; if I cling to some belief that my reason mocks, this is because I hope to find in it some power against myself.

As soon as a healthy day comes along, I shall blush at having written this.

2 September

Before closing this notebook and starting out for the south, I want to make a record of the month just past.

Read aloud, with Mlle Siller, the first four acts of Hebbel's *Gyges und sein Ring*[10] and Leopold Andrian's *Garten des Erlebnis*. Derived much good from resuming my reading of Pascal's *Pensées* and *Opuscules* in the Brunschwicg edition (chiefly the *Prières pour demander à Dieu le bon usage des maladies*).[11] Finished the excellent *Kidnapped* of Stevenson. Corrected the proofs of *Paludes* (the German translation by Félix-Paul Grève) and of my *Essai sur Wilde* (English translation by Millard).

Whipped into shape the first forty pages of my novel.

It was one of the emptiest months in the year for me.

Saturday

I am rereading almost from beginning to end *Le Visage émerveillé*[12] with as much rapture as the first day. What makes a masterpiece is an adaptation or a happy matching of subject and author. And I am inclined to doubt that such a fortunate coincidence will ever occur again in the life of Mme de Noailles. Her very faults, this time, set off, emphasized her good qualities; yes, I like in this book even "the little golden knife against my heart." But henceforth the "little golden knife" will be prejudicial to her.

Mme de R. congratulates me on *L'Immoraliste*, "that book in which there are such beautiful thoughts." Obviously she thinks they are sprinkled on afterward like nasturtium blossoms on a salad. How uncultivated these women of the south are, and how paradoxical you seem to them when you don't disguise yourself considerably!

Gérard was unable to appreciate Em.'s exquisite remark when, speaking of Octave, she said: "You are not grateful to him for the pity he excites in you." He is incapable of judging that type of wit.

Minutes of such excruciating joy that you think they might break the thread of life; then, between two such, the succession of monotonous days, spent merely in growing older.

[10] This play (1856) deals with the same legend as Gide's *Le Roi Candaule* (1901). When the latter was produced in Berlin in 1908 it was unfavorably compared with Hebbel's work.

[11] "Prayers to Ask God for the Good Use of Ill Health."

[12] *The Awe-Struck Face*, a novel (1904) by the Countess Anna de Noailles.

I find in Gaston Deschamps's latest article: "I should be
very glad to find some masterpieces among the innumer-
able novels that French publishers put on the world
market every day. I welcome new names and young
talents. And I do not think there could possibly be,
through my fault, any unknown Balzac, or neglected
Daudet, or unpublished Ferdinand Fabre, or forgotten
George Sand. . . ."

And yet he has never mentioned Paul Valéry, or Paul
Claudel, or André Suarès, or Francis Jammes, or me.

Today the big pine opposite the cedar is being cut
down. Three men worked at it all day. This evening the
desperate silhouette of its huge branchless trunk rises like
a nightmare against the wonderful pure sky.

Back in Paris, 8 November
Met little Louis Rouart, redder and more middle-class
looking than ever. As it is a long time since I have seen
anyone, my smile suggests an exaggerated joy; he comes
along with me. As spotty, as strained conversation as ever;
it seems like the spasmodic skirmishes of a fencing bout,
but of a bout without courtesy. With the very first words,
from the start, he attacks. With him, in spite of myself, I
throw up my guard, take on a false, tense attitude, and
say nothing natural. What silly things he made me say
yesterday! To be sure, I was already tired out by the
conversation I had just had with Gérard.

Louis Rouart went with me to Welter's bookshop, where
I ordered Nyrop's grammar for André Ruyters. He heard
me give the order and thought: three foreign names!!
Protestant, cosmopolitan, etc. . . . And as I asked him,
on the way out, if he knew that wonderful grammar: "I
don't mind telling you" (he in fact told me pompously)
"that I never felt the need of grammars to learn French."
Nothing could have been more insulting or more stupid.
And I, quite dumbly, out of weakness and kindness, bothered to explain that the first volume of that grammar was
"above all historical." Absurd! Absurd!

And so on. I drop him in front of the *Mercure* (without
going in, for I suddenly remember that Tuesday is Mme

Rachilde's *day* for receiving visitors), annoyed with him and even more with myself. But when he speaks of calling on me, I reply: "Yes, do." For, after all, I find him likable. Now I'll never shake him off.

23 *November*

. . . My mind still anxious at not being able to decide what to tackle. I have before me Collignon's *Sculpture grecque*, Nyrop's *Grammaire française* and the *Histoire de la littérature anglaise* by Jusserand—which all tempt me equally. For each of these works I need a month of un-broken study; my mind is still too restless to choose and to limit me exclusively to my choice. I have left everything in the air: Pascal, Taine's *Correspondance*, Stendhal's *Journal*. These are readings that one can easily drop and pick up anywhere and that I prefer not to read to the end at one time. But one must at least be able to pick them up conveniently at the point where one left them. At Auteuil I am going to have a special shelf where the books I have begun will stand waiting for me; each one will have its bookmark, which I shall occasionally move a few pages. That will allow me, dropping the book and picking it up at will, never to read anything without giving myself to it wholly.

From Athman's latest letter I copy this sentence that Mardrus would not understand and that I should like not to forget:

"I love her very much" (he is speaking of his very young wife) "and *yet I have been able to make her sincere* toward my mother and me; she is very good, and I only treat her very gently like how you treat a child."

23 *November*

Around four o'clock O. S., a young German, comes to call. I remember, or rather he reminds me, that he is the author of a book (rather mediocre), *Lothar*, which I read or skimmed through last spring on the recommendation of Félix-Paul Grève. I believe I even wrote him a note about it. . . . O. S. not at all unpleasant, but talking too much, like all foreigners (moreover, those who don't talk are even more tiresome). He praises my *Immoraliste*, adding that those who admire it have hardly understood it, that peo-ple always speak of me as a lyric writer, failing to appreciate my chief virtue, which is knowing how "to look through the cracks of culture." That's not bad at all!

I have just read, first to myself, then aloud, the extraordinary Sixth *Chant de Maldoror* (chapters i, ii, and iii).[13] How does it happen that I didn't know it until now? I have even begun to wonder if I am not *the only one* to have noticed it. "You feel as you draw toward the end of the volume that he is gradually losing consciousness . . ." writes Gourmont. Let's admit that he *never read* these pages; that is less insulting to Gourmont than to suppose that he read them without noticing them.

Here is something that excites me to the point of delirium. He leaps from the detestable to the excellent. Amazing, the exchange of letters between Maldoror and Mervyn, the description of the family dining-room, the figure of the Commodore, the little brothers, "their caps topped off with a feather torn from the wing of the Carolina fern-owl, with their velvet trousers ending at the knees, and their red silk stockings," who "take each other's hand and go into the drawing-room, taking care to touch the ebony parquet only with the tips of their toes," etc. . . . etc. . . . I must read it all to Copeau. What mastery in the "sheer cussedness" of these lines.

Immediately afterward I reread Rimbaud's *Poètes de sept ans*.[14] Then in Gourmont's book of *Masques* the few pages on Lautréamont and the ones on Rimbaud, which are a painful disgrace.[15] (Those on Lautréamont are sadly insufficient.)

25 November

Gérard had gone ahead on the rue Godot-de-Mauroy last night—where Jean and I are prowling. Suddenly we hear someone shout from the end of the street: "Stop! Thief!" In the distance we can make out the white apron of a barmaid who is apparently running, and galloping toward us a tall, thin, gaunt silhouette. A butcher-boy suddenly appears near us; sticking out his arm, he knocks

[13] By Isidore Ducasse, who took the pen-name of Count de Lautréamont. The now famous *Maldoror*, first published in 1869, was recognized as a work of genius by Léon Bloy and Remy de Gourmont in the early nineties and popularized by the surrealists in the 1920's.

[14] Rimbaud's poem "The Seven-Year-Old Poets" describes the revolts and visions of childhood.

[15] These pages are not found in the recent editions. [A.]

down the thief, who collapses on the edge of the sidewalk
at our feet and moans: "Oh, you hurt me!" He tries to get
up, all covered with mud, but is immediately seized by
three big chaps who look as if they are going to crush
him; but others intervene, for already a crowd has
gathered. "Leave him alone. No! Don't hit him! . . ." A
fat mulatto woman runs up who looks to me just like
Pierre Louÿs's old Zora. "He took my purse. I had no
money in it, but I'd like to have my keys back." All this
was said with great dignity. Her heart is pounding; she is
also out of breath from running; but she controls herself.
Meanwhile the man keeps repeating: "Give me my cap.
Give me my cap." It must have fallen on the sidewalk; no
one has seen it; it doesn't matter. Various voices lean
toward him and, almost in a whisper: "Give back the
purse and get out of here quick." The thief looks stunned.
He stays where he is. He gave back the purse, I suppose,
but I didn't see it. People say to him several times: "Get
along; *they* will be coming." The circle that had formed
around him opens to let him get away. He goes, very
slowly at first; then, at a little distance, he starts running.
    We were amazed by the charity of these people. It is
true that the poor fellow didn't look very frightening;
probably half dead with hunger; later on I reproached myself for not giving him something.

1 December

At Fontaine's. Paul Claudel, whom I have not seen in
more than three years, is there. As a young man he looked
like a nail; now he looks like a sledge-hammer. Not very
high forehead, but rather wide; face without subtlety as
if chiselled out; bull neck continued by the straight line of
the head, through which passion can rush to flood the
brain. Yes, I think this is the dominating impression: the
head is of one piece with the body. I shall study him more
fully next Tuesday (when he comes to lunch with us); I
was a bit too concerned with defending myself and only
half responded to his advances. He gives me the impression of a solidified cyclone. When he talks, it is as if
something were released within him; he proceeds by
sudden affirmations and maintains a hostile tone even
when you share his opinion.
    While I am talking with Fontaine, out of the corner of

my ear I hear him proclaiming his admiration for Baudelaire. Mithouard, tactlessly taking up the subject, speaks
of Baudelaire's "health," seeing in him above all a
"healthy" genius. Is that a necessary prerequisite before he
will allow himself to admire him?

"Poe and Baudelaire," declares Paul Claudel with a sort
of stifled rage, "are the only two modern critics." Then he
praises, most intelligently, the critical intelligence of
Baudelaire and Poe, but in terms so close to those recently used, on this very same subject, by Remy de Gourmont that I can hardly keep myself from pointing this
out. But I am afraid, at the mere name of Gourmont, of
provoking an explosion.

Claudel is wearing a little jacket that is too short and
that makes him look even more thickset and lumpish.
One's eyes are constantly drawn to and shocked by his
necktie, a four-in-hand the color of a locust-bean.

After the reading, as I compare Francis Jammes's series
of poems with Verlaine's *Sagesse*, Claudel at once declares
that *L'Église habillée de feuilles*[16] is a much finer work,
that he for one has "never liked *Sagesse* very much, in
which Verlaine's juggling is always apparent and spoils
even the best poems."

He talks in a not very loud voice, like a man very much
in earnest; I notice once more how unsuitable real passion
is to eloquence. Léon Blum, whom I went to see the day
before yesterday, talked loud, vigorously and easily; he
must have been audible in the next room.

5 December

Paul Claudel came to lunch. Too short a jacket, aniline-
colored necktie; his face still more square than the day
before yesterday; his speech both precise and full of
images; his voice staccato, clipped, and authoritative.

His conversation, very rich and alive, does not improvise
anything, you feel. He recites truths that he has patiently
worked out. Yet he knows how to joke and, if he only let
himself go a bit more on the spur of the moment, would
not be without charm. I try to discover what is lacking in

[16] *The Leaf-clad Church*, a collection of poems by Francis Jammes
published in 1906; Gide had just read the manuscript aloud to his
friends.

that voice . . . a little human warmth? . . . No, not even that; he has something much better. It is, I believe, the most *gripping* voice I have ever heard. No, he doesn't charm; he does not want to charm; he convinces—or impresses. I didn't even seek to protect myself from him, and when, after the meal, speaking of God, of Catholicism, of his faith, of his happiness, he added as I said that I understood him:

"But, Gide, then why don't you become converted? . . ." (this without any brutality, without even a smile). I let it be apparent how his words had upset my mind.

I should attempt to set them down here if I were not to find them in his *Traité de la co-naissance au monde et de soi-même*[17] that he has just finished. Likewise I should write down the few details he gave about his life if I did not think that life were to become famous.

L'Ode aux Muses, he tells us, begun in 1900, hung for a long time interrupted. He didn't know "how to finish it." It was only in 1904 that he added the invocation to Erato and the end.

"For a long time, for two years, I went without writing; I thought I must sacrifice art to religion. My art! God alone could know the value of this sacrifice. I was saved when I understood that art and religion must not be set in antagonism within us. That they must not be confused either. That they must remain, so to speak, perpendicular to each other; and that their very struggle nourishes our life. One must recall here the words of Christ: 'Not peace, but a sword.' That's what Christ means. We must not seek happiness in peace, but in conflict. The life of a saint is a struggle from one end to the other; the greatest saint is the one who at the end is the most vanquished."

He speaks during the lunch of a certain "frontal sense"

[17] "Treatise of the Awakening to the World and to Oneself," which forms part of the *Art poétique* of 1907. This title, inspired by Bossuet's seventeenth-century *Traité de la connaissance de Dieu et de soi-même* and untranslatable in its subtlety, rests on Claudel's typical identification of the two words *naissance* and *connaissance*: "*Nous ne naissons pas seuls. Naître, pour tout, c'est co-naître. Toute naissance est une connaissance. . . .*" ("We are not born alone. To be born, in brief, is to be born with something. Every birth is an acquisition of knowledge.")

that allows us, without reading them, to recognize in advance a good or a bad book, and always warned him against Auguste Comte. I should be more amused to hear him execute Bernardin if he did not at the same time demolish Rousseau. He demolishes many others! Beating about him with a monstrance, he devastates our literature.

(I remember my consternation, at Cuverville, when, pruning and cleaning out a peony plant, I noticed that a branch I had just removed because it seemed to me dead was still full of sap.)

He speaks with the greatest respect of Thomas Hardy and Joseph Conrad, and with the greatest scorn of English writers in general "who have never learned that the rule of 'nothing unessential' is the first condition of art."

He talks a great deal; you are aware of the pressure of ideas and images within him. As, apropos of I don't remember what or whom, I spoke of the weakening of the memory: "Memory doesn't weaken," he immediately exclaimed. "None of man's faculties weakens with age. That is a gross error. All man's faculties develop continuously from birth to death."

He talks endlessly; someone else's thought does not stop his for an instant; even a cannon could not divert him. In talking with him, in trying to talk with him, one is forced to interrupt him. He waits politely until you have finished your sentence, then resumes where he had stopped, at the very word, as if you had said nothing.

He shocked Francis Jammes some time ago (in 1900) when he replied to Jammes's anguish with "*I* have my God."

(The greatest advantage of religious faith for the artist is that it permits him a *limitless* pride.)

Upon leaving me he gives me the address of his confessor.

He also said:

"I attach absolutely no value to the literary quality of my work. Frizeau was the first one who, brought back to God by my dramas because he saw religion dominating everything in them, made me think: then I haven't written in vain. The literary beauty of my work has no other significance for me than that found by a workman who is aware of having performed his task well; I simply did my best; but, had I been a carpenter, I should have been just as conscientious in planing a plank properly as I have been in writing properly."

18 December

When I don't write is when I have the most to write. If I have a moment's relaxation, I use it to correct proofs, to write letters. I am barely sufficient unto my life. It is not so much the urgency of my occupations as their number and diversity; my mind is completely dislocated by them. My best time in Paris is when I am supposed not to be there. If I cease to write in this notebook for more than three days, it becomes painful for me to go back to it, and the moment I do not pay attention to details, I no longer enjoy noting anything down. Let us force ourselves.

(Raymond Bonheur, whom I saw yesterday, cannot conceive of *forcing* oneself. On the other hand it's my watchword. I want all my branches to be arched, like those the clever gardener torments to urge them to fruit.)

What especially shocked Paul Claudel when, after several years in the Orient, he returned to modern civilization was the waste.

"What!" he exclaimed, "when St. Francis of Assisi found in the mud of a path a bit of crumpled parchment, he picked it up in his hand, smoothed it out, because he had seen writing on it—*writing*, that sacred thing—and look at us, what we do with it today! It really pains me to think of that enormous mass of paper which is covered with printing for one day and then thrown into the garbage-pail. . . . We have not only no more respect for the writing of others, but not even for our own. . . ."

Waste, yes, that is also what spoils for me an evening like yesterday's. Waste of time, of money, of strength—and for what a petty pleasure!

Yet everything would have been all right if it had not been for that sort of obligation we felt (at least some of us) to go and finish out the evening at Maxim's. I had dined (rather pleasantly too) with Gérard and Ventura at the Café de Paris; it was my first time there. We met

the J. T. couple and Copeau at the Athénée, where
Tristan Bernard's *Triplepatte* was being played. On seeing it again, that delicate play seemed to me even better.

Christmas Day

Natanson reports to me these sentences of Maillol:

"A model! A model; what the hell would I do with a
model? When I need to verify something, I go and find
my wife in the kitchen; I lift up her chemise; and I have
the marble." And this said with a strong southern accent.

1906

Unbearable mental fatigue. Work alone could rest me,
gratuitous work, or play . . . I am far from that. Each
thought becomes an anxiety in my brain; I am becoming
that ugliest of all things: a busy man.

Stupidly missed yesterday the rehearsal of Curel's new
play, for which Copeau had given us two tickets.[1]

We have finished reading aloud the *Mémoires* of Mme
d'Épinay. Without Grimm she would be easier to bear.
Here and there, charming passages; I have noted several.
Nothing is up to the first half of the first book.

We try *Le Chevalier Destouches*,[2] but after twenty
pages the book falls from my hands. I want to go on
with it by myself. I find just as much profit in cultivating
my hates as my loves. From one end to the other there is
nothing but rhetoric and bluff in that man.

In two evenings we read *La Princesse de Montpensier*.[3]
I am too tired to say anything about it. Curious epoch
in which the art of writing is confused with politeness,
and manners govern the mind above all.

15 January

Style: not so much sagacious as prudent; cautious; a
man of infinite precautions.

Art would consist, despite the greatest explicitness, in
always holding a surprise in store.

Friday, at Charmoy's, a strange evening. In the studio,
cluttered with huge statues fantastically lighted by a score
of candles ingeniously stuck here and there, on the corner
of benches, in the folds of the robes of the enormous angels supporting the monument of Beethoven—in that
studio, overheated by a little cast-iron stove, José, his
wife, and I wait for the Princess de Broglie and Miss
Barney.

---

[1] *Le Coup d'aile* (*The Wing-Stroke*), three-act play that opened at
the Théâtre Antoine on 10 January 1906.

[2] A novel (1864) by Jules Barbey d'Aurevilly.

[3] A short-story by Mme de La Fayette, published anonymously in
1662.

Around ten o'clock we hear the Princess's automobile, which appears in the blackness at the door. The Princess is wearing an ermine wrap, which she drops into Charmoy's hands. A gown of black velvet covering only the lower half of her body sets off a vast expanse of lustrous skin; the gown hangs from jet straps. Her face is small and tired; her coiffure, almost virginal, strives unsuccessfully to make her look younger. No wrinkles, however, but her features are painfully tight.

As soon as she comes in, she stares at me through her lorgnette, whose gold handle is linked by a small chain to a delicate bracelet of rubies.

Her intention of charming is flagrant.

On the back of a wicker chair, which she considers "not very inviting," a fur is stretched; on the floor a footwarmer for her little feet, which she also wraps in a shawl. Near her, behind her, Miss Barney takes refuge in an eloquent silence and lets the Princess strut.

Cuverville, 3 February

Apropos of a very interesting letter from Tahiti published in the *Journal des missions,* I pick up Darwin's *Journal* and reread to Em. the wonderful account of his stay in the South Sea Islands.

I continue the reading alone.

It is a long time since I have read with such a healthy appetite and at the same time with so much gluttony. Each new idea drawn from my reading, as soon as it enters my head, links up with something; it seems to me that I was waiting for it; its place was ready.

I recall certain readings in my childhood, so voluptuously penetrating that I felt the sentence almost physically enter my heart. This evening I again felt that marvelous sensation.

I had stayed in the garden until five o'clock, pruning my rosebushes with Mius under the flurry of snow; came in chilled to the bone, inebriated by the clear air. How beautiful the livid, slate-colored sky was above the russet hill and the leafless trees of the avenue!

In the greenhouse an *Iris tuberosa* offers me a delicate green and black flower. In the garden almost all the hellebores are in flower.

13 February
The Van Rysselberghes, the Jean Schlumbergers, Ghéon, and I come out of the Schola (Monteverde's *Orfeo* very poorly executed). At the Closerie, where we stop a moment, we see at a table in the rear a residue of *Vers et Prose*[4] gathered around Paul Fort and his wife, B. R., and several others unknown to me. Handshakes. R. begins an enormous compliment directed at me: "I thank you, Gide . . . I thank you for the beautiful pages of *Vers et Prose* that you permitted us to read." Nothing is so silly as the expression of a man who is being complimented. One must avoid it. And as he insists, quoting me: "I don't know where to place in my sentence this monstrous toad. . . ." I interrupt him abruptly with: "Well, I am glad it has found a place in your mouth." It came out in spite of me.[5]

For the past three days I have been packing my books with the enthusiasm of a vandal. As my bookshelves progressively empty themselves I feel my brain being aired out. At one and the same time I feel the intoxication of a sort of havoc and the joy, as I arrange the books in their baskets, of neatness and precision, of ingenious juxtaposition.

6 March
Yesterday evening read to Copeau all I have so far written of *La Porte étroite*. I had dined at his house; in the afternoon I had taken him my *Amyntas* at Petit's; then the swimming-pool; then the *Ermitage*. It was beautiful weather; I felt very well.

After dinner Copeau first reads several passages of

[4] *Vers et Prose*, a literary quarterly edited by the poet Paul Fort from 1905 until 1914, was founded to publish the works of the surviving members of the symbolist movement and their disciples. Such writers as Maeterlinck, Verhaeren, Barrès, Régnier, Claudel, Jammes, Moréas, Louÿs, and Gourmont appeared regularly in its pages, and it contributed to the discovery of younger writers like Guillaume Apollinaire, Jules Romains, and Georges Duhamel. The following writings of Gide were published in *Vers et Prose*: *Bou Saada* (1905); *Alger* (1906); *Poésies d'André Walter* (reprint, 1907); *Le Retour de l'enfant prodigue* (1907); *Bethsabé* (1909); *Feuilles de route 1895–1896* (from the *Journals*) (1911); *Proserpine* (1912).
[5] Gide's description of the toad occurs in his *Alger*, published in the fourth issue of *Vers et Prose*, which had just appeared. In French "to swallow a toad" means "to pocket an insult."

Amyntas to his wife; then, taking the book from his hands, I read the passage about the flute, Droh, etc. . . .

Mme Copeau leaves us alone; I take my manuscript out of its envelope. The reading, rather well begun, sinks into a mire of ennui. Lamentable impression, not so much on Copeau, perhaps, as on me; moreover, he already knew almost all of it. I resented that sort of cowardice which had made me have recourse to him before having obtained more. How much work still ahead! I must start it all over again. Excellent profit from the evening. Copeau, a good doctor, without cruelty, with even too much indulgence, but yet strengthening my impression with his. And already I know him too well to be ashamed of showing myself to him without having dressed up more.

This morning I send an express letter to Rouart to refuse his luncheon (at Prunier's with Albert Sarraut and Michel). I hurl myself into work.

I was so stupid as to go and see Blanche this afternoon. The indignation that I feel toward him makes me believe in eternal life. Impossible to work after that, or even to play the piano. I must go out and get a change of air. There is not a single thought in my mind that does not rise up in revolt.

Ingenious in spoiling the happiness of others, not exactly through ill will, but through an inability to understand any other form of happiness than that which his fortune would allow him to enjoy—in short, through an incapacity to achieve happiness himself. I fancy that he seeks it rather in a convenient use of things than in a self-determination; he is an extraordinarily dependent creature. He naturally looks with pity on the happiness of others. He says, or seems to say: "Oh heavens! how can you consider that as happiness? In your place, I . . ." and instead of pitying, he advises.

Tuesday morning

Em. returned yesterday from Cuverville. At eleven o'clock I am at the Gare Saint-Lazare. The suburban train gets us here by midnight.

Impossible to find the key to the wardrobe. Em. insists that she put it in her basket, on top of four dozen eggs. Naturally, the eggs having moved, the key—heavier than they—must have slipped to the bottom. We burrow with great care for fear of breaking the eggs. We bring up a pair of gloves, a veil, a pair of scissors, a handkerchief, what else? and ten boxes of matches! [6] But no key. We decide to take the eggs out, one by one. Each egg is wrapped in tissue paper which we remove. The egg is cool in one's hand, clean, and dull off-white in color. In Eugène Rouart's cloisonné bowl, so blue, so green, they make a marvelous still-life. Now it is one o'clock in the morning; the basket is empty, the bowl full; we admire the effect. But no key.

28 March

From little Gérard's presence here I have now gained about everything that I could hope to gain. It is to be feared, if he stays too long with me, that I might become a Christian again. I am too keenly aware of the use he might derive from practicing certain maxims of the Gospels, and I cannot restrain a *profound* indignation upon seeing him squander without beauty a moral patrimony that generations have striven, *with abnegation,* to build up for him. (That seems almost to come from an article by Claretie; but if I begin trying to write "elegantly," I am lost.)

His monstrous fatuousness is unhealthy; one would like to treat it like a cancer, but perhaps without any greater hope of curing it. Perhaps he owes to his very constitution his inability to prefer any pleasure to that of vanity. He is bored.

He claims that he is better now; my fear is that he really believes this. Yet no, he cannot be taken in by this superficial semblance. Indeed, after an hour or two of calm work he still recaptures that clear complexion which I often think lost forever. . . . An hour later, his cheeks redden again, take on that dreadful brick shade; the look in his eyes becomes heavy, closed. . . . How can you

---

[6] I must note here the story of the boxes of matches.

"Why, of course," says Em., "I bought them at Criquetot. Do you know that in the country they are only a penny? Berthe filled her suitcase with them."

"But, my dear, these are sulphur matches! You must have taken them for safety matches. Look, smell it." And I light one of them under her nose. Em. chokes a bit and exclaims:

"Oh! the robbers!" [A.]

then distinguish him from any other dissipated wash-out?
He frequents them assiduously; that is in fact his environment; even his fatuousness brings him closer to them; that
is the only milieu in which his remaining distinctions are
legal tender.

9 April

I reread a few pages of Anatole France. . . .

I should like France more whole-heartedly if certain
rash people did not try to make of him a writer of importance. That sets me wondering. I fear that perhaps I
have not been fair. I reopen *La Vie littéraire* and especially *Le Jardin d'Épicure*,[7] where his thought is most
directly accessible. I read this sentence which I applaud:

"One thing above all gives charm to men's thoughts,
and this is unrest. A mind that is not uneasy irritates and
bores me."

I am reminded of Goethe's remark: *The tremor of awe
(das Schaudern) is the best in man.* Alas! this is just it;
no matter how I try, I do not feel any tremor in France;
I read France without a tremor.

He is fluent, subtle, elegant. He is the triumph of the
euphemism. But there is no restlessness in him; one drains
him at the first draught. I am not inclined to believe in
the survival of those upon whom everyone agrees right
away. I doubt very much if our grandchildren, opening his
books, will find more to read in them than we are finding.
I know that, as far as I am concerned, I have never felt
him to be ahead of my thought. At least he explains it.
And this is what his readers like in him. France flatters
them. Each one of them is free to think: "How well put
that is! After all, I wasn't so stupid either; that's just what
I was thinking *too.*"

He is well-bred; that is, he is always aware of others.
Perhaps he does not attach any great value to what he
cannot reveal to them. Besides, I suspect that he hardly
exists at all behind and beyond what he reveals to us.
Everything comes out in conversation, in relationships.
Those who frequent him appreciate being taken right
into the drawing-room and the study; these rooms are on

---

[7] *The Literary Life,* four volumes of literary criticism published between 1888 and 1892, and *The Garden of Épicurus,* a novel (1895)
full of random reflections.

one floor; the rest of the house doesn't matter. In my case, I am annoyed not to have any hint of the near-by room in which a crime is committed or of the room in which people make love.

27 April

I am rereading *Madame Bovary*. The difficulties that Flaubert plans to overcome are all of the same order, and to reduce them Flaubert always finds the same common factors.

Since yesterday we have adopted a poor black poodle that was starving to death and prowling around our door for three days. His coat is all thick and matted from the plaster debris on which he has been sleeping in the house that is being built next door. At two a.m. Em. makes me go down to see if he isn't barking in the cellar, where we locked him up. I don't think he is intelligent, but he is affectionate.

I have bathed, I have soaped my poor dog in my tub. I hoped that cleanliness would give some luster to his coat! But now he looks more than ever like a blind man's dog. And I who wanted a pedigreed dog, I've got what was coming to me! No matter; it is time to learn once more to prefer the events that choose me to those I should have chosen myself.

Saturday

After a period of passable work, went out to call on the good La Pérouse, whom I knew to be alone that day. I leave him just in time to go and pick up Copeau as he leaves the Petit Gallery and walk home with him, before dining myself at Auguste Bréal's.

Very nice dinner, with the Philippe Berthelots, Moréas, Bonnard, and a sculptor whose name I didn't recognize.

Moréas protests when you speak of his healthy look and declares that he is "very ill." When you look at him more closely, you see in fact that the apparent "health" is only a rather nasty puffiness. He is just the way I have always seen him, scrupulously dressed, careful in his speech, and constantly turning up his mustache with a twist. Every time he addresses me, his big cockatoo eye caresses me in a way that stirs me. I should like to tell him how much I like his poems, but cannot produce the least compliment.

He speaks of Victor Hugo with a slightly disdainful arrogance, which, however, is only a pose; he says he prefers Lamartine to him and recites some of his lines, which, picked out in this way and warmed by that brazen voice, seem, indeed, full of ambrosia. He does not talk much, remains unaffected, does not insist on silence all around him, and talks only to a few at a time.

Philippe Berthelot produced, as usual, the easy paradoxes of a superior mind. The ruin of San Francisco is "an unimportant little event"; the eruption of Vesuvius likewise; the May Day strike "exists only in the imagination of the frightened bourgeois"; the Bonmartino trial is "a very banal news item, which attracts a little more interest than the usual news items only because the names are Italian." And so on. Moréas inclines somewhat toward this failing too, which belongs to three fourths of the literary men and intellectuals of today (Paul Valéry, Gourmont, Vielé-Griffin—I have chosen the most dissimilar men). There are few failings more tiresome to me.

Monday morning, 7 May

I am suspicious of the *genuineness* of a feeling the moment that feeling can be of advantage to me. That is what made me side-step the Jammes article. But the story is rather comical (unfortunately I have not kept all *my* letters). That article would have been of great value to me; but I should have owed it to a misunderstanding. I am beginning to believe that I have even more pride than vanity—and terrifying reserves of malice against myself.

This need of mortification is worth meditating on.

10 May

I chose this very small notebook in order to be able to put it into my pocket. I like having it on me, busying myself with it anywhere whatever, just as abruptly as I am doing today while waiting my turn at the barber's. The other one, too large, permitted too much affectation.

I must hasten to Cuverville in a couple of days. That thought is enough to disorganize my days. Spent all of yesterday and all of the day before on errands. Having finished the Oxford notebook and not yet having this frightful little one, I have noted nothing since the 7th; moreover, I've done nothing worth while; my relaxed mind has drifted aimlessly. I must decide to go and see a doctor. I should have made up my mind to do so three or four years ago. I have resigned myself too long to being tired and to getting along on a reduced vigor. Absurd! What do I care about the severity of a regime if it allows me to work more! What have I produced up to now compared with what I should have produced? For the last four years I have been floundering and marking time.

. . . .

Sunday

Reached Cuverville yesterday. The weather is so beautiful that this day is related to the happiest days of my childhood. I am writing this in the big room above the kitchen, between the two open windows through which the sun's warm joy surges in. Nothing but my tired reflection in the mirror hanging above my table is an obstacle to the fullest development of my happiness. (I need to learn all over again, and methodically, how to be happy. This is a form of gymnastics, like exercise with dumbbells; it can be *achieved*.) My feet are in the sunlight, wearing green and blue list slippers. The warmth enters into me, rises within me like sap. In order to be utterly happy the only thing necessary is to refrain from comparing this moment with other moments of the past— which I often did not fully enjoy because I was comparing them with other moments of the future. This moment is no less full of delight than any other moment of the future or of the past. The grass of the lawn is deep like the grass in a churchyard. Each apple tree in the farmyard is a thick mass of blossoms. The whitewashed trunks prolong their whiteness right down to the ground. Every breath of air brings me some perfume, especially that of the wistaria, on the left, against the house, so loaded with blossoms that one can hear its bees from here. A bee has come into this room and won't leave. The light envelops each object as with honey.

Yesterday before sunset I had just time to visit the garden thoroughly. The big apple tree leaning toward the tennis court, smiling and rustling in the last rays of the sun, was becoming pink. A frightful shower, a few

hours before, had submerged the countryside and purged
the sky of all clouds. Every bit of foliage was brimming
as with tears, particularly that of the two big copper
beeches, not yet copper-colored, but transparent and
blond, which fell about me like soft hair. When, going
out by the little door in the bottom of the garden, I saw
the sun again and the luminous cliff in front of it formed
by the grove of beeches, everything struck me as so affectionately beautiful, so new, that I could have wept with
joy. With me tears are not the privilege of sorrow, but
also of admiration, of emotion, of a brusque and violent
sympathy, of excessive joy. I cannot remember ever having wept, since childhood, for a personal sorrow, and yet
I weep so easily; in the theater the mere name of Aga-
memnon is enough: I weep torrents. From this physical
accompaniment my emotion derives the guarantee of its
authenticity.

The violence of this emotion had all but overwhelmed
me. On going in I had a rather sharp headache and immediately after dinner, heavy with sleep, went to bed.

Read before going to bed the biography of Athenaïs
(Eudocia) and a few lines of Tacitus.

Read this morning a few chapters of Tacitus (beginning of Book XI), then began writing before going down
to the garden.

I know that, outside, a vegetative lethargy seizes me
and that, if I let myself go, I am lost to work.

Sunday, 3 o'clock

After lunch, went to sleep for an hour (read the indifferent article by Deschamps on Ferrero); woke up, my
head swimming from the buzzing of the bees. A swarm,
escaped from Frémont's, had got into the dining-room
chimney. This young swarm, which Frémont wanted to
capture, was still uncertain and you could see it, as if
elastic, above the top of the house. Burning a little paper
in the chimney drove it away and it lighted in the lawn
on one of the lowest branches of the cedar. Mius, his
wife and his three not very handsome children, F., and
Em. were watching; I joined them. The shrill swarm,
dazed with sunlight, surrounded the branch, a moving
cloud that gradually became tighter and denser. Soon a
large number of bees, some of them fixed directly to the

branch and others clinging to the first ones, formed a
sort of gourd, growing, swelling, lengthening out as we
watched, then occasionally letting fall on the lawn what
looked like thick tears of burning pitch.

Frémont, the farmer, then set out to fetch his hive.
When he returned, Mius was setting up the stepladder;
the swarm had not moved. Frémont measured the distance
from the ground to the branch and cut a forked pole
exactly of that length, to which he attached the hive. The
bees stirred a bit; that is, there took place on the surface
of the swarm a sort of sudden evaporation, when he
brought up the ladder and climbed onto it to fix the
forked pole against the branch. Finally everything was so
well arranged that, the weight of the forked pole and of
the hive bending the branch slightly, the whole business
came to lean against the ladder and was supported there,
the hive forming a cover over the swarm and protecting
it from the sun. To give even more shade, an umbrella
was opened over the whole thing, supported half by the
branch, half by the ladder, in an equilibrium so precari-
ous that the least breath would have upset it; but the air
is so calm today that in the distance the upper branches
of the avenue can hardly be seen to tremble.

I left the scene, crushed with sunlight. I am writing
these lines on the path in the flower garden, of which the
part next to the vegetable garden is in the shade. Opposite
me, above the dark curtain of Portuguese laurels, I see the
top of the house wall where the big firs are already throwing their shadow. On my left, in perspective, the line of
espaliers; above them the bright red of the new tiles; the
branch of a big snowy apple tree springs out and waves in
the joyous blue.

6 o'clock

We have had tea. I read aloud to Em. the first pages
of the *Voyage d'un naturaliste*,[8] then, sitting on a folding
chair down in the vegetable garden, after having read
some amusing articles by Ernest-Charles, I am letting myself be voluptuously soaked up by the evening.

8 o'clock

Frémont, who was waiting for the cool of the evening,
has come back carrying a forked pole at the end of which,

[8] *Journal of a Naturalist* by Charles Darwin.

like a sort of broom, he has stuck a bunch of elder leaves. The odor of these leaves, crushed under foot and then dipped in a pail of water, is supposed to be very unpleasant to the bees: "It is like poison to them," he explained. Having, therefore, raised the forked pole under the swarm, he waited about half an hour until the smell of the elder leaves forced the bees into the hive. But to no avail. Night was falling. He had either to give up the swarm or to hurry. I advised cutting the branch; Frémont had been careful not to suggest this. Mius went off to fetch a huge hand clipper. Frémont, up on the ladder, held the branch with both hands, above and below the swarm. A towel had been stretched on the grass, the hive had been placed on the towel, not flat on the ground but raised, leaning against a plank so as not to cause trouble for the few bees that had already settled in it. With one stroke Mius cut the branch. Everything proceeded in the best manner possible and Frémont, by raising the hive, was able to slip the branch with its swarm between the hive and the towel.

But when everything was over, Frémont noticed that he still had on his shirt-sleeve (he had taken off his coat) a rather viciously active squadron of bees. The most amusing—I was about to say the most piquant[9]—aspect of the whole business was formed by the efforts and odd movements of Mius and Frémont to get rid of the last bees, fortunately somewhat numbed by the night. Each of them had wrapped his head in a white cloth: the masquerade effect of those two men jumping about and gesticulating in the growing darkness considerably amused the maids and the children, and since no one was stung, the general good humor contributed to everyone's individual joy (or everyone's individual good humor contributed to the general joy—and so on—ridiculous sentences).

15 October. *Back in Paris*

Traveled with a seventeen-year-old tramp, the son of a Douai tinsmith who had come to Havre to ship out as a cabin-boy. The ship for which he had a recommendation had left for Brazil a month ago. After vain attempts to sail on other ships, he was getting ready to return to his home town.

[9] In French *piquer* means "to sting."

I fear that Paris will delay his return. He has eighteen francs in his pocket, to which I add two francs to pay the cab that will take him to "a friend of his parents, a warrant officer who lives Place de la République." His parents do not expect his return. And I am aware that he is rather amused to arrive alone and free in Paris with twenty francs that will be stolen at his first stop. I do not leave him until I have seen him get into his cab.

Curious, the psychology of the vagrant. I should have great difficulty in defining it, yet I glimpse the rather special nature of the mania. Violently interested by that youngster (especially compared with the few other tramps I have already met). I am beginning to grasp the essential common features. But still impossible to define exactly.

Tuesday morning at de Max's. I find Lugné-Poë there; as always, seeming at one and the same time both querulous and ferocious; the manner of someone whose feet have been trodden on. He has no sooner left the room than de Max exclaims: "And now that the humbug of Paris has left, my friend, I am the most unhappy man on earth. X. shot himself in the chest last night."

Cuverville, 27 November

It's a wonderful thought that there is probably not a woman in Paris who, when she is applauding Rostand, does not think she has more taste than the Englishwomen of Elizabeth's time, for example. Every public has the Shakespeare it deserves.

1907

1 January

Yesterday evening, family dinner at the Charles Gides'. First Jeanne, then Gérard, tell me of Arthur Fontaine's visit to Briand to get me a decoration. M., Briand's chief private secretary, told them on Saturday. Since M. knows nothing of Fontaine's friendship for me (which, moreover, would seem inexplicable to him), M. will certainly think that I have started a campaign, and yet I knew nothing about it. This is profoundly distasteful to me, and I was unable to eat all during the dinner.

M. does not like me; he doesn't hide his scorn and aversion for everything I write. He suffers in his affection for Gérard, and especially in his vanity, that Gérard prefers my society to his. Gérard does not hide his scorn from him. M. thinks that my company can only harm Gérard, and when Dr. Andréæ, who knows me well, convinced Gérard's mother to put the youth in my care last spring, M.'s disapproval became passionate.

M. is not exactly a hypocrite; yet he plays an underhand game. He is small. I am suspicious of small men. For a long time I have been telling Gérard he must be afraid of M. Some day I shall try to sketch this small character, held upright by moral principles so as not to lose an inch of his height. He appears full of affection, of responsiveness; but one always feels that he hasn't much to expend. Perfect type of climber. He succeeds by means of patience, of minute economy, of hygiene. He succeeds in everything. Forever up to his best, he considers his constancy as wisdom and calls virtue the lack of turbulence of his desires. But enough about him.

I have wasted my morning in writing him. Then went to the G.'s to show Gérard a rough draft of a letter, which he has the good taste not to consider excellent. It was merely a question of making M. understand that I had nothing to do with Fontaine's initiative. It was especially a question of not seeming annoyed that he, M., had known about it even though it did not succeed. Eventually I understood, as a result of recopying and beginning this letter over again, that, in order to achieve this last point, the best thing was not to write anything; and finally I threw everything into the fire.

Lost about three hours over that letter, four even if I count the time spent at the Ch. Gides'.

The Marcel Drouins came to lunch; around two o'clock, leaving them, I dozed for an hour. But lost the advantage of this sleep by still concerning myself with that exasperating letter to M. Other letters absorbed my remaining patience. It was no good to try to read or work. . . . After dinner, picked out the piano and violin sonata that Magnard has just sent me.

The best moment of the day is the half-hour I spent in my tub (in d'Aurevilly's manner) calmly finishing Ferrero's first chapter (*Antony and Cleopatra*).

2 January

Visit of Giovanni Papini, the editor of the review *Leonardo*. Younger than I had thought, with an expressive and almost handsome face. A bit too irrepressible, yet not so much so as the other Italians I know. Too full of compliments, but seems nevertheless to think a part of what he says. Like all the Italians I know, has too high an idea of his own importance; or at least shows it too much; or in a different way from a Frenchman's. If he only knew how hard it is for me to take myself seriously! . . .

After Papini has left, I read three chapters of Ferrero; and after dinner, a fourth.

The important thing for me now is not so much what I read as how I read it, the attention that I bring to it. I must struggle by every means against the breaking up and scattering of my thought. It is for *this reason* likewise that I have harnessed myself to this journal again, without any great pleasure, but as a means of getting myself into the spirit for work. But what can I dare to hope for if, as soon as I begin working again, sleep again quits me?

5 January

At two o'clock, call on Léon Blum. A very pleasant thing about him is that he always receives you as if he had seen you the day before. Conversation flourishes easily between us. His book on marriage must be finished in a month.[1] He is writing it almost as fast as his pen can func-

---

[1] *Du mariage* was in fact published in 1907.

tion. I am not sure he is wrong. The artist in him hasn't any great value, and his sentence, like Stendhal's, does not need to go out of its way to achieve anything more than the mere movement of his thought, which flows from his mouth or his pen at once abundant and clear—clearer, to be sure, than abundant, without any noticeable *Schaudern*—but, as a consequence, easily and completely expressible; having a beginning and an end and always properly clothed. You cannot imagine a more exact, clearer, more elegant, easier summary than Léon Blum can give, on the spur of the moment, of an event or a book or a play. What an excellent committee chairman he must be in the Conseil d'État! Oh, if politics did not bend all his thoughts, what a keen critic he would be! But he judges things and people according to his opinions and not according to his taste. He has less confidence in his taste than in his opinions and prefers to distort the former rather than to seem to contradict himself. You can't be always quite sure that he likes everything he says he likes, but you can be sure that he thinks he likes it and knows why.

Wednesday, 9 January

Good work after lunch and a short siesta. Correcting the translation makes me examine closely my *Prométhée* and feel with joy, and in detail, all the qualities of my style.[2] In the whole book there are not four sentences that I should like to change. I greatly admire the work of the Tharaud brothers on their *Dingley*, of which I am reading the excellent rewriting. But how this reworking after several years amazes me and how impossible it would be for me! I cannot, I have never been able to, rewrite a sentence later; all the work that I put on it must be when it is still in a molten state; and each sentence strikes me as perfect only when retouching has become impossible.

Thursday

Barrès's formal reception into the Academy. For the first time in my life I enter the small enclosure. Paul A. Laurens, at whose house we had lunched and who is with us, withdraws before the mob.

[2] *Le Prométhée mal enchaîné* (*Prometheus Ill-Bound*) of 1899 was translated into German by Franz Blei.

Why speak here of what all the newspapers will be full of? We leave before Vogüé's speech.

Barrès wears the frightful uniform as elegantly as one can. Of all of us he has changed the least. How I like his thin face, his flattened-down hair, even his common accent! What a flat speech he made! And how I suffered from the touches of cowardice, the flatteries, the concessions to the opinion of his audience, which are perhaps natural to him (I mean for which he probably did not have to distort his thought, but which met a too easy applause here); and also his thrust at Zola!

I was not the only one to notice the care with which, praising the family of Heredia, he said nothing of the sons-in-law.[3]

Will no one bring out with what strange and crafty cleverness this master sophist enrolled in his camp, in order to praise them, those two uprooted masters: Leconte de Lisle and Heredia? (And Chénier! and Moréas!)[4]

Left the Academy quite demoralized with fatigue and melancholy. Another day like this and I shall be ready for religion.

Berlin. The Museum

In the same gallery:

Michelangelo: *John the Baptist*, very Donatello, excessively youthful; mannerism without mawkishness, strangely long neck, frail torso; in the gait more rhythm than direction. In his left hand he holds a honeycomb and with his right hand he is raising to his mouth something bitter that puckers his mouth.

Wonderful work; greater perfection but perhaps not greater beauty than in the little sketch of an Orpheus [Apollo (?)] hardly as tall as a gladiolus, which, even in

---

[3] Barrès was elected to the chair vacated by the death of the poet José-Maria de Heredia. The daughters of the poet all married writers: Hélène first married the novelist Maurice Maindron and then the critic René Doumic; Marie became Mme Henri de Régnier; and Louise, after her divorce from Pierre Louÿs, became Mme Gilbert de Voisins.

[4] With his long novel *Les Déracinés* (*The Uprooted*) in 1897, Barrès became the apostle of stability and conservatism symbolized by the individual's roots in his provincial earth. Gide's *Nourritures terrestres* in the same year preached the necessity of fleeing all such restrictions, and his review of *Les Déracinés* in the *Ermitage* for 1897 clearly voiced this ideological conflict.

the still thick marble, is palpitating with glorious life. He is holding the lyre with an arm folded flat against his left side; with his other arm he is leaning against what is about to be the branch of a tree. By Michelangelo likewise a very small bronze under glass, among other Renaissance figurines, has kept the charm of softened wax. A mere torso of the Crucified Christ.

Gallery 30

GALLERY 30.

Domenico Veneziano:
Head of a woman, seen in a perfect profile against a background of blue sky, probably repainted, standing out against the delicate and rather pale tone of the face. The nape of the neck completely uncovered in the manner of a Piero della Francesca; dress of brocaded silk, indiscreetly sumptuous.

Pollaiuolo:
A little David, with nothing remarkable about the painting, but creating a rather odd impression. The folds of his cloak, the corners of which are caught in his belt, raised almost immodestly, uncover the legs painted with a nervous and very elegant line.

Verrocchio:
A Madonna and Child. As usual with him, he indicates shadows on flesh with a monotonous darkening.

A little sacred wood, almost symmetrical, yet full of mystery and charm, where a Christ child and a John the Baptist just a little older meet. Near them some does come down to drink; wild anemones sparkle against the very dark green of the grass. And not far off, St. Joseph and Mary are coming forward. (This is attributed to some pupil of Filippo Lippi.)

Dierik Bouts:
Magdalen anointing the feet of Christ. She is on the far left of the painting. At the corner of a table Christ, together with three disciples, is eating bread and fish. A donor, kneeling in the right corner, balances the Magdalen.

A very beautiful crucifixion by Dierik Bouts also.

| CARPACCIO | 1470–1522 |
| TIZIANO | 1477–1576 |

TINTORETTO	1519–1594
VERONESE	1528–1588

(Strange gap. Look into it.)

TIEPOLO	1696–1770
GUARDI	1712–1793
CANALETTO	1720–1780

6 February

Have forsaken this notebook the last few days, but for the sake of work. I am composing an *Enfant prodigue,* in which I am trying to make a dialogue of my spiritual reticences and impulses.[5]

This morning, from Claudel, a letter full of a sacred wrath, against the epoch, against Gourmont, Rousseau, Kant, Renan. . . . Holy wrath no doubt, but wrath all the same and just as painful to my mind as the barking of a dog is to my ear. I cannot endure it and cover my ears at once. But I hear it nevertheless and then have trouble getting back to work.

9 February

Valéry will never know how much friendship it costs me to listen to his conversation without an outburst. I go away black and blue all over. Yesterday I spent almost three hours with him. Afterward nothing was left standing in my mind.

Going out with me, he accompanied me to the Bois de Boulogne. I had taken my skates, which had been lying in a packing-case for the last ten years, and, to my surprise, I didn't find them too rusty on the ice. Valéry did not leave me an instant; I suffered to see him waiting for me, so that I hardly skated at all. Leaving there with him, I abandoned him in front of the Charles Gides', where I went up to get news of Gérard.

And, of course, impossible to work this evening. After such a "conversation" everything in my head is in a state of havoc.

Valéry's conversation throws me into this *frightful* alternative: either consider everything he says absurd or else consider absurd everything I am doing. If he suppressed

---

[5] *Le Retour de l'enfant prodigue* (*The Prodigal's Return*), a short prose poem, is one of Gide's most beautiful works. It was first published by *Vers et Prose* in 1907.

in reality everything he suppresses in conversation, I should no longer have any *raison d'être*. Moreover I never argue with him; he merely strangles me and I struggle back.

Didn't he declare to me yesterday that music (he is sure of this) was going to become purely imitative; or rather, a more and more precise notation of what speech cannot express, but without any further æsthetic aim: an *exact* language?

He also says: "Who is concerned today with the Greeks? I am convinced that what we still call 'dead languages' today will fall into putrefaction. It is already impossible to understand the emotions of Homer's heroes. Etc. . . . etc. . . ."

After such remarks my thoughts take longer to rise up again than grass does after hail.

16 March

Finished *L'Enfant prodigue* a few days ago. As soon as I had suddenly glimpsed the composition of the poem in Berlin, I set to work at once; for the first time the writing followed the conception immediately. I was afraid, if I brooded over it any longer, of seeing the subject expand and deform itself. Moreover, I was sick of not writing anything, and all the other subjects that I am carrying about with me offered too great difficulties to be treated at once.

So that I have hardly spent a fortnight in elaborating and writing that *Enfant prodigue*.

I spent a week correcting it. Between Drouin and Copeau, like *L'Homme entre deux maîtresses*,[6] I really enjoyed this job of perfecting and polishing.

I read today in Brunot's *Histoire de la langue française:*[7] "Corneille and Racine were subject to the rule; they did not create it. If later on, through the influence of their genius, they became stylistic authorities, yet in their lifetime they humbly corrected themselves, the first to please Vaugelas, and the second out of respect for Father Bouhours, official arbiter of style." (Preface, p. xv.)

Yet I don't know if I am doing right in yielding to

---

[6] The reference is to La Fontaine's *Fables*, Book I, 17: *The Middle-aged Man and His Two Mistresses*, in which the man is torn by the need of satisfying both at once.

[7] *History of the French Language*, an authoritative scholarly treatise.

Copeau on this point: he claims that *lui parler* is incorrect. Indeed I find nothing in Littré to authorize it, and still there is no other means of expressing this relationship: "Quiconque veut parler au Père doit *me parler.—Je lui parlais* fort aisément sans toi."
None the less I correct it.[8]

March

Yesterday went to hear Father Janvier at Notre-Dame. We had dined with Rouart. Notre-Dame, badly lighted, disappoints us, but not Father Janvier, to whom we listen to the very end without being tired or bored. Constant political allusions help him to give color to his speech. A few seats in front of us, Boni de Castellane listens to the explanation of his duties. Subject of the sermon: Error— sins through ignorance. Necessity of *informing oneself;* that is to say, of learning to know *Truth.* Ah, how beautiful it is! Let's rush out and imprison Galileo!

24 [April]

I go to consult Marcel Drouin about the Claudel proofs I am correcting. Wonderful *Connaissance de l'Est,*[9] which I am rereading with close attention. Certain less ample, less inspired chapters still do not mar the book; a large number of them are of the loftiest beauty.

Spent some time also on the edition of Signoret, which the *Mercure* has agreed to bring out for the support of the poor widow. Some of these poems (almost all the last ones) are among the most dazzling and stately that I know. And, indeed, it is not enough to speak in this manner: to tell the truth, in our whole language I do not know any more beautiful ones.

17 May

I take hold of Jaloux and Miomandre, then, and bring them home. Here we are in my study. It appears that I have nothing to say to them, nothing to learn from them. I have, however, read Jaloux's book and didn't find it at all bad; but when I try to talk to him of it, I get all wound up in restrictions to prove at one and the same time my

---

[8] "Whoever wants to speak to the Father must speak to me.—I spoke to him quite easily without you." The text of *Le Retour de l'enfant prodigue* has: ". . . et qui veut comprendre le Père doit m'écouter.—Je l'entendais très aisément sans toi."

[9] Translated into English as *The East I Know.*

frankness and the delicacy of my critical taste. Then, I don't know how or why—through the same absurd fatality that makes Muishkin approach the fragile vase he is afraid of breaking—I bring up the subject of Suarès (a dangerous subject on which I know that we shall not be able to agree). The letter I have just written to Mauclair about Suarès is in my pocket; I have kept it for three days since I don't know his address, which Miomandre gives me at once. I am unfortunate enough to be somewhat satisfied with this letter, and especially with having dared to write it. I am seized with an itch to show it to them. Come on, I can't resist any longer. Besides, the envelope isn't closed. Fully aware of my error, of my mistake, holding in a trembling hand this sheet that I read stumbling over each sentence, I read it. I read painfully, my forehead covered with sweat, *forcing myself*, interrupting myself, looking closely for the disastrous effect of the reading, altogether lucid and conscious; then I resume, I go on. . . .

I have slept on it; I am still sick about it. The least unfortunate result of this mistake is to keep me now from sending the letter. But the greatest harm it causes me is to fill and becloud my whole mind for so long.

I am writing all this down as a lesson to me; but what I should do is to strengthen myself against myself. For I already knew my failing well; and that absurd need heedlessly to hand myself over disarmed to anyone whatsoever.

22 May

Last night Strauss's *Salomé*. Ghéon repeats to us the remark of Mme Strauss (as reported by Vielé-Griffin), commenting on the fact that Parisian audiences do not sufficiently applaud her husband's work: "Well, it's about time that we came back here with bayonets." Perhaps apocryphal. . . .

Abominable romantic music, with enough orchestral rhetoric to make one like Bellini. Only the parts filled with comic (the Magi) or morbid relief, Salomé's hesitations when Herod wants her to dance for him—almost the entire role of Herod, show a remarkable ability. Lasserre notes the same excellence of comic truculence in Hugo— likewise in the *Meistersinger*—same causes. And same causes of the shortcomings: lack of discretion of the means and monotony of the effects, annoying insistency, flagrant insincerity; uninterrupted mobilization of all the possible resources. Likewise Hugo, likewise Wagner, when metaphors come to mind to express an idea, does not choose, does not spare us a single one. Fundamental lack of artistry in all this. Systematic amplification, etc. . . . A shortcoming that it is not even interesting to examine into. One might better condemn the work as a whole and wait for the bayonets, because such an art really is the *enemy*.

Lunched at the Tour d'Argent with the Van Rysselberghes, Count Kessler, and Rodin. We talk to the last of his "start." For a long time, to earn his living, he makes "Carrier-Belleuse" of terracotta.[10] It is one of these poor insipid things that Druet recently exhibited in his window.

With *The Bronze Age* he arouses a protest; he barely avoids a trial with great difficulty (he is accused of having exhibited a mere cast of a man). But at that moment some friends group around him to defend him. That is when he leaves Brussels for Paris.

"How old were you then?"

"FORTY-FIVE."

This dominated my day.

22 June

For the fourth time I take up again from the very beginning this miserable book, over which I have labored so much already. The great improvisers of today would call this impotence or mania. Today I am almost at the point where I could agree with them. Yet toward the end of the day, after a great effort, I think I have set the amorphous mass in motion again.

The piano came yesterday. Good study of Chopin's wonderful preludes, which I am reviewing all together.

Every time that "success" has approached me, I have made faces at it.

Already in '91, I remember: I was with Pierre Louÿs; we met Retté at the d'Harcourt, where we had gone for dinner, I believe. The latter begins an elaborate praise of

[10] Decorative statuettes so named for the popular French sculptor Albert-Ernest Carrier-Belleuse, who multiplied them to satisfy the bourgeois public.

Les Cahiers d'André Walter,[11] which has just appeared
and which he "has just finished reading." I can hear his
sentence: "It is one of the twelve (or twenty) important
books that have appeared since . . ." At these words I
get up to hang my coat a bit farther away, leaving Retté
with half of his compliment unspoken. When I sit down
again, Pierre Louÿs leans toward me and says in my ear:
"My boy, when someone compliments you, you could at
least listen. It looks as if compliments drive you away."
This was true. It still is today. Too much pride perhaps;
also fear of blarney. Flatterers catch on at once and don't
let themselves get caught again.

On 29 June, in reply to a note from Marcel Drouin
about Blum's book, I had written this—which I later considered it wiser not to send him:

"Yes, Blum's book can do harm. . . . People will seek
in it not a 'new light' on a question which belongs, I
should say, more to the field of ethics than to sociology—
but rather an *authorization.* As for me, I first read the
book very hastily, then, embarrassed at hearing everyone
talking about it and being too uninformed to say anything
myself, I reread the book carefully; and was able to tell
Blum himself how foreign to me was a point of view that
proposes 'happiness' as an aim, limits happiness to the
bedroom and claims to furnish a recipe for capturing it.

"However typical and well presented all the observa-
tions of this book are—which seems a clever preface to
the whole Jewish theater of today—they utterly overlook
the value of resignation and restraint and imply the monstrous argument that the tree never produces so much or
such fine fruit as in *the state of nature.*"

I am merely a little boy having a good time—com-
pounded with a Protestant minister who bores him.

24 October

Again snowed under. Worked yesterday from morning
until two o'clock on a letter to Haguenin intended to facili-
tate and favor his zeal. He talks of presenting my work in
Berlin.[12] He talks well. I am beginning to be tired *of not
being;* as soon as a great enthusiasm does not sustain me,

[11] André Gide's first volume.
[12] *Le Roi Candaule* (*King Candaules*).

I struggle. Wounded vanity has never produced anything that matters, but at times my pride suffers from a real despair. And I live certain days as if in the nightmare of the man who was walled up alive in his tomb. Frightful state, which it is good to know, to have known. I shall write about it later when I have got out of it.

No news from Berlin, where they *must* play me before the 28th.

I think of Keats. I tell myself that two or three passionate admirations like mine would have kept him alive. Useless efforts, I feel at times all *wilted* by the silence.

13 December

Frightful, wonderful squall all night long. My mind seems to be lifted up by the wind—carried off like a kite—a kite on the end of a rubber band.

I find and reread a letter from Paul Claudel (1899): "Your mind has no slope," he said to me. That is just what is needed. No praise is more precious to me.

Gourmont—a desperately opaque soul.

Absence of sympathy = lack of imagination. This goes well with ignorance of dizziness; but Gérard doesn't know that this comes from his inability to imagine what he does not feel. This is what is often called *sang-froid;* merely impotence of the imagination. The most gifted natures are perhaps also the most trembling.

1908

9 *January*

Last night, the opening of *Candaule* in Berlin; this morning I receive the following telegram from Haguenin:

"Well acted Gurlitt (Nyssia)[1] very good great success for half of the audience the rest recalcitrant."

15 January

The day after the opening the press launches its attack. Barnowsky (the manager of the Kleiner Theater), terrified, hastens to cancel the play.

Great exchange of letters with Haguenin, who shows on this occasion a devotion that embarrasses me. An excellent article by him in the—(?) attempted to prepare the public. The critics stifle any inclination the public might have had to applaud.

I fear that the playing of *Saül* may be dreadfully compromised. . . .

We made a bad start. I have kept a copy of my letter to Haguenin. I should like it to be published, if ever . . .

Try to be proud rather than ambitious, that is the whole secret. I am beginning to think, moreover, that one suffers more from justified accusations than from those one doesn't deserve. To be told that I speculated on . . . to be called a pornographer, a boulevardier, a writer of farces; to be accused of imitating Maeterlinck! or Donnay, of whom I have never read anything!! Really, the blows fall wide of the mark.

Not a single critic who fails to drag out Hebbel; probably the same critics strangled him when he was alive. They are all vying with one another in their insults; terrifying monotony of these articles, only the first of which I read entire. One of them begins thus: "*Le Roi Candaule* had a dazzling success in Paris. [!] This does not surprise us . . . etc.—*eine solche Schweinerei . . .*" etc.

25 January

Inquiry conducted by the *Berliner Tageblatt*.

On the occasion of the twenty-fifth anniversary of Wag-

---

[1] Gurlitt is the actress who played Nyssia, the heroine.

ner's death they are interested in sounding out "the leading artistic and intellectual figures of all Europe as to their opinion of the influence of Wagnerism, especially in France."

I reply:

"I hold the person and the work of Wagner in horror; my passionate aversion has grown steadily since my childhood. This amazing genius does not exalt so much as he *crushes*. He permitted a large number of snobs, of literary people, and of fools to think that they loved music, and a few artists to think that genius can be acquired. Germany has perhaps never produced anything at once so great or so barbarous."

26 January

Yesterday, having arrived too early at Mme Brandon's, I spend three quarters of an hour waiting for the stroke of four in the Trocadéro Museum. In just the right mood for criticism and contemplation. Got a great deal out of it.

Got less from my visit to Mme Brandon; in less than five minutes eight people arrived; the inanity of the conversations was terrifying. Moreover Mme Brandon hardly talked with anyone but me. And as I got up to leave: "The people with whom one enjoys talking are so rare . . ."; the expression of the others as they heard this compliment.

Left to meet Copeau at the Pousset.

The *Phalange* banquet.[2]

I had promised Copeau not to separate from him, but unfortunately this was not possible. The embarrassing honor of seating me on the right of Royère was paid me (on his left Vielé-Griffin, then Gustave Kahn). It would have been hardly decent to refuse and I could not have done so without too many explanations. On my right Robert de Souza, then Ghéon, then, as the table turned a corner, Han Ryner, Apollinaire, Copeau, Jean Schlumberger, then about thirty people unknown to me. In all we might have been a hundred and fifty.—Pleasant room

[2] *La Phalange*, a literary review edited by Jean Royère from 1906 to 1914, published the second-generation symbolists, many of them also contributors to *Vers et Prose*. It was in this review that the great critic Albert Thibaudet, later associated chiefly with the *Nouvelle Revue Francaise*, began his career.

qn the first floor of the Cardinal. Passable food; but a
nervous tension makes me incapable of eating. . . .

Interrupted story. Useless to relate it in detail. Very
much amused and attracted by Apollinaire's face. At the
moment of the toasts a young fool who is not given the
floor when he wants to recite some of Royère's poems goes
off in the wings and breaks the mirror in a private dining-
room. "Very Dostoyevsky," says Copeau, with whom I
walk home. Jean Schlumberger is with us; Ghéon had to
take his train at eleven. Vielé-Griffin and Robert de Souza
take us to the Weber, where the evening is prolonged
until after midnight. It is one thirty when I get home.

Abominable night; not able to fall asleep a minute. If
anyone catches . . .

12 February

One more clipping from Germany; it says:

"Hebbels Auffassung steht für unser Empfindung ebenso
hoch über der Gides, wie etwa Kleists Ausgestaltung des
Amphitryons Stoffes über der Molières" (Bühne und Welt,
Berlin).[3]

Radiant weather; an azure we had forgotten during the
last three months. My mind full of gaiety, I go to return
the Signoret proofs to the Mercure and get tickets at the
Odéon for tomorrow's lecture (Moréas on Electra); I
walk back with Henry Davray to his new apartment on
the rue Servandoni. Go to take his ticket to Eugène
Rouart, at the Ministry. It is too late to return home—besides, it is too beautiful. I go to lunch alone (for one
franc seventy-five, tip included) in the little restaurant on
the Square Sainte-Clotilde where Ghéon and I lunched a
month ago. Then obliged to drop in at the École Al-
sacienne (for the purpose of paying an old bill), I go up
the part of the boulevard Raspail that has been recently
cut through, going over fences and wallowing somewhat
through vacant lots dug up by the construction gangs, but
amused to the point of rapture by the odd aspect of these
gutted houses on which the laughing sun sparkles. Old

[3] "In our opinion Hebbel's interpretation stands just as far above
Gide's as, say, Kleist's handling of the Amphitryon legend above
Molière's."

gardens, a well; caged trees, drooping and blackened; ancient courtyards, entrance steps of tumble-down private houses; all this dazzled and looking like a night bird that has suddenly been plunged into the light. How beautiful the day was!

Went to ring at Jean Schlumberger's and he accompanied me for a moment to the Luxembourg while waiting for the school to open.—Old school; courtyard I hadn't entered in twenty years! I hardly recognized myself there or old Papa Braünig, who spoke to me.

Back by métro—and work (Dostoyevsky for *La Grande Revue*).

13 February

Went with Eugène Rouart to hear the lecture by Moréas at the Odéon—which preceded a playing of Euripides' *Electra* in a prose version by Ferdinand Hérold. Numerous friends in the audience created a kind of success for the lecturer, who took three bows. I too applauded most willingly, for it was evident that everyone was applauding the poet of *Les Stances* and *Le Pèlerin*.[4] As for the lecture, it was interminable and boring. Moréas's voice, beautiful in a drawing-room or a café, remained hollow, monotonous and pompous. Having, indeed, but very few ideas, the fear of lacking substance made him embrace as many subjects as possible; he emptied his bag at random, spoke very little or not at all of *Electra* or of Euripides, but of Corneille, Shakespeare, Nietzsche, Malherbe, Aristotle, Otway, Voltaire, etc., etc.—limiting himself, most of the time, to reading old articles from *La Gazette*, which I remembered well enough to recognize sentences and groups of sentences. What in those articles had seemed to be delicate and discreetly phrased did not carry, and with the best will in the world I no longer found any savor in them. Many in the audience opened books or newspapers; some left noisily; people very nearly booed.

We left soon after the curtain went up, exasperated by the pasty elocution and the actors' lack of art.

The *points* in a speech have much to be said for them; need of knowing *how far one has got*.

---

[4] *Stanzas* and *The Pilgrim* are the principal works of Moréas.

It is not the subject that Moréas exhausted, but rather himself. One felt that he was saying everything and that, having done this, he had nothing more to say.

14 February

But I didn't know that Molière worked slowly! Very *important,* the remark of Grimarest quoted by Lemaître in his third lecture: "He did not work rapidly, but he didn't mind having people think he was prompt."

7 April

Lunched yesterday at Albert Mockel's with Stefan George, Albert Saint-Paul, and a rather pleasant young man whom they called Olivier (I never could make out whether it was merely his first name). Wonderful head of Stefan George, whom I have long wanted to know and whose work I admire each time I manage to understand it. Bluish-white complexion, skin dull and more drawn than wrinkled, sharply defined bone-structure; impeccably shaved; full, heavy hair, still more black than gray and all brushed back. Hands of a convalescent, very delicate, bloodless, very expressive. He speaks little, but in a deep voice that forces attention. A sort of clergyman's Prince Albert with two clasps toward the top, which opens for a necktie-scarf of black velvet, above and overflowing the collar. The simple gold slide on a ribbon leading to a watch or monocle gives a discreet accent to all this black. Shoes (elastic-sided, I fancy!) of a single piece of leather tightly gripping the foot, which I didn't like, perhaps because I had seen similar ones on Charmoy.

He expresses himself in our language without a single mistake, though yet a bit cautiously, it seems, and shows a surprising knowledge and understanding of our authors, particularly our poets; and all this without self-satisfaction, but with an evident awareness of his evident superiority.

6 June

. . . As a reaction I have plunged deeper into Pascal; sketched out two important dialogues of *La Porte étroite.* Went swimming every day. Returned strengthened, but after three days in Paris have lost almost all the advantage. Fortunately we are staying here only twelve days.

Cuverville, 22 June

Sublime style—direct emanation from the heart; it is only through *piety* that it can be achieved.

27 June

One can find in them (letters to Mlle de Roannez)[5] very fine arguments, even in favor of the Pope; ardent arguments, the only ones that persuade (see Letter VI, Brunschvicg edition)—and that leave me shaken.

"He ardently delighted in this outrage to flesh, the enemy. . . ." (Suarès: *Visite à Pascal.*)[6]

It doesn't seem to me that Suarès is following Pascal at this point. The Jansenist feels a loathing for sin, not for the flesh, and imagines the flesh itself not necessarily as a sinner but as a victim.

He speaks readily of an "innocent body" that death "afflicts." He considers it possible to have "peace between the soul and the body" and sees nothing wrong in seeking to flee a death that would destroy that peace (letter on the death of the father).

And finally he writes (first letter to Mlle de Roannez) the strangest sentence: "God never forsakes his own, not even in the sepulcher, where their bodies, although dead in the eyes of men, are more living before God because sin has ceased to inhabit them." It must be remembered that the Church teaches the resurrection of the flesh.

28 July

Amusing, these poems of Valery Larbaud.[7] As I read them, I see that in my *Nourritures* I should have been more cynical.

Speaking of Valery Larbaud, Philippe said to Ruyters: "It is always a pleasure to meet someone in comparison to whom Gide seems poor."[8]

18 October

Visit of the Paul Laurenses from 2 October until the 12th.

I returned from Paris, where I had spent a week. Painful fatigue, which continues even after the Laurenses have left. Yet I finish *La Porte étroite* on the 15th—and on the

---

[5] By Pascal.
[6] *Visit to Pascal.*
[7] *Poèmes par un riche amateur* (*Poems by a Rich Non-professional*) were attributed by Larbaud, when they first appeared in 1908, to an imaginary South-American millionaire named A. O. Barnabooth.
[8] Charles-Louis Philippe lived in near poverty; Larbaud inherited a fortune accumulated from mineral springs at Vichy.

16th shave off my mustache. Shocked by the lack of expression of my upper lip (as if something that has never yet spoken could suddenly become eloquent). How old I seem! "My poor André!" exclaims Em. on seeing me, and: "You must see your mistake." (I do not see it so readily.)

Prodigiously beautiful, warm weather for the last three weeks at least. I return to Paris tomorrow.

1909

January

The vicar of Cuverville comes to see poor Mius, who is starting his twelfth week in bed. Typhus has successively attacked all his organs; he is, as they say hereabouts, "very low." Just as he thought he was over it and already could see himself on his feet again, phlebitis set in—which he calls "feeblitis."

"Well!" says the priest, "I have an idea. Joan of Arc has just been canonized; there's a saint that hasn't been used much yet or too much bothered; we shall do a novena for her. . . ."

At this poor Mius is delighted. At the end of the novena the priest comes to see him. The very day he should have been cured, his second leg is attacked. "Oh, how taken in the priest was!" the good man writes us.

"You understand," explains the priest, "there are so many saints; each one has his specialty; Joan of Arc's wasn't yet known; we had to try her out; we made a mistake . . . well, we shall look elsewhere."

A few days later, on market-day, Juliette Mius meets an old neighbor.

"If you had only told me this earlier! I have just the thing for you. For a swelling there is only one; I already prayed him for my man."

"What is his name?"

"St. Hydropique." [1]

"My child, you must have made a mistake," the priest says to Juliette. "You must have misunderstood your friend. St. Hydropique does not exist. It is doubtless St. Euterpe that you mean. I was thinking of him. By the way, he is the patron of Cuverville. I am inclined to think that he will be particularly interested in you."

2 March

Departure for Rome at the height of rapture.

14 May

Yesterday, Thursday, Francis Jammes and his young wife came to lunch. I went to meet them at the train from

[1] In French, *hydropique* means "dropsical."

Soissons. I found Jammes grown stout, looking very life-of-Reilly as a result of his marriage. "Doesn't he look happy!" says Ginette. Obviously he has found the life for him.

At his request I had invited the Lacostes, Arthur Fontaine, Bonheur, and Ruyters. The lunch went off very well.

After the coffee, Jammes read us some "*Proses sur Bernadette*" which he gave in part to the *Figaro*, then a *Lettre à P. C. Consul*, which he is putting in the hands of the *N.R.F.*[2]

"An all the more magnificent work since you are named in it," he had written me a few days before.

He leaves the others a moment, goes up with me into the library, and there, with a great sigh:

"You are certainly lucky not to have any disciples! I don't know how you manage. . . ."

"They are the ones who wouldn't know how to manage it."

Then suddenly:

"I am afraid that Bonnard will begin to cut the ground out from under me."

Blum said to me: "Ernest-Charles always insists on my finesse and discrimination" (we were talking about an article in the *Grande Revue* concerning the republication of the *Nouveaux Eckermann*[3]). "He would like to get me accepted as the Jules Lemaître of a generation of which he would be the Brunetière."

4 July

Going through Paris for the review copies of *La Porte étroite*, I stop at the Valérys' to get news of Jeannie Valéry, on whom there was some question of operating. Degas is with her and has been wearing her out for more

---

[2] The "Prose Lines about Bernadette" concern his little neighbor Bernadette Soubirous, later sainted; the letter was addressed to Paul Claudel. This is the first mention Gide makes of the *Nouvelle Revue Française*, which he founded with Copeau, Schlumberger, Eugène Montfort, and others. After the first number had appeared, in November 1908, a quarrel eliminated Montfort from the board and a new initial number appeared in February 1909. From then until 1940, the *N.R.F.* under the successive editorship of Copeau, Jacques Rivière, and Jean Paulhan, but always reflecting the influence of Gide, was the leading literary periodical in France, if not in Europe.

[3] Blum's *New Conversations of Goethe with Eckermann*.

than an hour, for he is very hard of hearing and she has a weak voice. I find Degas has aged but is just like himself; just a bit more obstinate, more set in his opinion, exaggerating his crustiness, and always scratching the same spot in his brain where the itching becomes more and more localized. He says: "Ah, those who work from nature! What impudent humbugs! The landscapists! When I meet one of them in the countryside, I want to fire away at him. Bang! Bang!" (He raises his cane, closes an eye, and aims at the drawing-room furniture.) "There ought to be a police force for that purpose." Etc., etc. And again: "Art criticism! What an absurdity! I am accustomed to saying" (and in fact I remember hearing him say exactly the same things three or four years ago) "that the Muses never talk among themselves; each one works in her domain; and when they aren't working, they dance." And twice more he repeats: "When they aren't working, they dance." And again:

"The day when people began to write *Intelligence* with a capital *I*, all was damn well lost. There is no such thing as Intelligence; one has intelligence of this or that. One must have intelligence only for what one is doing."

Cuverville, September and October

Criticisms of *La Porte étroite.*—It is hard for them to admit that these different books cohabited, still cohabit, in my mind. They follow one another only on paper and through the great impossibility of letting them be written together. Whatever the book I am writing, I never give myself to it utterly, and the subject that claims me most insistently immediately afterward, develops meanwhile at the other extremity of me.

It will not be easy to trace the trajectory of my mind; its curve will reveal itself only in my style and will escape most people. If someone, in my latest writing, thinks that he can finally seize my likeness, let him be undeceived: it is always from my last-born that I am most different.

Sunday, 7 November

The book now strikes me as a nougat in which the almonds are good (i.e., the letters and journal of Alissa), but in which the filling is pasty, nondescript writing; but it couldn't have been otherwise with the use of the first person, the flabby character of my Jérôme implying flabby prose. So that, all things considered, I think the book well done. But how eager I am to write something different! It will be ten years before I can again use the words: *love, heart, soul*, etc. . . .

3 December

Here are the first two issues of a very small, very red review called *Sincérité*. M. Nazzi nourishes it all alone. Who is M. Louis Nazzi? To introduce him to me these sixty pages are not enough. They inform me as to his opinions rather than as to his tastes—that is to say, as to himself. I cannot be interested in the opinions before being interested in the person.

The word *sincerity* is one of those that are becoming harder for me to understand. I have known so many young men who vaunted their sincerity! . . . Some were pretentious and unbearable; others, brutal; their very tone of voice rang false. . . . In general, every young man thinks he is sincere when he has convictions and is incapable of criticism.

And what a confusion between sincerity and cheek! Sincerity means something to me, in art, only when it is consented to reluctantly. Only very banal souls easily achieve the sincere expression of their personality. For a new personality can be expressed sincerely only in a new form. The sentence that is personal to us must remain as peculiarly difficult to stretch as the bow of Ulysses.

THE DEATH OF
CHARLES-LOUIS PHILIPPE

No! no, it wasn't the same thing. . . . This time, he who disappears is a *real* man. We were counting on him; we were dependent on him; we loved him. And suddenly he ceases to be there.

On the way to Cérilly

I am writing this in the train—where I am still chatting with him. Oh, already confused recollections! If I did not fix them today, tomorrow, already utterly crushed, I should get them all mixed up.

Saturday evening a note from Marguerite Audoux tells me that Philippe is ill.

Sunday morning I rush to his place, on the Quai Bourbon; his concierge sends me to the Dubois hospital; he is unknown there. I learn that three persons came to ask for him the day before, who went away as uninformed as I. Mme Audoux's card bears no indication. . . . What shall I do? . . . Doubtless Francis Jourdain can give me some news; I write him. The telegram I receive from him on Tuesday morning already deprives me of all hope; I rush to the address he gives me.

At the end of the corridor in the Velpeau hospital a room door remains open. Philippe is there. Ah, what does it matter now that the long windows of that room open directly into a big bright garden! It would have been good for his convalescence; but already he has lost consciousness; he is still struggling, but has already left us.

I approach the bed where he is dying; here are his mother, a friend whom I don't know,[4] and Mme Audoux, who recognizes and welcomes me. I lead her out to the parlor for a minute.

Philippe has been here a week. At first the typhoid fever seemed very mild and, in the beginning, of so ill-defined a character that it was treated as a mere grippe. Then, for several days, Philippe was treated as typhoid cases are treated today; but the regime of cold baths was very impractical in his little lodging on the Quai Bourbon. Tuesday evening he was carried to the Velpeau hospital; nothing alarming until Sunday; then suddenly meningitis sets in; his heart beats wildly; he is lost. Dr. Élie Faure, his friend, who, against all hope, carries on and will continue to surround him with care, from time to time risks an injection of spartein or of camphorated oil; but already the organism has ceased to react.

We return to the bedside. Yet how many struggles still and with what difficulty this poor suffering body resigns itself to dying! He is breathing very fast and very hard—very badly, like someone who has forgotten how.

The muscles of his neck and of the lower part of his face tremble; one eye is half open, the other closed. I

4 Léon Werth. [A.]

rush to the post office to send some telegrams; almost none of Philippe's friends is informed.

At the Velpeau hospital again. Dr. Élie Faure takes the invalid's pulse. The poor mother queries: "How is the fever developing?" Through her suffering she is careful to speak correctly; she is a mere peasant, but she knows who her son is. And during these lugubrious days, instead of tears, she sheds floods of words; they flow evenly, monotonously, without accent or melody, in a somewhat hoarse tone, which at first surprises as if it didn't properly interpret her suffering; and her face remains dry.

After lunch I come back again; I cannot realize this loss. I find Philippe only slightly weaker, his face convulsed, shaken; struggling with slightly less energy against death.

✳

Wednesday morning

Chanvin was waiting for me in the parlor. We are led, on the right side of the courtyard, to a little secret room, with an entrance on an angle—hiding as if ashamed. The rest of the establishment does not know of its existence, for we are in a *house of health,*[5] which you enter only to be cured, and this is the chamber of the dead. The new guest is led into this room at night, when the rest of the house is asleep; on the wall a notice specifies: "not before 9 p.m. or after 7 a.m." And the guest will leave here only by way of that low door, the bolted door I see over there at the end of the room, opening directly on the other street. . . .

There he is: very small on a large shroud; wearing a brownish suit; very erect, very rigid, as if at attention for the roll call. Hardly changed, moreover; his nostrils somewhat pinched; his little fists very white; his feet lost in big white socks rising up like cotton nightcaps.

A few friends are in the room, weeping silently. The mother comes toward us, unable to weep, but moaning. Each time another person comes in she begins a new complaint like a professional mourner of antiquity. She is not speaking to us but to her son. She calls him; she

---

[5] In French *maison de santé* is one of the expressions for "hospital."

leans over him, kisses him: "Good little boy!" she says to him. . . . "I knew all your little habits. . . . Ah, close you in now! close you in forever. . . ."

At first this sorrow surprises one, so eloquent it is; no expression in the intonation, but an extraordinary invention in the terms of endearment . . . then, turning toward a friend, without changing her tone, she gives an exact indication as to the funeral charges or the time of departure. She wants to take her son away as quickly as possible, take him away from everybody, have him to herself, down in their country: "I'll go and see you every day, every day." She caresses his forehead. Then turning toward us again: "Pity me, gentlemen! . . ."

Marguerite Audoux tells us that the last half-hour was horrible. Several times everyone thought all was over; the frightful breathing stopped; the mother would then throw herself onto the bed: "Stay with us a bit more, my dear! Breathe a bit more; once more! just once more!" And as if "the good little boy" heard her, in an enormous effort all his muscles could be seen to tighten, his chest to rise very high, very hard, and then fall back. . . . And Dr. Élie Faure, seized with despair, would exclaim sobbing: "But I did everything I could. . . ."

He died at nine p.m.

At the *Mercure de France*, where the edition of the works of Lucien Jean, for which he was to write the preface, is in abeyance; while I talk with Vallette, Chanvin is writing some letters of mourning. The mother wants to take the body away this very night; at eight o'clock a brief ceremony will gather together a few friends, either at the hospital or at the station. I shall not go, but want to see Philippe once more. We go back there. Léautaud accompanies us.

Here we are again in the mortuary room. Bourdelle has come to take the death-mask; the floor is littered with splashes of plaster. Yes indeed, we shall be happy to have this exact testimony; but those who know him only through it will never imagine the full expression of this strapping little fellow, whose whole body had such a special significance. Yes, Toulouse-Lautrec was just as short as he, but deformed; Philippe was upright; he had small hands, small feet, short legs; his forehead well formed. Beside him, after a short time, one became ashamed of being too tall.

In the courtyard a group of friends. In the room, the mother, Marguerite Audoux (oh, how beautiful the quality of her grief seems to me!), Fargue; Léautaud, very pale against his very black beard, is swallowing his emotion. The mother is still moaning; Fargue and Werth are examining a time-table; it is agreed that we shall meet tomorrow morning at the Quai d'Orsay station for the eight-fifteen train.

Thursday, 8 o'clock

Quai d'Orsay station, where Chanvin and I arrive, fortunately well ahead of time, for there we discover that the eight-fifteen train leaves from the Gare de Lyon. Alas, how many friends, ill informed as we were, will not have time to get to the other station as we do at once! We don't see one in the train. Yet several had promised to come.

All night long it rained and there was a strong wind; now the air, somewhat calmed, is warm; the countryside is drenched; the sky is uniformly desolate.

We have taken tickets to Moulins. From the time-table that I buy in Nevers, I discover that to reach Cérilly it still takes three or four hours from Moulins in a little dawdling train, plus a long ride in the stagecoach; and that the little train will have left when we arrive. Can we make that leg of the trip in a carriage?

In Moulins we get refusals from three hacksters; the distance is too great: we shall need an automobile. And here it is! We light out into the country. The air is not cold; the hour is beautiful. In a moment the wind wipes away our fatigue, even our melancholy, and speaking of Philippe, we say: if you are watching us from some part of heaven, how amused you must be to see us racing after you along the road!

Beautiful country ravaged by winter and the storm; on the lavender edge of the sky how delicate are the greens of the pastures!

Bourbon-l'Archambault. This is where your twin sister

and your brother-in-law, the pastry-cook, live. Ah! here is the hearse coming back from Cérilly. . . . Evening is falling. We enter the little village just before nightfall. The auto is put in the coach-house of the hotel where we have left our bags. Here we are on the village square. We are moving about in one of Philippe's books. We are told the way to his house. It is there on the road halfway up the hill, past the church, almost opposite the house of *Père Perdrix*.[6] On the ground floor the shutters of the only window are closed like the eyelids of someone plunged in meditation; but the door is ajar. Yes, this is the right place: someone opens the door as he leaves, and in the narrow room opposite the entrance, between lighted candles, we see the coffin draped with black cloth and covered with wreaths. The mother rushes toward us, is amazed to see us; was her child so much loved! She introduces us to some village people who are there: friends come from Paris on purpose; she is proud of it. A woman is sobbing in a corner; it is his sister. Oh, how she resembles him! Her face explains our friend's, which was slightly deformed by a scar on the left side of the jaw which the beard did not quite hide. The brother-in-law cordially comes up to us and asks if we don't want to see Charles-Louis's room before more people come.

The whole house is built on his scale; because it was very small he came out of it very small. Beside the bed-sitting-room, which is the one you enter, the bright empty room where the maker of sabots, his father, used to work; it gets its light from a little court, as does Philippe's room on the second floor. Small, unornamented room; on the right of the window, a little table for writing; above the table, some shelves with a few books and the high pile of all his school notebooks. The view one might have from the window is cut short by two or three firs that have grown right against the wall of the courtyard. That is all; and that was enough. Philippe was comfortable here. The mother does the honors of the place:

"Look carefully, gentlemen; this is all important if you are going to talk about him."

In the front of the house, the best parlor, in which is collected the little luxury of this humble dwelling: deco-

---

[6] *Papa Partridge*, a novel by Charles-Louis Philippe.

rated mantel, framed portraits, draperies; this is the room that is never used.

"Even though we are poor people, you see that we are not in dire poverty."

She intends that at the hotel where we are staying we should consider ourselves as her guests as long as we remain in Cérilly.

"Do you want to see Papa Partridge's house?" asks the brother-in-law; "it should interest you."

And we go with him to the last house in the village; but the room in which we are received has been redone. As we are leaving, the brother-in-law leans toward us:

"The man you see over there is Jean Morantin; you know, the *lord of the village*. When Louis spoke of him in his book, people wanted to get him worked up. He said: no, no, I know little Philippe! He's a good boy; he certainly didn't intend to say anything bad about me."

We return to the hotel, where we find Valery Larbaud, just arrived from Vichy, and we spend the evening with him.

The funeral takes place Friday morning at ten o'clock. No other friend has come; yes, Guillaumin, the author of *La Vie d'un simple;*[7] he lives on a farm thirteen kilometers from here. We still "hope" for a quarter of an hour more; Cérilly lies between several railroad lines and can be reached from several different directions. Finally the short procession starts moving.

Small gray and brown romanesque church, filled with shadow and sound counsel. The deacon comes toward us where we remain grouped around the coffin:

"This way, gentlemen! Come this way, where we have a big fire."

And we approach a brazier near the apse. Twice during the ceremony the brother-in-law comes toward us; the first time to tell us that Marcel Ray has just arrived from Montpellier with his wife; then, the second time, leaning toward us:

"You should visit the Chapel of the Saints; my brother-in-law spoke of that too in his books."

[7] *The Life of a Simple Man.*

. . .

The ceremony ends; we walk toward the cemetery. The sky is overcast. Occasionally a low moving cloud befogs the distant landscape. Here is the open grave. On the other side of the grave, opposite me, I watch the sobbing sister, who is being supported. Is it really Philippe that we are burying? What lugubrious comedy are we playing here? A village friend, decorated with lavender ribbon,[8] a shopkeeper or functionary of Cérilly, steps forward with some manuscript pages in his hand and begins his speech. He speaks of Philippe's shortness, of his unimpressive appearance, which prevented him from attaining honors, of his successive failures in the posts he would have liked to hold: "You were perhaps not a great writer," he concludes, "but . . ." Nothing could be more stirring than this naïve reflection of the modesty Philippe always showed in speaking of himself, by which this excellent man was doubtless taken in. But some of us feel our hearts wrung; I hear someone whisper near me: "He's making a failure out of him!" And I hesitate a moment to step up before the grave and say that only Cérilly could speak so humbly of Philippe; that, seen from Paris, Philippe's stature seems to us very great. . . . But, alas, wouldn't Philippe suffer from the distance thus established between him and those of his little village, from which his heart never wandered?

Moreover, Guillaumin follows the other speaker; his speech is brief, full of measure and tact, very moving. He speaks of another child of Cérilly who went away like Philippe and died at thirty-five like him, just a century ago: the naturalist Perron. A little monument on the square immortalizes him. I shall copy the pious and touching inscription:

> PERRON
> DRIED UP LIKE
> A YOUNG TREE
> THAT SUCCUMBS
> UNDER THE WEIGHT
> OF ITS OWN FRUIT

[8] The insigne of the Palmes Académiques, a minor distinction awarded by the state.

Another side of the monument bears a bronze relief showing François Perron seated under a mangrove dotted with cockatoos in an Australian landscape peopled with familiar kangaroos.

An automobile stops at the gate of the cemetery; it is Fargue arriving just as the speeches are ending.

I am happy to see him here; his grief is very great, like that of all who are here; but it seems, besides, that Fargue represents a whole group of absent friends among the very best and that he comes bearing their homage.

We return to the hotel, where Mme Philippe invites us to dinner; her son-in-law, M. Tournayre, represents her. I am seated beside him; he tells me certain details of his brother-in-law's early childhood:

"Already at the age of five or six little Louis used to play 'going to school'; he had made up little notebooks, which he would put under his arm and then say: 'Good-by, Mamma; I am going to school.'

"Then he would sit down in a corner of the other room, on a stool, turning his back to everything. . . . Finally, a quarter of an hour later, the class being over, he *would come home:* 'Mamma, school is over.'

"But one fine day, without saying a word to anyone, slipping out, he really went to school; he was only six; the teacher sent him home. Little Louis came back again. Then the teacher asked: 'What have you come here for?' 'Why—to learn.'

"He is sent home again; he is too young. The child insists so much that he gets a dispensation. And thus he begins his patient education."

O "good little boy," I understand now what made you like so much, later on, *Jude the Obscure.* Even more than your gifts as a writer, than your sensitivity, than your intelligence, how much I admire that wondering application which was but one form of your love!

We leave.

And during the whole return trip I think of that article which I had promised him to write, that I was getting ready to write, on the appearance of his book, which Fasquelle is to publish any moment now—that article which he was waiting for. I fix the various points in my mind.

Philippe's death cannot make me exaggerate my praise in any regard; at most by bending me more sadly over that stirring figure and by allowing me to study him better (in the papers he left behind), it will strengthen my admiration by sharpening the contours.

Some people only half knew him because they saw only his pity, his affection, and the exquisite qualities of his heart; with that alone he could not have become the wonderful writer that he was. A great writer meets more than one requirement, answers more than one doubt, satisfies various appetites. I have only moderate admiration for those who cannot be seen from all sides, who appear deformed when looked at from an angle. Philippe could be examined from all sides; to each of his friends, of his readers, he seemed very unified; yet no two of them saw the same Philippe. And the various praises addressed to him may well be equally justified, but each one taken alone does not suffice. He has in him the wherewithal to disorient and surprise—that is to say, the wherewithal to endure.

☼   ☼   ☼

30 December

Jammes's vanity.

Annoys me like the upsetting of an equilibrium; like something lacking; is permitted him only by an utter ignorance of everything that is not himself. Paying attention to what is not oneself he calls discussing; and naturally he hates *discussion*. Schwob having rashly told him one day that *Jean de Noarrieu* seemed to him more beautiful than *Hermann and Dorothea*, Jammes concluded from this that he is greater than Goethe. The idea never came to him for an instant that those who risk such a comparison consider *Jean de Noarrieu* as Jammes's best work; and what is *Hermann and Dorothea* in Goethe's work? However perfect the poem may be, suppress it and the total work is hardly diminished at all.

"*Jean de Noarrieu*," writes Jammes, "even though I never tried to embody any philosophy in it, is in Schwob's opinion, as well as in my own, superior to *Hermann and*

Dorothea—although I have never had the courage to read that work of Goethe."

There is a certain *sincerity* that consists in trying to *see truthfully,* and Jammes will never know that form of sincerity. "If water breaks a stick," as La Fontaine says, his mind never "rectifies" it.[9] I am well aware that it is essentially *poetic* not to allow the reason to intervene too quickly and that often rectifying one's judgment amounts to falsifying one's sensation; but art would consist in maintaining the sensation in all its freshness and yet not allowing it to prevent any other function. Odd lay-out of that mind! One cannot blame him for anything, so well aware is one that the spirit of inquiry would spoil him. He doesn't seek, either, to see the truth about himself; and besides he would have less genius if he were less convinced of having genius.

I am saying this rather sloppily. Let me sum up: to be a poet, one must believe in one's genius; to become an artist, one must *question it.* The really strong man is the one in whom *this* augments *that.*

[9] La Fontaine points out that a stick projecting from water appears broken at the water-line; but it only appears so, and our mind, rectifying the impression, straightens the stick.

1910

16 January

Copeau asks me to go with him to the Bibescos'; he is to be introduced to Chaumeix. I overcome my apprehension of the frightful bore that a society dinner is for me and get out of the closet the dress suit dating from my marriage, which I have not worn a dozen times. At Copeau's, on the rue Montaigne, where I go to pick him up, we notice that my trousers are terribly eaten by moths! Laughter and anguish; impossible to show myself this way: the white of my drawers appears in odd patterns; we light on the black felt ribbon of my panama hat and sit down to sew onto the drawers, opposite the holes, little squares and stripes.

I knew from Boylesve that Chaumeix was quite willing to write an article on *La Porte étroite* in the *Débats*, hence I was unable to say three words to him. Nothing freezes me up so much as knowing that my cordiality could be useful to me.

20 January

Pleasant visit from Boylesve; I am well aware that the conversation will not go very far with him, but each time I have greater enjoyment in seeing him. Ghéon is with me and in a moment will go with me to the Countess de Noailles's. We are going to get from her the review of *La Mère et l'enfant*[1] that she has consented to do for *La Nouvelle Revue Française*.

Mme de Noailles is at the hotel (Princess Hotel) on the rue de Presbourg; the windows of her room look out on the Arc de Triomphe. She was expecting us, and this is rather apparent: she is lying on a chaise-longue made up of two armchairs and a stool that all go together, sinuously draped in a sort of Rumanian or Greek robe of black Tussore silk with a broad band of whitish gray, of that soft white one finds in China paper and certain Japanese felts; the chemise floats amply around her bare arms loaded with Venetian bracelets. A scarf wanders around

---

[1] *The Mother and Child*, a book by Charles-Louis Philippe.

her, the color of the yolk of a hard-boiled, or rather a soft-boiled, egg; the color of dried apricots. Siren, her feet disappear mysteriously under a Tunisian cloth. Her hair is undone, abandoned, and jet-black; cut in bangs on her forehead, but falling as if wet onto her shoulders. She introduces us to the Princess de Caraman-Chimay (?), who trains on me a lorgnette that she doesn't put down during the entire visit.

Impossible to set down anything from the conversation. Mme de Noailles talks with an amazing volubility; the sentences rush to her lips, crush themselves, and become confused in their haste; she says three or four at a time. This makes a very tasty compote of ideas, sensations, images, a tutti-frutti accompanied by gestures of the hands and arms, of the eyes especially, which she turns skyward in a swoon that is not too artificial but rather too encouraged.

Speaking of Montfort in passing, she compares him to a tench with big pop eyes and imitates the fish when it comes against the glass of the aquarium. This very striking image makes us laugh, and as later on we allude to it, she becomes quite worried:

"Don't repeat that. Oh, I beg of you, don't say that I said it! You would make me an enemy of him. And I am always promising myself never to say anything bad about anyone!"

Ghéon, very much a wondering yokel just off the train at the Gare d'Orsay with heavy muddy shoes, but, as is customary with him, very much at ease, is much more interested, intrigued, than he expected. One would have to hold oneself very much in check not to succumb to the charm of this extraordinary poetess with the boiling brain and the cold blood.

Paris, 15 April

Yesterday, lunch at Rouché's with Gabriele d'Annunzio. I had originally refused, caring very little about seeing him again; and I replied to Rouché that I had too good a memory of my meeting with d'Annunzio fifteen years ago to risk spoiling it by seeing again a writer for whose talent I no longer had much esteem. But Rouché would not take no for an answer (I have kept this amusing correspondence), and my reluctance yields to his kindly insistence. There were present: Henri de Régnier, Desvallières, Besnard, Suarès, Saglio, Marcel, Ernest-Charles, and so on. I was placed between Henri de Régnier and Suarès, almost opposite d'Annunzio: I could not have been more pleasingly placed. D'Annunzio, primmer, more constricted, more contracted, and also more sparkling than ever. His eye lacks kindness and affection; his voice is more cajoling than really caressing; his mouth less greedy than cruel; his forehead rather beautiful. Nothing in him in which natural gifts yield to genius. Less will than calculation; little passion or else cold passion. He generally disappoints those who have been taken (that is, mistaken) with his work. "He sums up all of Italy," says Mme Rouché, who is among the latter. "Less Dante," adds Suarès, who eloquently declares to me how little he likes the "Bluffer." The amusing thing is that d'Annunzio has smiles for only two persons: Suarès and me (less for me than for Suarès, whose grandiloquence quite naturally impresses him).

After lunch we gather in the den, Desvallières, Suarès, I, d'Annunzio, and Saglio, who launches into an exaggerated praise of the last pages of the novel (*Forse che si, forse che no*)[2] which *La Grande Revue* has just finished bringing out. It must be said that d'Annunzio has just drenched Suarès and me with the greatest praise a moment before. Saglio's compliments are probably hardly enough for the "Master" (who rather anxiously looks toward Desvallières, toward Suarès, toward me; but he can search us without finding any sugar. He will get only Saglio).

A moment later, nevertheless, d'Annunzio insists on seeing me again. It is agreed that he will write to invite me to lunch (I doubt very much that he will do so). Meanwhile, one by one, the guests leave. There remain only the "Master," Henri de Régnier, Suarès, and I. D'Annunzio starts downstairs first; we follow close behind him.

From the entrance hall we see the rain pouring down. Suarès, on the threshold, somewhat wild-looking, hastily shakes hands and starts to rush out into the rain.

[2] *Perhaps So and Perhaps Not.*

"What!" I exclaim; "are you leaving without a hat?"
Suarès collects his wits. "Why, you're right! . . . Oh,
I often do this. . . ."

And he rushes to the coatroom and back out again.
Outside, I understand why he was upset: d'Annunzio is
taking him home in his car.

30 May

I shall probably be obliged to write a preface for my
Aveugle[3]—which otherwise would only add to the confusion.

In it I should say: If being a Christian without being
a Catholic amounts to being a Protestant, then I am a
Protestant. But I cannot recognize any other orthodoxy
than the Roman orthodoxy, and if Protestantism, either
Calvinist or Lutheran, attempted to impose its orthodoxy
upon me, I should turn toward the Roman, as the only
one. "Protestant orthodoxy"—these words have no meaning for me. I do not recognize any *authority;* and if I did
recognize one, it would be that of the Church.

But my Christianity springs only from Christ. Between
him and me, I consider Calvin or St. Paul as two equally
harmful screens. Oh, if only Protestantism had rejected
St. Paul at once! But it is to St. Paul, rather than to
Christ, that Calvin is related.

[Cuverville] 17 June

Mius is gaining skill in hybridizing certain flowers; and
I have finally succeeded in convincing him that, in the
beds of seedlings thus obtained, the least robust varieties
often gave the most beautiful flowers. But it is only with
great difficulty that I can get him to set aside the common,
vigorous varieties that can get along without his atten-
tions, in order to favor those that are harder to cultivate
and require his care.

If, among her artists, Greece does not count a single
Spartan, is this not because Sparta threw her puny children into pits?

Impossible to get Mius to admit that, in order to assure
selection, it is not enough to prefer the delicate and rare
variety, that its difficult victory over the commoner varie-

---

[3] Doubtless an early title for *La Symphonie pastorale* (*The Pastoral
Symphony*), first published in 1919.

ties must be assured by suppressing the latter in its vicinity.

To avoid argument, he pretends to clear my garden of them; but I find them a little later, transplanted in some corner, just as rugged as the rare variety is fragile, and infinitely prolific. In less than two years they have won back their place; the exquisite has disappeared, stifled by the commonplace. Because, for flowers too, "the exquisite is as difficult as it is rare"; and however beautiful the most modest flower of the fields may be, one's heart weeps to think that the most beautiful always has the least chance of survival. It is at one and the same time the least gifted for the struggle and the one that most arouses appetites and jealousies. Oh, if only man, instead of so often contributing to the spreading of the vulgar, instead of systematically pursuing with his hatred or his cupidity the natural ornament of the earth, the most colorful butterfly, the most charming bird, the largest flower; if he brought his ingenuity to bear on protecting, not on destroying but on favoring—as I like to think that people do in Japan, for instance, because it is so very far from France! . . .

Were a miracle to produce in our woods some astounding orchid, a thousand hands would stretch out to tear it up, to destroy it. If the bluebird happens to fly past, every gun is sighted; and then people are amazed that it is rare!

Winged, plumed, down-covered seeds, wrapped in lusciousness and attracting the bird! what ingenuity each plant shows in scattering its progeny as far as possible from itself!

A giant parsley bends its enormous stem terminated by the umbel now without petals; as soon as the seed begins to ripen, the stem curves, seems to bend under the weight of the carpels, and in a solemn gesture, having to let that seed fall without any device to propel it in the air, at least it carries it as far as possible away from its own feet.

O Barrès! How different from yours is the teaching that I read in the book of Nature! I wonder at the way each animal drives its young from it as soon as they are able to take care of themselves. If a soil cannot long continue to produce the same crop, this is not so much because it

becomes poorer, but rather, according to a recently discovered phenomenon of exosmosis, because each plant
distils through its roots a poison for the plant that resembles it. . . .

And moreover, however you explain it, the important
thing to note is that the same soil cannot long continue
to produce the same crop.

[Cavalière, August]

ÆSTHETICS

It is not enough merely to create the event most likely
to reveal character; rather the character itself must neces-
sitate the event. (See Coriolanus, Hamlet.) The succession of events is the development of the character. (Mac-
beth—who cannot escape his own *realization*.)

Or else, quite to the contrary, the revealing event
should already have taken place (Sophocles, Ibsen) and
the drama should then furnish the progressive explanation
of the event; the prototype of this kind of drama is
Œdipus, who advances from happiness in ignorance to unhappy knowledge.

In an automobile heading toward Marseille

There is no art except on a human scale. The instrument that allows man to go beyond his measure, to exceed his natural agility, escapes the conditions of the
work of art. O light feet of Achilles! you are not scorned
with impunity. Yes, the work of art was easy in a time
when Pegasus of the ideal flight alone outdistanced the
speedy son of Peleus. There can be no question of art
as soon as the idea of establishing a record enters in.

Locating the idea of perfection, not in equilibrium and
the middle path, but in the extreme and exaggeration is
perhaps what will most set off our period and distinguish
it most annoyingly.

To succeed on this plane, one must agree never to be
embarrassed by anything. The *"quod decet"* of art is the
first obstacle to be forgotten.

The young men I have known who were most crazy
about automobile-driving were, to begin with, the least
interested in traveling. The pleasure is no longer that of
seeing the country or even of quickly reaching a certain
place, where nothing really attracts them; but simply that

of going fast. And though one enjoys thereby sensations just as deeply inartistic or anti-artistic as those of mountain-climbing, it must be admitted that they are intense and indomitable. The period that has known them will not escape the consequences; it is the period of impressionism, of the rapid and superficial vision; one can guess what gods and altars it will choose; through lack of respect, consideration, and consistency, it will sacrifice even more on those altars, but in an unconscious or unavowed manner.

The work of art blossoms forth only with the participation, the connivance of all the virtuous elements of the mind.

VOYAGE IN ANDORRA

Ax-les-Thermes, Thursday

Arrived at ten p.m. No room in the Hotel Sicre; at this season of the year it amounts to insulting M. Sicre to suppose that he has one. The hotel porter leads us out on the road to Spain until we reach one of the last houses in the village where they take in roomers. The landlady is already in bed; dull wait in a dusty little drawing-room invaded by winged ants, under the stupid gaze of the family portraits.

To reach what is going to serve me as a room I am told to cross through the kitchen, then a sort of dark storeroom; on the way I can clearly make out, by the light of my candle, a heap of newly washed laundry, but not the handles of the wheelbarrow on which it rests. I bump into them, scattering on the floor my night things, my light, and myself stretched out full length. For lack of witnesses, forced to laugh myself, in the dark, while rubbing my bruises.

[Merens, Friday] 10 o'clock

We reach Hospitalet in the stifling heat; seven hours' walk to this stop; we decide to lunch at once. Here is the old guide we have notified; but it is his youngest son, a lithe handsome youth of sixteen, who will lead us.

Little by little the statice becomes mingled with blue pompons that I think are shepherd's scabious. Higher up, big stemless thistles fixed close to the earth like spits. Over a field of lavender euphrasy is flying a *Parnassian Apollo;* I remember my delight when as a child I first saw this superb butterfly in the Jura; I thought then that it was found only in the Alps. We follow the stream separating Andorra from France; for some time we have been in Andorra.

My burning feet were slipping in my overwide sandals; I was ashamed of feeling so tired. A little before reaching the pass, we sat down a moment beside a trickle of a spring without beauty. It filtered, ice-cold, between the sheets of shale; you think you are merely going to moisten your lips, but you cannot refrain from drinking. Companions! If I had been alone, there I should have stopped, lying beside the spring; I should have drunk more than one glass; then I should have gone down slowly toward Hospitalet.—We set out again.

The hay is being drawn; the peasants are bringing the shocks home on their heads. Herds of cows and bulls as we go through the pass; herds of horses.

Dead snow, before reaching the summit; on the edge of the snow, gentians. The vegetation does not seem to me different from that of the Alps; yet dwarf pines take the place of the annoying larches and spruces.

In short, these mountains have no other advantage over the Alps than that they are a bit less high, a bit more to the south, and, hence, bathed with a little less crude light. Yet the Greeks or the Latins would have experienced here the same terror of the chaotic: "This region that God created to be horrible," Montesquieu would have repeated nevertheless.

On the Spanish side, dark-blue aconites; lower down, the china-blue sword-shaped iris; surprised to find it here in the wild state.

Unable to go any farther than Soldeu (which is pronounced Soldéou), a paltry village where we can spend the night. For some time now I have been thinking only of a bath. As soon as we have made sure of a lodging in the inn, we go down toward the stream. A waterfall was foaming not far off, which we reached over huge slippery blocks of stone; more aerated, the water seemed less cold;

each of us in turn got under the deep shower; it was amidst a thick eddy of foliage into which the sun plunged its last rays.

[*Andorra la Vieja*] *Sunday*

Four o'clock; first sounds on the square; a cat is mewing its hunger in the corridor; I hear the eldest of yesterday's fishermen, the innkeeper's son, getting ready and going downstairs; already the two other boys are waiting for him on the square; I get up and lean over the balcony; the square is ash-gray. The children recognize me and call to me. They have got back into their soaked clothing of the day before. The top of the mountains is trembling and growing pale, but all the colors are still asleep; an old woman leads some thin horses by. . . . I have hardly closed my eyes all night. The air is full of a winy scent. I go back to bed for a few minutes.

Five o'clock; I start out ahead of the others to spend a minute with the fishermen, who signal to me from the other bank. They complain that their nets have been raised, for they have caught only one fish, just one! Here they are all soaked again, still laughing.

Extraordinary narrowness of this valley. Without noticing it, we are in Spain again; already in Andorra we had met some of these mules fringed with red. The stream is getting deeper; a canal branches off, which we follow, leaving the road, where from a distance we see our horses raising dust.

Seo de Urgel

The grapevines, locked in the wall up to the second story, spread out over the balcony. Narrow streets, overhanging roofs narrowly channel the sky. Dark cathedral; beautiful Romanesque cloister (see Baedeker), deep arcades in which shops are set up; frugal market.

Between Seo and San Vicente from three o'clock to five; it is very hot; my companions say nothing but inanities; if I were not more silent than they, I should doubtless say just as many as they.

Sunday to Monday: night spent at the baths of San Vicente.

The moon, by some wonderful mystery, has been full for four or five nights now. My room, at the end of the hotel, overhangs the stream at a great height, and through the branches a little upstream I can just make out the sparkling of the water; not another sound but that of the rushing water. How slowly the night flows on! Anything that fell from the balcony would hardly be heard in its fall. Oh, to remain here, drunken and naked under the moon, with no other concern than to sleep off the heat of the day! It is so beautiful that the silence of the night birds is incomprehensible; it is amazing; everything seems to be waiting. . . .

Left at five o'clock; an hour in a rattletrap carriage. At —— the road ends. We pass over a shaky and bent wooden bridge. The mules loaded with our duffel and blankets ford the stream. Immediately afterward the path climbs into the mountains.

☼   ☼   ☼

VIIIth Court.—Monday, 14 November

He had held up until this moment; I saw him come in fresh and pink, his features only very slightly drawn; but as soon as he had been led to the place of the accused, he looked for his father among the crowd filling the back of the hall, and as soon as he had made out the stooped, unhappy man, who used to crush him under his scoldings and reproaches, then all the muscles in his pale little face seemed suddenly to contract. Those who come in through that door come from the house of detention. I was able to observe him well; I was seated on the lawyers' bench, right beside him; without having to get up, just by leaning over the railing, I could even see his thin, bare calves; he was completely covered by a blue-black cape, thread-bare and worn to a fringe, caught in a hook at the collar. The old father is called to the stand. I learned from the questioning that the boy is only twelve; three older "comrades" were being judged with him; the lad had let himself be led by them into an easy robbery; by means of a broken window, without even going into a garden house, they had managed to carry off various carpenter's tools.

"There wasn't even fifteen francs' worth," said the eldest.

The old father would like to get his child back; he was satisfied with him until this day, he says. . . . When the judge finally reads: "Transferred to the care of . . . (?) until his majority," the boy, being led off by the policemen, sobs.

Finished my novel the night before last[4]—with too great ease, and this makes me fear that I did not put into the last pages all that I was *charged* to put in.[5]

It is now high time to break with certain habits, certain indulgences in writing. I wish to try at once. And since this notebook happens to be filled, begin another one in which I shall get in training, in which I shall cultivate *new relations*. Keep from living on one's impetus.

Edmond Jaloux came to dinner last night. I suffered to feel so far from him, for I have a very old (though somewhat hardened) affection for him. From contact with society, he is taking on ever more polish; he talks with great tact and sweetness. He had come in evening dress, obliged, upon leaving the Villa, to attend a supper, at which he could get over the boredom I caused him; for I had nothing but gloomy things to say to him; the sight of his tail-coat froze me up, together with the thought that this is his real costume, in which he is more comfortable than in an ordinary coat.

[4] *Isabelle*, which appeared in 1911.
[5] The word *chargé* also means "loaded" both in the sense of a creature or vehicle and in the sense of a firearm.

1911

6 *January*

Every evening I read for Dominique Drouin from eight thirty to nine o'clock. Read the first evening Töpffer's *Le Col d'Anterne*, then "*Kanut*" and "*Aymerillot*," both of which struck me as very bad; then "*Oceano Nox*" and the end of "*Les Malheureux*" and other bits of *Les Contemplations*, which plunged me into the deepest admiration. Yesterday "*Les Djinns*"; this evening Turgenyev's short story "The Dog." [1]

Then, withdrawing into the little recess in the hallway, I read an hour of English before going to bed (*Robinson Crusoe* and Macaulay's study on the *Life of Byron*).

Leaving the Palais de Justice, where I had gone so that Fargue could not suspect my zeal. (He had come the evening before, panic-stricken, to beg me to intercede for a friend whose signature had been misused by some scoundrels—and the worst of it is that Fargue himself was not there, at the Palais de Justice. . . . He wanted me to intercede with Judge Flory; fortunately Marcel Drouin, whom I went to consult in the morning about the advisability of such a step, pointed out how contrary it was to all decency—and I was aware of this myself; but nothing is harder for me than an act that seems to be a sidestepping of responsibility; that is why I felt myself obliged to go to the Palais!) In the VIIIth Court I had seen only a few vague robbers appear. I had left Auteuil very early, hoping to stop at the Louvre on the way; but my fear of missing Fargue made me get there a half-hour too early. (I didn't tell him this in my letter this evening, in order not to seem to be complaining; I wrote that I had waited for him from noon until one o'clock; in reality I was there at eleven thirty.)

[1] "Kanut or the Parricide" and "Aymerillot" are both narrative poems from Hugo's *Légende des siècles*; "Night over the Ocean," "The Unfortunates," and "The Jinns" are also poems by Victor Hugo, as is the collection of *Les Contemplations*.

27 March

Lunched with Barrès (at Blanche's). Great anxiety about the figure he cuts; he knows how to maintain silence in order to say nothing but important things. He has changed greatly since almost ten years ago when I last saw him; but he has kept his very active charm, though constantly holding back and knowing how to keep his reserve. What prudence! What economy! He is not a great intelligence, not a "great man," but *clever,* using everything in him until he achieves the appearance of genius. Especially using circumstances, and knowing how to take advantage of what he has, to the point of hiding what he lacks.

Nine days in Bruges

At Verbeke's printing-house to correct the proofs of *L'Otage,* of *La Mère et l'enfant,* of *Isabelle,* of *Corydon* and of the June issue of the review.[2]

The issue appears with Saint-Léger's *Éloges* bristling with printer's errors.[3] The experience makes me ill and, to divert my mind from it, I imagine what might have happened the first time Debussy was played:

The conductor attached great importance to the music; unfortunately he had against him the theater manager and the organizer of the concerts; at least they did not approve it, so that in the beginning he had to struggle to get the new composition accepted on his program.

He knew, moreover, that he was going to displease his public, but it was a point of honor with him to prefer pleasing the composer and himself; indeed, he felt that he had become a conductor solely for this reason: to make

[2] The N.R.F., following the custom of most French literary reviews, had founded a publishing house under the name of Librairie Gallimard—Éditions de la Nouvelle Revue Française. Among the first books issued over this imprint were Claudel's drama *The Hostage,* Charles-Louis Philippe's novel *The Mother and Child,* and Gide's novel *Isabelle. Corydon* appeared in a very limited private edition the same year, anonymous as to author and publisher, as *C.R.D.N.* Verbeke directed the St. Catherine Press, Ltd., of Bruges, which printed the first issues of the N.R.F. and is still known for fine work.

[3] The statesman Saint-Léger Léger has always written under the pseudonym of St.-J. Perse. His first published work was formed of the beautiful lyric poems of *Praises.*

possible the presentation, beside the most classic harmonies, of the newest harmonies.

Debussy himself, who feared an imperfect execution, would have preferred not to be played; to convince him, it took the conductor's insistence and the urging of a few rare friends.

An unfortunate precaution that Debussy had thought it necessary to take made everyone wait some time for the scores, so that this composition, especially difficult because of its originality, could not be rehearsed by the whole orchestra together. The players arrived quite green before their sheets of music the day of the concert and played in defiance of common sense. The conductor had any amount of courage to fight against the ill will of the public, but not to betray a musician he liked, who was hissing with the public and was right to hiss. He himself would have liked to hiss and then to explain. . . . Someone said to him on the way out, when he was attempting an explanation, an excuse: "With music like that what does one note matter in place of another? This simply proves that you are wrong to include it on your program; it deserved such an execution—which, as far as I am concerned, didn't seem so bad." It was this that put the finishing touch to the conductor's despair; he fell ill that very evening; the next day he swallowed his baton and died.

Cuverville

The bad weather and my work keep me from observing this year, as I did for three successive years, the finches that live in my garden. Now that they are more numerous it is harder to observe them. In the beginning a single couple nested in the bush near the bench where I was accustomed to sit. Couple? No, it was a triangular arrangement. For a long time I refused to accept the evidence, considering as accepted and indubitable the hatred of rival males; yet I was forced to admit it: the two males that I saw attending to the same female, feeding the same nest, got along perfectly together.

And if it is not the same trio that I saw the following year, then these customs must be current among finches.

What inclines me to believe this is that I encountered them at Arco, in the Italian Tyrol. At the end of the winter season—that is, at nesting-time—from the hotel terrace, almost deserted at that season, during a fortnight we were able to observe some rather tame finches that the hotel-keeper was protecting. There were three of them, a female and two males, very easily distinguishable one from the other but equally solicitous in regard to the female and equally good providers for the nest.

Not claiming to be the only one to have noticed these strange customs among finches or other birds, for a long time I planned to write Henry de Varigny, who was then writing for *Le Temps* an interesting column on rural life, was glad to answer unknown correspondents, and on occasion even would launch a little inquiry. But wouldn't such a subject seem to him to belong to the novel rather than to natural history?

Cuverville, 3 July

X. (I later on) was accustomed to say that age had not forced him to give up a single pleasure of which he did not just happen to be on the point of getting tired.

21 December

Les Caves.[4] Necessity of drawing the naked form under the clothing in the manner of David, and of knowing about my characters even the things I am not going to use—or at least that are not to appear on the outside.

Mlle Emma Siller is having trouble with her landlord. She writes to Em.: "It is enough to make you sick of life; and this is very sad at my age." (She is sixty.)

Finished *Rhoda Fleming*.[5]

DETACHED PAGES

I find a great danger in a too ready sympathy. It proposes in rapid succession divers paths, all leading to equally charming landscapes. In rapid succession the soul becomes enamored of that languid lush country which shelters only the soft, the flexible, and the voluptuous and

---

[4] *Les Caves du Vatican* (*Lafcadio's Adventures*) did not appear until 1914.

[5] Meredith's novel.

produces it abundantly; then it waxes enthusiastic over the glare of a sandy dune where everything glitters.

FOR MARCEL D.

He taxes me with having badly economized my appeal to the emotions since I exhaust it in the beginning of the book,[6] so that I cease to stir as soon as I try to persuade. This is because I am addressing myself and wish to address myself to the head and not to the heart; this is because I do not seek to win over the reader's sympathy, which would risk becoming indulgence; and it is precisely because, as I am well aware, certain words springing from the heart would touch the reader more deeply than all these more or less specious reasonings—it is precisely for this reason that I have kept from using those words. Compare the device of the lawyer who tries to pass off his client's crime as one dictated by jealousy. I do not want any of that. I intend that this book should be written coldly, deliberately, and that this should be evident. Passion must have preceded it or at most be implied in it; but above all it must not serve as an excuse for the book. I do not want to move to pity with this book; I want to embarrass.

I do not feel any imperious attraction (toward this book). It is undeniable that I am writing it out of season and when I no longer need to write it. This is what I explained yesterday to Marcel, fearing that he might see in it some almost unhealthy obsession, an impossibility of getting my mind off this subject. But, on the other hand, the difficulty comes rather from the fact that I must artificially revive a problem to which I have found (as far as I am concerned) a practical solution, so that, to tell the truth, it no longer bothers me.

PRODIGAL SON

When he returns to the house he blames himself for having left. . . .

And when he sees again this little garden from which

[6] *Corydon.* [A.]

he promised himself so much delight, he is amazed not to find the flowers larger, the fruits more tasty, and the affection of his family more joyfully effusive.

Whether he be named St. Paul, Luther, or Calvin, I see him as beclouding the whole truth of God.

It is worthy of consideration that the two most *solemn* dramas that antiquity has bequeathed to us, *Œdipus* and *Prometheus,* offer us, one the notion of good and evil, or rather of the permissible and the forbidden, in its most arbitrary terms, the other the sanction, etc. . . .

ADVICE TO THE YOUNG MAN OF LETTERS

With regard to praise or blame I cannot recommend to you an indifference I have never known myself and, moreover, have been inclined to envy. It is good to be moved to emotion, to vibrate under caresses and even more so under bites. And no doubt there is something to be gained from not protesting immediately against them, but . . .

(Education through one's enemies.)

The important thing is not to let oneself be poisoned. Now, hatred poisons. Etc. . . .

It is only through restraint that man can manage not to suppress himself.

All the causes of ruin are in us; but artificially dominated: culture.

DIMINUTIVE NOVEL

Avignon.

The smell of the pines, the scent of the lavender.

Behind the arches of the bridges, those great swells that the water slowly carries along.

I grieve to think that, later on, my weakened memory
will be unable to offer me my sensation of today, however
lively, which, losing all sharpness of outline, all accent,
will merely seem to me like one of those medals of which
the effigy has been effaced, alas, now blurred like any
other medal that one can guess to have been precious only
by the luster of the worn metal.

Later on, taking this perfumed memory in my hand,
pressing it affectionately against my lips, I shall think:

What was it? I no longer see it very clearly. The name
of that child? Shall I get it mixed, alas, with so many
others? The day was delightfully radiant; the water in
the *saqiyas*, I remember, charming. I should like to define
the line of the young body and again find it adorable.

I believe that never did the "rules" embarrass any
genius, neither that of the *unities* in France nor that of
the three actors in Greece, and that Racine and Corneille
as well as Æschylus have sufficiently proved this. (That
moreover they have no absolute value and that any great
genius masters them, whether he finds support in them or
negates them—and that to come along and claim that this
or that great man was embarrassed by them is just as
ridiculous as if a painter said that when painting he is
embarrassed by his frame and exclaimed: "Oh, if only I
could spread out a little farther!" and that those who protest against them are like Kant's dove, which thought it
would fly better in a vacuum.)

In general, insubordination with regard to the rules
comes from an unintelligent subordination to realism, from
a misunderstanding of the ends of art, from that specious
insinuation of empiricism which aims, through a scandal-
ous generalization, to scoff at art by attacking it only
where it has become artifice, and to label as factitious all
supernatural beauty.

"You don't seem to understand, sir," the worthy Lyon,
my teacher, used often to say to me, "that certain words

are made to go with others; between them there exist
certain relationships that must not be changed."
"I can't help it, dear teacher, but for words too I am a
firm believer in the virtue of bad company."

Let us mistrust "foregrounds"; everything that seems
to us big in them changes rapidly.

Creusa or Lot's wife;[7] one tarries and the other looks
back, which is a worse way of tarrying.

It is also Ariadne who, after he has killed the Minotaur,
makes Theseus return to the point from which he started.
There is no greater cry of passion than this:

And Phædra having braved the Labyrinth with you
Would have been found with you or lost with you.[8]

But passion blinds her; after a few steps, to tell the
truth, she would have sat down, or else would have
wanted to go back—or even would have made him carry
her.

In the *Thésée* this must be brought out—the apron-
string, to express it vulgarly. After having conquered the
Minotaur, he would like to go on.—He is held—obliged
to return.[9]

NOVEL

The Santa Margherita hotel-keeper (a lawyer, it seems),
Milanese, short, and with a beard pointing forward, bright
and excessively amiable, serves at table himself; and since
he is aided only by a single servant-girl (Austrian but

[7] Creusa, the daughter of Priam and Hecuba and first wife of
Æneas, delayed as she left the burning city of Troy and disappeared
in the flames; Lot's wife turned to a pillar of salt when she looked
back at the destruction of Sodom.
[8] The famous lines of Racine's *Phèdre* when the heroine contrasts
herself with her sister Ariadne, who remained at the entrance of the
labyrinth to guide Theseus' steps by a thread:

Et Phèdre au Labyrinthe avec vous descendue
Se serait avec vous retrouvée ou perdue.

[9] This reference to the project of a *Theseus* in 1911 is interesting
since the work did not appear until 1946.

Irredentist), whereas there are twenty of us guests, he hustles about, jumps from one end of the dining-room to the other, urges me to have a second helping of a poor dish of which there is too much: "Help yourself again; it's very light!" says to me as he rushes by: "It's not quantity we lack . . ." flies off to give bread to a neighbor, then, on his way by again, finishes the sentence: ". . . it's service." The table wine being almost undrinkable, I order a bottle of Barbera; nothing out of the ordinary, but he serves it *wrapped in a table-napkin.* That is the key to his character (worth examining what this might produce in the serious circumstances of life).

The 15th of August, a holiday, when we were too numerous in the little dining-room, when the lunch didn't begin until one o'clock, and when the "service" lost its head, the main course was a strange stew of *bones,* which he passed me, gallantly leaning over me and whispering very quickly, like a secret: "Knuckle of veal *à la milanaise!* What is called *ossa bucca* in Italian."

This morning, while I am writing this: "A rather delicate little dish: red mullet with tomato sauce. Do you like it? This is French cooking, nothing to do with Italy." All this said very rapidly and *confidentially.*

A little later:

"It's not for me to offer you sweets . . . but if you like them . . . Do you like this?"

"I don't know; what is it?"

"The most original and at the same time the commonest thing in the world: custard."

And he pours into my plate a sort of inedible paste.

✳

To the famous "three unities" I should be glad to add a fourth: the *unity of the audience.* It would imply the importance for the poetic creation, whether a play or a book, to address itself, from one end to the other of its duration, to the same reader or listener. These reflections rise in me while reading Wells's latest book, which his faithful translator Davray has just brought out in the *Mercure.* Wells has the most ingenious mind; he skillfully interests us by opening up before us the most unforeseen perspectives; but his reputation has no need of further praise. If he is addressing us today, why didn't he always address himself to us? Read by too large a public, which he recruited in all countries and from all social classes, he now addresses himself alternatively to people who are too different from one another. In this book there are pages that could only amuse children, or new people; other pages to interest old experienced people like us, but which would repel the former; and finally others in which he seems to be amusing only some alter ego or other; both children and I cease to listen. Occasionally I feel like pulling his sleeve: Mr. Wells! you are forgetting us! And yet it was for us that you began your story; don't make any mistake about it, we were your best public.

✳

"Milton's whole genius lies therein: he brought the sparkle of the Renaissance into the seriousness of the Reformation, the magnificences of Spenser among the severities of Calvin." (Taine: *English Literature*, Vol. II, p. 415.)

It is improper, it is almost paradoxical, to claim that we owe to Calvinist puritanism the wonderful English school (I mean the school of novelists), for we cannot easily distinguish in them what belongs to upbringing and what belongs to the race, nor to what a degree the former suits the latter. Furthermore, one must consider that, aside from a few very rare exceptions (Thackeray, for instance), it is by escaping from Calvinism, and only by escaping from it and often by turning against it, that those novelists were able to succeed. So that it could be said that if Calvinism helped them it did so as a sort of restraint that curbs and tightens one's strength and makes Joseph de Maistre utter the remark that has been somewhat misused: "Whatever constricts man strengthens him." This is also because the habit of a certain gloominess, the desire or even the need of finding oneself at fault, and the rejection of the most charming solicitations of life invite them to seek the source of an action and its most secret repercussion rather than what immediately follows it, as do a great many of our novelists.

Thus it is that Calvinism can be an excellent school of

psychology, but, let me repeat, on condition that one get away from it, and if . . . (Quote Taine, Vol. II, p. 415.)

✳

In the jury-box again I look at my colleagues. I imagine these same faces on the opposite bench; badly outfitted, unshaved, unwashed, their hair uncombed, with soiled linen or with none at all, and that fearful hunted look in the eyes that comes from a combination of worry and fatigue. What would they look like? What would I look like myself? Would the judge himself recognize under that frightful disguise the "respectable man"? He would have to be very clever to distinguish the criminal from the member of the jury!

✳

At times I deeply regret living in an epoch when respect is so rarely shown and so difficult. Not everyone can do without it with impunity. "My mind was naturally inclined toward veneration," Goethe (or at least his translator) says somewhere. If curvatures of the mind were as obvious as those of the spine, I know more than one that would not dare show itself in conversation, etc. . . .

✳

"What do you mean by manners?"
"I mean a general submission and conduct consistent with good or bad laws. If the laws are good, the manners are good," etc. . . . (Diderot: *Supplément au Voyage de Bougainville*, Part IV, p. 205, Centenary Edition.)[10]

"Manners are the hypocrisy of a nation." (Balzac.)

"If, as Buffon says, love lies in the sense of touch, the softness of that skin must have been active and penetrating like the scent of daturas." (Balzac: *Les Paysans*.)[11]

[10] Diderot was inspired to write in 1772 an argument of naturist philosophy (supporting Rousseau's theory that man is naturally good) by the account of Louis-Antoine de Bougainville's voyage to Oceania.
[11] The Peasants.

＊

"Leveling is not God's work and every proper man must have moments in which he is tempted to weep over that work of desolation." (Kierkegaard.)

"That ambitious woman [Cornelia] had early prepared for her sons all *the instruments of tyranny: eloquence,* in which they surpassed all the men of their time; *gallantry:* Tiberius was the first to climb the walls of Carthage; *honesty* itself; for such ambitions could not stop at avarice. *The Stoics who raised the two children,* as they had raised Cleomenes, the reformer of Sparta, *inculcated in them that policy of leveling which serves tyranny so well,* and the classic fables of the equality of wealth under Romulus and under Lycurgus." (Michelet: *Roman History,* Vol. II, p. 162.)

1912

Sunday, 8 January

I had promised myself to return to this journal and to keep it regularly from the first of January on. But I have crawled along so miserably these last few days that, even begrudgingly, I could not have written a thing. To tell the truth, I didn't even try.

14 January

. . . But it is true here as it is for music, where the chord of G sharp does not have the same meaning depending on whether you have reached it by way of the sharps or by way of the flats, and does not sound the same as the chord of A flat to the sensitive ear, though composed of the same notes.

The night before last, excellent conversation with Paul Albert Laurens, who showed me the possibility of writing *Corydon* in an entirely different mode. He would like me to make of it a work as serious as my *Enfant prodigue;* and this causes me to reflect at length.

Late afternoon yesterday at Mme R.'s, where, for an hour, my mind endured the torture of the boot. She is charming nevertheless and shows a disarming kindness and goodwill; but what was I doing there? Speaking of T., I said to her: "He lives on an income, and in literature I like only those who eat up their capital." "As you so well express it," she immediately remarks, "that charming fellow hasn't the means." It is not at all that she is incapable of understanding; but she simply wants to have understood too quickly.

Then Péladan came; strange lack of accent to his face; fat, soft aspect of his whole body. He makes a few remarks in the d'Aurevilly manner: "Coffee and tobacco are the riding-whip and spurs of the mind," etc. . . . He accuses Gautier of "being short on general ideas" and adds: "As for me, I consider it quite natural that M. de X., meeting Y. for the first time" (he is alluding to a real fact, as far as I could understand, and cites the names), "should ask him at once: 'What do you think of the infinite?' And whoever is amazed by that is an imbecile."

It is a great mark of wisdom to dare to appear an imbecile, but it takes a certain courage that I have not always had.

Hotel Bellevue, Neuchâtel

Have I reached the limit of experience? And shall I be able to catch hold of myself again now? I need to put my remaining energy to some studious use. How easy it would be for me now to throw myself into a confessional! How difficult it is to be at one and the same time, for oneself, he who commands and he who obeys! But what spiritual director would understand with sufficient subtlety this vacillation, this passionate indecision of my whole being, this equal aptitude for contraries? Depersonalization, obtained by an effort of the will and with such difficulty, which could be explained and excused only by the production of works that it authorizes and with an eye to which I have striven to suppress my preferences. Absurdity of the objective method (Flaubert). Cease to be oneself in order to be all. Danger of aiming toward a limitless empire. To conquer Russia, Napoleon had to risk France. Necessity of linking the frontier with the center. It is time to return home.

(This will be the subject of *Alexandre aux Indes*.[1])

Constant *vagabundance*[2] of desire—one of the chief causes of the deteriorating of the personality.

Urgent necessity to recover possession of oneself.

But can one still make resolutions when one is over forty? I live according to twenty-year-old habits. Did I know what I was doing at twenty? When I made the resolution to look at everything, never to prefer myself to anything and always to give preference to what differed most from me. . . .

Even my insomnia struck me last night as a form of perplexity, a kind of difficulty in making up my mind to sleep.

Never go out without a definite aim; hold to this.

Walk along without looking in every direction.

[1] No work by André Gide entitled "Alexander in India" has been published.
[2] The French text has the same made-up word from *vagabondage* and *abondance*.

In a train choose any compartment whatever; and enter the subway train by the first door you see, without looking for something better. Do not scorn little victories; as soon as it is a matter of the will, the *much* is only the patient addition of the *little*.

Forbid oneself every kind of vacillation.

Zurich, Tuesday evening

Everything I wrote this evening will strike me as silly in a short while. Already I feel better; this brisk air has put me back on my feet; I am again becoming aware of my strength. This state is the very one I wanted; but as soon as I weaken, I cease to be anyone because of having wanted to be all (state of the perfect novelist), for fear of being only *someone*.

It is as a conqueror, not as a traveler, that Alexander advances in new lands; he is seeking the *limits* of the world, etc. . . .

Zurich, Wednesday

I should like never to have known Claudel. His friendship weighs on my thought, and obligates it, and embarrasses it. . . . I can still not get myself to hurt him, but as my thought affirms itself it gives offense to his. How can I explain myself to him? I should willingly leave the whole field to him, I should give up everything. . . . But I cannot say something different from what I have to say, which cannot be said by anyone else.

How much more sensuality invites to art than does sentimentality—this is what I repeat to myself as I walk in Zurich. To tell the truth, I don't understand anything here; I feel more foreign to these people, and they to me, than I should be among Zulus or Caribs.

Andermatt, 27 January

Here I am again in this land "that God created to be horrible" (Montesquieu). The admiration of mountains is an invention of Protestantism. Strange confusion on the part of brains incapable of art, between the lofty and the beautiful. Switzerland: a wonderful reservoir of energy; one has to go down how far? to find abandon and grace, laziness and voluptuousness again, without which neither art nor wine is possible. If of the tree the mountains make a fir, you can imagine what they can do with man. Æsthetics and ethics of conifers.

The fir and the palm tree: those two extremes.

[Paris] Wednesday

In order to be more economical of it, I shall note in minute detail the manner in which I spend my time.

Seven thirty: bath, reading of Souday's article on A. S.

Eight thirty to nine: breakfast.

Nine o'clock: piano (first Bach-Liszt Prelude for organ). Practice interrupted by the arrival of Dr. D. to dress Em.'s arm.

Ten to eleven: letters to Rilke and Eugène Rouart.

Eleven o'clock to twelve: walk, then cleaning up my notes on *The Possessed.*

Lunch.

One o'clock to two: practice at the piano.

Two to three: reading of *Clayhanger;*[3] then intense fatigue and frightful let-down. I am going to sleep from three to four.

Through a desire and a need to attach myself to something solid, I am tying myself to the translation of Hebbel's letters (those dated from France). I find both hard work and great interest in it, so that I continue this work until dinner-time.

With all my heart and all my soul I listen to this call of virtue.

Friday

A slightly better day which I spend altogether in the little room beside the library, between a fire of wood-blocks and the little electric radiator. Translated Hebbel all morning and part of the afternoon; I finally stop, not discouraged, but more and more convinced that these letters will hardly interest ten readers and that the *N.R.F.* cannot be willing to publish them.

I write a few lines of the *Traité des Dioscures,*[4] which I have been carrying in my head for so many years; but it doesn't go very well either. Right now I think that it is better to keep these ideas on Greek mythology for the

---

[3] By Arnold Bennett (1910).
[4] The *Treatise on the Dioscuri* was published only fragmentarily in 1919 as *Considerations on Greek Mythology.*

novel I shall write after *Les Caves*. I shall have them
developed by some character, with all the slowness and
complexity that is necessary. So that this work too is
dropped.

Read the first chapter of *Clayhanger*, which I leave to
go back to *Captain Singleton*.[5]

Monday

That state of equilibrium is attractive only when one is
on a tightrope; seated on the ground, there is nothing
wonderful about it.

This, however, checks my restlessness a bit: the memory
of having already gone through such periods of *lack of
interest*. Probably it is connected with a physiological
state; but I cannot succeed in establishing a relationship.
. . . To be always oneself, in mediocrity or genius! . . .
From me to me what a distance! This is why I never dare
plan or promise anything and never achieve anything
without using evasions and deceiving myself, through
what shilly-shallying! . . .

Wednesday, 7 February

If I were to disappear right now, no one could suspect,
on the basis of what I have written, the better things I
still have to write. What temerity, what assumption of a
long life, has allowed me always to keep the most important for the end?! Or, on the contrary, what shyness,
what respect for my subject and fear of not yet being
worthy of it! . . . Thus I put off *La Porte étroite* from
year to year. Whom could I persuade that that book is the
twin of *L'Immoraliste* and that the two subjects grew up
concurrently in my mind, the excess of one finding a secret
permission in the excess of the other and together establishing a balance.

Saturday, 17 February

I can only note in haste the rather whirlwind life of the
last few days. I am writing seated on a bench in the
Bois; the weather was radiant this morning; this is the
secret of my happiness. But already the sky is clouding
over again; I need Apollo; I must set out.

· · ·

[5] *The Life, Adventures, and Piracies of the Famous Captain Singleton*, by Daniel Defoe (1720).

How hard it is for me to remember what I have done since Wednesday!

Let's try: Wednesday afternoon I went to see the Valéry ladies; I had not had the heart to write them the bad news I had received from Switzerland about the Bataglia muds on which Paule G. was counting: those muds are not exported. Then went to pick up Eugène Rouart, who has just got back to Paris. Together we made an excursion to the exhibit of Italian futurists; then went to discover at the M. Bank that Ruyters, whom we hoped to see there, had not been in all day. Right after dinner I rush to ask after him; too late; the whole household is down with grippe.

Thursday morning at Valentine Gilbert's with Em. to liquidate the affairs of Édouard.

After lunch, visit of Verhaeren, then of Élisebeth R. accompanied by her two daughters and a young nationalist poet, who "wanted to meet me." Impossible to recall how I spent the rest of the day. . . .

Oh yes, I can: I had promised to be present at the little lecture that Jacques Rivière gives every week at the Gallimards' on French literature. He was to speak that evening on Rabelais and had asked me to read some passages for him. To tell the truth, I wanted to give the reading and had arranged it so that Jacques would ask it of me; petty pretense that I don't believe took anybody in; everything went off very well, however; but I had the embarrassment of thinking that Rivière would have read better than I; of feeling that the others thought so too and considered my intrusion into their group rather indiscreet, as it indubitably was. I became clearly aware of this as soon as I entered the drawing-room, and the feeling of my indiscretion deprived me of all assurance: I read miserably, almost dolefully, modestly, with an air of excusing myself, a text that on the contrary called for cynicism and bravura. Well, it's my fault!

Such little mortifications and blows to my vanity are very good lessons.

Took Ghéon to dinner. He drags me off to spend the evening at the Théâtre des Arts, where the first performance of *Mrs. Warren's Profession*[6] is being given. I arrived

[6] The comedy by George Bernard Shaw.

bristling, predisposed against it by the author's unbearable immodesty. And the first scenes were worse than I expected; you cannot imagine anything harsher, drier, or more abstract. But during the second act I let myself be captivated without thinking of resisting (it is only fair to say that the actress who played Mrs. Warren was excellent). I recovered myself toward the end of the third act. It is annoying that the fourth should be so bad. What a grimacing art and what creaking thoughts!

Unable to go to sleep before dawn.

Cuverville, Wednesday

Beautiful weather at last. I let myself be won over by the serenity of this beautiful light, and rest in the certainty of my forthcoming departure.

Copernicus: The wonderful revolution effected by Christianity consists in having said: the kingdom of God is within you. Happy paganism saw no enemy that was not outside man.

The Augean stables, the hydras, the swamps to be cleaned up are *within us.* It is within us that Hercules must labor. Christianity = the inner operation.

Radiant morning of the world; man's powers undivided.

It is altogether that Ajax, suddenly, turns against himself; he no longer finds anything whatever in him to defend itself.

Theseus adventuring, risking himself *amidst* the labyrinth, assured by the secret thread of an inner fidelity
. . . etc.

Written in the train, Thursday

My whole day yesterday was spent in copying the subscriptions and the complimentary lists of the *N.R.F.*, of which I had taken the collection of cards with me.

At this date we have five hundred and twenty-eight subscribers and we distribute two hundred and forty-four complimentary copies. I note a rather large number of errors in our list.

Driving rain this morning; reinvasion of gray ideas.

The notary comes at ten o'clock and with him Em. and I go to see Mme Freger, who is to sign some deed or other by which she yields the succession of her farm-rent to her son Louis.

Wonderful dignity of the old woman (she has just

recovered from pleurisy and wanted to put her affairs in order, though she still has a year and a half of her lease). Near the door, a little apart from the others, her son Louis; he is now twenty-eight. The brothers and brothers-in-law are to get together soon and sign a deed bearing witness to the fact that they consent to the mother's yielding to Louis four thousand francs' worth of furnishings, equivalent to the sum that Eugène, the elder son, received at the time of his marriage, in addition to two thousand francs coming to each of them from the father's estate.

The notary has prepared a letter; but instead of asking Mme Freger simply to sign, he invites her to write above her name: "good for security." The poor old woman, somewhat bewildered, calls her son to her aid; but Louis cannot write for her. The notary offers her a model. Em. has the better idea of writing the letters in lightly in pencil, so that she will only have to cover them in ink. Her hand casts a shadow; she doesn't see very well and twice has to clean her glasses. We urge her to change her place and to sit facing the window; then the notary dictates the letters to her one by one; or says to her: "*o*, a circle; *n*, two downstrokes; two more downstrokes. . . ." And while she is writing, I look at the old wooden table on which the notary has laid the deed, in which successive scourings have hollowed little valleys (where the wood is soft between the harder lines of the grain). So many memories *inscribed* in this table; the story of each one of those spots, of those scratches. . . . What the story of the Freger family must be! Character of the father: the harsh upbringing of his sons, sending them out to gather dung on the roads despite the gibes of passers-by; making a point of honor of always having the best-kept fields in the district; beauty, *nobility,* of that form of avarice; the children taught always to give us the least attractive eggs, saving the heaviest ones for the market, etc. . . . Ferocious sense of property: the time he shot at our dog after he had strangled one of their ducks (although Em. had immediately gone to pay them for it) and not trying to hide it; the barbs of the wire fence cut off at the spot where the cows could take advantage of the grass in the avenue by sticking their heads through the fence. Recall the father's childhood, a mere farm-hand in the beginning and *raising* himself by dint of severity. The beauty of his children—the daughter in particular, who now (as always happens) reaches marriage already quite out of shape. The night work in the fine season; the harvesting; the full bucket of cider that Louis, the second of the sons, used to drink daily at that time, whence diarrhea; his shame to admit his illness. The marriages of the elder son, Eugène, planned and missing fire one after another, as Mme Freger related to my brother-in-law: "I don't know how for us to go about it. M'sieur Georges, wouldn't you perhaps ask for her hand in place of us?"

Saturday, 2 March

I leave this evening for Marseille—and Monday sail for Tunis.

7 May

Rather embarrassed by the quotation Péguy makes of a sentence from *Isabelle* in his *Mystère des Saints Innocents.*[7] He takes the sentence and sets it in italics, but nothing indicates that it is a quotation. He counts none the less on my gratitude. But I don't know what to say to him; and, in my uncertainty, say nothing.

Anything that turns (or even *can turn*) into a device becomes hateful to me. As soon as the emotion decreases, the pen should stop; when it continues to run on just the same (and it only runs on the more easily), writing becomes detestable. Whole pages of this most recent Péguy, and groups of pages, he could have had written by a secretary; they cease to be *really animated;* they imitate the good ones, those in which the emotion *demanded* this intellectual stuttering.

The craft I wish, may it be so discreetly original, so mysterious, so hidden, that it can never be seized in itself! I should like no one to be aware of me save by the perfection of my sentence and, because of that alone, no one able to imitate it.

I intend to prevent its ever being said of anyone that he is imitating me or that he resembles me (or else that it should be for a very fundamental reason), as it can be currently said today of this or that one: he is indulging

[7] *The Mystery of the Holy Innocents,* by Charles Péguy, a long poem of religious inspiration, appeared in 1912.

in a little Francis Jammes or a little Henri de Régnier, and as it will be said tomorrow: a little Péguy. I don't want to have any *manner*—but that which my subject demands. (What is needed here is the English *but*). Amen.

Written on 8 May

I did not go to Tunis. Met Mme Mayrisch at Marseille. Let the Monday boat leave without me; slept in Toulon; then to Cannes, where I found Valery Larbaud and Arnold Bennett (the latter, installed at the Californie, earns around a thousand francs a day; he is paid at the rate of a shilling a word; he writes without stopping every day from six a.m. to nine a.m., then gets into his bath and doesn't think of his work again until the next morning). Through fear of bad weather and through impatience, I drop Tunisia and head for Florence, where, the very day of my arrival, I manage to get settled at 20 Lungarno Acciaioli in a very pleasant bedroom and sitting-room (*primo piano* on the quay) at three lire a day. I was still so tired and reduced to so little that Vannicola and Papini, whom I saw in the very first days, wondered what I had been suffering from (they have told me this since). I was able to get back to work and to myself only after a week of constant efforts. Nevertheless, little by little, work won me back and I was able to bring my book to the point I had hoped to reach in Italy. Neither churches nor museums (except for Santa Croce and the Etruscan Museum), but I felt that everything was there within reach, ready to consult. Almost daily letter to Em.; voluminous correspondence with Claudel; all my time spent at my table and at my piano, hardly going out except for meals and, in the evening, a bit of a spree. What a city Florence is!! Poor Vannicola's decline. Larbaud comes to join me and considerably upsets my work; but so nice! And how interesting his conversation!

Finally, the 16th, putting all my papers in the drawer, I go to meet Ghéon at Pisa, bring him back to Florence that same evening (a bed is set up for him in my sitting-room), and for six days we lead an amazing, unrelatable life, of inestimable value—interrupted, just as we were going to set out for Siena and Assisi, etc., by the bad news of Ghéon's little niece, which calls him suddenly back to Orsay. I haven't the heart to prolong my trip without him and return at the end of April.

Cuverville, 7 June

GOSPELS

I consider detestable all moral teachings that are not dictated by the love of humanity—but I tell you that these counsels are dictated by the love of humanity and that, through the apparent and resolute severity of that voice, I feel stirring a great suffering love, that only the dryness of your hearts, O skeptics and rationalists, prevents you from recognizing.

30 June

Beethoven's ample phrase. Absurd habit I had got into of letting the breath drop in the middle. It should swell with a single *inspiration* from one end to the other. It is just a fortnight ago that I became convinced of this (I should even say: that I became aware of it) and I am striving to correct myself to give nuances to the content of the phrase. Important progress.

11 November

From day to day I put off and carry a little farther into the future my prayer: may the time come when my soul, at last liberated, will be concerned only with God!

This morning at work at six o'clock. Spenser and Skeat, then Conrad. I write to my teacher to resume my lessons.

12 November

Stupid use of my morning (yesterday). I took an auto to save time; went to reserve the little dining-room of the Vian restaurant, where Em. and I can lunch comfortably with the young Iehl couple; then to the *Mercure*, where I did not find Vallette (I was taking back the volume of *Prétextes*[8] corrected for a new printing); then to the N.R.F., where I did not find Rivière; then to rue d'Assas, where I did not find Schlumberger; back at the N.R.F., I learned from Tronche that Rivière no longer came in the morning, but in the afternoon. I went after him at his place on the rue Froidevaux; he was working on the sequel to his article on Faith, of which we talked

---

[8] Originally published in 1903, *Pretexts* contains the two lectures on influence and on the limits of art, the series of three articles on Barrès and "uprooting," and some articles and book reviews on contemporary subjects. Most of the contents had appeared in *L'Ermitage.*

at some length. I repeated to him the word of Christ that is opposed to his article, and as I was reading it, I kept hearing within me: "No man cometh unto the *Father* but by *me.*" And I want to take these words literally, which Rivière does not appreciate.

I thought also of going to find Bourdelle, who wanted to show me his new work; but I didn't have time.

Charming lunch with the Iehls. I come home and close myself in to work until evening in a state so close to bliss that I wish for nothing better here below.

I have read much of Jusserand's *Histoire de la littérature anglaise*[9] and made synoptic tables. Worked wildly on Skeat. Read before going to bed Keats's notes on *Paradise Lost* and the quotations he makes from it.

Today I have not left the house; distracted from work only by my correspondence and various tidyings-up.

Begun my English lessons again. But the worthy W. W., my teacher of last year, now seems to me sinisterly insufficient. He could not believe that I had read the whole of *Paradise Lost.*

19 November

Went to see Paul Claudel yesterday at his sister's. He receives me with great cordiality. I enter right away the little room he is occupying, which is dominated by a crucifix above the bed.

Paul Claudel is more massive, wider than ever; he looks as if he were seen in a distorting mirror; no neck, no forehead; he looks like a power-hammer. The conversation immediately starts on the subject of Rimbaud, whose complete works in one volume prefaced by Claudel, which the *Mercure* has just published, are on the table. He has recently had an opportunity to talk with some employee or business representative who, for some period of time, had frequented Rimbaud at Dakar or Aden;[10] who depicted him as an absolutely insignificant creature, spending all his days in smoking, sitting on his haunches in the Oriental manner, telling silly gossip stories when he had

[9] *History of English Literature.*

[10] After renouncing literature in 1873 at the age of nineteen, Arthur Rimbaud lived as an adventurer until he settled in Harar, Abyssinia, in 1880 as representative of a French firm of Aden. By Dakar André Gide doubtless means Harar.

a visitor, and occasionally putting his hand in front of his mouth as he laughed the sort of private laugh of an idiot. At Aden he used to go out bareheaded under the hot sun at hours when the sun on one's head is like a blow from a club. At Dakar he lived with a native woman, by whom he had had a child, or at least a miscarriage, "which is enough to upset" (says Claudel) "the imputations of homosexuality still occasionally attached to his name; for if he had had such tastes (and, it seems, nothing is more difficult to cure), it goes without saying that he would have kept them in that country where they are accepted and facilitated to such an extent that all the officers, without exception, live openly with their boy."

As I chide him for having, in his study, glossed over the ferocious side of Rimbaud's character, he says he wanted to depict only the Rimbaud of the *Saison en enfer*, in whom the author of *Les Illuminations* was to *result*.[11] Led, for a moment, to speak of his relations with Verlaine, Claudel, with an absent look, touches a rosary in a bowl on the mantel.

He talks of painting with excess and stupidity. His speech is an unceasing flow that no objection, no interrogation even, stops. Any other opinion than his own has no justification and almost no excuse in his eyes.

The conversation, by a natural slope, reaches matters of religion; he rises up violently against the group of Catholic politicians of the Action Française,[12] then against Sorel and Péguy, whose "motives he begins to understand better."

In too great a hurry to get back to my book, I cannot note here all the turns of our conversation.

23 November

Slept well; thanks perhaps to a generous libation of orange-flower water. Work all morning. At one o'clock Iehl arrives, who is returning to Fronton two days from now. I go out with him to pick up Vannicola at his hotel, lunch with him, then, as soon as possible, get back to

---

[11] Rimbaud's two great works are the poems in verse and prose of *The Illuminations* and the prose *Season in Hell*.

[12] The Royalist group of L'Action Française, with its newspaper of the same name, remained militantly Catholic even after its leader, Charles Maurras, was censured by the Vatican.

Auteuil to work. I write the greater part of the conversation between Julius and Lafcadio after the crime, without too much nervous irritation, but incapable of judging right away the quality of what I have written. Perhaps when I reread it tomorrow, I shall find it abominable; nevertheless, I think at least that the general outline of the scene is good.

Em. went to see Allain at the house of education where he is still being kept. She gets back at about tea-time with a number of *L'Opinion*, which she bought to read on the way, expecting to find in it Pierre de Lanux's article on Serbia. Instead she falls upon Pierrefeu's article against Iehl and against me, which infuriates her; but the article is written in such a way that on the contrary it greatly encourages me. Such disparagements, instead of crushing me, exalt me, and even more completely than praises.[13] After dinner, I go back to work after having finished the second canto of *The Faerie Queene*, of which I read a few stanzas to Em.

Stupidly, after a good session of work, not making up my mind to go to bed yet, I go back to reading Conrad, then Spenser again—and this considerably upsets my night. Great trouble going to sleep afterward, and for a sleep all shot full of holes.

. . . .

Rather good work all these last days; I interrupt this journal, which is reduced to the dull notation of facts. Good solely as a way of getting into the habit of writing.

[13] I write to Pierrefeu: "Sir, a single thing displeases me in your article: the reproach you make me of seeking to hide what I owe to Dostoyevsky. I have the greatest gratitude toward Dostoyevsky and yet cannot proclaim it any louder than I have done, not having, as you have said, a strong voice. I beg, etc. . . ." (And I enclosed with my letter my booklet on Dostoyevsky.) [A.]

1913

Yesterday evening reread fifty pages of *La Porte* *étroite;* each time I pick up that book again, I do so with an indescribable emotion; but if the dialogues, the letters, and Alissa's journal strike me as excellent—as well turned out as possible—on the other hand the intervening passages are not devoid of preciosity. Could it be said that the subject demanded this? Then I should have taken another subject. I no longer want to choose a subject that does not permit, that does not require, the frankest, the easiest, and the most beautiful style.

Monday, 19 May

Back from Italy since last Wednesday.

Everything I am writing this morning should have been noted earlier, but I didn't have time. This work of simplification, of arrangement, in which my mind engages in spite of myself in regard to everything it takes up—excellent exercise if it leads to the work of art—is deplorable here where the particular is more important than the essential.

Interrupted again in the very first lines (went with Em. to see the David exhibit and the Bonnard exhibit). This evening my ink is muddy and my pen blunted. Before writing the first word of my sentence I wait until the whole sentence has taken shape in my head; deplorable; rather the incorrect expression. Need of rereading some Stendhal. Dare to write without order.

21 May

First finish my book.[1] Spurn everything that distracts me from it.

[Cuverville] 26 June

It seems to me at times that I have never yet written anything serious; that I have always presented my thought in an ironic manner, and that, were I to disappear today, I should leave an image of myself from which even my guardian angel could not recognize me.

[1] *Les Caves du Vatican* (*Lafcadio's Adventures*), which he did finish on 23 June.

(The belief in angels is so disagreeable to me that I hasten to add that this is only a manner of speaking—but one that expresses my thought rather well.)

Perhaps, after all, my belief in the work of art and the cult that I make of it prevent that perfect sincerity which I henceforth demand of myself. What interest have I in any limpidity that is not a quality of style?

29 June

Every day I read a chapter of *Marius the Epicurean* (with the greatest delight); aloud, for an hour, *The Merry Men;*[2] I spend from three to five hours (and more often five than three) in piano-practice (exclusively Bach and Chopin). When one adds Ransome's book on Wilde, some Milton, some Keats, some Byron, etc., plus the correspondence, which every day takes one or two hours more, there is hardly any time left for personal work. I am putting it off until I travel again, when I shall have neither the piano nor any reading to finish.

Ransome's book strikes me as good—and even very good in spots. Perhaps he admires a bit too much the trappings with which Wilde liked to cover his thought and which still seem to me rather artificial—and on the other hand he fails to show to what a degree the plays *An Ideal Husband* and *A Woman of No Importance* are revelatory—and I was about to say confidential—despite their apparent objectivity.

Certainly in my little book on Wilde I was not altogether just to his work and turned up my nose at it too readily—I mean before having known it sufficiently. As I think it over I wonder at the good grace with which Wilde listened to me when, in Algiers, I criticized his plays (very impertinently it seems to me today). No impatience in the tone of his reply, and not even a protest; it was then that he was led to say to me, almost as an excuse, that extraordinary sentence which I quoted and which has since been quoted everywhere: "I put all my genius into my life; I put only my talent into my works." I should be interested to know if he ever said that sentence to anyone else but me.

Later on I hope to return to the subject and relate

[2] *Marius the Epicurean* is by Walter Pater; and *The Merry Men,* by R. L. Stevenson.

everything that I didn't dare tell at first. I should like, too, to *explain* Wilde's work in my own way, and especially his drama—of which the greatest interest lies between the lines.

✿　✿　✿

[*Summer, 1913*]

Trip to Italy. Sojourn at Tivoli, at Vallombrosa, at Santa Margherita.

I reproach myself bitterly for not having gone to see poor old Papa La Pérouse as I went through Paris on my return journey. Probably he has no one to hold out a hand to him and is wallowing about in the darkness.

2 September

At that time he used to repeat to himself, not without anguish, that the last act would perhaps not be a comedy ending and that life would fail him, not even all at once in screams and tears, which still involve a sort of glory and solemnity, but slowly in silence.

He felt all his faculties weakening and wildly regretted all the joys and all the beauty of life that he had not hugged to his flesh and to his heart.

4 September

The most extraordinary visions—he will have them when he is no longer in a state to describe them. . . .

Milton's blindness is frightful; but how much more horrible is Baudelaire's loss of speech!

8 September

I long ago became reconciled to not having anything glorious in my manner. If only the work is born, even at the price of a tremendous effort! . . .

25 September

Excellent visit of Paul A. Laurens and his wife (they spend four days with us); I talk with him as of old. I read him *Les Caves*. He recalls that I already talked to him about it at Biskra; that is farther back than I remembered.

It seems to me that everything I have written up to now has been nothing but barking and outside show before the *real* show begins and that it is only now that the public is going to enter the booth.

DETACHED PAGES

I mean to speak of the rules.

If it is true that genius escapes the rules, this puts me at ease.

I was just seeking in what way that genius escapes which I so often see anxious to force into the strictest forms the impulse least likely to submit to authority; and I shall try to find out why.

Art is just as far from turmoil as from apathy.

Neuchâtel

How much I love this calm lake ringed by low shores and peopled by gulls, where neither my eyes nor my mind encounters anything accidental or foreign!

How does it happen that I, generally so susceptible to cold, felt nothing but comfort this morning seated on the bench when it was barely five degrees above freezing, and with nothing in front of me but water and fog? I should be glad to live here.

That abominable effort to take one's sin with one to paradise.

Beware of artistic protestations; the real artist does not sport a red waistcoat and is not eager to talk of his art. Among those who shout so loud, you can be sure that there are not many who, to the immediate success of Pradon, preferred the attentive perfection of the other *Phèdre*.[3]

Indeed, he cannot doubt of our affection; but perhaps he is not yet aware how much pride, ambition, and exigence it involves.

The scent of the hay near Pavia.

The oleanders near Genoa.

The truth is that, as soon as the need to provide for it ceases to force us, we don't know what to do with our life and we waste it wantonly.

[3] A cabal organized by the Duchesse de Bouillon and her brother the Duc de Nevers produced Pradon's inferior play, *Phèdre et Hippolyte*, simultaneously with Racine's *Phèdre* (1677), and assured its success by buying out the house at both theaters for the first six performances.

NOVEL

Almost at the start of the book, dining together in a restaurant, they examine the wrinkles they *will have.*

Hasn't there been any bankruptcy in their life, any surrender—any renunciation?

He who protests will later on make of the ability to renounce the wisdom of his whole life.

(That too can be a rule of conduct based on complacency.)

The fox with his tail cut off: he who pretends to have wanted and to prefer everything that happens to him; from this alone he wins a reputation for wisdom.

The friend to whom he had confided his youthful dreams is well aware that this is a form of bankruptcy.

Establish the bankruptcy of Christianity—those who wanted to practice it had to withdraw from the world; Christianity was unable to form a world in the image of Christ as Buddha or Mohammed did—show that this is the *superiority* of Christ. But Catholicism set out to form a society and succeeds in doing so only by getting rid of Christ.

(All this wants to be said very mildly; horror of the tone of voice that belongs to the dispenser of justice or to the revolutionary.)

That the first duty of the Christian is to be happy; and so long as he has not achieved happiness he has not put into practice the teaching of Christ.—Christ's wonderful words: "Why weepest thou?" (To be commented on.)

Richard Feverel, *waking up* after the accident (it is essential that the accident should be caused by love), has completely forgotten that he had reached happiness (the odd feeling he has however: apprehension).

Subject: the two lovers who wake up after having drunk of Lethe (but one after the other).

They will not begin their love all over again—quite the contrary. . . . If they disliked each other. (She, sure of the past love, of which he is ignorant, seems *bold* to him.)

CAVES

Funeral of Fleurissoire.
I must put:

In the first carriage: Blaphafas and the widow. (Conversation.)

In the second carriage: Mme Armand-Dubois and the Countess de Baraglioul.

In the third: Anthime Armand-Dubois, Baraglioul.

CHOPIN

For Beethoven surely the *quantity* of sound is important; for Chopin only the *quality* (pianissimo in the Barcarolle).

No more limpid diamond.

No pearl of finer water.

(To say after the Algiers night in the *Mémoires*.[4])

How often the joy of love, particularly the most charming, left me in such an exasperated, atrocious delirium of all the senses that, for a long time afterward, I could not relax and overexerted my frenzy, not consenting to be released, to take leave of the instant, but insatiably avid and as if pursuing through pleasure something beyond pleasure.

---

[4] Gide commonly refers to his *Si le grain ne meurt* (*If It Die* . . .) as his *Memoirs*. This volume was openly published in 1926; a private printing, without name of publisher, had been made in 1920–1.

1914

Yesterday I had left Auteuil early in the morning to stop at the *Mercure*, at the Theater, and at the Review.[1] I planned to lunch with Paul A. Laurens and, not having found him in his studio, was walking up and down in front of 126 boulevard Montparnasse. Instead of Paul, Léon Blum came along. To avoid an invitation to lunch with M., I thought it expedient to invite him at once. I was not shaved; after a sleepless night, or rather one in which I was constantly awakened by the sick cat, I had got up with a bad headache. I felt ugly, dull, and stupid, and since Blum has the precise kind of mind that congeals mine at a distance and whose lucid brilliance keeps mine muscle-bound as it were and reduced to impotence, I said nothing during the whole meal that was not inane.

As I reflect tonight on Blum's character—in which I cannot fail to recognize nobility, generosity, and chivalry, even though when applied to him these words must be considerably distorted from their usual meaning—it seems to me that his apparent resolve always to show a preference for the Jew and to be interested always in him, that predisposition to recognize talent and even genius in him, comes first of all from the fact that a Jew is particularly sensitive to Jewish virtues. It comes above all from the fact that Blum considers the Jewish race as superior, as called upon to dominate after having been long dominated, and thinks it his duty to work toward its triumph with all his strength.

Perhaps he glimpses the possible dominance of that race. Perhaps he glimpses in the coming to power of

[1] Almost since its beginning in 1890, André Gide had been a contributor to the literary review *Le Mercure de France*, and from 1896 until 1911 the publishing house of the same name had been the principal publisher of his books. The theater is the Théâtre du Vieux-Colombier, founded by Jacques Copeau in 1913 as an offshoot of the *Nouvelle Revue Française* or *N.R.F.*, the monthly literary periodical established by Gide and a group of writers in 1909, to which he refers here as the Review.

that race the solution of many social and political problems. A time will come, he thinks, that will be the age
of the Jew; and right now it is important to recognize and
establish his superiority in all categories, in all domains,
in all the divisions of art, of knowledge, and of industry.
He has a marvelously organized, organizing, clear, and
classifying intelligence, which ten years later would be
capable of finding each idea exactly in the place where
his reasoning had put it, just as you find an object again
in a cupboard. Although he is sensitive to poetry, he has
the most antipoetic brain that I know. I believe also that
in spite of his value he overestimates himself somewhat.
His weakness lies in letting this be seen. He likes to give
himself importance; he wants to be the first to have
recognized the value of this or that one; speaking of little
Franck, he says: "I must have sent him to you some time
ago"; and speaking of Claudel: "That was the time when
Schwob and I were among the very few to admire him."
He also says: "T. has only to mention my name to the
fencing-master X., who will give him some help." He
always talks to you as a protector. At a dress rehearsal,
when he meets you by chance in a theater lobby, he puts
his arm around your waist, neck, or shoulders and, even
if you have not seen him in a year, makes everyone think
that he saw you yesterday and that he is the most intimate
friend you have in the world.

But why should I speak here of shortcomings? It is
enough for me that the virtues of the Jewish race are not
French virtues; and even if the French were less intelligent, less long-suffering, less virtuous in all regards than
Jews, it is still true that what they have to say can be
said only by them, and that the contribution of Jewish
qualities to literature (where nothing matters but what
is personal) is less likely to provide new elements (that
is, an enrichment) than it is to interrupt the slow explanation of a race and to falsify seriously, intolerably even, its
meaning.

It is absurd, it is even dangerous to attempt to deny the
good points of Jewish literature; but it is important to
recognize that there is today in France a Jewish literature
that is not French literature, that has its own virtues, its
own meanings, and its own tendencies. What a wonderful

job could be done and what a service could be rendered
both to the Jews and to the French by anyone who would
write a history of Jewish literature—a history that would
not have to go back far in time, moreover, and with
which I can see no disadvantage to fusing the history of
Jewish literature of other countries, for it is always one
and the same thing. This would clarify our ideas somewhat and would perhaps check certain hatreds that result
from false classifications.

There is still much more to be said on the subject. One
would have to explain why, how, and as a result of what
economic and social reasons the Jews have been silent
until the present. Why Jewish literature hardly goes back
more than twenty years, or at most fifty. Why during these
last fifty years its development has followed a triumphant
progress. Had they suddenly become more intelligent?
No, but before that they did not have the right to speak;
perhaps they did not even have the desire to, for it is
worth noting that of all those who now speak, there is
not one who does so through an imperious need to speak
—I mean whose eventual aim is the word and the work,
and not *the effect* of that word, its material or moral
result. They speak with greater ease than we because they
have fewer scruples. They speak louder than we because
they have not our reasons for speaking often in an under-
tone, for respecting certain things.

I do not deny, indeed, the great worth of certain Jewish
works, for example the plays of Porto-Riche. But how
much more willingly I should admire them if only they
reached us in translation! For what does it matter to me
that the literature of my country should be enriched if it
is so at the expense of its significance. It would be far
better, whenever the Frenchman comes to lack sufficient
strength, for him to disappear rather than to let an un-
couth person play his part in his stead and in his name.

THE TURKISH JOURNEY

April

When you look at the aridity of the soil in the immense
vacant space between Adrianople and Chatalja, you are
less surprised that the Turks never defended it more bit-

terly. For miles and miles there is not a single house, not a single soul. The train follows the circuitous way suggested by the meanderings of a little stream, and these continual curves force it to go very slowly. Not a tunnel, not a bridge, not even an embankment. M. Loucheur, who is traveling with us, explains that Baron Hirsch, who was in charge of the undertaking, was paid by the kilometer. He must have made a fortune!

Nomadic dogs run from a distance toward the train; from the dining-car people throw out the remains of their meal in paper bags that the dogs tear open.

Among the clumps of blossomless iris and of reeds on the edge of a ditch half filled with gray water—tortoises, families of tortoises, hordes of tortoises, stuck against the mud, flat and mud-colored; they look like bedbugs.

Delight at seeing storks again. Here are even a few camels. Here and there flaming clumps of wild peonies, which our neighbor, a rich Armenian woman from Brusa, insists on calling poppies.

My companion enters into conversation with a young Turk, the son of a pasha, who is on his way back from Lausanne, where he was "learning painting." It is seven months since he left his family for the first time; he is returning home with a volume of Zola under his arm, *Nana,* which he says he likes very much, as much as he likes "the books of Madame Gyp." He declares himself to be a fervent member of the "Young Turk" movement, and he believes in the future of Turkey; but this is enough to keep me from believing in it.

1 May

Constantinople justifies all my prejudices and joins Venice in my personal hell. As soon as you admire some bit of architecture, the surface of a mosque, you learn (and you suspected it already) that it is Albanian or Persian. Everything was brought here, as to Venice, even more than to Venice, by sheer force or by money. Nothing sprang from the soil itself; nothing indigenous underlies the thick froth made by the friction and clash of so many races, histories, beliefs, and civilizations.

The Turkish costume is the ugliest you can imagine; and the race, to tell the truth, deserves it.

Oh Golden Horn, Bosporus, shore of Scutari, cypresses of Eyoub! I am unable to lend my heart to the most beautiful landscape in the world if I cannot love the people that inhabit it.

2 May

The joy of leaving Constantinople, the praises of which I shall have to leave to others. Laughing sea in which the dolphins rejoice. Charm of the Asiatic shores; great trees near by under which the herds seek out shade.

9 May

Oh, how beautiful the light was when, after having gone through the pass, I discovered the other slope! . . . I had let my companions go back to the carriages and had continued upward on foot, taking a short cut and hastening my step, eager to reach the pass before them and to tarry there a moment. But it constantly withdrew into the distance, as it happens in the mountains, where what seems the last height hides another more distant one from which you discover a new peak. It was the hour when the homing flocks people the slopes of the mountain and I had been walking for some time in the growing darkness filled with the singing of the birds before they go to sleep.

On the other slope everything was golden. The sun was setting beyond the Lake of Nicæa, toward which we were going to descend and which was sparkling in a single horizontal ray. We could make out, half hidden by the foliage, the little village of Isnik, rattling around loose within the walls of the ancient fortified city. Urged on by the hour, our brakeless carriages rushed down as if falling, scorning the bends in the road, taking dangerous short cuts. I fail to understand what upsets carriages since ours were not upset. . . . At the foot of the mountain the horses stopped to catch their breath; a spring was near by and I think they were watered also. We had set out ahead. The air was strangely warm; clouds of day-flies were dancing in the golden light of the setting sun. To our right, although the sky was already dark, not a star was to be seen; and we were amazed that Venus could already shine so strong, alone, above the glow in the sky. As we were about to enter through Hadrian's gate, the moon began to appear above the shoulder of the mount, the full moon, enormous, sudden, and surprising as a god. And since my first arrival at Touggourt, I don't think I ever enjoyed a stranger emotion than this entry by night into the little village of Isnik, ashamed, musty, rotted with poverty and fever, huddling in its solemn ruins and its too large past.

Konya

This afternoon we go to the Mosque of the Dervishes. A closed garden surrounds it; opposite the entrance to the mosque a succession of little rooms, probably inhabited by the dervishes, open onto the garden, which they surround. Other larger and more handsome halls are reserved for dignitaries. With exquisite courtesy one of the latter invites us, in the name of the leader of the dervishes, to sit down for a moment. We go into a sort of kiosk, opening wide onto the garden on two sides, at the end of the building containing the dervishes' lodgings.

No furniture; nothing but these lateral benches on which we sit down. Oh, how gladly I would take off my shoes and squat on these mats in the Oriental manner as I used to do in the Green Mosque! . . . We are served coffee. With our dragoman interpreting, I express our regret not to be at Konya on the proper day to see one of their bimonthly ceremonies. Even more than their monotonous whirling dance, which we were able to see at Brusa, I regret missing their music. I should like to know how old that music is and whether or not it is the same in all the convents of the dervishes. What are their instruments? . . . To answer my insistent questions, one of the dervishes goes and gets two long bamboo flutes with the mouthpiece on the end and a rather voluminous notebook in which they have recently transcribed according to the Occidental system of notation the complete repertory of their tunes. I wonder if the outline of their subtle melodic arabesques has not suffered considerably from that noting down and if they did not often have to mar the melody to fix it to our scale. Are they henceforth going to play and sing according to this transcription?

At my request they very kindly begin to blow their pipes; but one of the flutes is too dry and comes to life slowly; the other, with which it was playing in unison, gets out of breath; and this complimentary concert, very ordinary moreover, soon ends.

We go back out into the garden. It is filled with the perfume of flowers and the discreet laughter of a fountain. Returning to the mosque, we pass close to the rooms of the other dervishes; each one is like a bay opening onto the garden, the broad cell of a honeycomb filled with shadow and meditation. In several of these alcoves we see gatherings of dervishes seated in the Persian fashion as in a miniature.

These dervishes are surely very holy men, but so little austerity enters into the great calm of this spot, this fountain is so unlikely to recommend prayer, that one would not be very much surprised if the miniaturist had indulged a fancy and added a few dancing-girls here and there.

In the mosque a large, bright room is devoted to the whirling practices of these gentlemen. Right next to it a no less large but much darker hall is sanctified by the tombs of famous marabouts. Hideous modern rugs cover the ground. From the ceiling hang an unbelievable number of lanterns and lamps of all kinds, all shockingly new and in the worst taste. If by chance I look closely at a copper hanging lamp that seems to be Byzantine in form, I see at once that it is modern, very ordinary in workmanship, and garishly bright. The dervish who is guiding us explains that the real lamp has gone to America and that this is just a copy, which the college of dervishes accepted in its place. He says this as the most natural thing in the world, without the slightest embarrassment, and ready I fancy to accept some new exchange of this type—if only there remained in this venerable spot anything whatever that deserved to be coveted.

[*On way to Greece*]

It is better to come from Turkey rather than from France or Italy to admire as one should the miracle that was Greece—to have been "the weary, way-worn wanderer . . . on desperate seas long wont to roam" of Poe's *To Helen* who feels brought "home to the glory that was Greece." [2]

[2] Gide quotes the poem in Mallarmé's French translation.

The very educative value that I derive from this trip is in proportion to my disgust for the country. I am glad not to like it more. When I feel the need of the desert air, of wild and strong perfumes, I shall go seek them again in the Sahara. In that woebegone Anatolia humanity is not so much undeveloped as it is definitely deteriorated. Should I have gone farther? To the Euphrates? To Bagdad? No, and now I don't want to. The obsession of that country, that painful curiosity that had so long tormented me, is now conquered. What a relaxation it is to have enlarged on the map the space one no longer wants to go and see! For too long I believed (out of love of exoticism, out of fear of chauvinistic self-satisfaction, and perhaps out of modesty), for too long I thought that there was more than one civilization, more than one culture that could rightfully claim our love and deserve our enthusiasm. . . . Now I know that our Occidental (I was about to say French) civilization is not only the most beautiful; I believe, I know that it is the *only one*—yes, the very civilization of Greece, of which we are the only heirs.

On the Adriatic, 29 May

Voluptuous calm of the flesh, as much at rest as this unruffled sea. Perfect equilibrium of the mind. The free flight of my thoughts is supple, even, bold, and voluptuous, like the flight of these gulls through the dazzling blue.

✿ ✿ ✿

11 June

Repeat to myself every morning that the most important remains to be said, and that it is high time.

The synovial sheaths in my right wrist have again become inflamed; most likely the cold and humidity we have had since my return are the cause; but even more so piano-practice, which I have exaggerated of late and which has considerably distracted me from work. I had been so long cut off from music! And I feel, I now know so well how to work. I have gone back to Chopin's *Études* (second book) and his Scherzos, Schumann's Allegro, Beethoven's Variations in E flat and in C major—and the first book of Albéniz's *Iberia*.

Probably it is fortunate that the pains and ankylosis of

the wrist have stopped me. One must get oneself to give the best moment in the day to what most deserves it. The piano should come along only to rest me from work. The best hour is the first; the hard thing is to protect it.

Just as I finish writing these lines, a big package sent by the *N.R.F.* is brought from the station. It contains the other volumes of Albéniz, the Symphonies of Beethoven (Liszt), Fauré's Impromptus, the Transcriptions of Bach (J. Herscher), and the complete work of Chopin in the big Ricordi edition.

I cling to my work-table.

15 June

Yesterday finished the morning most unpleasantly with the memory of M. E., to which I returned or which returned to me several times during the day. Last night my nerves were on edge and I was barely able to sleep a few hours.

Today the weather is clear and the air balmy. I feel all right again.

It is almost seven o'clock. I expect the Copeaus at any moment; I think I shall be less distracted than stimulated by their presence. The rewriting of my Turkish notes progresses with absurd slowness; yet I keep at it and shall get them as far as the arrival in Greece; but I cannot look upon them as anything but a training and preparation for a more important and more serious work. At times, when I think of the importance of what I have to say, of my *Christianisme contre le Christ,* of *Corydon,* and even of my book on Chopin, of my novel, or merely of my *Traité des Dioscures,* I tell myself that I am mad to delay and to temporize in this way.[3] If I were to die right now I should leave only a one-eyed image of myself, or an eyeless one.

---

[3] No such work as *Christianity against Christ* or *Treatise on the Dioscuri* was ever published. *Corydon* first appeared, anonymously and without place or publisher's name, in 1911 as *C.R.D.N.;* a second, enlarged edition appeared in 1920 with the same anonymity. *Notes on Chopin,* not written until 1931, first appeared in the *Revue musicale* for December 1931. The "novel" is of course *The Counterfeiters.* Fragments of the *Treatise on the Dioscuri* appeared in 1919 as *Considerations on Greek Mythology.*

19 June

Yesterday Cuverville went to sleep in a cloud, which this morning is still chilling the surrounding country. Perhaps this numbing climate is partly responsible for the contraction, the strangling of almost all my books, which we discussed with Copeau last evening. I had to finish almost every one of them in Cuverville, contracted and striving to recapture or maintain a fervor that in a dry climate (in Florence, for example) came easily and naturally. I am inclined to believe that, with a little help from the climate, my production would have been easier and, hence, more abundant.

To say nothing of the physiological equilibrium that is so difficult and dangerous to find here.

22 June

I found in the driveway yesterday morning a little starling that had fallen from the nest but was almost ready to fly. While I am writing now, he is right here beside me on the table, or more exactly between the fingers of my left hand, which are holding this notebook in place; that is the spot he most likes. He folds up his legs, puffs up like a little ball; you can tell he is comfortable. I had tried to put him into a cage, but he beat against it; I had to leave him free in the room, where he soils everything. Every ten minutes he lets fall anywhere and everywhere a little liquid, corrosive dropping. I give him bread soaked in milk to eat, mixed with the yolk of a hard-boiled egg; or little earthworms, which he is very fond of. He just flew from the table to my shoulder as soon as he saw me come in. After he has sat for some time on my hand, I feel an odd little itch moving over the back of my hand; this is tiny parasites moving from him to me. Another dropping.

23 June

Finally finished those lamentable Turkish notes. I am ashamed to produce such ordinary stuff. My ideas become numbed and shrunken here to such a degree that, some days, nothing I have in my head seems worth the trouble. . . .

I have regained my self-control in regard to the piano and played yesterday—with Agnès Copeau listening—almost as well as I can ever play when I don't practice more.

My starling amuses me as much as he bothers me; besides the fact that I never get tired of observing him, he is never satisfied unless he is perched on my shoulder, where I should be glad to leave him if he did not soil me. I picked him up about twenty times to put him back on the table and finally I got tired; I went to get a rag and wrapped the upper part of my body in it, but now he is no longer interested in perching on me.

He throws himself so hungrily on the earthworms that I haven't time to chop them up; he snaps them up all at once, then a moment later strangles and gurgles as if he were stifling once and for all. He follows me when I walk up and down in the hall, trotting along behind me, and when I stop climbs fluttering up my leg.

To air out the linen-room I leave two windows open, but with the shutters closed, and this darkens the room rather lugubriously. To divert my starling I risked taking him down onto the lawn at tea-time, when only the Moune, Miquette, and Toby were with us. The last-named was so excited that he trembled all over; Em. ran in fright to get the lead and tie him up. As for the Moune and Miquette, they are so obedient that I had no fear about them; the bird even approached and hopped around Miquette, who, probably finding her position humiliating, turned her head aside and pretended not to see him. I left the starling out about ten minutes; then I took him back into the linen-room, without holding him, freely perched on my finger.

29 June

This afternoon Copeau asked me to help him in his translation of Whitman—that is, to act as his secretary.

We had sat down on the bench behind the house that is sheltered by a hazel tree; then soon, leaving the bench, we stretched out on the lawn beside the path. We were about to leave our work and go in for tea when there came toward us, hopping through the grass in great haste, my little starling. By himself he came right up close to my hand and made no effort to get away when I tried to catch him. In my hand he didn't struggle at all; he seemed perfectly happy to be there. I ran into the kitchen to ask for some bread and milk and, for fear of the cats, I carried the bird into the aviary. He ate quite willingly

but without throwing himself on the food with such eager-
ness that it seemed that mere hunger brought him back. I
could have shouted with joy. I prepared his mush with a
hard-boiled egg, changed the water in his tub, and stayed
for some time with him. Very sorry to have to leave tomorrow. As soon as I get back from Paris I shall give him
his liberty.

30 June

I find in Paris both Souday's article and Lucien Maury's
article on *Les Caves*. The latter article interests me because it could not have been written—or not just as it is—
if I had kept the preface I had almost finished writing;
among other things, I ended the preface thus:

"Whether tales or satirical farces, I have written up to
now nothing but ironic—or, if you wish, critical—works,
of which this is probably the last."

There is a certain amusement and even some advantage
in letting the critics make a mistake at first. But how
could I be surprised that they didn't immediately see in
my *Porte étroite* a critical work? Now, in *Les Caves*,
Lucien Maury thinks he sees an affirmation of nihilism.

How beautiful were the vast fields of grain under the
broiling sun today! How ugly were the men in the train!

7 July

The difficulty lies in letting one subject get ahead of
all the others; as always, the lightest is the most agile and
gets out ahead. I am concerned this morning with the
Traité des Dioscures. But, even here, the tangle of my
ideas is such that each of them in turn seems to me capable of serving as an opening, as the crux of the argument,
or as a closing. Probably I shall be satisfied to note them
down on separate sheets, without seeking to give them
any order. Furthermore I have found in my papers
brought from Paris a certain quantity of materials intended to be used in the construction; I shall leave all this
in a fragmentary state.

12 July

I receive this morning, forwarded by Tronche, the issue
of *L'Éclair* (22 June) in which Henri Massis thinks it
necessary to sound the alarm about the *Caves*.

It has been of great help to me; for even if the accusations he directs against me are false, at least I must admit that I behaved in such a way as to provoke them.

After all, what Massis and the others reproach me with is having made a mistake in their first judgments of me.

In the judgment they formulate today they are making an even greater mistake and will be less inclined to forgive me it. I believe my books would have been judged quite differently if I had been able to publish them all at once, just as they grew up in my mind.

"Publish one's complete works all together for the first time"—I remember how this remark dazzled me when I read it in Flaubert's *Correspondance*. But that would not have been *natural*.

And how could I have agreed to reject the enlightenment I get from the reaction of my books on the public?

I write to Beaunier:

"Consequently I am calling out all my patience" (a letter from him, the day before yesterday, tells me that his article on the *Caves* which was to appear in the *Revue des deux mondes* for June will not be out until September); "you did well to write me, for already I was on the point of thinking: he is giving it up.

"But, if you will permit, I am going to take advantage of this delay to bring to your attention the preface I had written for the *Caves* and then deleted from the proofs.

"In it I told the reader that *Les Caves du Vatican* had been in my mind for more than fifteen years just as I had been big with *La Porte étroite* for more than fifteen years and scarcely less *L'Immoraliste*, the first to come out.

"All these subjects developed parallelly, concurrently— and if I wrote one book before another it is because the subject seemed to me more 'at hand' as the English say.[4] If I had been able to, I should have written them *together*. I could not have written *L'Immoraliste* if I had not known that I was one day to write also *La Porte étroite*, and I needed to have written both of them to be able to allow myself the *Caves*.

"Just as I also need to have written the *Caves* in order to write . . . the rest.

"Why do I call this book a *Sotie* or satirical farce? Why *tales* the three preceding ones? In order to bring out quite

[4] The expression *at hand* appears in English.

clearly that they are not *novels*. And I ended my preface thus: Satirical farces or tales, I have up to now written nothing but *ironic*—or, if you prefer, critical—books—of which this is doubtless the last.

"Then I suppressed this preface, thinking that the reader had no concern with such confidences. But perhaps the critic . . . and that is why I am rewriting all this for you. But after all you are quite free not to pay any attention to it and you can go on as if you didn't know it if this upsets your article.

"Most sincerely yours. . . ."

14 July

The secret of almost all my weaknesses is that frightful modesty of which I cannot cure myself.

I can never persuade myself that I have a right to anything.

They took me for a rebel (Claudel and Jammes) because I was unable to get—or unwilling to force—myself to that cowardly submission which would have assured my comfort. That is perhaps the most Protestant trait I have in me: my horror of comfort.

18

This morning the new issue of *Les Marges* reaches me. Not satisfied to strangle me in an ample article signed Le Cardonnel, it also quotes, in the section devoted to reviews, the most unkind passages from Massis's article and ridicules Souday's meager praises.

The two quotations that Le Cardonnel makes from the *Caves* are shot with obvious errors which make an amorphous thing of my text: "the vague stream of the town" for "the vague sound," etc.[5]

I try not to let myself be too much poisoned by such examples of meanness. I expect help and support solely from *the unknown*.

This evening, moreover, I feel well and strong enough —despite an entirely sleepless night following on a too long tennis game that I couldn't refuse to play with K. (the poor fellow has no distractions here)—and I convince myself that the situation created for me by these

---

[5] This error in copying has substituted "*le vague ruisseau*" for "*la vague rumeur.*"

combined hatreds is unique and decidedly the one I should have longed for.

But no wincing!

I left my bird outside almost all day. He comes when I call; he rises from a bush, first flies around me, then goes off in the distance, and finally returns to perch on my shoulder or arm. He does not fly away when I walk, and I go for a walk with him in the garden. At about tea-time the cats noticed him on the grass and, if I hadn't rushed to him, it would have been all over with him. He let me take him back to the aviary without leaving my shoulder, where he had again perched.

21 July

That odd habit I have always had of putting to work, to begin with and by preference, the laziest parts of myself.

This morning I had to go and fetch Toby, who ran away yesterday to the Dumonts', attracted by their bitch. He allowed himself to be brought home without resisting; I didn't even have to attach his leash. Miquette went along with me, like a legitimate wife going to get her husband at a prostitute's. I should like to know whether or not bitches are capable of jealousy. I doubt it. I fancy that, even among birds, jealousy belongs only to the male.

Jean Schlumberger told me, in this connection, of the extraordinary scene witnessed by Roger Martin du Gard and his wife. They are very proud of the pigeons they are raising and keep a close eye on them. This year the broods succeeded wonderfully; but the male pigeons soon began to be jealous of the little ones; they pursued the females and tried to keep them from approaching the nests. Then, one morning, changing tactics, they all at once hurled themselves on the little ones, both male and female, and raped them with such brutality that all the little ones, bashed in, died of it. Not one of them escaped.

No matter how unbelievable this may seem, it is sworn to be true, and Martin du Gard is not a man to invent anything of this sort.

Offranville, 25 July

I stupidly left at Cuverville, in the excitement of leaving, the little notebook just like this one, only four days

old, but in which I had written last night, or this very
morning, some rather somber reflections about K. Will the
fate we associate with fiction arrange it so that he reads
them? I am almost inclined to wish so, if only this would
lead to some protest, some salutary reaction on his part.[6]

But since I don't want to help fate too much, I write
to Em. to get hold of the notebook and send it to me at
J.-É. Blanche's.

I am writing these lines in the train taking me to Offranville, whence I plan to set out tomorrow for London.

27 July

A certain easing of the strain this morning. People are
relieved and at the same time disappointed to hear that
Serbia is giving in. The wind has fallen too; a thick fine
rain has followed the squall; I should leave, but J.-É.
Blanche suggests going this afternoon to see Walter Sickert
and J. T. R., whom he described to me rather curiously
yesterday. We spent long hours yesterday reading and
patching up his manuscript. This morning I completely re-
wrote three pages of it, changing hardly anything, moreover, except the word-order and arrangement of the sentences, which were tied together any which way. The extraordinary weaknesses of his style enlighten me as to those
of his painting: he never embraces his object; his good
points always spring from *impatience:* he is easily satisfied.
As soon as he has made four slight changes on a page as
he copied it, he thinks he has "worked over it considerably," and since he paints even more easily than he writes,
he is amazed not to get ahead faster. He asks me: "When
you were writing *La Porte étroite,* did you make many
corrections?"

Three titled and rich ladies came this afternoon; one
of them (Countess de C.?) I liked; great traveler with a
free and easy manner . . . but it was the other one who
especially talked with me, embarking on the subject of
La Porte étroite, which she had "read almost ten years
ago, but which was an event in her life." [7] She leads me
to a corner where we are alone and at each compliment
she pays me, I feel like sticking out my tongue at her or

---

[6] In *Les Faux-Monnayeurs* the novelist Édouard arranges to warn
his nephew Georges by leaving some notes for him to read.

[7] The tale had first been published five years before, in 1909.

shouting: Shit! "You so delicately depicted spiritual solitude. It's an entirely different thing from *Mensonges* or
La Dame devant le miroir;[8] you have discovered a new
psychological law that no one had ever stated before. The
wall! Monsieur! The horrible wall! And we ourselves
built it. . . ."

I: "And without windows! Madame, without windows!"

SHE: "No possibility of communication. When you
sense it between two others you would like to knock it
down."

I: "But the others would be angry at you for doing so,"
etc. . . .

And it goes on and on. . . . It was time to write the
Caves.

28 July

The auto took me to Dieppe, where I expected to get
on board at noon. Already I had sent a telegram to Valery
Larbaud announcing my arrival at Newhaven in the
thought that he could come from Hastings to meet me.
A half-hour later I sent him another telegram saying that
I was delaying my departure. Meanwhile we had gone to
the newspaper office, where the latest developments are
posted (Mme Blanche and her sister came to Dieppe with
me), and had met Xavier Léon, who puts the finishing
touch on our anxiety. Impossible to go away with this
terrible worry. I shall probably return to Cuverville tomorrow. My bags were already on the quay beside the
steamer; they were loaded back on the auto. Mme Blanche
went to get a little money at the Dieppe branch of the
Crédit Lyonnais. Xavier Léon plans to return to Paris
tomorrow. The hotel busses are loaded with the trunks of
departing guests. Everyone expects the worst.

1 August

A day of painful waiting. Why don't we mobilize?
Every moment we delay is that much more advantage for
Germany. Perhaps we owe it to the Socialist Party to let
ourselves be attacked. This morning's paper tells about
the absurd assassination of Jaurès.

---

[8] *Mensonges* (*Lies*), short stories by Paul Bourget, had first appeared
in 1897; the other title is doubtless an error for *La Danse devant le
miroir* (*The Dance before the Mirror*), a psychological play by François de Curel, first presented in January 1914.

Under pretense of gathering some apricots, I went to talk with Mius. I spoke of my departure and of my worry at having to leave so many women and children here almost without protection. He then told me of his intention not to leave the house in September.

"No, no, I'll not go away like that; you needn't worry, sir. I'll pay the three hundred francs' penalty if need be. But I'll not go away." He says this in the same grumbling, obstinate tone in which he used to say that he didn't want to do the buying at the market. But we both had tears in our eyes as we shook hands.

At about three o'clock the alarm-bell began to toll. Nevertheless J. insisted at first, in order not to miss a chance to contradict, that it was tolling for a funeral as it had been all morning. I ran to find Mius in the garden and to warn him; and as I returned, having met no one but Edmond, I saw Em. on the flower path, who, with drawn features, said to us, barely restraining her sobs: "Yes, it's the alarm; Hérouard has just come from Criquetot; the order to mobilize has been posted."

The children had set out for Étretat by bicycle. Feeling a need to keep busy, I wanted to go to Criquetot to mail two letters and to get the registered envelope that I knew had arrived. The bell was silent now; after the great alarm throughout the whole countryside, there was nothing but an oppressive silence. A fine rain was falling intermittently.

In the fields a few fellows all ready to leave were going on with their plowing; on the road I met our farmer, Louis Freger, called up on the third day, and his mother, who is going to see her two children go away. I was unable to do anything but shake their hands without a word.

2 *August*

I am writing in the train carrying me to Paris, the last one, it is said, to be left open to civilians. I was tormented at the thought of being cut off at Cuverville. . . . T. is with me.

In Paris we shall make out somehow and shall look for something to do. Before leaving Em. this morning, I knelt down beside her (something I hadn't done since . . .) and asked her to recite the Lord's Prayer. I did this for her sake and my pride yielded to love without difficulty;

moreover, my whole heart participated in her prayer.

K. was indeed very moved to see us leave. Mius accompanied us; he wanted to go get news of his daughter at Yvetot. I had his ticket, which I stupidly let the collector take at the entrance, for they are not admitting third-class travelers for local stops.

Crowd on the platform, both serious and vibrant. A workman shouts as he goes by: "All aboard for Berlin! And what fun we'll have there!" People smiled but did not applaud.

In Paris only an hour late. Our train was filled to overflowing. We lost time letting all the others get out ahead of us so that it was impossible for us to find an auto or even a mere carriage. But the suburban line took us to Passy; from there an auto took us to rue Decamps. I left my bag at Uncle Charles's and started out again almost at once. My uncle struck me as having aged very much; his clothes were worn thin and his gaiters split; he looked like Marmeladov.[9] How I like him this way!

When I left him I hurried to rue du Dragon. Poor Copeau must have got under way too late and now he is going mad with the responsibility of his mother, mother-in-law, wife, and children. How tormenting not to know where to find him in order to help him! He left no word with the concierge. . . . I hurry to the office of the Review; fortunately Tronche is still there, for he is not called up until tomorrow. He is with Mme Suarès and a young man whom I must have met once somewhere or other. All are leaving or have already left. . . . The air is full of a loathsome anguish. Fantastic appearance of Paris, its streets empty of vehicles and full of strange people, calm but hypertense also; some are waiting with their trunks on the sidewalk; a few noisy fellows at the entrance to cafés are bawling the *Marseillaise*. Occasionally an auto loaded down with luggage passes at great speed.

Agnès Copeau, the three children, the mother-in-law, and the governess must have left for Cuverville. I am tormented by the thought of them.

[9] Marmeladov is a disreputable retired functionary in tatters whom Raskolnikov meets in a bar at the beginning of Dostoyevsky's *Crime and Punishment*.

5 August

Germany declares war on Belgium, and England on Germany.

6 August

The idea of a possible collapse of Germany gains strength little by little; one struggles against it, but one does not convince oneself that it is impossible. The wonderful behavior of the government, of everyone, and of all France, as well as of all the neighboring nations, leaves room for every hope.

One foresees the beginning of a new era: the United States of Europe bound by a treaty limiting their armaments; Germany subjugated or dissolved; Trieste given back to the Italians, Schleswig to Denmark; and especially Alsace to France. Everyone talks of this remaking of the map as of the forthcoming issue of a serial.

Monday, 10 August

This morning, at last, a long, exquisite, and comforting letter from Em. Everything seems to be going all right at Cuverville.

Édouard put in an appearance the Sunday before last, before joining up.

"For forty-four years now they have seen nothing but our rear. Now we are going to show them our face and they will remember it!"

The evening of the 8th, dinner with Valery Larbaud, then evening at Suarès's where we find Copeau and Pierre de Lanux.

As Larbaud and I were going up the rue de Rennes, we are accosted in the darkness by a tall woman wearing an old, brownish traveling-cloak and carrying under her arm a bundle wrapped in newspaper. Her face was covered with a veil. Her voice, like her whole body, trembled. She said to us: "*Sprechen Sie Deutsch?*" and when I replied: "*Ein wenig,*" she told us, without tears but in a desperate tone of voice, that she hadn't eaten in two days, that they would not let her return to her hotel, where she hadn't been able to pay for her room, and that she had been wandering in the streets since morning, dead tired.

We told her first that she had only to go to the police station.

"I already went there this morning," she replied in German; "I couldn't register."

"Come back there with us."

She protested that she was too tired; we saw that what she wanted was a little money that would allow her to spend one more night in her room. She lived rue du Dragon, almost opposite Copeau's apartment. We accompanied her that far and went in to make arrangements with the hotel proprietor. She owed only five francs, which we paid; and since she was paying by the week, she could have stayed on Monday; but we urged her to go and hand herself over tomorrow. She was a seamstress, who had been in this place for three months and seemed quite respectable. . . .

12, 13, 14

Seen nothing, done nothing, heard nothing. One buys eight papers a day. First *Le Matin* and *L'Écho*—then *Le Figaro* for Ghéon, who telegraphed for it to be sent to him at Nouvion; then the *Daily Mail;* then *Paris-Midi;* then *L'Information,* the evening *Matin, La Liberté*, and *Le Temps*—and although each sheet repeats the preceding one in the same terms, one rereads the least bit of news, constantly hoping to know a bit more.

Spent the evening before last with Élie Allégret after having dinner with Marcel. This good Élie, to whom I had expressed my desire to find something to do, has found a place for me: I am going to be commissioned by the Mairie of the XVIth Arrondissement to register all the boys between twelve and eighteen who come and to think up ways of keeping them busy . . . ! I told him that I didn't think I was quite the right man for the job.

15 August

The sky clouded over during the night, and in the early morning a big storm broke east of Paris.

The first rolling of the thunder at about four o'clock seemed enough like the explosion of bombs to make one think a flight of zeppelins had raided Paris. And in my half-sleep I imagined for some time that Paris was being bombarded and that it was even the end of the world. From my lack of emotion I realized that I was ready for anything and everything; but it was only a dream. Yet can I know how I might react when faced with real danger? Of what simple stuff are they made, the people who can guarantee their reactions at any hour of the day or night! How many soldiers anxiously wait for the event that will prove whether or not they are brave? And he who doesn't react as *he would like to*—whose will alone is brave! . . .

The despair of the man who thinks he is a coward because he yielded to a momentary weakness—when he hoped he was courageous (*Lord Jim*).[10]

Copeau came to dinner at the rue Laugier; I walked part of the way home with him and told him of my visit to poor old La Pérouse. Yes, yesterday afternoon I thought I could do nothing better than call on him. Mme de La Pérouse opened the door and immediately buttonholed me, bursting forth in recriminations against her husband, who, she claims, does whatever he can to be disagreeable to her and has now thought up the idea of letting himself die of hunger. For several days, ever since the declaration of war, I believe, he has been refusing almost all nourishment. After a few affected courtesies, she got up to "announce" me. And since she warned me that "Monsieur de La Pérouse" was in bed, I spoke of going into his bedroom.

"Oh! sir, you could hardly get in; Monsieur de La Pérouse is so finicky that no one is allowed to clean up his room. . . ."

But when she returns she announces to me that M. de La Pérouse is expecting me.

The room I now enter for the first time is rather dark because of the only half-open shutters. The open, uncurtained window looks out on a court, and the position of the shutters keeps people across the way from seeing into the room.

Old La Pérouse is not in bed. Up against the bed he lies deep in a mahogany armchair covered in worn red velvet that reveals the stuffing. I sit down in another armchair just like it. He hardly makes a gesture when I come in; he lets me grasp his inert left hand; he is leaning on the right against a square table, and his elbow is resting on two little cushions in the shape of a tea-cozy; on a lower level of the same table two metal bowls are lying one in

[10] Joseph Conrad's novel.

the other. I hold his hand in mine and put my arm behind him without saying a word. He doesn't say anything either. I observe his face, mottled with red and yellow, deathly pale in spots, which seems made of such a strange material that if one scratched the skin anything but blood would run from the scratch. I look at the room's odd disorder: on the right a pile of hatboxes rising almost to the ceiling; then a bureau, one half of which is covered with a pile of unbound books; on the other half, a bottle of cider standing in a saucepan, a dirty glass, a small hotplate, and several spirit-lamps, one of which is burning imperceptibly. On the left, in front of the fireplace, a low table holds a collection of mysterious pots, all of the same size and each with a cover on it. In the middle of the room another table with toilet articles on it and, under the table, a garbage-can filled with old shoes.

Eventually the poor old man raises his head a bit and murmurs: "I am very weak."

I try then to persuade him to accept a little nourishment. Finally he confesses that, in addition to a lack of appetite, he has decided not to eat any more, to end it all. Then turning toward me: "Be good; give me a drink. Just a little cider." And with a flabby hand he points at the bottle.

I refuse to give him more than a quarter of a glass.

"Ah! I could drink the sea itself!" he sighs.

However, while talking, I lead him gradually to the idea of accepting a gruel that Mme de La Pérouse is going to prepare for him. And while the soup is heating, he returns to old complaints: particularly his wife's jealousy toward all those who show esteem and affection for him:

"She has all the faults," he says; then, correcting himself, he adds: *all the petty ones.*

For the first time I inquire about his reasons for marrying Mme de La Pérouse. As one could well imagine, those reasons were altogether sentimental: he loved her. And going back into the past, he tells me about his brother, that brother he loved most tenderly and passionately and who died at the age of seventeen. La Pérouse himself was hardly more than twenty-one at the time. A few months later he got married. In a little trunk to which he kept the key, he had locked up his brother's letters, which he did not *dare* read for several years. Then one day (most likely after his first conjugal disappointments) he locked himself in a room where he knew he would not be disturbed, opened the little trunk, and reread that correspondence. From that day on, he got into the habit of seeking consolation and support in that reading; these were hours when he could be almost sure of not being watched by his wife. But he soon became convinced that she was spying on him and suspected his little trunk; for some time she had already been rummaging in his drawers among his other papers. The day finally came when, opening his trunk, La Pérouse found his brother's letters in disorder. "It was," he told me, "just as if someone had put them back in a hurry, someone who had been surprised while reading them and hadn't had time to put them in order." He had no words with Mme de La Pérouse, but he burned those papers at once.

Next he tells me of his excessive shyness, which so often made people misjudge him. This is why he could never express his gratitude to Mme de Rothschild, who, on many occasions, had obliged him most charmingly. Eager to speak with her, he accepted an invitation to a dance, arrived among the first, could not screw up his courage to approach her at the rare moments when he saw her alone, stayed until the end, and, since the only person he knew at the dance constantly dragged him off to the buffet, he must have looked like the kind of person who comes to stuff himself. This stuck in his mind as a burning remorse.

He talks with extreme slowness, without turning toward me, his eyes staring into space; occasionally I hear an odd sound in his mouth as if he were chewing his teeth. But then he becomes lively; once more I succeed in reassuring him, in consoling him; probably the soup he ate ("with pleasure," as he confesses) is doing him good; now, surprised at it himself, he asks me to help him get up; he looks for his hat; he wants to go out. We go downstairs together and, after I have said good-by to him in the street, I feel his eyes following me for a long time and, when I turn around again, he waves to me. . . .

21

Copeau arrives at the rue Laugier just as we were about to go up to bed and delays our curfew an hour. He seems younger, more Diderot than ever, eagerly embracing every new project. He talks of reopening the Vieux-Colombier for theatrical presentations and recitals improvised for the occasion, and he would like to organize them at once. He also talks of going abroad since he is doing nothing in Paris; he would like to become more involved; he would like to write for the newspapers, the articles he reads— even those by Barrès—striking him as very ordinary and unsatisfactory; he thinks he could do better; and I can easily believe it, at least for the first ones he wrote. . . .

There begin to be seen walking the streets, hugging the walls, odd lucifugous creatures such as the tide uncovers when the water withdraws.

Yesterday a sort of Colonel Chabert,[11] stiff-jointed and almost voiceless, who nevertheless did his best to sing in order to attract the charity of passers-by. People didn't hear him at all and no one stopped. He was holding a little boy by the hand and another smaller one was following. Both of them ugly, gaunt, and looking as if they had forever forgotten how to smile. I asked for their name and address and this morning I went to rue Bolivar, near the Buttes-Chaumont, to see their poverty at closer hand. The two little boys were not there; on the first floor of a low house I found the old man of the other day beside an enormous, whining, panting woman who told me her story. Twice married, she has given birth to seventeen children, of which ten—all tubercular—are still alive. The two eldest sons are in the services. The municipality supports them in an almost satisfactory fashion, after all. I expected to find an even worse poverty in these sorry quarters; that is also because it was very beautiful weather.

Read Yeats's preface to W. Blake as I was walking.

26 August

The French, who were playing fair, were indignant at the fact that in war the Germans did not observe the rules of the game.

As for the latter, it seemed as if they were aiming to discredit war forever; and as if to prove that war was an evil thing—if it is true that in war the aim is to conquer —they won by the worst means.

[11] The hero of Balzac's story by the same name returns to life and civilization after having been buried alive during the Napoleonic Wars.

[*28 August*]

Characters:

He who deceives himself with fine words, who feels that he is not believed and is annoyed by it, but little by little becomes aware that people were right not to believe him.

At the moment of danger he is not there; it isn't exactly that he wanted not to be there; without thinking he just happened to favor the little circumstance that would let him out. He did not cling to his post.

On the other hand, those on whom you didn't count and who do their duty wonderfully. You suffer for having spoken ill and thought ill of them.

At certain hours everything that seemed as if it were to our advantage turned against us. The "dash" of our troops—who are constantly overstepping the line of artillery protection so that our own soldiers are killed by our projectiles.[12] The fury of our black troops and their excessive fierceness, which drags all their officers to death after them because there is no way of getting them to let go and to re-form their units.

At first he is pleased to hear that all the wounded men arrive with rather slight wounds; then he learns that this is merely because of the lack of stretcher-bearers, so that all those whose wounds prevent them from escaping themselves remain on the field of battle.

7 September

I do not recall ever having seen in this region such a long succession of uniformly beautiful days. One's heart is overwhelmed by the sky's serenity.

8 September

All you could get from him was an aphorism like this: "It is a rule of nature that the common should triumph over the exquisite."

His *despair* derived above all from the fact that he knew that the German armaments were in no wise factitious or sham but just as natural to that race and to that country as a shell and claws are to a crustacean. Between this and that there were deep and essential relationships.

---

[12] On 4 September Joffre gave special instructions about this. [A.]

With us the army remained an instrument; with them it is an organ; so that, without much exaggeration, it could be said that, for that organ, war was the necessary function.

16 September

The impossibility of keeping oneself in a state of tension (which is after all artificial) as soon as nothing in the *immediate surroundings* motivates it. X. goes back to reading, to playing Bach, and even to preferring the fugues with a joyful rhythm from the *Well-Tempered Clavichord*, which he can forbid himself only with great reluctance.

Meanwhile, in the old house where he had remained alone with his wife, the clan begins to gather. Jeanne was still tarrying in Étretat, where she had gone against her will since her mania for contradicting common sense and the facts kept producing optimism. She declared: "They will never come this way," in the same tone that she assured us that the Russians were going to cut off the Austrians headed toward Belgium.

But since, after all, the Germans hadn't come, the discussion became retrospective and X. was reduced to asserting that they could have come. This was enough to dispute about endlessly.

Forced to take part again in the family worship. His discomfort. His horror of the gesture that might exceed his feeling.

His embarrassment when commissioned to choose the verses to read; he understands why ministers so often turn to the texts of St. Paul, which are less specific, more suitable for any emergency, than those from the Gospels. He also looks for a Psalm and a chapter from the Prophets, but everything strikes him as too "improvised for the occasion."

This pushes him farther in that direction than he would like to go.

My dear André (Ruyters):—Of all my recent companions of whom I think insistently every day, it seems that you are one of the least favored. To go off to the wars and then end up at a rear echelon in front of a cook-stove or a wash-tub is not very exciting. I know also that you were seriously upset the first few days as a result of the change of diet; I know too that your discomfort did not last.

I should most likely have written you earlier, but I have very little liking for general reflections about the events and I find nothing new or special to tell you. You probably know that I returned to Cuverville as soon as conditions began to appear not too favorable and a dreadful cloud temporarily darkened our outlook. Copeau became somewhat alarmed at the thought that his wife and children were in a spot that might seem dangerous; it was my mission to send them across the water. At the same time I emptied Cuverville of my nephews, nieces, and sisters-in-law, who were then pleasantly but unwisely filling the place; and I remained alone with my wife and K. (who was to get back to Havre by bicycle at the first serious alarm), Em. and I with our minds made up to remain to the last like my brother-in-law Georges, mayor of Cuverville, as you know. On the day of my return here the "official communiqué" proclaimed the Germans' onslaught on "the Somme"—the lack of preciseness had the effect of spreading panic throughout the Caux district. Étretat, Fécamp, even Criquetot were literally emptied of everyone who could afford flight. The spectacle was rather disgusting and its repercussion on the poverty-stricken and on those detained by their functions was most painful. On the other hand, I was able to notice the comfort they took from my wife's calmness and courage. My return likewise contributed toward reassuring them, for they thought: "Since Monsieur Gille[13] is coming back, there can't be any danger!" Fortunately they couldn't read my heart! I lived through ten days of frightful anguish, expecting the worst from one hour to the next—and perhaps not entirely without reason. . . . And when the "communiqués" gave us reason to believe that the flood no longer threatened Normandy, they showed it to be so close to Paris that our anguish merely changed form. . . .

How easily life takes shape again, closing up its gaps! Too easy healing of wounds. Surrender to that paltry comfort which is the great enemy of real happiness.

· · ·

[13] A local mispronunciation of Gide.

The position of X., who stays behind while those who insisted on the necessity of staying all go.

The converse position of the L.'s at Yport—whom F. urges to leave, even fixing an appointment with them at such and such a station—then abandons after making up his mind to stay till the last moment, as if he lacked the courage of his cowardice.

18 September

This morning, before eight o'clock, a telegram brought by the postmistress's great-nephew: "Charles Péguy fell before the enemy Argonne." Théo sent it to me.

25

Yesterday Jacques Raverat left. We had read together Milton's wonderful *Ode on the Nativity* and several of Shakespeare's *Sonnets*. Talked endlessly of ethics and religion. He believes in the devil; he even told me that he believed in the devil before believing in God. I told him that what kept me from believing in the devil was that I wasn't quite sure of hating him. Certainly there will be someone in my novel who believes in the devil. These conversations will prove to have been of rather great advantage to both of us. He tells me that he is leaving full of new vigor for work.

Ride to Étretat in the afternoon in a carriage. I regret not having learned until too late that one could visit the wounded (from one to three on Thursdays and Sundays).

This morning Marcel arrived unexpectedly just while I was in the act of writing him.

5 October

Every day I make Françoise practice two hours; I should like to teach her to practice alone. The chief difficulties (I was about to say the only ones) I find in her are due to bad habits picked up some time ago; particularly the habit of never giving its full value to each note, so that it yields only to the following note. She plays in strict time, but does not hold the notes she strikes. Because of this, I make her practice the first of Handel's *Little Fugues*, which calls for the perfect linking of each note to the following one and the holding of the white and full notes through the black ones.

· · ·

Took Miquette back to Fellow; the bitch is just as willing as can be and even tries to help, but he insists on being out of line despite all I do to help him. Since, eventually, I left him to himself and he got nowhere, he came to get me, pulling and pushing me toward the bitch, again begging for my help.

I wish it were forbidden for anyone to make statements about sex who had not had experience in breeding and observing animals. Perhaps they would finally come to understand that many difficulties, deviations, and irregularities that they insist on calling abnormal and "against nature" are no less *natural* than others.

15 November

An American came just the other day to the Foyer Franco-Belge[14] to inform us that he would give our institution a large sum of money if we could succeed in putting him into direct contact with a child who had been mutilated by the Germans.

Richepin, in an indignant article, spoke of *four thousand* children who supposedly had had their right hands cut off. That assertion without any proof had irked Romain Rolland (see his letter) and doubtless a number of Swiss people also.

However, Mme Edwards, at the end of August (check the date), had told me of the arrival at rue Vaneau of a procession of children, all boys from the same village and all similarly amputated.

The day before yesterday I went to her, pointing out the great interest we would have in definite proof of such monstrosities. She told me then that she had not seen the children herself, that she knows they were coming from the Cirque de Paris, where they had first been sent. She invites me to come back and lunch with her on the following day (yesterday), promising me—until I find better proof—photographs of those mutilations.

Yesterday she had not been able to get the photographs, but she was expecting Cocteau right after lunch, who was to bring them. Cocteau came after lunch without the photos, which he promised me for tomorrow evening. Meanwhile he led me to the clinic on rue de la Chaise,

[14] Franco-Belgian Center, of which André Gide was assistant director.

where we could speak with a Red Cross nurse who had taken care of those children. The lady was not there yet and, expected at the Foyer, I had to leave Cocteau before learning anything.

Ghéon also tells me that two amputated children, one fifteen and the other seventeen years old, were being cared for at Orsay right now. He is to bring me further information.

Not one of these statements could be proved.

1915

I tell you that a new civilization is beginning. Yesterday's was based too much on Latin civilization; that is to say, on the most artificial and empty culture. In contradistinction to the thoroughly natural Greek civilization. . . . But it must be admitted that its very shortcomings made Latin culture appeal to us.

24 September

Until then I wrote in the overflow of my joy. Through lack of expression, today my suffering is increased. I am awkward in grief. And I am even inclined to attribute to some secret fatigue any decrease in my happiness. How tired I am! . . .

25 September

I have recovered my balance only at the piano, where I am continuing to practice the Albéniz compositions. I know three of them by heart and more than half of a fourth. Picked up again in the same manner Franck's Prelude, Choral, and Fugue and some of Chopin's Études.

28 September

Hope still hesitates, not daring to open wide its wings and take flight toward new skies. . . . What patience our waiting calls for! How long will I have to keep silent? And when the time comes will I have enough strength and time left to speak?

I am diverted from the Foyer and now go there only in the afternoon to find little to do. I am tired of it and constantly break away. I can't stick it. . . . Before my recent short trip to Cuverville I had again been completely absorbed by a new branch (the distribution of clothing) that had to be thoroughly reorganized. Right now the keeping of our list of grants, perfectly organized, does not call for any further initiative. The regular work on it has become almost entirely administrative. Perhaps I shall settle down for a while at rue Taitbout to keep an eye on the way the restaurant is functioning. Most likely it would be worth reconsidering many things there, but I fear that Charlie Du Bos might be hurt. I cannot half give my services or lend myself. For eleven months at the Foyer I managed to let myself be completely absorbed by my task and become utterly interested in it. Now that the machine is running properly, is it permissible for me to get away from it, as from a finished book? . . .

No. Nothing in the material world is ever finished. Everything goes on. And what you have once taken upon yourself has a claim upon you.

Darius Milhaud came yesterday, late in the afternoon, to play the symphonic poem he has just composed on one of the Tagore poems I translated. It was nothing but noise to me.[1] Then he played us most delicately some rather ordinary melodies of Mendelssohn. The day before I had accompanied Marianne Delacre. She sang some Chausson and some Duparc. A purpose or psychological meaning always bothers me in music. For me it loses its real meaning when it tries to take on too definite a meaning.

1 October

I almost left for England. I was already leaving the Théos' with my bag and steamer-rug; I had an appointment to meet Mrs. Wharton tomorrow morning at the Gare du Nord. Henry James and Arnold Bennett were expecting me. Yesterday I had written to Raverat to announce my arrival and had taken leave of the Foyer. Fortunately I encounter insurmountable difficulties at the prefecture. Before getting my passport I have to go to the Invalides to regularize my military status or at least to prove that it is regular; then to the local police station with two witnesses and my photograph; then to the British Embassy; then to the Ministry of Foreign Affairs. . . . And, since there was not enough time for all these formalities, I suddenly found myself extraordinarily relieved to give up the project altogether. If I got some pleasure from the idea of going away, my pleasure at the idea of staying was certainly much greater, and I enjoy this late afternoon, here, like someone who has just had a narrow escape.

[1] Milhaud's *Melody* for voice and piano (rather than symphonic poem) was inspired by the Tagore-Gide poem beginning: "*Les nuages s'entassent sur les nuages.*" It has been published only once, by *La Revue Française de Musique.*

I rushed to Mrs. Wharton's, for she was to get my ticket. Yet it would have amused me to travel with her. But this was not the moment.

8 October

This evening I finish *The Autobiography of Mark Rutherford*. Wonderful integrity of the book. I do not know any literary work that is more specifically Protestant. How does it happen that the book is not better known? How grateful I am to Bennett for having told me about it! The exquisite qualities of Hale White's style (this is the author's real name) are the very ones that I should like to have.

16 October

Having resumed my life as a philanthropist and parasite, I no longer have a moment to write in this notebook. At the Foyer morning and afternoon; I am caught again by the extreme interest of certain cases, by the atmosphere of affection and bewilderment that pervades that place, and the dangerous intoxication that self-sacrifice brings. Em. is to come to town Monday.

21 October

Frantically busy from morning to evening. These last few days we have had an avalanche of pathetic cases. Unable to note anything.

24 October

I have never produced anything good except by a long succession of slight efforts. No one has more deeply meditated or better understood than I Buffon's remark about patience.[2] I bring it not only to my work but also to the silent waiting that precedes good work.

All the same, by dint of waiting, I wonder if I have given all that I might have. At times it seems to me that everything I have produced up to now was only to prepare for the rest, merely to train my hand, and that everything important remains to be said. (I have already expressed this idea elsewhere, but I feel the need of repeating it as I do so often to myself.) At times it strikes me painfully that I have delayed too much and that many of the books that remain to be written should already have been written.

[2] Buffon is reported to have said: "Genius is but a greater aptitude for patience."

Thursday, 11

Hateful sluggishness. At times it seems to me that I have already ceased living and that I am bestirring myself in a sort of posthumous dream, a sort of supplement to life, without importance or meaning. This state of apathy is probably the natural result of the emotional strain of the Foyer.

Mme Théo is again giving herself to our organization and this permits me a little leisure; but I don't take real advantage of it and neither work properly nor rest properly.

Yesterday, at the Prisoner of War Organization where I had gone to get a piece of information, M. C. de W., who is the head, I believe, asked me if I had been able to resume my "little literary relaxations."

Friday, 12

I had had the absurd weakness to accept an invitation to dine at Mme Edwards's with the Philippe Berthelots; I come away quite upset. I don't understand very well why people invite me: not famous enough for it to be flattering to have me; my conversation remains desperately dull, and there is nothing to be got out of me.

I got into rather hot water by suddenly taking up the defense of Souday, raising my voice and exaggerating my praise, through simple exasperation at the summary judgment of Philippe Berthelot and the others: "And to think that the war will not rid us of fellows like that!"

Philippe Berthelot utters aphorisms of paradoxical flavor and impeccable form, which denote his assurance of his superiority and that of his family, his friends, his tastes, etc. He affects a great calm like that of Renan, which is due, I believe, to an utter insensitivity. In his look, his voice, his gesture, there is something inhuman that paralyzes me. I am also bothered by the narrowness of his forehead; and since despite this he has a prodigious memory, it seems that his ideas must have lost one dimension in order to store themselves in his brain.

Mme Philippe Berthelot arrived in a sheath gown without any waist at all, a sort of silk slip of solid apple-green; excused herself, as she has done on every other occasion I have seen her, for wearing "a tea-gown"; and Mme Edwards, as on every other occasion, exclaimed:

"But, my dear, I too am wearing a negligee." It had a very low neck prolonged by transparent gold lace, a cream-colored silk skirt, very short and edged with fur, and over it all a sort of broad-sleeved jacket, likewise edged with fur and considerably shorter than the skirt. These two women sit close together on a low divan with the manners of odalisques. Mme Edwards laughs and clucks and coos, puffing out her neck and letting her head roll on her bare shoulders. Sert is there, plumper and more sententious than ever. I try in vain to listen to him. He tirelessly lectures me on the superiority of "baroque" art and distills boredom as much as I do myself. It seems to me that, with all the time he has been living in France, he might have deigned to lose a little of his accent. F. is the sixth: thin, courteous, insignificant.

At table, the Heredia family is discussed: charming group, a bit noisy, but so amusing, so whimsical! . . . And Philippe Berthelot begins relating his earliest recollections of them. The eldest daughter was barely sixteen then; the youngest was merely a child. Was it the first time that Philippe Berthelot had entered that drawing-room? I don't know. . . . Two days before, the maid had had a slight "accident" which was now the young ladies' subject of conversation. One of them suddenly announced that she was going to fetch the fetus, went out, and shortly returned from the sixth-floor room with a jar. And since, in the middle of his tale, Mme Edwards protests, Philippe Berthelot insists, asserting that it was not a sham, that the fetus was very definitely in the jar, where the young ladies, with the aid of a long buttonhook, amused themselves by whirling it around.

The G. couple and the J. R. couple came after dinner. About books, things, and people much nonsense was said; and if I said perhaps a little less than the others, this is because I talked less.

I was asked with such insistence to play that refusing became most difficult. To encourage me Mme Edwards sat down before a book of Chopin and played some mazurkas with fluidity and charm, but in the artistic manner, with that *tempo rubato* I dislike so much, or, to speak more precisely, without paying any attention to the time and with sudden accents, stresses, and effects much more apt to show off the player's temperament than the excellence of the composition. This took place between two drawing-rooms, in a tiny room hung with gold and on a piano completely out of tune. The Philippe Berthelots having left, I wanted to get away too, but since it was raining hard, Mme Edwards insisted on having an automobile brought round for me and led me meanwhile toward the piano in the other room, the large drawing-room with the charming Bonnard decorations. I began the Prelude in E-flat major. But just as it occurs to me when talking with an Englishman to take on an English accent, I assumed, out of politeness, the same *tempo rubato* that Mme Edwards had just used and stopped after twelve agonized bars.

The auto that was taking me home to Auteuil ran out of gasoline two kilometers from the Villa, so that I had to walk in the dark and under a driving rain. I was unable to close my eyes all night long, and all today I shall go about with a headache and a grudge against yesterday's hosts and against myself.

From 22 to 26 November, an automobile trip with Mrs. Wharton.

Hyères, 26 November

I have made the acquaintance of Paul Bourget. He received me most cordially at Costebelle, at his estate named Le P., to which Mrs. Wharton had taken me. He felt a great need to captivate someone he knows to represent another generation, another side of the fence, another point of view. The introduction took place in the garden.

"To enter here, Monsieur Gide," he said to begin with, "you have no need to go through *the strait gate.*"

This didn't exactly mean anything but a way of showing his kindly attitude. And shortly thereafter he managed to allude to my *Immoraliste;* then, returning to the subject, after Mrs. Wharton had left us for a moment to go and see Mme Bourget, who was kept in her room by a slight indisposition:

"Now that we are alone, tell me, Monsieur Gide, whether or not your immoralist is a pederast."

And, as I seem somewhat stunned, he reinforces his question:

"I mean: a practicing pederast?"

"He is probably more likely an unconscious homosexual," I replied as if I hardly knew myself; and I added: "I believe there are many such."

At first I thought that he had taken this way of showing me that he had read my book; but he especially wanted to develop his theories:

"There are," he began, "two classes of perversions: those that fall under the head of sadism and those that belong to masochism. To achieve sexual pleasure both the sadist and the masochist turn to cruelty; but one, etc. . . . while the other," etc. . . .

"Do you class homosexuals under one or the other of these perversions?" I asked just to have something to say.

"Of course," he replied; "for, as Régis points out . . ."

But at this moment Mrs. Wharton returned and I never learned whether, according to him, the homosexual fell under the head of sadism or of masochism. I was sorry that he turned the conversation into another channel; it would have amused me to have Mrs. Wharton's opinion, if she had one.

Paul Bourget still seems extremely hardy for his age, as if gnarled and hewn out of chestnut. His least remarks are redolent of literature; he splatters you with literary allusions like the spaniel that shook off precious stones.[3] "You are welcome to—what is anything but Elsinore," he said as we left the garden to enter the house. In less than a half-hour he managed to speak of Régnier (Mathurin), Shakespeare, Molière, Racine (whom he confesses not to be very fond of), Baudelaire, Boileau, Zola, Balzac, Charles-Louis Philippe, etc., all this with an extraordinary lack of real literary taste, I mean an odd lack of appreciation of poetry, art, and style. It is this that allows him to admire such paltry productions as those of Psichari, for instance, for which he has just written a preface. He reads us a few pages from the *Voyage du Centurion*,

[3] "The Little Dog Shaking Off Money and Precious Stones" is the title of the thirteenth tale in the third part of La Fontaine's *Contes*.

from the proofs;[4] his voice catches as if he were on the point of weeping. Out of the corner of our eyes Mrs. Wharton and I glance at each other, not knowing which deserves more wonder, Paul Bourget's emotion or the mediocrity of those pages. He insists on our reading the whole book, of which he gives us the proofs. And a little later, as I am walking down the corridor of the Coste-belle hotel with him, after tea and a short walk, then a new conversation in Mrs. Wharton's room, in which we talked of Pascal and of the *Mystère de Jésus*[5] . . . he takes me familiarly by the arm and, leaning toward me:

"So you will promise me to read the *Voyage du Centurion?*" And, in a whisper of solemn secrecy, he adds: "Believe me: it is worth the *Mystère de Jésus.*"

On this odd declaration we separated.

Bourget told me also:
"I am a panpsychist! I no longer believe in matter."

8 December

My wonder as a child on seeing the first eucalyptus tree in blossom. We had just reached Hyères. I ran quickly to the hotel and was not satisfied until I had led my mother out to look at those wonderful flowers with me. I shall have to relate also the trips I made at that time to the islands; perhaps the most enchanted memory of my childhood is that of the moments, the hours, that I spent on Sainte-Marguerite (or Saint-Honorat), leaning over the rocks on the edge of the water, watching the fairyland formed, at that time, by the natural aquariums among the rocks. Sea-anemones, starfish, sea-urchins besprinkled the rock walls down to depths where the eye ceased to make them out clearly; everything was palpitating according to the rhythm of the waves, but there were shelters to which not even the slightest undulation reached; there creatures and flowers breathed indolently; by keeping still and quiet for a long time, one could see strange, almost a little frightening animals issuing from dark lairs. I would stay there without stirring, lost in a contemplation—or rather an adoration—that nothing inter-

---

[4] *The Centurion's Journey* (1916) by Ernest Psichari.
[5] *The Mystery of Jesus* is a brief series of devotional reflections by Pascal, both profound and beautiful.

rupted until Marie's call, toward evening, in time to catch the return boat.

I am very much afraid that the shores of those islands, so charming in my childhood, have been as lamentably spoiled as the immediate surroundings of Cannes itself; as was also the coast of England of which Edmund Gosse speaks so eloquently in *Father and Son;* and as are all the most charming spots on this earth as soon as man begins to sprawl on them.[6]

13 December

I am anxious for this notebook to be finished; I am not writing anything worth while in it; but I shall not drop it until it is finished. . . .

20 December

(For the novel.)

X. went so far as to say that the best way to triumph over Prussian militarism was not to try to conquer Germany, but on the contrary— He was never allowed to finish. He would continue, a little later and in a somewhat lower voice:

"The best way to overcome them would be to make their whole attack useless. Their offensive increases in direct ratio to our resistance. Faced with a nation that did not defend itself, all the Krupp cannon wouldn't be any good. . . ."

The others swallowed their indignation and gave up trying to make X. understand in what way Christian renunciation (and that non-resistance which the Gospels teach us) becomes unbearably shocking as soon as a collectivity, rather than individuals, is involved—and even more so when the collectivity is a nation entrusted with a past. X. was not convinced by the little that they did say, however. He cited the early Christians and asserted that it was precisely through their non-resistance that they had triumphed over all oppressions. He maintained that a nation that does not defend itself is essentially invincible. "A nation of cowards!" exclaimed the others. He replied: "A nation of martyrs." He claimed that this would have been the real way to win out over Germany and that France would thus have conquered her without fail,

[6] André Gide is speaking of the Iles de Lérins, off the coast of Cannes, and not of the Iles d'Hyères, as might be at first supposed.

as Christianity had conquered ancient Rome, and that it was mad to claim that our disorganized nation could win out otherwise over Germany's organization. The only victory toward which we could and should aim today, he concluded, is a mystical victory; and it is the only real one.

In vain they tried to make him see that for such a victory there would have had to be, throughout France, an agreement and organization, the lack of which was our greatest weakness.

"And if any party had been mad enough to propose such a thing," Marcel said, "the indignant revolt of the others would have brought on a revolution even more harmful than war."

"Harmful!" X. replied; "are you quite sure? Yet you know very well that all the half-victories that the superhuman feats of our army allow us to hope for will hardly decrease the permanent danger threatening us, that France may exhaust herself."

"In that case I am for Corneille's 'He should die!'" [7] Marcel answered, "and I much prefer to end up sharp than to fizzle out. My two sons are at the front, where I have already lost three of my brothers and I don't know how many cousins and nephews. We shall all die if need be, but at least the world will see France die entire and we shall be saving her from a survival due to some shameful compromise."

Immediately the others began to boo X. and to raise their glasses (this takes place at the Café Vachette) in honor of France and of Marcel, who had just spoken so eloquently.

27 December

Intellectually tired, apathetic; I no longer achieve anything. . . .

Ghéon, on a week's leave, reads us the poems he has just written; some of them strike me as excellent. I deeply regret that his long piece on Romain Rolland employs arguments that are often dubious. He repeats the story of the hands cut off the little children, even though we have

---

[7] In Corneille's *Horace*, Act III, scene vi, the father, when asked what he would expect his son to do in unequal battle against three opponents, heroically says: *"Qu'il mourût."*

striven everywhere in vain to get back to a proved fact, even though all the inquiries we conducted at the Foyer, with a view to winning the huge prize offered by America to whoever could confirm such atrocities, led only to ultimate denials.

This is the place and the occasion to set down the strange, pathetic tale that Mme Théo has brought home from the Foyer. She has it directly from Mme Théâtre, a good, reliable woman of the lower classes whose odd name amused us at first, but whose exaggerated reserve kept her somewhat at a distance from us. Every week she would come to our section to get her grant. A little boy three or four years old usually came with her. I remember my faintness the first day when, wanting to give the child one of the hard candies we always kept on hand, I noticed that he didn't have any right hand: the sleeve of his jacket hid as best it could a hideous stump, which did not however show any sign of seam or scar; at wrist-level the arm simply stopped short. . . . The mother, who was watching my eyes, told me then that the child "was born like that." I was amazed, for I didn't think such a thing possible; but I could only accept what the mother told me. And now here is the story:

During the Germans' incursion into Reims, there was great confusion among the civilian population, rubbing elbows as it was with enemy soldiers and officers. Chance brought Mme Théâtre into a delicatessen where she had to queue up next to a German lieutenant; she had her son in her arms. The lieutenant was to be waited on ahead of her. Out of the silver coin with which he paid he was given back two pennies. Eager to make a good impression, and perhaps also through natural kindness, he turned around and held out the pennies to the child. (I must add here that the mother, who now hides the stump under a sleeve that is intentionally too long, then wrapped it up rather awkwardly in a cloth that only served to call attention to it. The child, as if to accept the offer, made a gesture that revealed his deformity.

"Then," says Mme Théâtre, "I saw the officer change color, his jaws set, and his lips tremble; he looked toward me; I felt that he wanted to speak but didn't know what to say; but I didn't need words to understand his question. Surely he was thinking: 'So it's true then, what they accuse us of? This is what we Germans have done?' . . . And I too was unable to find any words to tell him: 'No, it's not what you think.' I merely shook my head from left to right as if to say: 'No.' I thought he would understand. . . . But I must tell you that for several days I had been without news of my husband and thought him dead, so that my face had such a sad expression that he must have been misled by it. He hurried out of the shop, his hand before his eyes and shaken with sobs."

1916

16 January

Had a good night; got up at six thirty; if I could sleep well as a regular thing, I should like to get into the habit of getting up early (as Em. always does) and of putting myself right with myself before starting off for the Foyer. There is no reason to give up everything; from seven to eight I could practice the piano, for instance; or busy myself with a translation if I fear to wake M., who is our boarder for three weeks. In a short while I shall perhaps even be capable of beginning to write again.

This morning I go over the text of J.-É. Blanche's book before giving it to the printer.

My conversation with Copeau did me much good, the day before yesterday. My attention constantly brought back to ruins, in my life at the Foyer, it was hard for me to imagine that anyone could still aim to build something. I am aware that the atmosphere in which I have lived for more than a year is the most depressing possible. Faced with that uninterrupted parade of misfortunes constantly tearing my heart, I became ashamed of any superiority and repeated to myself the words of Montesquieu's Eucrates: "For one man to rise above humanity is too costly to all others." [1]

17 January

Ghéon writes me that he has "taken the jump." It sounds like a schoolboy who has just taken a crack at the brothel. . . . But he is really talking of the communion table.

Shall I set down here the odd dream I had last winter?

Ghéon, until then a boarder of the Van Rysselberghes at rue Laugier like me, had just left for the front. I dreamt this: I was walking, or rather *floating*, beside someone whom I soon recognized to be Ghéon. Together we were advancing in an unknown countryside, a sort of wooded

[1] The fictitious interlocutor speaks thus to the despotic Sulla in Montesquieu's *Dialogue de Sylla et d'Eucrate* (1745).

valley; we were advancing with delight. The valley constantly became narrower and more beautiful and my delight was reaching its height when my companion suddenly stopped and, touching my forearm, exclaimed: "No farther! Henceforth between us there is *that.*" He did not point at anything but, lowering my eyes, I made out a rosary hanging from his wrist, and I suddenly awoke in unbearable anguish.

18 January

While writing to Ghéon, I reread the fifteenth chapter of the Gospel according to St. John and these words are suddenly illuminated for me with a frightful light:

"If a man abide not in me, he is cast forth as a branch, and is withered; and men gather them, and cast them into the fire, and they are burned."

Truly was I not "cast into the fire" and already a prey to the flame of the most abominable desires? . . .

19 January

Everything in me calls out to be revised, amended, re-educated. The trait I have most trouble struggling against is my sensual curiosity. The drunkard's glass of absinthe is not more attractive than, for me, certain faces encountered by chance—and I would give up everything to follow them. . . . Why, to be sure this involves such an imperious urge, such an insidious, such a secret counsel, so inveterate a habit that I often wonder if I can escape it without outside aid.

"I have no man, when the water is troubled, to put me into the pool." (John, v, 7.)

21 January

Forenoon at the *N.R.F.* with Copeau; no visits. All negotiations are suspended while waiting for G.; a telegram announces his arrival for Monday. We talk at length of the possibility of forming a small company of actors sufficiently intelligent, clever, and well trained to improvise on a given scenario and capable of reviving the *commedia dell' arte* in the Italian manner, but with new types: the bourgeois, the noble, the publican, the suffragette would take the place of Harlequin, Pierrot, and Columbine. Each of these types would have his own costume, his own way of speaking, his own bearing and psychology. And each of the actors would personify only one type, limiting himself to it and never getting away from it, but constantly enriching and amplifying it.

If this plan is realized, I foresee and long for an audience in complicity with the actors, urging them on and communicating enthusiasm to them. Very soon these performances (which I do not see as filling the whole program, but rather as preceding, following, or breaking the main show) would make the theater's success and would take on a bold importance; they would constitute a *satire of parties*—an excellent, healthy satire in the name of common sense.

Sunday, 23

Yesterday evening I yielded, as one yields to an obstinate child—"to have peace." Lugubrious peace; darkening of the whole sky. . . .

On my return to the Foyer I had to preside over a meeting in which nothing was going satisfactorily. My annoyance was so great that I feared to express it and forced myself to keep silent.

I no longer have any justification at the Foyer and don't like it there. For more than a year charity kept it alive and throbbing; now it is becoming a philanthropic undertaking in which I have neither intellectual nor emotional interest.

24

Yesterday an indescribably odd and beautiful sunset: sky filled with pink and orange-tinted mists; I admired it especially, as I was going over the Pont de Grenelle, reflected by the Seine heavy with barges; everything melted into a warm and tender harmony. In the Saint-Sulpice tram, from which I was watching this sight with wonder in my eyes, I noticed that no one, absolutely no one, was aware of it. There was not a single face that didn't look preoccupied with cares. . . . Yet, I thought, some people travel to a great distance to find nothing more beautiful. But most often man does not recognize beauty unless he buys it, and this is why God's offer is so often disdained.

25

Very bad night. I again fall as low as ever.

This morning, up before seven, I go out a moment and

hear a blackbird's song, odd, so precociously springlike, so pathetic and pure that it makes me even more bitterly aware of the withering-up of my heart.

I read in Rutherford (Vol. II, p. 113) a passage about the devil and hell that just happens to back up my thought wonderfully: "The shallowest of mortals is able now to laugh at the notion of a personal devil. No doubt there is no such thing existent; but the horror at evil which could find no other expression than in the creation of a devil is no subject for laughter, and if it do not in some shape or other survive, the race itself will not survive. No religion, so far as I know, has dwelt like Christianity with such profound earnestness on the bisection of man—on the distinction within him, vital to the very last degree, between the higher and the lower, heaven and hell. What utter folly is it because of an antique vesture to condemn as effete what the vesture clothes! Its doctrine and its sacred story are fixtures in concrete form of precious thoughts purchased by blood and tears." [2]

For several days now I have been striving to free myself from the Foyer, to cease being interested in it. I have great difficulty in doing so, and the time I spend trying to interest myself in something else (not to say in myself) is put to poor use, almost lost. And since Saturday I have been again assailed by abominable imaginings, against which I am defenseless; I find no refuge anywhere. At certain moments, sometimes for hours, I wonder if I am not going mad; everything in me yields to my mania. Yet I strive to organize the struggle. . . . What patience and what deception it would take!

And this evening, however, an excellent letter from Ghéon brings me a little comfort.

Sunday, 30

If I had to formulate a credo, I should say: God is not behind us. He is to come. He must be sought, not at the beginning, but at the end of the evolution. He is terminal and not initial. He is the supreme and final point toward

---

[2] Though André Gide gives his reference as to a second volume of the *Autobiography*, the passage is actually found in *The Deliverance of Mark Rutherford*. Gide quotes it in his own translation.

which all nature tends in time. And since time does not exist for Him, it is a matter of indifference to Him whether that evolution of which He is the summit follows or precedes, and whether He determines it by propulsion or attraction.

It is through man that God is molded. This is what I feel and believe and what I understand in the words: "Let man be created in Our image." What can all the doctrines of evolution do against that thought?

This is the gate through which I enter into the holy place, this is the series of thoughts that lead me back to God, to the Gospels, etc. . . .

Will I some day succeed in setting this forth clearly?

For a long time already I have believed this without knowing it, and now it becomes clear in me through a series of successive illuminations. The reasoning follows.

1 February

I give up the reading of Bossuet's *Élévations* before my disgust overflows and carries away with it what I should like to keep. I have gone on as far as I could, but no reading is more likely to hurl me into the opposition, and I am stopping out of precaution.

I am trying to put aside a half-hour every evening and every morning for soothing meditation, self-analysis, and expectation. . . . "Remain simply attentive to that presence of God, exposed to His divine observation, thus continuing that devout attention or *exposition* . . . at peace under the rays of the divine sun of justice."

I long ardently to write that book of meditations or elevations which will balance the *Nourritures* and fuse in places with the *Conseils à un jeune écrivain* that I am preparing.[3] May I. . . .

Francis Jammes annoys me most when he believes, or pretends to believe, that it is through reasoning and an exaggerated need for dialectics that I withdraw and stand in opposition, whereas quite the contrary. . . . But what is the good of starting a discussion on this point? It is not ignorance, humility, or renunciation—it is rather falsehood that I detest. And that pretense by which the soul dupes itself and offers itself to God as a dupe.

[3] *Advice to a Young Writer* was never completed or published.

2 February

Tried to write to Gosse in reply to his article on France. I spent the better part of my morning on it and produced nothing worth while. Practiced Albéniz.

Our cats break the most beautiful vase in the drawing-room, the only beautiful one: a large gray and blue Persian vase that I had got at an auction. Its narrow base gave reason to fear and I had taken care to weight it heavily with lead shot. In order to put some flowers from Saint-Clair into it, Em. recently removed the shot (otherwise, she says, it would have been too heavy to lift), but when she removed the flowers, she forgot to put back the shot. Right after the war, things like that will go on in this country.

3 February

I have given up reading the Bible in English; my expectation must not be caught by words, even were it to enjoy them. Nevertheless I sometimes open the book to find the text I have just read in French. And at times a sudden new light is thrown on the text: "Except a man be born again." [4] All this morning I repeated these words to myself and I am repeating them this evening, after having measured all day long the frightful shadow that my past cast onto my future.

6 February

Yesterday, following my visit to W. M. regarding Rilke, having some time ahead of me before the committee-meeting at the Foyer, I went into the Saint-Séverin Church and stayed there about a half-hour meditating and reading the end of the Rutherford. I was sitting on the right side of the church; there were only a few silent, worshipping women; the outside light reached me subdued and colored by the stained-glass windows, and the sounds of out of doors were muffled when they reached me. The peace in which I was bathed had nothing especially religious about it, or at least did not incline me toward a particular devotion. I simply savored to what a degree contemplation is useful to me.

7 February

I have never been so modest as when constraining myself to write every day in this notebook a series of pages

[4] The quotation appears in English in the original.

that I know and feel to be so definitely mediocre; repetitions, stammerings so little likely to make anyone appreciate, admire, or like me.

Always have I been pursued by the desire to shake off all affections but those of a quite exquisite and superior quality. If these notebooks should come to light, later on, how many will they repell, even then! . . . But what affection I feel for him who, despite them, or through them, will still want to remain my friend!

I cling desperately to this notebook; it is a part of my patience; it helps keep me from going under.

8 February

Yesterday two very important committee-meetings; following the second one, at the Foyer, long explanation before del Marmol, Lauris, Mme Théo, etc. I shall tell of this elsewhere.

Dined at Darius Milhaud's. He asks my advice about the "cantata" he wants to make of my *Retour de l'enfant prodigue*.[5]

This morning at the *N.R.F.* I find on the office mantel a little volume (Romanica series) of the *Journal* of Maurice de Guérin—which I open at random to find this excellent page that I enjoy copying down here:

"*7 September. I get lost in conversations. Most often I derive nothing from them but dejection and bitterness. In them I compromise my inner life, everything that is best in me. In order to keep the conversation going, I throw into it my favorite thoughts, the ones to which I am most secretly and solicitously attached. My shy and awkward speech disfigures, mutilates them, throwing them out into the bright light in disorder and confusion and only half-dressed. When I go away ·I gather up and hug to my breast my scattered treasure, trying to put back into place dreams that are bruised like fruit fallen from the tree onto rocks.*"

I have never very much liked, nor even carefully read, Maurice de Guérin, always irritated to be told that I resembled him. But it is true that I *feel* that page, even

[5] Milhaud's cantata using the dialogues of Gide's *Return of the Prodigal Son* was in fact composed in Rio de Janeiro in 1917. Written for five voices and twenty-one instruments, it has been executed in Paris, in Brussels, and at the Baden-Baden Festival of 1928.

to the slightest detail of its rhythm and vigor, as if I had written it myself—and that I should have liked to write it.

Bothered also by the calligraphy of the *Centaure* and of the *Bacchante* (which are both almost unendurable to me), by the latent *whimpering* of his mind ("The loveliest days," he says, "the most absorbing studies fail to quiet in me that restless and *whimpering* thought which is the basis of humanity"), by his sister, by his friendship for Barbey d'Aurevilly, etc. . . .

Friday, 11

Noted nothing yesterday. In the morning, work—or at least an attempt at work. But since the beginning of the week I have not yet managed to have a morning to myself. Little things to take care of arise at the last moment, and my equilibrium is not yet sufficiently assured so that I can resume my meditation as soon as the cause of this upset is gone. Yet I am better and keep myself in a state of vigilance. The best way of struggling against temptation is still not to expose oneself to it. One cannot hope to reach paradise in one single leap. It takes resolve and, even more, patience. Nothing could be less romantic, nothing could be more tiresome at times than the minute detail of this moral hygiene; no great victories; it is a constant struggle without glory, like the one that is being fought in the trenches.

Each defeat, on the other hand, is sudden and complete and seems to hurl you back to the lowest point. It is often delightful. At least it can be, and I keep telling myself this. And the Evil One is always ready to whisper in my ear: "This is all a comedy that you are playing to deceive yourself. With the first blush of spring you will pass over to the enemy. The enemy? What do you mean by enemy? You have no other enemy than your own fatigue. If it were more open, your sin would be glorious. Be frank, then, and admit that you use the word *sin* in this connection only because you find this dramatic effect convenient and a help in recovering that agility you were on the point of losing: namely, the free control of your flesh and mind. Today you take your physical fatigue for moral decay; soon, when you are cured, you will blush for

having thought you had to have recourse to such means
to cure yourself." Meanwhile I am still ill—and shall
remain ill as long as I listen to that voice.

Saturday [25 February]

Too brief days; the slow succession of hours. Snow
outside; nothing to do and not even any letters to write,
for I should not dare to mail them from Paris; no visit
to fear since I am thought to be in Cuverville, where our
mail is awaiting us. Day entirely spent in work, meditation, and reading. Far back into the past I should not find
such a pure one.

I pick up *Jean-Christophe* again from the beginning and
make a great effort at sympathy without my consideration
for Romain Rolland, or for his book at least, being increased.

It breathes a sort of rough heartiness, vulgarity, and
guilelessness—which will please the reader to whom the
artist always seems to be putting on airs. But that's that.

What bothers me is the ease, the thoughtlessness, with
which he makes a German of his hero—or, if you prefer,
he makes his hero of a German. As far as I know, there
is no other example of this, for even Stendhal takes care
to point out that his Fabrice was born of a French father.[6]
What more are we expected to see in this? The Germanic
quality of his tastes, tendencies, reactions, and impulses,
which allows Romain Rolland, if not to paint Jean-Christophe precisely in his own image, at least to infuse life
into him through sympathy? Or else the illusion of a
generous but uncritical mind abstractly creating in Jean-
Christophe a creature who is no more German than he is
French, a musician, a vague personality to whom he can
attribute any sensations and emotions he wants?

Oh, how Germanic is that very psychological inadequacy! How inexpressive it is! [7]

[6] Stendhal, who wanted the false statement that he was a Milanese
engraved on his tombstone, chose Italy as the scene of his famous
novel *The Charterhouse of Parma*, of which Fabrice del Dongo is the
hero.

[7] What I said no longer strikes me as just right today (21 May).
When he made his hero a German, Romain Rolland was especially
looking for a certain perspective that would allow him to judge French
manifestations. [A.]

2 March

Reached Cuverville the night before last at about midnight; considerably done in by an eighteen-hour trip, embellished by a collision at Serquigny; four or five dead and about twenty wounded. (See the papers.)

Both those who were giving aid and those who were receiving it behaved in seemly fashion, certainly having already learned their lesson from the war; enjoyed talking with people of all ranks. As for me, again noticed my great difficulty in taking tragically, even seriously, a chance accident. I remain amused, as at a show, or excited rather and ready to put forth a great reserve of sudden activity. Somewhat prevented, however, in helping to extricate the wounded and in giving them first aid by my anxiety for Em., accompanied by two maids, without counting the two dogs and five cats. The good wife of a sea captain clung to us, carrying in her arms a beautiful baby boy, two years old. We had to lug baskets and hand-baggage and help all these people to climb the embankment, etc.

We were, moreover, rather far from the crumpled cars, and the shock we felt was not very great; it did not give me any idea of how serious the accident was and hence I did not approach the scene until after the victims had already been extricated. I should have liked to be of greater help.

The extreme quiet of Cuverville, after the fatigue and late night, acted yesterday like a bromide on my mind. Read on the way and after getting here the second volume of *Jean-Christophe*, some of Nietzsche's *Thoughts out of Season* (wonderful beginning of the study on Strauss), the Lasserre on German influence, some excellent articles by Souday that I had gone to get the day before at the office of *Paris-Midi*.[8]

3 March

During these periods of restlessness I ought deliberately to give up all reading, set nothing in front of me but blank paper. But I flee work, begin six books at a time, not knowing which one to hide behind so as not to have to reply yet to the demands. . . .

[8] The Nietzsche work, referred to in French, is *Unzeitgemässe Betrachtungen*; the book by Lasserre is *Le Germanisme et l'esprit humain* (*Germanism and the Human Spirit*).

There is no more time to lose; I must convince myself of this and give myself formal notice beginning tomorrow. There is no good longing for the time when I could still make resolutions; I must still make them just as in my youth—and make up my mind rather to do nothing than to do something *else*.

Put off until later any other reading, translation, letter-writing—and *first* start my work again.

Sunday, 5 March

This morning wrote a half a page of my *Chopin*.[9] In the afternoon finished putting my papers in order; that is, classifying in series the pages of old notebooks that seem to me worth keeping and tearing up all the rest. I tore up and tore up and tore up just as the day before I had cut and torn out the dead wood from the espaliers. How much there was! And how mediocre the little that I spared still seemed to me! Between certain covers I came upon very old piles. I recognized certain sentences that I had once thought full of strength and vigor, but from which the sap had completely withdrawn by now. I was ashamed of them and even suffered from the very appearance of the handwriting, so unsimple, so unnatural. . . . I do not like anything in me but what I achieve at the expense of the most modest, most patient effort.

Even the pages I have preserved will have no value unless they are completely melted down, completely *lost* in the ensemble.

My sight, during the last few days, has failed considerably.

6 March

How far can my intellectual humility go. . . . I have a horror for all rhetoric and romanticism and that verbal effort of the mind to try to "add an inch to one's height."

Shrove Tuesday

Heavy fall of snow last night. The sound of little snow-slides on the roof keeps us long awake. On awakening, the countryside is white; the big cedar looks like the Himalaya. Under their load of whiteness the bushes are prostrate. The least twig is supporting an enormous burden. The wire netting around the tennis court has become a spar-

[9] The "Notes on Chopin" were not published until December 1931 in the *Revue musicale*.

kling wall. Above the immaculate plain shines a cloudless
azure. Not a single bird singing; not a sound. It occurs to
us that on the battlefield a like shroud must be spread,
hiding the dead, smothering the dying, covering the
horror.

The children have come, according to the local custom,
to recite what they call "the farce" for us. They come
along in little groups of two or three, each one carrying
a large basket; they go from door to door and, in gratitude
for their little song, everyone gives them an egg—or, for
want of an egg, an apple, a penny, a piece of chocolate.
I have set down several of their songs, almost amorphous,
but which come from the depths of the past.

Unsatisfactory work. My eyes are too tired for me to
read.

Bad ending to the day.

Wednesday

Yesterday evening wrote several pages of Memoirs.[10]
This morning commentary on Christ's words to the Samari-
tan woman. The piano has come, an upright piano to
save money and also because we should not have had
enough men here to carry the other.

I am training myself to play with my eyes closed, for
they hurt me. I doubt that I shall succeed and believe
that I should give up if I were never to see again.

Sunday [19 March]

Insomnia the last few nights, rather painful because of
the nervous disorders that reappear—as they always do,
alas, as soon as I begin working seriously. Yet I am being
very good, observing a continence that it seems to me I
have not known since my childhood, or except in very
rare periods. I threw into the fire the day before yesterday
two packages of cigarettes I had brought back from
Havre. Smoking makes me dizzy almost at once; I light
a cigarette from habit rather than out of pleasure.

The pruning of our fruit trees is dreadfully behindhand;
the sap is rising. I have taken an active part in it and
every day have spent almost four hours at it. I get furious

[10] Under the title of *Si le grain ne meurt . . . (If It Die . . .)*
the Memoirs were first printed privately in 1920–1 without name of
publisher. They were finally published openly in 1926 by Librairie
Gallimard.

with Mius when I discover the absurd arrangement of his espaliers. Since he sacrifices everything to appearances and since the least empty spot upsets him, he contrives to bring a branch forward from anywhere whatever to take the place of the missing one, which he should have known how to get the tree to produce. Impossible to describe the acrobatic contortions and odd arrangements my trees were forced to by that limited mind. His dream would have been to write his name everywhere in bent branches; on the espaliers I find the shape of every letter in the alphabet. And in order to achieve somewhat reasonable outlines again, I have to risk real havoc, which the trees won't get over for a long time.

22 March

One struggles effectively so long as one thinks it a duty to struggle; but as soon as the struggle appears meaningless and one ceases to hate the enemy . . . Yet I am still resisting, though less from conviction than from defiance.

Recovered myself at once.

Easter Monday, 22 or 23 [April]

I get to the point of being unable even to understand, at times, to what I owe the friendship that certain people bear me. I countermand it . . . so unpleasant and exasperating do I find the things I hear myself saying. Without doubt, if I heard them from another, they would be enough to make me hate him. What poverty! what complacency! what a need to climb on top of others, to crush them! . . .

The evil is so deep and long-standing and carries such impetus that it upsets all the attention I give it, which consequently only succeeds in making my remarks seem more deliberate. I find a little relaxation only at the piano, at work, or in the garden.

3 May

The day before yesterday I had got up at six o'clock, although having gone to bed late, in an excellent state of mind for work; but soon a sharp neuralgic pain killed my enthusiasm. It was like a knife in my right side; the pain continued to get worse for three hours and brought on vomiting, then stayed about the same until four p.m.; at that time I was able to sleep a little, and on awakening it was all over. Nothing remained but a general fatigue and a slight tenderness on that side. The fatigue still subsists two days later. . . . Ashamed to have so little resistance to pain. Without doubt that attack was of the mildest type; and yet I don't know how I could have stood anything worse.

I read in a letter from my mother to my father: "André would be very nice if he didn't have a mania for standing a long time absolutely still at the foot of a tree watching snails."

The letter must date from '73 (the year of Isabelle Widmer's marriage, which it mentions earlier). I was therefore four years old.

16 September

I shan't succeed without a constant effort, an hourly effort, constantly renewed. I shan't succeed without deceit and attention to detail.

Nothing gained if I aim to note here only things of importance. I must make up my mind to write everything in this notebook. I must force myself to write anything whatever.

Last night was a bit better (frightful anguish the night before). During the evening I had read a few pages of Bossuet (first sermon on Providence), so copious and so charmingly true that I had gone to sleep quite calmed.

Late in the afternoon my headache returned; such an intellectual torpor that I need great courage not to despair. With great difficulty I managed to write a few letters (one of them to that odd fellow Labasque); I went out; I hoped that walking would restore me, but it only increased my discomfort to the point of dizziness.

In this morning's *Temps* appeared an article by Souday ("*Le Pauvre Subjonctif*"),[11] containing fragments of the letter I had written him. I rather regret having asked him not to name me, for everything he quotes from my letter seems good to me. I always have a tendency to lay it on a bit too heavily. . . .

17

Abominable torpor. I have great trouble convincing myself, if this state of imbecility continues, that my role

[11] "The Poor Subjunctive."

is to shelter myself, to hold myself in reserve. As soon as my worth decreases, as soon as it ceases to appear clearly to me, I should like to be used in some more direct fashion, offer myself to some active service or other. And I know that I should be good at it. How can I believe that I am *better* by remaining here? Get thee to a depot!

19 September

Yesterday, an abominable relapse. The storm raged all night long. This morning it is hailing heavily. I get up, my head and heart both heavy and empty, full of the entire weight of hell. . . . I am the drowning man who is losing heart and now struggles only weakly. The three calls have the same sound: "It is time. It is high time. It is no longer time." So that you do not distinguish one from the other and already the third one is sounding while you still think you are at the first.

If at least I could relate this drama; depict Satan, after he has taken possession of a creature, using him, acting through him upon others. This seems an empty image. Even I have only recently come to understand this: you are not only a prisoner; active evil demands of you a reverse activity; you must fight in the other army. . . .

This evening I am going to Paris; my pretext is to meet Gosse, whom Briand has invited here. Besides, I shall be extremely happy to see him again; and I am not doing anything worth while here, for I do not count my piano lessons to the children and my translation of *Typhoon,* which has progressed considerably of late.

The great error is to form a romantic image of the devil. This is what made me take so long to recognize him. He is no more romantic or classic than whomever he is talking to. He is as diverse as man himself; more so, because he adds to his diversity. He made himself classical with me, when it was necessary to catch me, and because he knew that I could never willingly assimilate to evil a certain happy equilibrium. I did not understand that a certain equilibrium could be maintained, for a time at least, in the worst. I took to be good everything that was regulated. Through measure I thought to dominate evil; and it is through that very measure on the contrary that it took possession of me.

3 October

Back in Cuverville. I had left Paris Friday; spent a night at Offranville at J.-É. Blanche's, a night at Varangeville at the Godebskis', and last night at Offranville. (Visit to Calmont.)

I had gone to meet Gosse at the Hôtel Crillon, where the Propaganda Ministry had reserved a very pleasant apartment of three rooms for him. He was expecting me. I was taken up; it was on the third floor. I found the same old Gosse barely a bit older-looking; slightly shriveled, thinned out in spots. As in the past, his movements seemed to me prompted perhaps a bit more by his mind than by his heart, or at least by a sort of *self-respect*.[12] Intelligence, which with him always has a weather-eye out, intervenes and checks him on the slope of surrender. He begins to catch himself at the moment when I was beginning to like him. Moreover, it is perhaps not so much me as himself that he distrusts.

As soon as I come in, effusion; our four hands are joined for some time; then I sit down. And he, after a very brief silence, which seemed intended to catch his breath, as if yielding to an irresistible impulse (yet it was a trifle put on):

"Ah, dear friend, let us embrace once more!"

Seeing an invitation in these words, I rise from my chair and, rushing toward him, apply to both his flabby cheeks two big kisses in the French manner. He jumped a bit, drew back almost imperceptibly with a slight grimace immediately hidden, but from which I recognized that he intended to remain master of the situation and tell me just how far to go and no farther, that by taking literally his "let us embrace" I was forgetting that he spoke French only half well and that, in short, for the English, so chary of demonstrations, a prolonged handshake was better than any embrace. I can imagine Gosse later on asking Millet, his guide, or someone else: "But tell me, sir, when you want to shake someone's hand in the middle of a conversation, how do you say this in good French? Just imagine that the other day, having had the imprudence to say to Gide: 'Let us embrace,' I find him actually embracing me! It was absurd."

[12] This expression appears in English in the original.

We lunched together at the Crillon; I was tired out in advance and also by the necessity I have just pointed out of skillfully mixing the most extreme cordiality with an imperceptible reserve. It would be less obvious on his part if we were speaking English; this would be entirely up to him since he speaks English in the clearest possible manner and I am sure I should understand him; but he is getting a little practice, for he is to lunch tomorrow at Briand's. He asks me what wine I prefer, suggests sauternes, and I have no sooner accepted than he orders a less expensive one he has just discovered on the card. Later on, he shows that he is slightly hurt that I have not drunk more of it.

At dessert he suggests: "A cigar?"

I refuse.

"What! You don't smoke?"

Then, as if in spite of myself, nervously:

"Why yes, a cigarette, if you wish."

And this is just what I know that I ought not to say, for Gosse, who doesn't smoke them, has none on him and is going to have to order some. The waiter, as might be expected, brings the most expensive packages on a tray. Gosse is not a miser the way X. is, but he is *close,* and all the more so since he is a guest of France and a discretion that is only common decency checks him. The amusing thing is his need of making me feel, subtly, what I am only too well aware of since it covers me with embarrassment:

"Take this little package as a souvenir of our lunch."

I had only to slip the package into my pocket with a few words that would have shown I was not taken in. I might have said, for example: "If I offer one, I shall do so in your name," or else simply: "I shall think of you when I smoke them," but I found nothing to say, I didn't even look for anything, filled to overflowing with a vast melancholy . . . which was like drowsiness. And the worst of it is that when we got up I left the package of cigarettes on the table.

I have set down other bits of our conversation in a letter to Em.

At the slightest material obstacle, whether it come from the ink or the paper, my thought contracts, stops. My fingers' numbness leads to the numbness of my brain. A scratchy pen and my style is embarrassed. Today I forbade myself the piano. I force myself to write despite my headache and that sort of stupor which so often paralyzes me here. At least my fountain-pen is all right. I am writing on a bench on the avenue. I am lost if I do not manage to catch hold of myself before winter. These summer months were hateful, full of utter waste of time, with no work accomplished. I do not think I have ever been farther from happiness. With ever the vague hope that, from the depths of the abyss, will arise that cry of distress that—no—I have forgotten how to utter. . . . One can, while being at the lowest ebb, still look toward the azure; no, however low I was, I always looked still lower. I gave up heaven. I ceased defending myself against hell. Obsessions and all the prodromes of madness. Truly! I frightened myself; and incapable in my own case of the advice I should have been so able to give to someone else.

Does this fact of already talking about my state indicate that I am already so sure of being cured?

There is in J.-É. Blanche something contented, facile, and light that causes me an indescribable discomfort. Blanche has too many trumps in his hand, and his oddest intellectual quirk is the need of proving to all and sundry that with a single trump less life is not worth living. His most sincere remarks begin: "I don't know how you can . . ." His house is surrounded by a beautiful garden: "I don't know how you can live in a street." During the fine weather he is in Normandy: "I don't know how you can spend the summer in Paris."

Occasionally this commiseration is veiled. He asks me where the Théos are now living. I reply: "Rue Claude Lorrain." And already in his manner of repeating: "Rue Claude Lorrain?" in his tone, in the ironic and painful interrogation of his eyebrows—which rise unequally so that the left one remains frowning while the right one goes way up—you can guess that he foresees that the rue Claude Lorrain must be an unmentionable, impossible street in an uninhabitable section of town. He adds: "I don't know it." (Now, he knows everything that it is proper to know.) "Where is it?"

"It runs into the rue Michel-Ange," I told him, "right after the Auteuil viaduct."

"In short, Billancourt."

This "in short," to judge from the tone, means "dare to say it," "confess it," and "this is just what I was expecting." . . . "How can anyone live in Billancourt?" [13]

If I were to write many novels, I should fill one with Blanche.

6 October

Most likely I shall have neither the strength nor the constancy to write the wonderful novel I glimpse on this theme:

A man, equally capable of passions, even of dissipation, and of virtues, marries, when still young, a woman whose love exalts in him only nobility, disinterestedness, etc.; for her he sacrifices, without even being quite aware of it, everything ardent, adventurous, luxurious in his nature; or at least, he holds all this in reserve.

An abominable nostalgia seizes hold of him, soon after the death of that wife. He still feels young. He wants to begin his life over again, a different life which will give him everything of which the virtue, the reserve, the voluntary poverty of the first life deprived him. He hurls himself into a luxurious life. Disgust, scorn of himself that derives therefrom. . . .

"It is impossible to love a second time what one has truly ceased to love," says La Rochefoucauld. And this is true even when what one has ceased to love is oneself.

The subjects of my books, of each one of them, would have seemed idiotic if I had related them in this fashion. I am convinced that this one, however ridiculous it may appear in this bare state, could be most pathetically beautiful. It is the story of him who would deny his virtue.

7 October

A few words from Em. plunge me back into a sort of despair. As at last I make up my mind to speak to her of that plan of spending the winter at Saint-Clair:

"*I certainly owe you that,*" she said with an effort of her whole nature, which at once made her face so sad, so

[13] Billancourt is a continuation, then an unfashionable one, of Auteuil.

grave, that immediately I think only of giving up this plan like so many others, since it costs her so much and since I should have to buy my happiness at the expense of hers—so that it could therefore no longer be my happiness.

There was a time when I abominated all literature, all art, when it did not spring from joy, from an excess of *joie de vivre*. And my unnamable melancholy of today should now urge me to continue speaking?

9 October

I read in the *Revue des deux mondes* that the Yungs send us this morning Gosse's article on Anglo-French intellectual relations.

Gosse is playing with words. It was never a question of "European literature," as he claims, but of "European *culture*," which involves a participation of the various literatures of our old world, each of them powerfully individualized. And only the particularization of each literature, only its nationalization, could permit the Europeanization of culture. So that . . . and so on.

Received a letter from Souday, who complains bitterly that he is not given press copies of Péguy's works. I write to Souday; I write to Gallimard. I spend the better part of my day on this. I made a copy of my two letters.

I have no desire to dictate and don't want to give Gallimard a pretext for taking offense. I have no importance and do not want to have any. But, in order to avoid being made responsible for attitudes and acts that friendship alone keeps me from disavowing, it would be better to change the firm's imprint at the earliest opportunity and give up a compromising and misleading solidarity.[14] I believe with Copeau that it is right for Gallimard to make decisions and to do so alone; but then it becomes necessary that he should sign, alone, his decisions, that the Librairie de la *N.R.F.* should become Librairie Gallimard.

10 October

In the rare moments she manages to give me, I con-

[14] As is usual with French literary reviews, *La Nouvelle Revue Française* led to the foundation of a publishing house, which between about 1911 and the present has become one of the most important in France. The last name of its director, Gaston Gallimard, was eventually taken as the firm nme.

tinue with Em. the reading of Dupouey's wonderful letters. I should like, if I can attain a pure enough ardor, to write a preface for the publication of these letters. Their beauty often sparkles before my eyes like a sword of ice.[15]

20 October

Somewhat better work, the result of an enormous effort. I cannot believe that, under a slightly better physical regime, I should not succeed in furnishing a larger sum of work with less wear.

A draft of a letter by Dupouey, found in his papers, is finally going to give me the occasion to write to Maurras:

"You cannot but be touched by the posthumous evidence of one of the most beautiful souls I have ever known. I copy these lines with a deep emotion and all the more gladly since I most heartily associate myself with them.

"PS.—Thank you for sending me *L'Étang de Berre*.[16] I rather regret that you maintained this title: 'the two fatherlands,' which runs the risk of misleading and even deceiving the reader, most disagreeably for my thought. . . . But perhaps, after all, it is not the mere title that would have to have been changed. Unless you added, as in your latest book, a 'twelve years later' along these lines:

" 'I recognize that I was mistaken about A. G.'s thought; and this is doubtless somewhat his fault, for he is often careful to hide his thought, it seems, rather than to express it; but upon rereading him (and no longer 'from memory' as I once did and now recognize that it is not always wise to do), it strikes me that he never sought anything in his articles but French unity, nor proved anything except that that unity was naturally composed of the harmonious diversity of our provinces, and that this unity was realized, more specifically than in anyone else, in the man whose cross-bred heredity mingled the blood of Languedoc, for

---

[15] The letters were in fact published in 1922 with a preface by Gide.

[16] Maurras took the title for this book of essays, first published in 1915, from the name of a large lake in his native region, not far from Marseille. The essay to which Gide alludes, entitled "The Two Fatherlands or the Choice of a Burial-Place," was reprinted as it had originally appeared in 1902. Starting with Gide's assertion of 1897 that he had been born in Paris of a Norman mother and a father from Languedoc, Maurras claims that Gide will eventually reveal to which province he is most loyal when he chooses his final resting-place.

instance, with Norman blood as it happened in his case, or with Breton blood, as it happened in the case of Léon Daudet.' "

Outline of a second letter:

"No, my dear Maurras; there is nothing new there; and if you had deigned to lend my books the same attention that you granted one day to my *Roi Candaule,* I suspect that you would have found in each one of them at least as many of those 'profound and subtle truths' (I believe these are your very words) as in the least important of my writings. Instead of which you have always let me be decried by your carping lieutenants. What do you expect? I do not write for fools, but I cannot demand that intelligent people should understand me without having read me. This is why I have never protested but have always remained, despite you and despite your followers, very close to your thought and, I assure you, most cordially yours. . . ."

21 October

That morning, more specifically, he had waited for her —one can say "desperately"—in her room, where he had gone down the earliest he could, rushing his dressing and putting off both work and prayer. It must be said that the day before she had promised to be there, and it was as to a rendezvous that he hastened, with a new and joyful soul; it would act as a springboard for his whole day.

When he had entered, the room was empty; he had found, placed on the table, D.'s letter, which the day before she had promised to read to him. She had placed it there opened, as if to say: "Read it without me," which he did not do, for he found no pleasure in it. He sat down in the window-seat, opened a book he had brought with him; but he could not fix his attention on it. He kept thinking: where is she? what is she doing? what shall I say to her when she eventually returns? Obviously she is not inactive; I am willing to admit that some urgent problem may have called her as it constantly happens, all day long, every day. He made an effort not to be vexed and planned to say to her simply, sweetly: I was beginning to believe you had forgotten me; or: you had rather forgotten that I was waiting for you. . . .

At this moment he heard her step in the vestibule; but she still was not coming upstairs; she was going back and forth; she was busying herself about something or other; there were now but very few minutes before the bell that was to gather the household for breakfast. . . . Then it was that he heard her beginning to wind the clock. It was the big grandfather clock at the foot of the stairs; obviously as she was going by she had seen the clock stopped and, on the point of joining him, had stopped to set it. He heard it strike twice, then the half-hour, then three times. . . . The worst of it is that the clock, an old-style one, struck double. It was after eight o'clock; he calculated that he still had to hear it strike fifty-four times; and each one of these notes unbearably spaced out. . . . He couldn't stand it any longer and went out into the hall.

"I had left the letter on the table so that you could read it," she said as if it were the simplest thing in the world. "You see that I had things to do. When this clock is not on time, the whole house is late."

"I notice that; it is now twenty minutes that I have been waiting for you."

But she made no excuses; she remained so calm and he so upset that he began to think he had been wrong to wait for her and she right not to have come. He said nothing, but thought:

"My poor dear, you will always find clocks to set, along your way, whenever it is a question of meeting me."

25 October

At the rate at which we are going, there will soon be formed a Germanophile party in France, which will be recruited not among anarchists and internationalists, but among those who will be obliged to recognize the constant superiority of Germany. They will judge, and rightly, that it is good, that it is natural, for superiority to govern. And perhaps they will reflect that something in France remains superior to that very superiority; but alas! that something divine is powerless and mute. Would Germany be able to recognize that something? Would she strive to stifle it? Or would she not perhaps consent to exploit it? . . . Exploit that in which the enemy excels! What a fantasy! And indeed would that something permit itself to be exploited by the enemy?

Sunday [*17 December*]

I reread this morning the beginning of the second note-book of my Memoirs, to try to start myself off again. Several anecdotal passages seem to me rather well turned; but most often the languid, lullaby tone is unbearable to me. I admire nothing so much as that friskiness of Stendhal in his letters, which I pick up immediately after-ward in order completely to disgust myself with myself.

Saturday

With a very great emotion finished reading to Em. the first four chapters of my Memoirs; gave her the beginning of the fifth to read. My work has just happened to stop at the story of my furtive visit to rue de Lecat. . . . To tell the truth, the impression from this reading is not bad and even of such a nature as to encourage me greatly. But, to my taste, it is all overwritten, in too precious, too con-scious a style. . . . I always write better and more easily what I have not carried too long in my head; as soon as my thought precedes my pen, it checks my hand.

Yesterday, late in the day, great fatigue and depression to the point of making me think I shall have to interrupt everything. But this morning, after an almost sleepless night, I get up in fairly good fettle.

NUMQUID ET TU . . . ?

To Charles Du Bos
Allow me, dear Friend—whose affection sus-
tained me in difficult hours—to write your name
at the head of these few pages. Indeed, they
would have remained in a drawer were it not for
the attention you kindly granted them.

(1916–1919)

"Numquid et vos seducti
estis?" (John, vii, 47)
"Numquid et tu Galilæus?
. . ." (John, vii, 52)[17]

*What do I care about the controversies and quibbles of
the doctors? In the name of science they can deny the
miracles; in the name of philosophy, the doctrine; and in
the name of history, the facts. They can cast doubt on His
very existence, and through philological criticism throw
suspicion on the authenticity of the texts. It even pleases
me that they should succeed in doing so, for my faith in
no wise depends on that.*

*I hold this little book in my hand, and no argument
either suppresses it or takes it away from me; I hold it
fast and can read it when I will. Wherever I open it, it
shines in quite divine fashion, and anything that can be
brought against it will do nothing against that. This is
where Christ escapes the very ones who have come to lay
hold of him, and not through cunning or force; and where
they, back among the chief priests, when the chief priests
and Pharisees ask them:* Why have ye not brought him?—
Quare non adduxistis illum?—*reply:* Nunquam sic locutus
est homo.—Never man spake thus—sicut hic homo—like
this man. (John, vii, 46.)

*I read, in the preface to the Gospels in my Vulgate,
that if "instead of making of the apostles witnesses who*

---

[17] "Are ye also deceived?" and "Art thou also of Galilee?"

are reporting what they have seen and heard, one tried to make of them, as the rationalists suppose, writers who are inventing what they say, it would be appropriate to say with Rousseau that the inventor is much more surprising than the hero." I did not know that Rousseau had said that, but I think it also, and that it is not so much a question of believing in the words of Christ because Christ is the Son of God as of understanding that he is the Son of God because his word is divine and infinitely above everything that the art and wisdom of man offer us.

This divinity is enough for me. My mind and heart are satisfied with this proof. Anything you contribute in addition obscures it.

It is because Christ is the Son of God, they have said, that we must believe in his words. And others came who ceased to bear his words in mind because they did not admit that Jesus was the Son of God.

O Lord, it is not because I have been told that you were the Son of God that I listen to your word; but your word is beautiful beyond any human word, and that is how I recognize that you are the Son of God.

Through what absurd modesty, what humility, what shame have I put off writing until today what has for so many years been impatient within me? . . .

I was always waiting for more wisdom, more study, more knowledge, as if the wisdom of men were not folly before God.

O Lord, I come to you like a child; like the child that you want me to become, like the child that becomes whoever yields to you. I resign everything that made up my pride and that, in your presence, would make up my shame. I listen and surrender my heart to you.

The Gospels are a very simple little book, which must be read very simply. There is no question of explaining it, but merely of accepting it. It needs no commentary and every human effort to throw light upon it only dims it. It is not addressed to learned men; science prevents one from understanding anything in it. Access to it can be gained through poverty of spirit.

· · ·

It is true, this opening of the Epistle to the Romans is confused, full of repetitions, annoying to anyone who is not aware of the pathetic effort of the apostle to bring forth so novel a truth, which he feels with all his soul, and not confusedly, but which eludes his grasp and wrestles with him like an angel and struggles.

Not the law but grace. It is the emancipation in love—and the progress through love to an exquisite and perfect obedience.

One must feel here the effort of the tender young Christian doctrine to burst the tight swaddling-clothes of Semitism that enfold it. This cannot be fully understood before having first grasped the Jewish spirit.

For I was alive without the law once: but when the commandment came, sin revived, and I died.

To be sure, it is only too easy to distort the meaning of this extraordinary word and to lend to St. Paul an intention that was never his. However, if one grants that the law precedes grace, cannot one admit a state of innocence preceding the law? *For I was alive without the law once.* This sentence is lighted up and filled, despite St. Paul, with a fearful significance.

Except a man be born again.[18]

See everything with novelty; is it not true that the Kingdom of God is nothing else? The innocence of the little child: *If you do not become like unto these*—these little children who *are naked and feel no shame.*

For I was alive without the law once. Oh, to achieve that state of second innocence, that pure and laughing rapture!

The Christian artist is not he who paints saints and angels, any more than edifying subjects; but rather he who puts into practice the words of Christ—and I am amazed that no one has ever sought to bring out the *æsthetic* truth of the Gospels.

Oh, to be born again! To forget what other men have written, have painted, have thought, and what one has thought oneself. To be born anew.

9 February (1916)
If ye were blind, ye should have no sin: but now ye

---

[18] This line appears in English in the original.

say, We see; therefore your sin remaineth. (John, ix, 41.)

How could you fail to be conquered in advance, poor soul, if in advance you doubt of the legitimacy of the victory? How could you fail to resist feebly, when you doubt whether you must really resist?

There is, besides, much more craze than real desire in your case—the craze of the collector who *owes it to himself* not to let this item escape—as if his collection of sins could ever be complete! As if one more were necessary to complete his perdition!

My time is not yet come: but your time is alway ready. The world cannot hate you. (John, vii, 6.)

Journalists *alway ready* and ready for anything whatever at any time whatever. *The world cannot hate you.*

15 February

That Christ should have cried out: *Now is my soul troubled,* this is what constitutes his greatness. This is the point of debate between the man and the God.

And when he goes on: *Father, save me from this hour,* this is still the human speaking. When he finishes: *But for this cause came I unto this hour,* the God prevails.

The words that precede throw light on this one: *Except a corn of wheat fall into the ground and die . . .* and again: *He that loveth his life shall lose it.* Here Christ renounces man; here truly he becomes God.

18 February

The predominance of the mediocre and the sudden advantage of the second-rate is expressed and explained in the book of Genesis (vii and viii) with extraordinary eloquence. In equal quantities, in seven couples each, all the "clean" animals are preserved in the Ark; they issue from the Ark and immediately Noah takes a levy from among the best; the best are sacrificed, offered as a sacrifice to the Eternal. What faith, what belief in progress this sacrifice implies! At the very moment that he escapes disaster with what he has been able to save, at the moment that he sets foot on dry land and in this terrestrial life, of the little that remains to him, of these few unique representatives of each species (and what a value each one had for him!), of these irreplaceable individuals he at once offers the best. . . . No, the sacrifice of Isaac, more atrocious though it may be, is not more eloquent to my mind. I find here again that confidence that everything progresses toward the best and in spite of everything, and even because of the perpetual sacrifice of this best, to which the chain of beings reaches. It leads to renunciation, joyous and voluntary. It is in the negation of self that springs up and takes shelter the highest affirmation of self.

(On rereading more carefully chapter viii of Genesis, I notice that this selection is not specified. It is said that Noah took, to offer them in holocaust, *of every clean beast, and of every clean fowl*—now it was said in chapter vii that God had enjoined to take with him in the Ark *seven* couples of each of the latter and only *one* couple of the others—the unclean beasts—which the sacrifice does not touch, does not seek. But they are the most prolific.)

Et nunc . . .

It is *in eternity* that right now one must live. And it is *right now* that one must live in eternity.

What care I for eternal life without awareness at every instant of the duration?

Just as Jesus said: *I AM the way, the truth,* He says: *I am the resurrection and the life.*

Eternal life is not only to come. It is right now wholly present in us; we live it from the moment that we consent to die to ourselves, to obtain from ourselves this renunciation which permits resurrection in eternity. *He that hateth his life in this world shall keep it unto eternal life.* (John, xii, 25.)

Once more, there is neither prescription nor command here. Simply it is the secret of the higher felicity that Christ, as everywhere else in the Gospels, reveals to us.

If ye know these things, happy are ye, says Christ later. (John, xiii, 17.) Not: *Ye shall be happy*—but: *happy ARE ye.* It is right now and immediately that we can share in felicity.

What tranquillity! Here truly time stops. Here breathes the Eternal. We enter into the Kingdom of God.

20 February

Knowing the time, that now it is high time to awake out of sleep: for now is our salvation nearer than when we believed. (Romans, xiii, 11.)

Strange word—I should like to know apropos of what it was pronounced. Forcibly it preserves, and ever takes on more, present-day interest; every day it postpones the promise a bit further.

The important thing is that for many a soul, in many a different epoch, it assumed a particularly urgent character. But how far it is from the permanent and eternal character of Christ's words! We are plunged back into time. *The night is far spent, the day is at hand.*

21 February

. . . But not to doubtful disputations.

For one believeth that he may eat all things: another, who is weak, eateth herbs. Let not him that eateth despise him that eateth not; AND LET NOT HIM WHICH EATETH NOT JUDGE HIM THAT EATETH: FOR GOD HATH RECEIVED HIM. (Romans, xiv, 1–3.)

And why not pursue the quotation farther:

Who art thou that judgest another man's servant? to his own master he standeth or falleth. Yea, he shall be holden up: for God is able to make him stand.

This chapter xiv of the Epistle to the Romans is moreover unanswerable throughout. A little farther this can be read:

I know and am persuaded by the Lord Jesus, that there is nothing unclean of itself: but to him that esteemeth any thing to be unclean, to him it is unclean.

Obviously this concerns foods; but to how many other passages of the Bible has a double, a triple meaning been assigned? (*If your eye*, etc. . . . Multiplication of the loaves.) There is no need of quibbling here; the meaning of that word is broad and deep: the restriction must not be dictated by the law, but by love; and St. Paul formulates it immediately afterward: *But if thy brother be grieved with thy meat, now walkest thou not charitably.*

My Lord, preserve me from everything that can wither up and divert my heart.

And Paul continues, and this enters me like a sword:

Destroy not him with thy meat, for whom Christ died.
What! for a little pleasure shall I deny the death and
mercy of Christ! *For meat destroy not the work of God.*
*For the kingdom of God is not meat and drink; but
righteousness, and peace, and joy in the Holy Ghost.*
And this is the final word, the boundary-stone against
which my whole intellectual protest stumbles:
*Happy is he that condemneth not himself in that thing
which he alloweth.*
I must return to this.

25 February
*And these things I speak in the world, that they might
have my joy fulfilled in themselves.* (John, xvii, 13.)
That they might have in them my perfect joy, says the
Segond translation.
*I pray not that thou shouldst take them out of the
world, but that thou shouldst keep them from the evil
one.*
Segond says: *from evil,* which is much less eloquent.
And it is not a matter here of a simple literary effect.
Whereas evil expresses only the absence of good, or a
personal state of sin, the Evil One is an active power,
independent of us.

Si quis vult me sequi deneget semetipsum (in Matthew:
abneget semetipsum) *et tollat crucem quotidie, et sequa-
tur me.*
*Qui enim voluerit animam suam salvam facere, perdet
illam; nam qui perdiderit animam suam propter me et
Evangelium, salvam faciet eam.* (Matthew, xvi, 24; Mark,
viii, 34; Luke, ix, 23.)

4 March
This text is suddenly made clear by virtue of another
version. (John, x, 17.)
The Segond translation has: *Je donne ma vie, afin de
la reprendre* (I give my life in order to take it back).
Here is the text of the Vulgate:
Pono animam meam ut iterum suman eam.
Wonderful word—to be compared with: *Whosoever
shall seek to save his life shall lose it,* etc.
One would have to see the Greek text.
Whereas the two French versions I have at hand

(Segond and A. Westphal) and the English all speak of
life, the Vulgate says *soul*, more expressly. The meaning
becomes something like this: I renounce what makes up
my life, my soul, my personality, to assume it anew, to re-
new my mastery over it—and it is for this that the Father
cherishes me: *Propterea me diliget Pater*.

That life, that soul, no man taketh it from me by force.
Of myself, quite willingly, I lay it down. For it is in my
power to lay it down; it is in my power likewise to seize
hold of it again. Such is the commandment I received
from my Father:

*Nemo tollit eam a me; sed ego pono eam a me ipso, et
potestatem habeo ponendi eam, et potestatem habeo
iterum sumendi eam: hoc mandatum accepi a Patre meo.*

This is the mysterious center of Christian ethics, the
divine secret of happiness: the individual triumphs in the
renunciation of the individual.

*Quicumque quæsierit animam suam salvam facére, per-
det illam: et quicumque perdiderit illam, vivificabit eam.*
(Luke, xvii, 33.)

(Notice that the text of the Vulgate always gives
anima and not *vita*.)

And this finally, in which Christ's thought is clarified
and strengthened:

*Qui amat animam suam, perdet eam: et qui odit ani-
mam suam in hoc mundo, in vitam æternam custodit eam.*
(John, xii, 25.)

He who loves his life, his soul—who protects his personality, who is particular about the figure he cuts in this
world—shall lose it; but he who renounces it shall make
it really living, will assure it eternal life; not eternal life
in the future, but will make it already, right now, live in
eternity.

*Amen, amen, dico vobis, nisi granum frumenti cadens
in terram, mortuum fuerit, ipsum solum manet: si autem
mortuum fuerit, multum fructum affert.* (John, xii, 24.)
Resurrection in total life. Forgetfulness of all particular
happiness. Oh, perfect reintegration!

This is likewise the teaching to Nicodemus: *Amen,
amen, dico tibi, nisi quis renatus fuerit denuo, non potest
videre regnum Dei.* (John, iii, 3.)

6 March

Unumquemque sicut vocabit Deus, ita ambulet. (I Corinthians, vii, 17.)

Unusquisque in qua vocatione vocatus est, in ea permaneat. (Ibid., 20.)

Unusquisque in quo vocatus est, fratres, in hoc permaneat apud Deum. (Ibid., 24.)

. . . ut sim fidelis. (Ibid., 25.)

12 March

Oh words of Christ, so completely misunderstood. Eighteen centuries have passed, and this is where we are in regard to you! And some people go about saying: "The Gospel has ceased to live: it no longer has either meaning or value for us." *They blaspheme that of which they are ignorant,* and I want to shout to them: the Gospel still awaits us. Its virtue, far from being exhausted, remains to be discovered, to be constantly discovered.

The word of Christ is always fresh with an infinite promise.

The cross appears in the Gospels well before the executioners bring it in. (Luke, xvi, 27; Matthew, x, 38.)

3 April

There is always a danger in defining precisely the meaning of the words of the Gospel, for in doing so one limits their implication.

Thus I read in Westphal, apropos of Christ's word: *Signum non dabitur ei, nisi signum Jonæ prophetæ*—this note: ". . . Jesus refers the Pharisees of his generation, proud and scornful, to 'the sign of Jonas'; in other words, to the lesson given all of us by the story of that faithless servant brought back to duty by chastisement and disconcerted witness of the return to grace of a condemned city." That is simply comical.

The miracle of Jonah—there is no shilly-shallying about it—is Jonah issuing alive from the whale after having spent three days in its belly. A mystical comparison has been established between this and Christ's disappearance in the tomb for three days, but this remains none the less the most enormous, most unbelievable, most monstrous of miracles.

The divine virtue of Christ's words is recognizable by

the fact that they are addressed, over the crowd of
Pharisees and Sadducees before whom they were pronounced, directly to each one of us: You ask for a miracle
to convince you. If only a sign came from heaven, something extraordinary, then you think you would believe. I
offer you, to rest your reason, an unheard-of miracle, in
which your reason refuses to believe, which you can verify
neither with your senses nor with your mind, something
absurd and nothing else. *No other sign shall be given you
but that of the prophet Jonah.*

It is not *because of* that that you can believe, that you
must believe, poor soul! It is *despite that.*

—No, I shall not help you to believe. You know well
that on the contrary . . . so that there may be nothing
but what is absurd and loving in your faith; and so that
it may be withdrawn from the learned and permitted to
the humble.

Faith is made of confidence in God and renunciation of
self.

7 *April*

I reproach Westphal likewise for reducing the solemnity
of the text for the sake of a certain familiarity that he considers appropriate not to frighten his readers. He attempts
to establish a text on the ground floor, which can be entered without effort, and which does not contrast sharply
with everyday life. Thus it is that he translates: *The
opportune moment has not come for me. For you whom
the world cannot hate, the occasion is good at all times;
but the world hates me because, etc.* . . .[19] allowing only
the most accidental interpretation of this dazzling word:
TEMPUS MEUM *nondum advenit, tempus autem* VESTRUM
SEMPER EST PARATUM. (John, vii, 6.)

What! I meet you here again, Nicodemus! you who first
came to Jesus by night, *nocte primum*—and who later on
will bring aromatics to embalm him, for you are rich and
you think that without your riches Christ would rot. . . .
Phariseus, princeps Judæorum: such you appeared to

---

[19] "Le moment opportun n'est pas venu pour moi. Pour vous que le
monde ne peut haïr, en tout temps l'occasion est bonne; mais le
monde me hait, moi, parce que, etc. . . ."

me at first; such you remained, although you deserve already that it be said to you: *Numquid et tu Galilæus es?* —*Art thou also of Galilee?* But with you at least it is possible to talk. If you take up the defense of Christ, you do so in the very name of the law you represent. You say: *our law* and you ask those who want to lay hands upon Him: *Doth our law judge any man before it hear him?* You like to listen and you like to be listened to. You know how to talk; you have an open mind; you listen to Christ; what am I saying? you even question him. But you are not among those at least who allow themselves to be led astray. *Numquid et vos seducti estis?* (John, vii, 47.)

When Christ said to you: *Except a man be born again . . .* you exclaimed: *How can a man be born when he is old? can he enter a second time into his mother's womb?* After having talked, you are the same as before, so that, even in your presence, Pharisee and prince in their midst, it can be said: *Have any of the rulers or of the Pharisees believed on him?* (John, vii, 48.)

Too long have I cherished your hesitations, your marks of integrity, your scruples—the display of your cowardice.

Sed turba hæc, quæ non novit legem, maledicti sunt.

From word to word of this sacred text I see sparks of light. . . .

But this people who knoweth not the law are cursed.

Give me, O Lord, to be among these latter, and cursed by the orthodox men, by those "who know the law."

Search and look, they say to Nicodemus, *for out of Galilee ariseth no prophet.*

A Galilæa propheta non surgit. (John, vii, 52.)

This is what they are still saying, those who believe in nations, in races, in families and fail to understand that the individual constantly rises up to give them the lie.

And every man went unto his own house. Et reversi sunt unusquisque in domum suam. (Ibid., 53.)

O Lord! he who comes to You no longer has a house.

20 *April*

Amen, amen, dico vobis: quia omnis qui facit peccatum, servus est peccati. (John, viii, 34.)

Sin is what one does not do freely.

Deliver me from that captivity, O Lord!

Si ergo vos Filius liberaverit, vere liberi eritis.
If the Son therefore shall make you free, ye shall be free indeed.

And the Evil One whispers to my heart:
What good is that liberty to you if you cannot use it?
It is with these words in his heart that the Prodigal Son ran away.

23 April
Unus autem ex illis, ut vidit quia mundatus est, regressus est, cum magna voce magnificans Deum. (Luke, xvii, 15.)

The translators give: "when he saw that he was healed" —which hardly renders the *mundatus.*

Osterwald dares: *cleansed.*[20] I am not going to quibble; but this morning the words: *ut vidit quia mundatus* act upon me with a strange power.

Frightful blemish, oh stain of sin! Ashes left behind by that impure flame, slag. . . . Can you cleanse me of all that, O Lord? that I may glorify you.

"How happy you will be if you learn what is the occupation of love!" (Fénelon: *Lettres spirituelles.*)

28 April
The Bible of Crampon gives in a note the Greek word of the text of Luke (xvii, 33) that it was so important for me to know.

And the whole text is illuminated by it.

Whosoever shall seek to save his life shall lose it, and whosoever shall lose his life shall find it, Osterwald's version gave, thus emptying that word, in which would soon be seen nothing but a balancing of the thought, a somersault paradox such as "the first shall be last" or "blessed are the unhappy"; but this is making it too easy for the enemy. The Greek word is: ζωογονήσει, for which Crampon proposes *will regenerate,* or literally: *will engender him to life.*[21] Here indeed is the *be born again.*[22]

It is likewise in chapter xvii of Luke that is specified: *regnum Dei intra vos est.* And Crampon, who translates like Osterwald and Westphal by: *The kingdom of God is*

[20] *Nettoyé.*
[21] *L'engendrera à la vie.*
[22] These three words appear in English.

among you, at least feels the need of adding in a note:
"Among you in the sense: The kingdom of God has therefore come to you in the person of Christ and his disciples. Others translate: *it is within you,* in your heart, thereby indicating the inner and spiritual nature of this kingdom."

12 May

Written nothing further in this notebook for the last fortnight. Gave up my readings and those pious exercises which my heart, utterly dry and listless, had ceased to approve. See nothing in it but a comedy, and a dishonest comedy, in which I convinced myself that I recognized the hand of the demon. This is what the demon whispers to my heart.

O Lord! Oh, do not leave him the last word. I do not wish any other prayer today.

2 June

Period of indifference, of dryness and unworthiness, my mind wholly concerned with ridiculous anxieties that fatigue and dim it.

This morning I read in St. Paul (I did not go back to my Bible until yesterday): *And if any man think that he knoweth any thing, he knoweth nothing yet as he ought to know.*

But if any man love God, the same is known of him. (I Corinthians, viii, 2–3.)

16 June

I am no longer able either to pray or even to listen to God. If he perhaps speaks to me, I do not hear. Here I am again become completely indifferent to his voice. And yet I scorn *my* wisdom, and, for lack of the joy He gives me, all other joy is taken from me.

O Lord, if you are to help me, what are you waiting for? I cannot, all alone. I cannot.

All the reflections of You that I felt in me are growing dim. It is time that You came.

Ah, do not let the Evil One in my heart take your place! Do not let yourself be dispossessed, Lord! If you withdraw completely, he settles in. Ah, do not confuse me completely with him! I do not love him that much, I assure you. Remember that I was capable of loving You.

What! Am I today as if I had never loved Him?

17 June

It is never of Christ but of St. Paul that I run afoul—and it is in him, never in the Gospels, that I find again everything that had driven me away. . . . I believe in miracles more easily than I follow this reasoning: *But if there be no resurrection of the dead, then is Christ not risen.*[23] Here it is he who denies the miracle exactly as if he said: "If water does not become wine naturally, Christ did not perform the miracle of the wedding-feast at Cana." I am willing not to reason; but here it is he who reasons; and it is precisely that lame reasoning that leads him to this conclusion where my heart and mind balk:

If in this life only we have hope in Christ, we are of all men most miserable. (I Corinthians, xv, 19.)

Atrocious remark and which St. Paul succeeds in making true—to which fortunately all the Gospels are opposed.

Nothing could be more foreign to the Gospels than: *If the dead rise not, let us eat and drink; for tomorrow we die.*[24]

22 June

Gratuitousness of the gift. Gift beyond question.

Surrender of mortal anxiety.

Oh, paradisaical fruition of every instant!

To share in that immensity of happiness, yes, I feel that You invite me, Lord! And sometimes I remain on the watch, trembling at the immediate promise of so much joy.

If therefore I do not reply better to your voice, do me violence. Seize a heart that I am incapable of giving you.

Your lightning love, may it consume or vitrify all the opacity of my flesh, everything mortal that I drag after me!

I am bored with everything in which I do not feel your

[23] Worthy counterpart of this other: *Doth not even nature itself teach you, that, if a man have long hair, it is a shame unto him?* (I Corinthians, xi, 14.) [A.]

[24] My remark no longer strikes me as quite correct. Does not St. Paul wish simply to invite us to see in the resurrection of Christ a guarantee of our own resurrection and of our eternal life? It is on this belief that he aims to base all possibility of real joy. (January 1934; written while correcting the proofs of this text.) [A.]

presence and recognize no life that is not inspired by your love.

23 June

Be not amazed to feel melancholy; and melancholy because of Me. The felicity I offer you excludes forever what you used to take for happiness.

Joy. Joy. . . . I know that the secret of your Gospel, Lord, lies altogether in this divine word: Joy. And is not that just what makes your word triumphant over all human teachings?—that it permits as much joy as the strength of each heart proposes.

Any Christian who does not attain joy renders the passion of Christ useless and thereby augments it. Wishing to carry Christ's cross, longing to assume his sufferings— does this not amount to slighting his gift? At least, Lord, at the memory of your adorable suffering let my heart weep with gratitude and love. Lamb of God, you who cancel the sins of the world, who else but God himself would have had the power and the right? Our sins nailed you to the cross, Lord, but your crucifixion redeems us. That God should offer himself, son of man, for the redemption of our sins, that he should thereby hurl his love into agony. . . . Contemplate, my soul, this ineffable mystery.

"Go, *and sin no more,*" says Christ to the woman taken in adultery. The truly Christian soul conceives a horror for sin, which caused Christ his suffering.

26 June

I was happy; You have spoiled my happiness. Jealous God, You have poisoned with bitterness all the springs where I used to quench my thirst, so that I have no thirst but for the water that You offered to the woman of Samaria.

"God himself is the enemy of those whose covetousness he troubles," I read this morning in Pascal.

". . . Cupidity makes use of God and enjoys the world; the contrary is true of charity."

"Can it be therefore that you do not believe in his miracles?"

"Do not drive my reason to resist. You know that I do

not attack with it. If it were proved to me today that
Christ did not accomplish his miracles, my confidence in
his voice would not be shaken; I should believe in his
teaching just the same."

"In short, you do not believe in his miracles."

"What! it is His miracles that make you consider Him
divine? What! you too need a miracle to believe in Him?
Like the 'evil and adulterous crowd' that said: 'Master,
we should like to see a sign from You.' "

"In short, you do not believe. . . ."

"I leave you the last word."

3 October

His hand forever stretched out, which pride refuses to
take.

"Do you then prefer to sink ever, slowly, ever more
deeply into the abyss?"

Do you think that this rotten flesh will fall away from
you by itself? No, not unless you tear yourself away from
it.

"Lord! without your intervention it will first rot on me
utterly. No, this is not pride; you know it! But to take
your hand, I should like to be less unworthy. My filth
will soil it before its light will whiten me. . . .

"You know well . . ."

"Forgive me, Lord! Yes, I know that I am lying. The
truth is that this flesh that I hate, I still love it more than
You Yourself. I am dying from not exhausting all its
charm. I beg you to help me, but without any true renunciation. . . .

"Miserable one who aims to marry heaven and hell in
you. One cannot give oneself to God except wholly."

Are you really surprised if, after having left God for so
long, you do not attain, as soon as you turn to Him again,
to felicity, to communion, to ecstasy? One can attain these
only through intimacy.

20 October, in the evening

My God, make me awake tomorrow morning fit to serve
you, and my heart full of that zeal without which I am
well aware that I shall never again know happiness.

21 October, in the evening

Lord, grant me that I may have need of You tomorrow
morning.

22 October

Lord, remove from my heart everything that does not belong to love.

It is the image of God that we must purify in ourselves.

Lord, may my prayer, like that of very pure souls, be but a reflection of You returning to You when You look upon me.

Lord, do not interrupt your grace, so that I may not cease to pray to You.

26 October

Raise me up, Lord, for I bend down before You.

It is at the joints of our love that the Evil One attacks us.[25]

29 October

(After reading a *Lettre spirituelle* by Fénelon.)

My Lord, I come to You with all my sores that have become wounds; with all my sins under the weight of which my soul is crushed. . . .

7 November

My Lord, grant me not to be among those who cut a figure in the world.

Grant me not to be among those who succeed.

Grant me not to count among the fortunate, the satisfied, the satiated; among those who are applauded, who are congratulated, and who are envied.

20 June (1917)

After seven months of neglect, I take up this notebook again, which S. A., to whom I had lent it, gives back to me yesterday. The few words she says to me after her reading enlighten me at one and the same time as to the meaning of these pages and the boldness that certain people might find in them—but also, but above all, as to their inadequacy. To push farther the affirmation of one's thought, to give it form in a satisfying expression—one waits for age and maturity of mind; one hopes that that maturity will be ever greater; but in its place come fatigue and that sort of submission to the rule and to established conventions, made up less of modesty perhaps, than of fear, weakness, and cowardice.

[25] Surely the expression *défaut de l'amour* is suggested, perhaps unconsciously, by *défaut de l'armure* ("joints in the harness"); alone, *défaut* means "lack, flaw, deficiency."

I now find the trace of old trails I cut, which I allowed to be covered over by a thousand branches, and which I did not even blaze.

It was when my thought was boldest that it was truest. I was frightened, not by it, but by the fear that certain friends had of it. O my heart, harden yourself against that ruinous sympathy, counselor of all compromises. Why did not I always remain unchanged and always obstinate in following my line!

15 June (*1919*)

The English version suddenly opens my eyes as to a verse of Matthew that (as it happens then) takes on an extreme importance for me:

And he that taketh not his cross, and followeth after me, is not worthy of me.[26]

The three French versions that I have at hand translate: *He who does not take his cross* AND DOES NOT FOLLOW ME *is not worthy of me.* And yet is that really what Christ means? Is it not rather: *He who does not take his cross* AND WHO FOLLOWS ME—that is to say, he who would follow me without first taking up his cross? I turn to the Vulgate. Yes, that is it: *Et qui non accepit crucem suam, et sequitur me, non est me dignus.*

Lord, it is only weighed down with one's cross that one can follow You.

But did you not likewise say: *Come unto me, all ye that labor and are heavy-laden—and I will give you rest; for my yoke is easy and my burden is light.*

It is pleasure that bends the soul, and everything that one is alone in bearing; the weight of the cross straightens it up, and everything that one bears *with You.*

One of the gravest misunderstandings of the spirit of Christ comes from the confusion frequently established in the Christian's mind between future life and eternal life.

The eternal life that Christ offers, and in which all his teaching invites us to share, that eternal life has nothing future about it. It is not beyond death that it awaits us; and indeed, if we do not attain it at once, there is no hope that we may ever achieve it (find again the very beautiful passage by Mark Rutherford on this subject,

[26] This verse is quoted in English.

Vol. I, pp. 108–10).[27] The words of Christ are divinely luminous and it has taken nothing less than all the ingenuity of man to dim or change the obvious meaning. But they shine anew for whoever rereads them with a new heart, with a childlike spirit.

It is to eternal life, it is to participate at once in the eternity of life, it is to enter the Kingdom of God that Christ invites Nicodemus when He says to him: *Except a man be born again, he cannot see the kingdom of God—* for *whosoever shall seek to save his life shall lose it,* but whosoever is born again, whosoever surrenders up his life to be reborn, whosoever renounces himself to follow *Him,* makes his soul truly living, is reborn to eternal life and enters the Kingdom of God.

And is this not likewise what Christ teaches, on the edge of the well, to the woman of Samaria: *But whosoever drinketh of the water that I shall give him shall never thirst?*

Once more, the meaning of this teaching, for an unprejudiced mind, is so obvious that, rereading the story this morning in the Crampon translation, I was struck

---

[27] The passage, which Gide does not quote, is probably this one: "The dissolution of Jesus into mythologic vapour was nothing less than the death of a friend dearer to me then than any other friend whom I knew. But the worst stroke of all was that which fell upon the doctrine of a life beyond the grave. In theory I had long despised the notion that we should govern our conduct here by hope of reward or fear of punishment hereafter. But under Mardon's remorseless criticism, when he insisted on asking for the where and how, and pointed out that all attempts to say where and how ended in nonsense, my hope began to fail, and I was surprised to find myself incapable of living with proper serenity if there was nothing but blank darkness before me at the end of a few years. As I got older I became aware of the folly of this perpetual reaching after the future, and of drawing from tomorrow, and from tomorrow only, a reason for the joyfulness of to-day. I learned, when, alas! it was almost too late, to live in each moment as it passed over my head, believing that the sun as it is now rising is as good as it will ever be, and blinding myself as much as possible to what may follow. But when I was young I was the victim of that illusion, implanted for some purpose or other in us by Nature, which causes us, on the brightest morning in June, to think immediately of a brighter morning which is to come in July. I say nothing, now, for or against the doctrine of immortality. All I say is, that men have been happy without it, even under the pressure of disaster, and that to make immortality a sole spring of action here is an exaggeration of the folly which deludes us all through life with endless expectation, and leaves us at death without the thorough enjoyment of a single hour."

by these words: *the water that I shall give him shall be in him a well of water springing up* INTO EVERLASTING LIFE.[28] What? could I have been mistaken? Does Christ speak of eternal life, just as it is generally taught, as a future state? This *jusqu'à* implies that; but isn't it a mistranslation? I open the Vulgate and read: *Sed aqua quam ego dabo ei, flet in eo fons aquæ* SALIENTIS IN VITAM ÆTERNAM.[29]

(The Segond translation and the Osterwald translation say likewise: *une source d'eau qui jaillira* JUSQUE DANS *la vie éternelle.* The meaning of these words is thereby falsified.)

But the hour cometh, AND NOW IS, says Christ right after this. *Venit hora,* ET NUNC EST. Whoever waits for that hour beyond death waits for it in vain. From the very hour at which you are born again, from the very moment at which you drink of this water, you enter the Kingdom of God, you share in eternal life. *Verily, verily, I say unto you,* Christ repeats everywhere, *He that heareth my word and believeth on him that sent me* HATH (not: *will have,* but *already has*) EVERLASTING LIFE . . . *he is passed from death unto life. Transiit a morte in vitam.* (John, v, 24.)

F O R E W O R D
TO THE 1926 EDITION

A collection of intimate writings, you told me. Under such conditions I am willing that this little book should be reprinted.

If words that have once been whispered should happen to be shouted, their intonation is distorted.

I hold that there is nothing secret that does not deserve to be known, but intimacy does not endure broad daylight. I hold also that the soul's recesses are and must remain more secret than the secrets of the heart and of the

---

[28] The Crampon translation gives *jusqu'à la vie éternelle,* which suggests "until eternal life."

[29] It is thus that A. Westphal translates, and most happily. But the Latin *in* could, if need be, justify *jusqu'à.* I must have recourse to the Greek text. [A.]

body. If it happened to me to be "converted," I should not endure that that conversion be made public. Perhaps some sign of it would appear in my conduct; but only a few intimate friends and a priest would know it. And should it be bruited about, this would be against my will, offending and wounding my modesty. I hold that this is no matter to be amazed at or to joke about. It is entirely a matter between God and me. This at least is my own feeling; and I have no intention, through these words, to throw blame on some very much discussed conversions.

Were I a convert, I should probably not speak thus. A convert, I should seek to convert, through my writings and my example, just like our famous converts. I am neither a Protestant nor a Catholic; I am simply a Christian. And as a matter of fact, I do not want anyone to make a mistake as to the testimonial value of these pages. Most likely I should still sign them today quite willingly. But, written during the war, they contain a reflection of the anguish and confusion of that period; and if, probably, I should still sign them; I should perhaps not still write them.

I do not claim that the state that followed this one is superior to it; it is enough for me that it is not quite the same. It is only fair to warn the reader.

One word more:
I had taken care, when rereading the notebook from which the pages of *Numquid et tu . . . ?* were extracted, to let none appear that the most orthodox Catholic, it seemed to me, could not approve. My desire was one of conciliation rather than of discord; good faith and good will guided me. I thank Monsieur Massis for having shown me that his religion could not be mine. There can be no further doubt in that regard, thank God.

DETACHED PAGES

"He believes neither in God nor in the Devil."
(*Popular saying*)

Until then I had never realized that it was not necessary to believe in God in order to believe in the devil. To tell the truth, the devil had never yet appeared before my imagination; my conception of the devil remained utterly negative; I condemned him by default; I limited his contour by God; and since I extended God everywhere, I did not let the *Other One* begin anywhere. In any case I admitted him only as a metaphysical entity and merely smiled at first that autumn evening when suddenly Jacques Raverat introduced him to me.

✳

But I was full of scruples, and before I surrendered, the demon who addressed himself to me had to convince me that what was asked of me was permitted me, that this permitted thing was necessary to me. Sometimes the Evil One reversed the propositions, began with the necessary; he would reason thus—for the Evil One is the Reasoner: "How could it be that what is necessary to you should not be permitted you? Just consent to call necessary what you can't do without. You cannot do without that for which you thirst the most. Just consent not to call sin what you cannot do without. You would acquire great strength," he would add, "if instead of wearing yourself out struggling against yourself in this manner, you only struggled against the external obstacle. For anyone who has learned to struggle, no obstacle can hold up. Go, learn to triumph over yourself at last and over your own sense of decency. Haven't I taught you to see a hereditary habit in your uprightness, and the mere prolongation of an impetus; shyness and embarrassment in your modesty; less decision than carelessness in your virtue . . . ?"

In short, he drew argument and advantage from the fact that it cost me more to yield to my desire than to continue curbing it. To be sure, the first steps I took on the sloping path required, to risk them, a certain courage and even a certain resolve.

It goes without saying that I did not understand until much later the diabolic element in this exhortation. At that time I thought I was the only one to speak and that I was carrying on this specious dialogue with myself.

I had heard talk of the Evil One, but I had not made his acquaintance. He already inhabited me when I did not yet distinguish him. He had made me his conquest; I thought myself victorious, to be sure; victorious over myself because I was surrendering to him. Because he had convinced me, I did not feel myself to be conquered.[30] I had invited him to take up his residence in me, as a challenge and because I did not believe in him, like the man in the legend who sells his soul to him in return for some exquisite advantage—and who continues not believing in him despite having received the advantage from him!

I did not yet understand that evil is a positive, active, enterprising principle; I used to think at that time that evil was simply a lack of good, as darkness is a lack of light, and I was inclined to assign all kinds of activity to light. When, in 1910, my friend Raverat first spoke to me of him, I merely smiled. But his words entered my heart no less deeply. "I began," he explained to me, "by believing in the devil. . . ." (We were in the office at Cuverville, and a reading together of Milton in the afternoon had brought our conversation to the subject of Satan.) "And it is believing in him, *whom I actually felt*, that led me to believe in God, whom I did not yet feel." And since a great deal of irony was mingled with my amazement, and since I feared that he himself was not altogether serious: "Satan's great strength," he went on soberly, "comes from the fact that he is never just the way you think he is. You have already accomplished considerably against him when you are convinced that he is there. To recognize him properly it is better never to lose sight of him."

It took all my great friendship for Jacques Raverat to make me pay attention to his words. Henceforth I bore them in me, but like those seeds which germinate only after a long stratification; to tell the truth, they did not sprout until the beginning of the war, when, having given myself completely to a relief organization, I was able to see the face of the Evil One more sharply against this background of philanthropy.

The great mistake, which allows him to slip incognito into our lives, is that, ordinarily, people are willing to recognize his voice only at the moment of the temptation itself; but he rarely risks an offensive without having prepared it. He is much more intelligent than we, and he

[30] There is an untranslatable play here on the words *convaincu* and *vaincu*.

hides most often in reasoning; if we were more humble we should recognize him in the *Cogito ergo sum*. That *ergo* is the cloven hoof.[31] He knows that there are certain souls that he cannot conquer in open battle and that he must persuade.

I know that to many minds it might seem absurd, as it would still have seemed the day before yesterday to my own, to go out of one's way to postulate this existence, this presence of the demon in order to explain by upheaval what cannot be explained through logic; a less lazy or more subtle psychology would succeed in again putting this phantom out of countenance, they say. These are the same minds that think that the evolutionary explanation has succeeded in supplanting God. What shall I reply except that I had no sooner *assumed* the demon than my whole biography was at once made clear to me: that I suddenly understood what had been most obscure to me, to such a point that this assumption took on the exact shape of my interrogation and my preceding wonder.

What is more glorious than a soul when it liberates itself? What is more tragic than a soul that makes itself a prisoner just when it thinks it is liberating itself?

I am utterly indifferent, afterward, as to whether or not this name of demon is the right name for what I mean, and I grant that I give it this name out of convenience. If someone should come along later and show me that he lives not in hell but in my blood, my loins, or my insomnia, does he believe that he can suppress him thus? When I say: the Evil One, I know what that expression designates just as clearly as I know what is designated by the word *God*. I draw his outline by the deficiency of each virtue.

And since he is more intelligent than I, everything he thought up to hurl me toward evil was infinitely more precious, more specious, more convincing, more beautiful, more clever than any argument I could have brought up to persevere in honor. I should never have stumbled upon such arguments by myself. *Cogito ergo Satanas.*

Now, this is how He proceeds:

"To begin with, thank you for having brought me into

[31] A good pun is lost here on *ergo* and *l'ergot du diable*, "the devil's spur."

being! Yes, you are well aware that your kindness creates me. You are well aware that I didn't exist, but probably you needed to take off from me in order to believe in God—a God that might help you to fight me."

"Good Lord, how complicated all this is! I believe in God. The existence of God alone matters to me, and not yours; but the proof that you exist is that you want to make me doubt it."

"Come! Come! You are not so stupid as all that! You created me in order to make me responsible for your doubts, your dejections, your fits of boredom. Everything that bothers you is I, everything that holds you back. If your pride protests against the bent of your mind, it is I. It is I if your blood boils, if your mood is flighty. When your reason balks it is I. When your flesh revolts, it is I. Your hunger, your thirst, your fatigue are all I. Your inclination is I. In short, you give me such a wonderful role that I wonder if sometimes you do not confuse me with God. The amusing thing, I tell you, is that henceforth you cannot believe in One without the Other. Just listen to the fable of the gardener. . . ."

"By heaven! I knew it: you too know how to talk in parables."

"Oh, I'm not limited to just one form of expression."

"This is because you speak in turn to the mind, to the heart, to the senses; and since, while protecting myself on one side, I am always uncovering myself on the other, you, who keep moving around me, always address yourself to the unguarded side."

"How well we know each other! You know, if you wanted to—"

"What?"

"What good friends we should be! . . ."

1917

Weather excessively foggy and melancholy. This morning we have to endure the respects of all the good people
of the township.

1 January

Yesterday evening I was shocked by the tremendous
amount of work that revising the translation of *Victory*
would require.[1] I cursed out Isabelle Rivière and her
childish theories about how *faithful* a translation must be
—which makes her present hers studded with errors, awkward expressions, cacophonies, ugly passages. Yet I hoped
to have finished with this job and to have only to reread.
. . . But now this ages me a fortnight.

11 January

For several days I have been seeking what title to give
to these Memoirs; for I should not exactly like *Mémoires*
or *Souvenirs* or *Confessions*. And the awkward thing about
any other title is that it allows of a meaning. I am hesitat-
ing between: *Et Ego* . . . but which limits the sense, and
Si le grain ne meurt . . . but which slants it, while en-
larging it.

I believe, however, that I shall decide on the latter.

19 January

Toby died last night. I reproach myself for not having
noted from day to day the phases of his illness. I have just
written to the Criquetot pork-butcher, who has assumed
the veterinary's functions since the mobilization, to come
with the necessary instruments to perform an autopsy.
I have no idea of what he died . . . ? Of a tumor, says
Mathilde Roberty. Whatever the complaint was, it was
strangely complicated by his nervous state. He was certainly the most neurasthenic dog one could possibly
imagine. He had every possible phobia: hugged hedges

---

[1] André Gide had undertaken the supervision of the translations of
Conrad to be published by Librairie de la N.R.F. Isabelle Rivière, the
wife of Jacques, then a prisoner in Germany, had translated *Victory*.
The biographer of Conrad, G. Jean-Aubry, shared responsibility with
Gide.

and walls; always took the longest way around to come to a call; was seized with dizziness as he climbed the stairs; dared to eat only when no one was looking. He adored sugar; but if you offered him a piece, he would let it fall on the floor and go off into a corner to play the martyr. Whence it was impossible ever to reward him; untrainable, you could have got him only through hunger, and even then—I believe he never forgave me the spoonful of sugared coffee that I had made him take just after his arrival, when I did not yet know him and thought I could tame him. But the least approach to a blow put him in a snarling mood, or else he would run miles away as soon as I would raise my cane, or else he would squirt on the ground. It was just as impossible to help him; if you wanted to take a tick off of him, you had to put on gloves or else muzzle him; even then I had to give up more than once. And with his mania for rubbing up against old walls and bushes along the way, he swept up everything bad on his path; even to comb him required a thousand precautions and I had to give up combing his belly. How often he bit me like a mad dog!

With other dogs he tried to be dashing and would offer himself to their caresses. Although excited to the point of frenzy by the odor of our bitch in heat, he could never achieve anything with her, any more than with any other bitch whatever and any more, it goes without saying, than with our old cat, although she nevertheless excited him as much as a bitch and, on her side, would provoke and pursue him as much as if he had been a tomcat. You cannot imagine a more absurd and more dumbfounding game; Toby would wear himself out after her for hours and days on end.

He would spend most of the day seated, like a macaque, on his lumbar vertebræ with his legs and his whole hindquarters paradoxically brought forward between his front legs and sporting his cock like a rosette of the Légion d'Honneur on a lapel.

Porto-Riche had given him to me after having learned from Copeau, who frequented him, that we had a bitch of the same breed. Most certainly he wanted to get rid of him. Probably after having seen him at work, he had named him Joseph.

And for the last six weeks Toby had refused to eat. Em. kept him alive with pieces of sugar, which, I believe, stopped the diarrhea that he had first had very seriously. We thought he was going to die of inanition, when suddenly— But I shall tell that after the autopsy has been made.

It is possible to write properly, it is possible to think properly only what one has no personal interest in thinking or in writing. I am not writing these Memoirs to defend myself. I am not called on to defend myself, since I am not accused. I am writing them before being accused. I am writing them in order to be accused.

1 February

I am striking out of my Memoirs, of this first part at least, all the reflections and considerations thanks to which one earns the reputation of a "thinker." They do not seem to me to be at home here; and everything, for me, yields to the artistic consideration.

This is likewise what makes me strike out in my preface to the *Fleurs du mal* the few paragraphs that, yielding to Helleu's invitation, I had eventually added.

Cuverville, 27 February

A few hours before my arrival Em. had been brought a little hare three weeks old that had been found in the farmyard, huddling behind a bundle of firewood. Em. thought that I could perhaps raise it; but I still have a sorry memory of my experience of four years ago. Yet I tried, first with a spoon, then with an eye-dropper, to make him take a little warm milk. The baby hare did not struggle, but simply contracted his throat so that one could make him swallow almost nothing. I had put him into a basket half full of wood-shavings near my room. Last night, hearing him stir, I got up to try to feed him again; and while I was warming the milk over a candle, I heard outside strange animal cries, which I am certain must have been a doe-hare's cries. It occurred to me that the baby hare heard them likewise and that this was what made him stir. Despairing of the possibility of nourishing him, I went out, taking him in my pocket, and having climbed the fence, put him back in about the place where he had been found during the day. (It was two a.m.) How I should like to know what he did! The night was unfortunately very cold; this morning hoar-frost silvered the grass; I fear he was unable to come through. . . .

1 March

Extreme difficulty in getting back to work. Everything I have written of my recollections seems to me, when I think it over, deplorably *profane* and light. That pendulum movement to which my mind yields, despite all resolutions, would plunge me back into extreme license if only outside circumstances and my physical state permitted greater exaltation. It strikes me that I was foolish and guilty to bend my mind artificially so as to make it better understand the Catholic teaching. That is where the real impiety lies. I recognize that *tendency toward veneration,* which was doubtless a fortunate attitude in my youth but which is quite out of place today; in which I am now willing to see only weakness, deplorable modesty, inept confidence in the superiority of others, doubt of myself, surrender of my own thought simply because it is mine, repudiation.

There is no question of humility before God, but rather of that humility before men which has always been my secret malady, which, moreover, I find likewise in Dostoyevsky and Baudelaire. Something that a Francis Jammes, for example, could never manage to understand, who sees danger only on the side of pride, and of modesty knows only the outward simpering. (This comes from the fact that he knows nothing of and denies everything in which he does not show himself to be superior.)

8 March. Evening

The thought of death did not leave me once all day. It seems to me that it is right here, close beside me.

10 March

Yesterday, after a somewhat better day, during which I at least succeeded in working a little, a strange dizziness overcame me in the evening, just as I was going to go up to bed—yet without nausea and, if I may say so, without discomfort, but so violent that I wondered whether or not I should be able to get out of the armchair in which I was seated.

This morning I am quite unable to stand up; since, when

I tried to, everything began whirling around me, I first thought I was going to fall on the floor and barely had time to get back to bed—where I am writing this, more for the sake of filling up the time than through a need to write. I am like a man who has been bled white.

Monday

Night haunted, devastated, laid waste by the almost palpable phantom of X., with whom I walk for two hours or in whose arms I roll on the very steps of hell. And this morning I get up with my head empty, my mind distraught, my nerves on edge, and offering an easy access to evil. Yet last night I did not quite yield to pleasure; but this morning, not even benefiting from that repulsion which follows pleasure, I wonder if that semblance of resistance was not perhaps worse. One is always wrong to open a conversation with the devil, for, however he goes about it, he always insists upon having the last word.

Tuesday

Equilibrium almost recovered. Rather good work. Last night, great disappointment at discovering, in an article by Sainte-Beuve, that I am not reading Mme de Sévigné's letters in a good edition. Yet it is hard for me to leave her and to wait for the large Paris edition. Is there anything better than her reflections on death in the letter of 16 March 1672? It is turned out in a way that could not be equaled.[2]

[2] The following is the passage, which Gide does not quote:
"You ask me if I am as fond of life as ever: I must own to you that I experience mortifications, and severe ones too; but I am still unhappy at the thought of death: I consider it so great a misfortune to see the termination of all my pursuits that I should desire nothing better, if it were practicable, than to begin life again. I find myself engaged in a scene of confusion and trouble: I was embarked in life without my own consent, and know I must leave it again: that distracts me; for how shall I leave it? in what manner? by what door? at what time? in what disposition? Am I to suffer a thousand pains and torments that will make me die in a state of despair? Shall I lose my senses? Am I to die by some sudden accident? How shall I stand with God? What shall I have to offer to him? Will fear and necessity make my peace with him? Shall I have no other sentiment but that of fear? What have I to hope? Am I worthy of heaven? or have I deserved the torments of hell? Dreadful alternative! Alarming uncertainty! Can there be greater madness than to place our eternal salvation in un-

We are reading aloud *Mr. Britling Sees It Through* by Wells.

22 March

Until the week before last, I got as far ahead as I could in the writing of my Memoirs (pathetic conversation with Albert Jalaguier—I changed the name—and the reflections that followed it).[3] But there is a certain point of exertion I know it is unwise to go beyond. I long for a diversion that would take me outside myself for a time, away from my desk, from my piano, where my memory is likewise worn out by the effort I demand of it. I had decided to leave for Paris, but various reasons kept me from day to day—among which my anxiety at leaving Em. alone here. So that, for a week now, day after day, I exercise patience and grow impatient, neither daring to work seriously nor able to distract myself sufficiently. The weather is frightful; the air frigid; for the last two days it has been snowing.

I am eagerly reading Sainte-Beuve with unequal pleasure—discover his profession of faith, so important (or more exactly his program) in the second part of his article on Chateaubriand (*Nouveaux Lundis*).[4]

---

certainty? Yet what is more natural, or can be more easily accounted for, than the foolish manner in which I have spent my life? I am frequently buried in thoughts of this nature, and then death appears so dreadful to me that I hate life more for leading me to it than I do for all the thorns that are strewed in its way. You will ask me, then, if I would wish to live forever? Far from it; but if I had been consulted, I would very gladly have died in my nurse's arms; it would have spared me many vexations, and would have ensured heaven to me, at a very easy rate; but let us talk of something else." (Letter 189 in the Carnavalet Edition, Vol. II; no translator mentioned.)

[3] In *Si le grain ne meurt . . . (If It Die . . .)* Albert Jalaguier bears the pseudonym of Bernard Tissandier.

[4] The entire second part of the article entitled "Chateaubriand Judged by an Intimate Friend," which appeared in Vol. III of *The New Mondays*, outlines Sainte-Beuve's method "in examining books and talents." He begins: "Literature, literary production, to me is not distinct, or at least separable, from the rest of the man and his organization; I can enjoy a work, but it is impossible for me to judge it independently of my knowledge of the man himself; and I am wont to say: *as the tree is, so is the fruit.* The study of literature thus leads me quite naturally to the study of character." He then shows the importance, in this study, of the background, upbringing, parents, brothers and sisters, children, friends, and even disciples of a writer.

30 April or 1 May

Already in the last weeks of 1914 I wrote in one of my notebooks: There are many chances that if the war goes on, as many claim, for several years, each country will eventually be back on its own frontiers, exhausted.

Just the same it takes a certain dose of mysticism—or of something—to go on speaking, writing, when you know that you are absolutely not being listened to.

From top to bottom, and starting from the ground up, I see nothing but negligence, thoughtlessness, and dishonesty. In the midst of which the mere honest man appears as a hero—or as an easy mark.

The feeling of duty, or to speak in more secular fashion: of the law, has relaxed to such a degree that just a slightly strict application of the law would make people cry tyranny. What is more ridiculous than the word "enforcement" of a law!

The pleasure of corrupting is one of those which have been least examined; this is true likewise of everything we begin by stigmatizing.

From Geneva to Engelberg [August]

Although he is too taciturn, I like traveling with Fabrice. He says, and I believe him, that at forty-eight he feels infinitely younger than he was at twenty. He enjoys that rare faculty of starting off anew at each turning-point in his life and of remaining faithful to himself by never resembling anything less than he does himself.

Today when he is traveling first-class (this hadn't happened to him for some time now), in new clothes of an unaccustomed cut and under a hat that is wonderfully becoming, he is amazed when he encounters himself in the mirror, and he charms himself. He says to himself: "New creature, today I can refuse you nothing!" Just because he has indulged in a box of delicate Oriental cigarettes, he immediately feels like more of a millionaire than Barnabooth.[5] Heavens! what beautiful weather it is. Having

[5] Valery Larbaud's hero, the imaginary multimillionaire A. O. Barnabooth, traveled throughout Europe in great luxury analyzing his soul.

compressed itself this morning for rain, it is now bursting. All alone in this empty region of the Swiss first-class carriages, he walks up and down the corridor with a triumphant air—favored by the German script that has been rife since he left the Valais.

Engelberg, 7 August

He confessed to me that he had first experienced a strange disappointment on meeting Michel at Chanivaz. He hardly recognized the youth. After barely a month's absence could this be? The fear of seeing the adolescent grow up too rapidly constantly tormented Fabrice and precipitated his love. He loved nothing so much in Michel as the childlike qualities he still preserved, in his tone of voice, in his ardor, in his caressing ways—all of which he recaptured shortly afterward, wild with joy, when the two of them stretched out beside each other on the edge of the lake. Michel, who lived most of the time with his collar wide open, had bundled himself up that day in some stiff collar or other that changed even his bearing; and this is why Fabrice did not recognize him at first. Furthermore, it must be confessed that Michel had already let himself be deeply marked by Switzerland. And Fabrice began to detest that raw and starched element that Helvetia adds to every gesture and every thought. Were it not for this, one might have thought oneself at Oxford or in Arcady.

9 August

Michel was at the age when one is still ignorant of almost everything about oneself. His appetite was barely awakening and had not yet measured itself with reality. His curiosity seemed turned only in the direction of barriers; this is the disadvantage of a puritan upbringing when it is applied to someone who is not inclined to be hedged in.

Michel's soul offered Fabrice rapturous perspectives, which were still clouded, it seemed to him, by the morning mists. To dissipate them the rays of a first love were needed. It was of this, not of the love itself, that Fabrice felt he might be jealous. He would have liked to suffice; tried to convince himself that he might have sufficed; he grieved to think that he would not suffice.

Lucerne, 10 August

What cleanliness everywhere! You dare not throw your cigarette into the lake. No graffitti in the urinals. Switzerland is proud of this; but I believe this is just what she lacks: manure.

In the morning, Geneva, on a bench on the Bastions

One of Fabrice's most disconcerting intellectual peculiarities for his neighbors (I mean for his companion of the present moment, whoever he might be) was to break away from himself constantly.—From himself? No, I have expressed it badly: Rather, to break away from circumstances. Without resolve or defiance, his whole soul would slip beyond, and the event would no more manage to seize him than Jason did in taking Proteus prisoner. Adversity exalted him rather; he yielded only to fatigue; but he was often fatigued.

Saas-Fée, 21 August

On certain days that child took on a surprising beauty; he seemed clothed in grace and, as Signoret would have said, "with the pollen of the gods." From his face and from all his skin emanated a sort of blond effulgence. The skin of his neck, of his chest, of his face and hands, of his whole body, was equally warm and gilded. He was wearing that day, with his rough homespun shorts, only a silk shirt of a sharp, purplish red, swelling out over his leather belt and open at the neck, where hung amber beads. He was barefoot and barelegged. A scout's cap held back his hair, which otherwise would have fallen tangled on his forehead, and, as if in defiance of his childlike appearance, he held in his teeth the brier pipe with an amber bit that Fabrice had just given him, which he had never yet smoked. Nothing could describe the languor, grace, and sensuality of his eyes. For long moments as he contemplated him, Fabrice lost all sense of the hour, of the place, of good and evil, of the proprieties, and of himself. He doubted whether any work of art had ever represented anything so beautiful. He doubted whether the mystical vocation of the man who used to accompany and precede him in pleasure would have held firm, and his virtuous resolve, before so flagrant an invitation, or whether, to adore such an idol, the other would not have declared himself a pagan again.

20 September
What good is it for me to resume this journal if I dare not be sincere in it and if I hide my heart's secret occupation?

21 September
Almost uninterrupted dizziness all day today. But rather good work—if the clearing away of a pile of correspondence can be called work. Letters to Alibert, to Lady Rothermere, who is translating my *Prométhée*,[6] to Ida Rubinstein about the contract to be drawn up for the translation of *Antony and Cleopatra*, etc., etc. I read the first of Walter Pater's *Portraits* (Watteau) with the greatest pleasure, which is unfailingly accompanied by a desire to translate.

Paris, 1 October
Back from Dieppe yesterday with Mme Mühlfeld. In the train I gave her to read, to make the time pass, *Le Prométhée*, which she had never read and of which I was lugging about a copy to correct Lady Rothermere's translation. At every page, rapturous admiration of Mme Mühlfeld, who naturally declares that she has never read anything more beautiful.

Went to the Gare de l'Est to meet the Élie Allégrets. Spent the night at the hotel opposite the Gare Saint-Lazare, where I had had to take a room because of the impossibility of getting anyone to take me to Auteuil at once. The following morning (yesterday) to the Gare de l'Est to pick up the eight hundred pounds of luggage that had been left there the day before. Slept at the Villa.

Today glorious weather. My inner sky is even more radiant; a vast joy softens and exalts me.

22 October
Returned to Cuverville yesterday.
I have lived all the time of late (and, altogether, since 5 May) my head swimming with happiness; whence the long empty space in this notebook. It reflects only my clouds.

25 October
I am no longer mistaken about it: Michel loves me not

[6] *Prometheus Ill-Bound* did in fact appear in a translation by Lady Rothermere in London (1919).

so much for what I am as for what I allow him to be. Why should I ask more? Never have I enjoyed life more, nor has the savor of life seemed more delicious to me.

I have not yet advanced in my Memoirs, but I am copying into the oblong notebook the part (chapter vii) that I had not yet put into final form. I have got back to the translation of *Antony and Cleopatra*—and above all I have written letters, a pile of back letters that were obstructing the horizon for me. I am reading *Phèdre* to the little girls. I prolong the evening in my bed until midnight (for three nights now and I haven't felt any the worse), reading, deciphering with difficulty the book sent by W., *Sons o' Men* by G. B. Lancaster—a rather remarkable book but written in a New Zealand dialect that is almost incomprehensible to me.

30 October

I rest myself with Keats, resuming his letters with infinite delight: "Better be imprudent moveables than prudent fixtures." (*Letters*, II, p. 80.)[7]

Never have I aspired less toward rest. Never have I felt more exalted by that excess of passions which Bossuet considers the attribute of youth, in his wonderful *Panégyrique de Saint Bernard*,[8] which I was rereading this morning. Age cannot manage to empty either sensual pleasure of its attractiveness or the whole world of its charm. On the contrary, I was more easily disgusted at twenty, and I was less satisfied with life. I embraced less boldly; I breathed less deeply; and I felt myself to be less loved. Perhaps also I longed to be melancholy; I had not yet understood the superior beauty of happiness.

31 October

Dramatic character: the despised bastard who discovers that he is the son of a king. His re-establishment above his brothers, legitimate sons.

Fictional character: the man whom the doctors give only a year to live. And at the end of that year he finds himself ruined, but healthier than ever—and resolute, having got the *habit of happiness* (lack of preoccupation with the future).

---

[7] The quotation appears in English.
[8] Panegyric of Saint Bernard.

1 November

At moments it strikes me, and as if in a sudden flash, that I have only a little time still to live, and that this is why I take such a lively interest in everything I read, that everything I see seems so beautiful to me, and that I enjoy life so completely.

I received from Michel yesterday a letter full of exquisite fancy and grace that lighted up all my thoughts. Half of the day was given, alas, to correspondence. Read considerable English (Santayana—chapter on Browning, on the Platonism of the Italian poets, and on Shakespeare's lack of religion—in *Poetry and Religion*, which Guillaume Lerolle lent me; and *Simon the Jester* by Locke); got ahead with the rewriting of the Memoirs; went over a chapter of the translation of *End of the Tether*.[9]

16 November

The thought of death pursues me with a strange insistence. Every time I make a gesture, I calculate: how many times already? I compute: how many times more? and, full of despair, I feel the turn of the year rushing toward me. And as I measure how the water is withdrawing around me, my thirst increases and I feel younger in proportion to the little time that remains to me to feel it.

18 November

The above lines will seem prophetic if I am to die in a short while; but I shall be really ashamed if it is given to me to reread them fifteen years from now. If I could simply not know or forget my age, how little I should be aware of it! I ought never to remind myself of it except to urge myself to work.

Somewhat tired these last few days, having slept less well. Rather out of patience also with this job of translating and revising the translations of others, which takes almost all my time. I hope to be rid of it before the end of the year (even before my forthcoming departure for Paris, perhaps) and to be able to concern myself solely with the Memoirs.

One of the Hérouard sons, the youngest of those who are in military service, has just been killed. Em. went this

[9] This is another work by Conrad, for whose French edition Gide had editorial responsibility.

morning to Cuverville to attend the funeral service for Georges's deputy mayor, old Crochemore. As people were preparing to leave the church, an old woman began to shout in a high-pitched voice:

"There's God! There's God!"

Em., who is afraid of crazy people, ran out terrified, while her neighbor reassured her:

"Don't be afraid, Mam Gille! She's seized like that every time."

And for some time we amuse ourselves by imagining the panic caused by the arrival of God in the church.

15 December

Ride to Criquetot. The sky was overcast, very dark, heavy with showers; a great sea wind swept the clouds. The thought of M. keeps me in a constant state of lyricism I had not known since my *Nourritures*.[10] I no longer feel my age, or the horror of our time, or the season, unless to draw from it a new source of exaltation; were I a soldier, with such a heart, I should meet death joyously.

I believe I have ceased to prefer "the fine weather" to these late-autumn skies, so pathetic, so serious in tone, so tragic in sonority. Vast flights of crows spread madly over the plain.

As soon as I got home I wrote at one breath the preamble to *Corydon,* as a reaction to the *Préface aux Lettres de Dupouey,* which I had finished that very morning. Then I practiced the irritating toccata (finale) of Beethoven's little Sonata in F major, which, almost completely mastered, becomes charming.

Read with Em. *Under Western Eyes* and corrected the rest of *End of the Tether* (soon finished).

16 December

Labored over *Corydon* all day yesterday and today. I lose myself in the accumulation of notes, outlines, and rejects that I had left pretty much topsy-turvy—and I am angry with Marcel Drouin for having stopped me in my work at the moment when the iron was hot. It seems to me, however, that what I had to say is important. I repeat to myself Ibsen's remark: "Friends are to be feared, not so

---

[10] Written largely in 1895, *The Fruits of the Earth* was published in 1897.

much for what they make us do as for what they keep us from doing." It's a pity, but I shall succeed.

Outside it is snowing; all the rays of sunlight are dead on the desperate plain. . . .

1918

Back in Cuverville since the first of January. Worked
on *Corydon.*

Monday, 7 January

Read yesterday and the day before various passages of
my Recollections in the presence of Mathilde Roberty,
who came to spend a week with us. Great dissatisfaction
with almost all I have written of them. It all lacks tremor,
elasticity, richness. The often happy expressions appear
to have been sought out. It seems to me that I see better,
now, how the rest should be written.

In Paris I reread to Jean-Paul Allégret a few pages of
Proust—dazzled.

I write to Lady Rothermere upon sending her a copy
of *Prétextes,* of which she would like to translate some
passages:

"The chief difficulty comes from the fact that my sentence constantly suggests rather than affirms, and proceeds by insinuations—for which the English language,
more direct than the French, feels rather a repugnance.
It has always seemed to me that in my writings the
thought mattered less than the movement of the thought:
the gait." [1]

Monday, 14

Forsaken this notebook for a week. I get no pleasure, or
profit, from writing in it; if I open it again today this is
because my work is slackening. I have almost finished
Corydon; at least, to advance it further I shall need a bit
of perspective; but the most important part is done.

I wanted to harness myself to the Memoirs again, but
I have no further taste for them; the few passages that I
read aloud in the presence of Mathilde Roberty disappointed me; and the comparison I made between them
and the pages of Proust's marvelous book, which I was
rereading at the same time, overwhelmed and finished me
off.

Could the reserves of health and joy that this summer

---

[1] The expression in italics appears in English.

accumulated in me be exhausted now? A secret relapse
makes me fear this. I am already thirsty to plunge into
life anew.

Practice of Beethoven and Granados.

15 February

I am beginning to think that our Commune is the only
one in France in which the rules are observed. As mayor,
Georges did not think he could grant himself more than
two hundred grams of bread a day. And he has restricted
Em. and me to this same minimum allowance. People are
poking fun at us. The mayors of the neighboring com-
munes began by granting themselves the lion's share. We
are a subject of ridicule. . . . But I do not mind being
made fun of.

Each time a new ruling is imposed on France, every
French citizen begins worrying not as to how he can
follow it but as to how he can escape it. I keep coming
back to this: people talk of a lack of organization when
it is a lack of conscience they mean.

3 March

Lucien Maury, with whom I was lunching the other day
in Paris, is greatly worried about the wave of socialism
he feels rising, which he foresees as submerging our old
world after we think the war is over. He believes revolution inevitable and sees no way it can be opposed. When
I speak to him of the resistance organization that *L'Action
française* is working to form, he becomes indignant. Maurras exasperates him and Léon Daudet makes his blood
boil.

"I can understand," I told him, "that they should not
satisfy you. But you will be forced to side with them if
you are anxious to resist. There will be no third choice.
It will be like the Dreyfus affair: you will have to be *for*
or *against,* willy-nilly. You don't like the *Action française*
group? It is not so much that I consider it the best—*but
it is the only one.*"

6 March

Examined with Em. the accounts of which she has just
finished making the statement. The item *Gifts* absorbs
about a quarter of the annual expenditures (which, moreover, considerably exceed the "income"). Happy to see
Em. approve that expenditure as much as I. I know that

if she let herself go, she would give even more—even to
the point of depriving herself completely. Oh! I should
like to succeed in giving still more. I should like to succeed in giving everything away, to enjoy only what I gave
or what I received from others.

18 April

Returned to Cuverville yesterday—after two sojourns in
Paris—interrupted by a week at Carantec, with M.—at
Godebski's.

"Yes, I am very fond of Mme E.," said Cocteau, "and I
admire her. She is so sincere. Just take this for instance—
she went to see Debussy's body laid out; but when, later
on, she was asked: 'Well, how did he look?' 'Why, I
don't know,' she replied; 'I didn't see him at all. *I* see
nothing but colors.' And that's true. Isn't that wonderful:
she sees nothing but color!"

Nothing is more foreign to me than this concern for
modernism which one feels influencing every thought and
every decision of Cocteau. I do not claim that he is wrong
to believe that art breathes freely only in its newest manifestation. But, all the same, the only thing that matters to
me is what a generation will not carry away with it. I do
not seek to be of my epoch; I seek to overflow my epoch.

Propose this definition of *sin:* everything that involves
the injurious.
This is simply displacing the question, not answering it.
Often a superior good is obtained only at the cost of a
particular injury.

20 April

Frigid weather. Completely done in by a cold.
I occasionally wonder if I am not quite wrong to try
to correct M.; if *I* have not more to learn from his shortcomings than *he* would profit from acquiring the virtues
I should like to teach him. I inherit from my mother that
mania for always wanting to improve those I love. And
yet what attracts me in M. is also what I call his shortcomings—which are perhaps only poetic virtues: thoughtlessness, turbulence, forgetfulness of the hour, complete
surrender to the moment. . . . And how could that bold

self-affirmation which I like so much in him go without some egotism?

9 *May*

What a wonderful subject for a novel:

X. indulges in a tremendous effort of ingenuity, scheming, and duplicity to succeed in an undertaking that he knows to be reprehensible. He is urged on by his temperament, which has its exigences, then by the rule of conduct he has built in order to satisfy them. It takes an extreme and hourly application; he expends more resolve, energy, and patience in this than would be needed to succeed in the best. And when eventually the event is prepared to such a point that he has only to let it take its course, the let-down he experiences allows him to reflect; he then realizes that he has ceased to desire greatly that felicity on which he had counted too much. But it is too late now to back out; he is caught in the mechanism he has built and set in motion and, willy-nilly, he must now follow its impetus to its conclusion. The event that he no longer dominates carries him along and it is almost passively that he witnesses his perdition. Unless he suddenly gets out of it by a sort of cowardice; for there are some who lack the courage to pursue their acts to their conclusion, without moreover being any more virtuous for this reason. On the contrary they come out diminished and with less self-esteem. This is why, everything considered, X. will persevere, but without any further desire, without joy and rather through *fidelity*. This is the reason why there is often so little happiness in crime—and what is called "repentance" is frequently only the exploitation of this.

Rather languishing, the interest of Fielding's *Amelia*, which I am reading aloud to Em. Eager to look for the possible connection (or rather the similitude of tone) with *Gil Blas*, I pick up in the latter *L'Histoire de Scipion* and am above all amazed to find it better.[2]

1 *June*

I sometimes think, with horror, that the victory all our hearts wish France to have is that of the past over the future.

. . .

[2] *The Story of Scipio* is a section of the picaresque novel *Gil Blas* by Lesage, published in sections from 1715 to 1735.

In Paris I read (in part) Douglas's abominable book, *Oscar Wilde and Myself*. Hypocrisy can go no further, nor falsehood be more impudent. It is a monstrous travesty of the truth, which filled me with disgust. Merely from the tone of his writing it seems to me that I should be aware he is lying, even if I had not been the direct witness of the acts of his life against which he protests and which he claims to whitewash. But even this is not enough for him. He claims that he was ignorant of Wilde's habits! and that he upheld him at first only because he thought him innocent! Whom will he convince? I do not know; but I hope not to die before having unmasked him. This book is a villainy.

8 June

Busy these last few days perfecting *Corydon*. Most likely I shall still have many slight changes to make in the proofs and numerous additions to the appendix—but such as it is I could hand it over to the printer. I should have liked to have thirteen copies printed—not one more —and should have taken care of this at once if Gouchtenaere (Méral) were still in Paris and if his printer had not been upset by the bombardment.

I should likewise like to bring out before the end of this year:

A new edition of *Les Nourritures;*
The big edition of *Typhoon;*
The letters of Dupouey;
A third volume of *Prétextes;*
And an edition of three hundred copies of *Le Prométhée*.

Perhaps also my translation of *Antony and Cleopatra*. And finally I hope very much to have finished my *Symphonie pastorale*.[3]

18 June

I am leaving France in a state of inexpressible anguish.

[3] A new edition of *The Fruits of the Earth* did appear in 1918, as did the translation of Conrad's *Typhoon* and the *Œuvres choisies* (*Selections*) of Walt Whitman. The *Lettres du Lieutenant de Vaisseau Dupouey* did not come out until 1922 and *Antoine et Cléopâtre* until 1921. A new edition of *Le Prométhée mal enchaîné* (*Prometheus Ill-Bound*) with thirty drawings by Pierre Bonnard was issued in 1920. *The Pastoral Symphony* was indeed finished in 1918.

It seems to me that I am saying farewell to my whole past. . . .

Cambridge, 2 September

I have been living at Merton House for a fortnight. In all my life I have never been better set up, except of course at Cuverville and at the Villa. Norton, whose guest I am, is absent.

Cuverville, 10 October

Back in harbor for several days now. I don't know whether or not I shall recover the constancy to keep this journal unbroken—as I did before my trip to England? . . .

Some difficulty in getting back to work; the books I have brought back from London interest me more than those I might write. Deplorable, but a passing state. Browning especially, of whom I am just finishing the biography (study by Chesterton[4]) and whom I am tackling everywhere at once. Amazing *Mr. Sludge, the "Medium"*—the short piece *Prospice* particularly touches me, and the wonderful opening of *The Worst of It*. Read likewise some poems from the end.

Laziness in making my thought explicit; tendency to prefer it left in the poetic state—I mean: nebulous. Struggle against this.

Obsessive fear of death and that the ground may suddenly give under my steps. I love life passionately, but I have ceased to have confidence in it. And yet this is necessary.

13 October

It is from the point of view of art that it is most fitting to judge what I write—a point of view the critic never, or almost never, takes. And if, by a miracle, someone takes that point of view, he has the greatest trouble getting his readers to accept it. It is, moreover, the only point of view that does not exclude any of the others.

[4] Some very perspicacious remarks drowned in a flood of dialectic, exasperating need to convict some imaginary adversary of absurdity. A large number of his paragraphs begin thus: "This is a truth little understood in our time," etc. . . . , or "None of the students of Browning seems to have noticed . . ." sentences by means of which he seems to want to give rarity to what are often the most banal of remarks. I cannot endure this bluff. [A.]

19 *October*

Reading and work. I am somewhat worried to see my-self reach so quickly the end of my *Symphonie pastorale;* I mean that I shall have exhausted my subject while the proportions and equilibrium of the book called for a more extended development. . . . But perhaps I am wrong; and, besides, the sudden change of situation could stand some expanding.

Read considerable Browning. Perhaps I shall use as an epigraph for the second part of my Memoirs this stanza from *By the Fire-side:*

> *My own, confirm me! If I tread*
> *This path back, is it not in pride*
> *To think how little I dreamed it led*
> *To an age so blest that, by its side,*
> *Youth seems the waste instead?*[5]

20

I am reading the life of Cardinal Manning in Lytton Strachey's *Eminent Victorians,* and Renan's *Souvenirs.* I can endure neither the flaccidity of his thought nor the amenity of his style. But this book nevertheless seems to me of great importance.

23

Read Browning's *Ivan Ivanovitch* and *Bishop Blougram's Apology.*

26

And while reading Browning (*Saul, Fra Lippo Lippi, Andrea del Sarto,* etc.), I thought: but we have Victor Hugo. Consequently, this morning, I pick up *La Légende des siècles* (Volume II of the little definitive edition)[6] and make a great effort to read *Eviradnus.* Appalled by the gigantic silliness of those sublime lines. Just imagine a foreigner plunged into that! Beyond the technical interest, what remains?—begging Souday's pardon. Beautiful lines, admirable lines (the envelope of the song of *Eviradnus* is extremely beautiful—and even particularly rare in

---

[5] No epigraph is used for either Part I or Part II of *Si le grain ne meurt.* . . .

[6] Hugo's *Legend of the Centuries* is a collection of narrative poems on legendary and historical subjects.

quality), but of a beauty that is almost solely verbal and sonorous. One can imagine nothing more empty, more absurd . . . nor more splendid.[7]

DETACHED PAGES

I

All great works of art are rather difficult of access. The reader who thinks them easy has failed to penetrate to the heart of the work. That mysterious heart has no need of obscurity to defend it against an overbold approach; clarity does this well enough. Very great clarity, as it often happens for the most beautiful works of French art, by Rameau, Molière, or Poussin, is, to defend a work, the most specious girdle; you come to doubt whether there is any secret there; it seems that you touch the depths at once. But ten years later you return to it and enter still more deeply.

It is for the same reasons that the French language at first seems childishly easy to learn, then more and more difficult as you begin to hear it better.

Obviously what shocks me in the case of Romain Rolland is that he has nothing to lose as a result of the war: his book (*Jean-Christophe*) never seems better than when translated. I shall go further: he can only gain by the disaster of France, by the disappearance of the French language, and French art, and French taste, and all of those gifts which he denies and which are denied him.

He is animated by such perfect good faith that at times he almost disarms you. He is an unsophisticated person, but an impassioned unsophisticated person. He early took his frankness for virtue and, since it is somewhat summary, he considered hypocrites those who were less rudimentary than he. I am sure that too often his attitude was permitted by a lack of sentiment and taste, even of compre-

---

[7] The poem *Eviradnus* is a heavy melodramatic narrative of medieval knights. Lines 640–710 contain a song in lyric stanzas together with four stanzas forming a frame for the song and setting the mood.

hension that the mind brings to art, to style, and to that
sort of Atticism that now has no other home but France.
Nothing is more amorphous than his book; it is a Kugelhupf [8] in which you sometimes encounter a good raisin.
No affectation, no artifice; I am well aware that this is
why some like him.

The day that La Rochefoucauld bethought himself of
referring and reducing the impulses of our heart to the
instigations of self-esteem,[9] I doubt whether he so much
revealed an extraordinary perspicacity or simply nipped in
the bud any attempt toward a more indiscreet investiga-
tion. Once the formula had been found, people held to it
and for over two centuries they lived with that explanation. The psychologist seemed most experienced who
showed himself to be most skeptical and who, when faced
with the noblest and most exhausting gestures, was best
able to expose the secret egotistical incentive. Thanks to
which everything contradictory in the human soul escapes
him. And I do not blame him for exposing "amour-
propre"; I blame him often for stopping there; I blame
him for thinking he has done everything when he has
exposed "amour-propre." I blame especially those who
came after him, for having stopped there.

One will find more profit in meditating this remark of
Saint-Évremond (which I deeply regret not finding in the
selection published by the *Mercure* any more than in any
anthology):

"Plutarch judged man too coarsely and did not think
him so different as he is from himself: wicked, virtuous,
equitable, unjust, humane, and cruel; *whatever seems
contradictory to him he attributes to outside causes,*"
etc. . . .

This is a wonderfully educative remark.

No theory is good unless it permits, not rest, but the
greatest work. No theory is good except on condition that
one use it to go on beyond. Darwin's theory, Taine's,
Quinton's, Barrès's. . . . Dostoyevsky's greatness lies in
the fact that he never reduced the world to a theory, that

---

[8] A Kugelhupf is a German cake.
[9] Gide uses La Rochefoucauld's term: amour-propre.

he never let himself be reduced by a theory. Balzac constantly sought a theory of passions; it was great luck for him that he never found it.

The most important discoveries are most often due only to *taking into consideration* very small phenomena that had been previously noticed only because they threw calculations off slightly, insensibly crippled forecasts, imperceptibly tipped the arm of the scale. I am thinking of the discovery of those new "simple bodies" in chemistry, so hard to isolate. I am thinking especially of the decomposition of elements, of "bodies" that chemistry considered as "simple" until today. I am thinking that in psychology there are no simple feelings and that many discoveries in the heart of man remain to be made.

How much I like what Saint-Évremond says of Plutarch: ". . . I think he could have gone further and penetrated more deeply into human nature. There are recesses and deviations in our soul that escaped him. . . . If he had defined Catiline, he would have presented him to us a miser or a prodigal: that man *alieni appetens, sui profusus,*[10] was beyond his knowledge, and he would never have untangled those contradictions that Sallust separated so well and that Montaigne himself understood much better."

In these lines of Baudelaire:

> *Là, tout n'est qu'ordre et beauté,*
> *Luxe, calme et volupté,*[11]

in which the inattentive reader sees only a cascade of words, I see the perfect definition of the work of art. I take each one of these words separately, next I admire the garland they form and the effect of their conjunction; for no one of them is useless and each of them is exactly in

---

[10] "Avaricious of another man's property, extravagant of his own."
[11] There, all is order and beauty,
Luxury, calm, and voluptuousness.
These lines form the refrain of the famous *Invitation au voyage,* which has been several times set to music.

its place. I should quite willingly take them as titles of the successive chapters of a treatise on æsthetics:

1. *Order* (logic, reasonable disposition of the parts);
2. *Beauty* (line, dash, profile of the work);
3. *Luxury* (disciplined richness);
4. *Calm* (tranquilization of the tumult);
5. *Voluptuousness* (sensuality, adorable charm of matter, attractiveness).

The novelist does not long to see the lion eat grass. He realizes that one and the same God created the wolf and the lamb, then smiled, "seeing that his work was good."

II

IN AN ALBUM . . .

To the memory of Émile Verhaeren
February (1918)

A little country whose vast horizon pushes its frontier to the edge of the sky and whence the soul springs forth with ease; a sky, and often a fog that forces one to seek the sun within oneself, in which the impassioned wind reigns supreme; a black soil, rich in latent ardor, in secret fervor, and in concentrated energy; an excessive toil that keeps the muscles taut and makes man find his greatest beauty in effort; and then nevertheless comfort but without flabbiness; luxury but without complacency; voluptuousness without languor.

And you, great overpopulous cities, crowded harbors, and especially you, well-off, clean little towns, well painted and well drawn, still quiet just yesterday, at peace with men and trusting God—today ground down, painful, having had to pay for imaginary debts, having an immense injustice and a bad quarrel to settle. . . .

I see all this again in your living eyes, Verhaeren, great departed friend, more living today, more vivid by your absence than when we knew you to be among us—I hear a great love singing, and a great indignation, in your more active voice, which knows nothing of death.

You would like to know what to believe in regard to my political opinions. It seemed to you that too often, to the right or the left I took one step forward only to take two backward immediately after, so that nothing was less trustworthy than the declarations I might have made. This is just why I did not make any, knowing full well the indecision of my mind, but nevertheless believing that indecision preferable to inconstancy.

To tell the truth, political questions do not much interest me; I have trouble convincing myself that one regime is preferable in itself; and if I get to the point of wishing France a king, even if he were a despot, this is because everything proves to me, alas, that of all the peoples I know, the Frenchman is the one who most lacks a feeling of the public weal and of that solidarity without which a republic results in the greatest prejudice to all.

Yes, political questions interest me less, and I believe them less important, than social questions; and social questions less important than moral questions. For after all I hold it a fact that the "bad organization," of which people are constantly complaining here, can be most often imputed to the negligence or lack of conscience of the employees, from the most modest to the highest, in the exercise of their functions. It is not so much the system as man himself that must be reformed, and Paul Valéry seems to me on the right track when he protested, the other day, that the most important ministry was that of education.

I am well aware that if the very stuff of the mind is bad, nothing good can be embroidered on it; but it is not proved that the stuff is bad. It seems to me that here, as so often in France, it is not so much the scarcity that is to be deplored as the bad utilization of what we have.

The French nationalist can be recognized by his love for what is Spanish. Happily he can be recognized by a few other signs as well.

The nationalist has a broad hatred and a narrow love.

He cannot stifle a predilection for dead cities. His most violent hatred is directed against the French literary provinces that do not belong to France—I mean Belgium and Switzerland in particular. He regrets that all French Protestants are not Swiss, because he has a mind that likes simplification and he hates Protestants as much as he does the Swiss.

The nationalist is quite willing to believe that Christ was a Catholic.

If you have any love for your country, you will find in yourself more than one idea in common with them, but the nationalist cannot endure having any idea in common with you.

CORYDON

I do not feel any imperious attraction (toward this book). It is undeniable that I am writing it out of season and when I have ceased to have any need to write it. This is what I explained yesterday to Marcel Drouin, fearing that he might see in it some almost unhealthy obsession, an impossibility of getting my mind off this subject. But, on the other hand, the difficulty comes rather from the fact that I must artificially revive a problem to which I have found (as far as I am concerned) a practical solution, so that, to tell the truth, it no longer bothers me.

All my will-power is needed to keep me at this work, in which I seek no advantage. (Likewise for *La Porte étroite*. Only what has ceased to serve is a suitable subject for art.)

What made me undertake it at first, or at least gave me the first rudimentary idea of it, was the disavowal of that false holiness with which my disdain for ordinary temptation clothed me (in the eyes of J., for instance, and which she used to help crush M. by comparison).

You meditate for months; in you an idea becomes flesh; it palpitates, it lives, you caress it; you adopt it intimately; you know its contours, its limits; its deficiencies, its reliefs, its recesses; at once its genealogy and its descendants (?). As soon as you present in public some exposé of this prolonged meditation, immediately a critic rises up to declare in peremptory fashion that you know nothing about it, and he does so in the name of common sense, that is to say of the most general opinion, that is to say the most conventional—to get away from which your entire effort tended.

Had Socrates and Plato not loved young men, what a pity for Greece, what a pity for the whole world!

Had Socrates and Plato not loved young men and aimed to please them, each one of us would be a little less sensible.

If only, instead of getting angry, people tried to find out what is being discussed. Before discussing, one ought always to define. Most quarrels amplify a misunderstanding.

I call a *pederast* the man who, as the word indicates, falls in love with young boys. I call a *sodomite* ("The word is *sodomite*, sir," said Verlaine to the judge who asked him if it were true that he was a *sodomist*) the man whose desire is addressed to mature men.

I call an *invert* the man who, in the comedy of love, assumes the role of a woman and desires to be possessed.

These three types of *homosexuals* are not always clearly distinct; there are possible transferences from one to another; but most often the difference among them is such that they experience a profound disgust for one another, a disgust accompanied by a reprobation that in no way yields to that which you (heterosexuals) fiercely show toward all three.

The pederasts, of whom I am one (why cannot I say this quite simply, without your immediately claiming to see a brag in my confession?), are much rarer, and the sodomites much more numerous, than I first thought. I speak of this on the basis of the confidences I have received, and am willing to believe that in another time and in another country it would not have been the same. As to the inverts, whom I have hardly frequented at all, it has always seemed to me that they alone deserved the reproach of moral or intellectual deformation and were subject to some of the accusations that are commonly addressed to all homosexuals.

I add this, which may seem specious but which I believe altogether exact: that many heterosexuals, either through diffidence or through semi-impotence, behave in relation to the other sex like women and, in an apparently "normal" pair, play the role of true inverts. One is tempted to call them *male Lesbians*. Dare I say that I believe them to be very numerous?

It is the same as with religion. The kindest thing those who have it can do for those who don't is to pity them. "But we are not to be pitied. We are not unhappy."

"All the more unhappy since you don't know that you are. We shall cease to pity you, then. We shall detest you."

We are accepted if we are plaintive; but if we cease to be pitiable we are at once accused of arrogance. No, not at all, I assure you. We are merely what we are; we simply admit what we are, without priding ourselves on it, but without grieving about it either.

That such loves can spring up, that such relationships can be formed, it is not enough for me to say that this is natural; I maintain that it is good; each of the two finds exaltation, protection, a challenge in them; and I wonder whether it is for the youth or the elder man that they are more profitable.

FRANCE AND GERMANY

The nationalist parties, on both sides of the frontier, vie with each other in exaggerating the differences of temperament and mind that, according to them, would make any understanding between Frenchmen and Germans impossible. It is certain that differences do exist; they are known moreover; some writers have detailed them masterfully and I do not have to speak of them here. I believe, however, that they are less fundamental and native than jealously magnified by the family upbringing, the teaching of the schools, and finally the press. During the war I saw the people of our countryside get along very well with the German prisoners employed in agriculture. On the other hand, it is rare that a Frenchman traveling in Germany was not struck and charmed by the graciousness of the people toward him, regardless of the social class to which they belonged. In the domain of culture, just as much in the sciences as in arts and letters, the shortcomings and advantages on both sides are complementary to such a degree that there can only be advantage in an understanding, and prejudice in a conflict.

I cannot, alas! forget that the present problem does not concern simply direct relations among individuals. To be sure, a writer does not have the competence necessary to establish the precise conditions of a political agreement between states, but he has the right and the duty to state to what a degree that understanding seems to him desirable; let me go farther and say: *indispensable* in the present situation of Europe.

There is no more fatal error today, both for nations and for individuals, than to believe that they can get along without one another. Everything that sets the interests of France and Germany in opposition to one another is injurious to both countries at once; beneficial, on the contrary, everything that tends to bring those interests closer together.

It is properly the dispute between the colossal and the individual, as it has been said. Everything French tends to individualize itself; everything German, to dominate or to submit.

Many inanities have been said and written against individualism—by those who did not understand or were unwilling to recognize that the triumph of the individual is in the divine word of the Gospel: "Whosoever shall seek to save his life shall lose it; and whosoever shall lose his life shall preserve it."

1919

19 May

Long explanation-plea with André Ruyters, whom I had the extraordinary luck to find alone. Glad to have finally been able to talk to him, but not altogether satisfied with the manner.

The point of view of almost every one of my friends changes extraordinarily with age; they all have a tendency to blame me for my constancy and the fidelity of my thoughts. It seems to them, naturally, that I was unable to learn anything from life, and because they thought it prudent to age, they consider my *imprudence* madness.

A sentence from Eugène Rouart's letter that I have just received is revelatory: "I am pleased," he says, "that Ghéon, without any close family responsibilities, has been able to recover the tradition of his fathers, and . . . (illegible word) wisely; he had to find his limits," etc. Oh, how sad all this is! What sophisms to hide from oneself one's failure! My God, preserve me from intellectual wrinkles! And above all keep me from not recognizing them as wrinkles!

26 July. On arriving at Dudelange

Not a day passes but what I say to myself: all the same, old man, take care, for tomorrow you might wake up mad, idiotic, or not wake up at all. That marvel which you call your body, that even more astonishing marvel, your mind —just think what a little accident would suffice to put their machine out of order! Already I am full of admiration when, without holding onto the bannister, you go down the stairs; you might stumble, bash your head in, and that would be the end. . . . The idea of death follows my thought as the shadow follows my body; and the greater the joy, the light, the blacker the shadow.

7 August

I have abandoned this notebook for the other one, in which I am noting, inch by inch,[1] each progress of my novel.[2]

---

[1] This expression appears in English.
[2] *Le Journal des Faux-Monnayeurs* (*The Journal of "The Counterfeiters"*). [A.]

1920

Yesterday came home too tired to write anything. I *Tuesday*
had lunched at the Drouins', then attended the first stage
rehearsal of *Antoine et Cléopâtre*. The actors' monotonous
delivery equalizes the text and sandpapers it, so to speak.
It does not seem that any of them is sensitive to the
beauty of words in themselves. It is like the roller that is
pushed over the clods of earth after plowing. I am surrounded by twenty-five men who would be my enemies if
it were *my* play that I had to defend. Yet each one of
them is charming and is obviously doing his best. But I
am once more convinced of the impossibility of making a
play a work of art.

I shall attend all these rehearsals, for my education;
but the gap is too great; they can do what they want
with the play; its staging bores me and I have completely
lost interest in that "realization."

Today went after Drésa, whom I had not found in his
studio yesterday. There is a misunderstanding between
Ida Rubinstein and him as to the costumes; as to hers at
least, for she claims to be delighted with all the others.
It is a question of letting Drésa decide as to the tones of
the gowns that Worth is to design and make. I make some
diplomatic efforts between them, while not giving a damn
about the result.

This morning at the *N.R.F.*, where Trevelyan, with
whom I am lunching, picks me up. Then rehearsal. Then
visit, with Ida, to the business man who is to handle the
dispute. All this takes a dreadful amount of time. I should
most likely have done better to go away on a trip.

While waiting for M., I am rereading Baudelaire's
intimate journals. Incomparable distress of that soul, every
one of whose efforts is a desperate one. Souday, the other
day in *Le Temps*, tried to prove that Baudelaire is only a
"false thinker." Why "false"? Baudelaire is not a "thinker"
at all. Obviously, seen from that point of view, not a line
of these journals that is not lamentably silly. Baudelaire's
value is above all of an emotive nature.

Paris, 3 October

I pick up this notebook again after a very long interruption. Back in Paris for three days now; settled fairly well in the Villa; obliged to go out for my meals, busy from morning until night, I succeed only with great difficulty in saving a few moments of solitude and leisure. Yet never have I felt more fit, and the very evening of my arrival, despite my fatigue (or perhaps because of it), I should have written all night long if I had not forced myself to sleep.

Finished *Crochet Castle* by Peacock and began *The Old Wives' Tale*.[1]

Obtained the six-thousand-franc fellowship for Rivière.[2]

I pick up this notebook without trying to go back to yesterday; I am writing today as if I had written in it the day before.

Tuesday, 4 October

Lunched with Charlie Du Bos. Talked at great length of Henry James and of himself. Spent the late afternoon at the Villa going over with M. the photographs from the museums of Vienna and Berlin. I love that attention, ever greater the more informed it is, with which M. looks at everything, and I already admire the sureness of his taste and judgment. The day before we had been to the Cluny Museum in the morning, and to the Jacquemart-André Museum in the afternoon.

5 October

Lunched at Martin du Gard's with his friend Marcel de Coppet, on his way through Paris and about to return to the Chad region, where he has already spent four years in succession. Handsome face of a bishop with already completely white hair. His calm in contrast to our bustle. Most interesting conversation (which Gallimard joined, after the meal), that I should have noted down that very evening.

The 6th, day of my departure for Cuverville, Roger Martin du Gard comes to the Villa at nine thirty. He brings back *Si le grain ne meurt . . .* of which I had

---

[1] By Arnold Bennett.

[2] Jacques Rivière received in 1920 the General Pershing Fellowship offered by the Fondation Blumenthal (6,000 francs a year) to a French citizen having contributed signally to French thought or art.

taken him a copy two days before. He informs me of his deep disappointment: I have side-stepped my subject; from fear, modesty, anxiety about the public, I have dared to say nothing really intimate and only succeeded in raising questions. . . .

Since I have been here, received from him a long, excellent letter in which he goes over all the points our conversation had touched upon. Yet I feel that I have related of my childhood everything of which I have any recollection and as indiscreetly as possible. It would be artificial to put more shadow, more secret, more deviation into it. Perhaps, however, Jacques Raverat is right when he tells me (he came yesterday from Montivilliers) that often my account, in an effort to be clear, simplifies my acts a bit too much, or at least my motives—and that it is true here as it is of all my books, each one of which taken by itself falsifies my figure. "In order to have a somewhat lifelike portrait of you," he told me very correctly, "one would have to be able to read them all at once. As soon as one knows you well, one understands that all of the states which, out of regard for art, you depict as successive can be simultaneous in you; and this is just what your Memoirs do not make one feel."

Cuverville, 11 October

The children (Odile and Jacques) have left two goldfish here; Em. put them, with a big stone and a bit of moss, in a crystal bowl in the room I am occupying and, while I work, I watch them from the corner of my eye. Yesterday they took a little bread I had broken up for them. This morning old Virginie tells Em.:

"Monsieur is wrong to give them bread. A fish, you know, lives on his excrements; or on human flesh."

28 October

Calm at last; alone in this big Villa, which I should perhaps not be so mad to have had built if only I could live in it.

I let all these last few days be devoured by errands, visits, etc. The necessity of going and getting my meals outside, or at least of going after supplies, left me very little time for work; for it to be good, it is important not to lose sight of it.

Yesterday evening I took out all my youthful "journals."

I cannot reread them without exasperation—and were it not for the salutary *humiliation* I find in reading them, I should tear up everything.

Each progress in the art of writing is bought only by the surrender of a self-satisfaction. At that time I had them all and used to approach the blank page as one does a mirror.

3 November

Invited to lunch by Mme Mühlfeld, with Paul Valéry and Cocteau; I go to join them. I had not exchanged three sentences when I was already exasperated. Whatever subject the conversation drifted to, the minds of Valéry and Cocteau strove to disparage; they vied with each other in lack of comprehension, in denial. Repeated, their remarks would seem absurd. I can no longer put up with that sort of drawing-room paradox which shines only at the expense of others. Péguy used to say: "I am not judging; I am condemning." In this way they executed Régnier, Mme de Noailles, Ibsen. Octave Feuillet was brought up and they agreed in granting him more talent than Ibsen, whom Valéry declared "tiresome." Seeing me reduced to silence —for what would have been the good of protesting?— Cocteau declared that I was in a "dreadful mood." I could not have seemed "in good form" except on condition of joining their chorus, and already I was blaming myself enough for having come to hear them.

Yet each one of them, taken separately, is charming; and for Valéry in particular, if I esteemed him less, I should not suffer so much from his negative attitude. How could it be surprising if, after having disenchanted the world around him, after having strained his wits to lose interest in so many things, he is bored!

23 November

On leaving the Palais de Justice (I find the Law Library closed, where I had been planning to work), I meet Duhamel on the Place Saint-Michel and he walks up the boulevard with me and, through the Luxembourg, as far as the Lion de Belfort (I was on my way to lunch at the Allégrets'). Excellent conversation about the novel. Like me, he is struggling against Martin du Gard's criticisms. He protests that I was not wrong to write *first* those monographs which Martin du Gard regrets not seeing fused together and confused in one thick cluster; and that those little purified tales that Martin du Gard criticizes have more hope of enduring than the complex novel that I now long to write.

When one tries to set down the substance of a conversation (as I am doing here), nothing remains; the very words themselves are needed—just as the resurrection of the flesh is needed to permit that of the spirit.

22 December

Spent two days at Clermont, at Roger Martin du Gard's, for he calls me in consultation for his novel, of which he reads me the first six chapters and outlines the general plan.[3] Uninterrupted conversation, which I believe to have been most profitable to both of us. He greatly encourages me to continue writing my Memoirs and to dare to write of my life everything that I relate to him.

But it is especially toward the novel that I now turn. I open the brown notebook and want to get in the harvest of these last few days.[4]

I enjoy keeping this journal up to date only when I have hope of writing in it almost every day, even if only a few lines.

Time flies and each day escapes me without my succeeding in embracing anything. I envy Martin du Gard and his calm solitude at Clermont.

End of December

Miquette's death.[5] Long blind, deaf, frightfully swollen, she seemed to remain attached to life only through fidelity to her mistress.

[3] The novel in question is *Les Thibault* (*The World of the Thibaults*), of which the first part was to appear in 1922.
[4] The brown notebook must be *Le Journal des Faux-Monnayeurs* (*The Journal of "The Counterfeiters"*).
[5] Miquette was a dog belonging to the Gides.

1921

Arrived last night at Cuverville. All the way down I read *The Breaking-Point* by Artsybashev; strongly recommended by Roger M. du G., but I do not like it much. As for raw material, it is better to seek it in life; in books it is craft that interests me especially—and in this one, no more of one than of the other. Shall I go on?

I played myself the trick of not bringing any cigarettes (in Paris I was getting to smoke much too much), but this morning I am maddened.

In a tremendous effort of virtue, I force myself this morning to do the gymnastic exercises recommended by Roger M. du G.; plus, this afternoon, an hour's walk, to the detriment of the piano.

I have ahead of me the preface to *Armance*,[1] the intermediary chapter of *Si le grain ne meurt . . .* , and that enormous novel that I must begin to block out.

Before my departure, went to see *Parade*[2]—of which I don't know what to admire the more: pretense or poverty. Cocteau is walking up and down in the wings, where I go to see him; aged, contracted, painful. He knows that the sets and costumes are by Picasso, that the music is by Satie, but he wonders if Picasso and Satie are not by him.

The *Contes russes* delighted me.

12 January

When the path your mind begins to follow saddens unto death creatures who are infinitely dear to you, you can, at one and the same time, believe that that is the

---

[1] Gide wrote a highly original preface for Stendhal's novel, *Armance*, which appeared in the edition of Stendhal's works published by Librairie Champion, after having appeared in the *Nouvelle Revue Française* for August 1921.

[2] A satirical ballet (book by Jean Cocteau, music by Erik Satie, scenery and costumes by Pablo Picasso, choreography by Leonide Massine), *Parade* was first presented by the Diaghilev company in Paris on 18 May 1917. Together with it, a ballet named *Contes russes* (Russian Tales; music by Anatoly Liadov, scenery and costumes by M. Larionov, choreography by Massine), made up of Russian folk tales, was given.

path you must follow and yet advance in it tremblingly; remain with a divided heart; know hesitations and backings—in which Ghéon would see the mark of an irresolute mind, though it is only a matter of heart and sympathy. It is not constancy that I lack; it is ferocity.

14 January

There is taking place in my inner being what happens with "little countries": each nationality claims its right to existence and revolts against oppression. The only classicism admissible is the one that takes everything into account. Maurras's classicism is hateful because it oppresses and suppresses, and I am not sure that what he oppresses is not worth more than the oppressor. Today it is time to hear what has not yet spoken.

I like this praise, in C. Du Bos's article on me: "infinitely respectful of the sensitivity of others."

Paris, 4 May

One might say that there are two kinds of attention: one intense, and the other half listless and discursive; it is the latter that one is most inclined to lend; I really believe that most people are capable of the former kind only in case of danger and when it can serve as a warning. But, not having any gift whatsoever at telling stories, when I begin to tell a story aloud I am always afraid that it will be too long and that people will not listen to the end; I have often had even this mortifying experience (if, suddenly, I had to cut my story in the middle) of waiting in vain for a voice to say: "And so? . . ."

And perhaps indeed the lack of confidence that results from this, that fear of not being able to retain the reader's attention (even much more than my "impatience," as has been said), is the cause of that contraction or shrinking of the end of my books.—Just a moment more, gentlemen, and I shall have finished.

It is because I do not count on that prolonged attention, the second kind, that I appeal to the first kind, intense attention, infinitely rarer, harder to obtain, and granted more sparingly—but without which one cannot penetrate my writings.

Related elsewhere (in the gray notebook of the novel) the story of that little schoolboy from the Lycée Henri

IV—whom I surprised yesterday in the act of stealing.[3]

14 May

Spent an hour of yesterday evening with Proust. For the last four days he has been sending an auto after me every evening, but each time it missed me. . . . Yesterday, as I had just happened to tell him that I did not expect to be free, he was getting ready to go out, having made an appointment outside. He says that he has not been out of bed for a long time. Although it is stifling in the room in which he receives me, he is shivering; he has just left another, much hotter room in which he was covered with perspiration; he complains that his life is nothing but a slow agony, and although having begun, as soon as I arrived, to talk of homosexuality, he interrupted himself to ask me if I can enlighten him as to the teaching of the Gospels, for someone or other has told him that I talk particularly well on the subject. He hopes to find in the Gospels some support and relief for his sufferings, which he depicts at length as atrocious. He is fat, or rather puffy; he reminds me somewhat of Jean Lorrain. I am taking him *Corydon,* of which he promises not to speak to anyone; and when I say a word or two about my Memoirs:

"You can tell anything," he exclaims; "but on condition that you never say: *I.*" But that won't suit me.

Far from denying or hiding his homosexuality, he exhibits it, and I could almost say boasts of it. He claims never to have loved women save spiritually and never to have known love except with men. His conversation, ceaselessly cut by parenthetical clauses, runs on without continuity. He tells me his conviction that Baudelaire was homosexual: "The way he speaks of Lesbos, and the mere need of speaking of it, would be enough to convince me," and when I protest:

"In any case, if he was homosexual, it was almost without his knowing it; and you don't believe that he ever practiced. . . ."

"What!" he exclaims. "I am sure of the contrary; how can you doubt that he practiced? He, Baudelaire!"

And in the tone of his voice it is implied that by doubt-

[3] This true incident, told in the *Journal des Faux-Monnayeurs,* reappears transposed in the novel of *The Counterfeiters.*

ing I am insulting Baudelaire. But I am willing to believe that he is right; and that homosexuals are even a bit more numerous than I thought at first. In any case I did not think that Proust was so exclusively so.

Just from having heard, at Darius Milhaud's, Mlle X. dash off with extraordinary assurance and charm, to perfection, a number of compositions by Chabrier and Debussy (particularly the *Études*) and (very poorly these) by Chopin—I remained discouraged, not daring to open my piano for twelve days. Small wonder after that that I don't like pianists! All the pleasure they give me is nothing compared to the pleasure I give myself when I play; but when I hear them I become ashamed of my playing —and certainly quite wrongly. But it is just the same when I read Proust; I hate virtuosity, but it always impresses me, and in order to scorn it I should first like to be capable of it; I should like to be sure of not being the fox of the fable. I *know* and *feel* for instance that Chopin's *Barcarolle* is to be played much more slowly than Mlle X. does, than they all do—but in order to dare to play it in the presence of others as *leisurely* as I like it, I should have to know that I could just as well play it much more rapidly and especially feel that whoever hears me is convinced of this. Played at that speed, Chopin's music becomes *brilliant,* loses its own value, its virtue. . . .

Wednesday

Last night I was about to go up to bed when the bell rang. It was Proust's chauffeur, Céleste's husband, bringing back the copy of *Corydon* that I lent to Proust on 13 May and offering to take me back with him, for Proust is somewhat better and sends a message that he can receive me if it is not inconvenient for me to come. His sentence is much longer and more complicated than I am quoting it; I imagine he learned it on the way, for when I interrupted him at first, he began it all over again and recited it in one breath. Céleste, likewise, when she opened the door to me the other evening, after having expressed Proust's regret at not being able to receive me, added: "Monsieur begs Monsieur Gide to have no doubt that he is thinking constantly of him." (I noted the sentence right away.)

For a long time I wondered if Proust did not take advantage somewhat of his illness to protect his work (and this seemed quite legitimate to me); but yesterday, and already the other day, I could see that he is really seriously ill. He says he spends hours on end without being able even to move his head; he stays in bed all day long, and for days on end. At moments he rubs the side of his nose with the edge of a hand that seems dead, with its fingers oddly stiff and separated, and nothing could be more impressive than this finicky, awkward gesture, which seems the gesture of an animal or a madman.

We scarcely talked, this evening again, of anything but homosexuality. He says he blames himself for that "indecision" which made him, in order to fill out the heterosexual part of his book, transpose "*à l'ombre des jeunes filles*" [4] all the attractive, affectionate, and charming elements contained in his homosexual recollections, so that for *Sodome* [5] he is left nothing but the grotesque and the abject. But he shows himself to be very much concerned when I tell him that he seems to have wanted to stigmatize homosexuality; he protests; and eventually I understand that what we consider vile, an object of laughter or disgust, does not seem so repulsive to him.

When I ask him if he will ever present that Eros in a young and beautiful guise, he replies that, to begin with, what attracts him is almost never beauty and that he considers it to have very little to do with desire—and that, as for youth, this was what he could most easily transpose (what lent itself best to a transposition).

3 June

Good piano-practice the last few days. Have been able to devote three hours to it daily. Went back to Chopin's *Barcarolle*, which it is not so hard as I thought to play more rapidly; I manage to do so (I let myself be intimidated much too easily by others' *brio*)—but when I do, it loses all character, all emotion, all *languor;* and that is above all what this wonderful piece expresses: languor in

[4] A *l'ombre des jeunes filles en fleurs* ("In the shadow of blossoming girls") is the original title of the second part of Proust's long work, which Scott Moncrieff freely translated as *Within a Budding Grove.*

[5] *Sodome et Gomorrhe* (*Cities of the Plain*) forms a fraction of Part IV and all of Part V of Proust's work.

excessive joy. It seems that there is too much sound, too many notes as soon as one ceases to understand the complete meaning of each one. Any good execution must be an *explanation* of the piece. But the pianist, like the actor, strives for the *effect;* and the effect is generally achieved at the expense of the text. The player is well aware that I shall be more impressed the less I understand. But that is just what I want—to understand. Being impressed, in art, is worth nothing unless it yields at once to emotion; and most often it stands in the way of emotion.

8 June

How much I like this that I read in Sainte-Beuve (*Les Cahiers*):[6] "The Latins, in their language, did not dislike a certain vagueness, a certain lack of determination of the meaning, a touch of obscurity. . . . Take it as you will, they seem frequently to say: understand it in this sense, or in this other sense which is close to it.—You have a certain latitude of choice.—*The principal sense is not absolutely exclusive of another.*" (I am underlining.) Delight in feeling myself to be very Latin, in this regard.

20 July

Struggle against that impulse to pour personal experiences into the novel, and particularly those which have made one suffer, in the fallacious hope of finding some consolation in the treatment one gives them.

"They appear particularly interesting to us only because they happen to us."

"No, no; on the contrary, that is the sophism: everyone has the adventures he deserves; and for choice souls there are privileged situations, special sufferings, of which vulgar souls are simply incapable."

21 July

I should long ago have ceased to write if I were not inhabited by the conviction that those to come will discover in my writings what those of today refuse to see there, and which nevertheless I know that I put there.

30 September

I am rereading the book of *Maximes* with the greatest admiration.[7] It seems to me that the position I tried to take with regard to La Rochefoucauld could not be main-

---

[6] *The Notebooks*, a posthumous publication.

[7] The famous collection of La Rochefoucauld's *Maxims*.

tained without injustice. My first mistake was to try to assimilate what he calls "amour-propre" to egotism. Despite everything, the maxims having to do with self-esteem are of less interest than those that are not linked to any theory, to any thesis, and some of which are singularly penetrating and *turned* in a way that can be imitated but which belongs only to him; or at least if it can be found in the drawing-rooms of the classical period, *he* carries it to perfection.

3 October

Back to Cuverville.

Spent three to four hours relearning pieces 1 and 4 of the *Goyescas* (and I am far from completely possessing the first). I ought now to tackle *Les Faux-Monnayeurs;* but through timidity, through indolence, through cowardice, I welcome every distraction that offers itself and do not know how to embrace my subject. I advise myself to walk back and forth in my room for an hour, forbidding myself any reading whatever. And repeat this like a novena, preferably before going to bed. Without letting oneself be discouraged if one sees no results the first few evenings.

I write, almost without any difficulty, two pages of the dialogue with which I hope to open my novel. But I shall not be satisfied unless I succeed in getting still farther from realism. It matters little, moreover, if, later on, I am to tear up everything I write today. The important thing is to get accustomed to living with my characters.

1 November

Arrived yesterday evening at Roquebrune. . . . As the moment of leaving her approached, I felt more painfully everything that attached me to her and I came to wonder if reason really counseled this departure. How hard I find it not to prefer the austere, or at least not to believe in its superiority! Instinctive distrust for everything that pleasure adorns.

26 November

Returned to Cuverville the evening of the 24th. It seems to me now that I dreamed this trip . . . Pisa, Siena, Orvieto, Rome; perfect weather, if it had not been taken from work. Immediately I plunge into it again, cursing that lecture on Dostoyevsky for which Copeau, on my way through Paris, extracted the promise.

Yesterday evening reread Browning's *Ivan Ivanovitch* and considerable Coleridge. I am waiting until I have brought my correspondence up to date before getting back to the piano.

29 November

Big article by Massis in *La Revue universelle* on (or rather: against) me. Massis sets up against my books a remark of Claudel: "Evil does not compose." As if it were by lack of composition that my books sinned!

All together, the article, although denouncing my influence as a public danger, is full of unconfessed admiration. What rather irritates me is seeing Massis ascribe to me not only sentences by me but also sentences written by others about me. Even then the quotations he makes are not always exact, and the reader is never warned when it is merely a character from one of my novels speaking; I must take responsibility for everything indifferently; everything that can harm me. He does not try to sketch a lifelike portrait, but simply to prejudice his readers against me.

This article, prepared in advance, appears the very day that the volume goes on sale;[8] as already, some time ago, when he demolished *Les Caves*. When shall I ever see such haste in praise? But for Massis it was a matter of sounding the keynote for the critics.

For the last four months that I have resubscribed to the *Courrier de la Presse*,[9] I have received nothing but violent attacks. It is enough to make one think that I am paying for them. A Spanish critic, obviously well informed, goes so far as to speak of my hardness of heart and my avarice. The article is, besides, rather funny; but what a caricature it draws of me! Will it be possible, later on, to make out my real features under such a heap of calumnies? Three quarters of the critics, and almost all those of the newspapers, form their opinion, not according to my books themselves, but according to café conversations. I know

[8] A little volume of *Morceaux choisis* (*Selections from André Gide*), containing a few unpublished fragments, was brought out by Librairie Gallimard in 1921.

[9] A clipping-service.

moreover that I have on my side neither the cafés, nor the drawing-rooms, nor the boulevards; and these are what make successes. Consequently it is not that kind of favor which I seek, nor which I have ever desired. I shall let my books patiently choose their readers; the small number of today will form the opinion of tomorrow.

I do not want to pretend to be stronger or more self-assured than I am, and some of these misjudgments are extremely painful to me; but finding in my *Morceaux choisis*, as I reread them, a sentence that does not satisfy me would affect me much more. I have difficulty in not yielding to that tendency of mine to agree with criticisms; but I am often reassured by the fact that the accusations made against me contradict one another. Then too, I think of Baudelaire and that most of these accusations are the very ones that were likewise directed against him.

Only today have I returned to the piano. I am rereading *The Idiot* and have again plunged with intoxication into *The Ring and the Book*, which I understand much more easily.[10] There is nothing headier than Browning, not even Dostoyevsky. Yet perhaps I should get less excited if I knew his language perfectly. The slight fog that occasionally floats between the lines lends them imaginary depths.

2 December

I have read Proust's latest pages (December issue of the *N.R.F.*) with, at first, a shock of indignation. Knowing what he thinks, what he is, it is hard for me to see in them anything but a pretense, a desire to protect himself, a camouflage of the cleverest sort, for it can be to no one's advantage to denounce him. Even more: that offense to truth will probably please everybody: heterosexuals, whose prejudices it justifies and whose repugnances it flatters; and the others, who will take advantage of the alibi and their lack of resemblance to those he portrays. In short, considering the public's cowardice, I do not know any writing that is more capable than Proust's *Sodome et Gomorrhe* of confirming the error of public opinion.

[10] *The Idiot* is the novel by Dostoyevsky; *The Ring and the Book* is a long narrative poem by Browning.

7 December

Every evening I plunge again, for a half-hour, into the *Kunst der Fugue*. Nothing I said of it the other day strikes me as quite exact now. No, one does not often feel in it either serenity or beauty, but rather an intellectual torment and an effort of the will to bend forms as rigid as laws and inhumanly inflexible. It is the triumph of the mind over figures; and, before the triumph, the struggle. And while submitting to restraint—through it, in spite of it, or *thanks to it*—all the play of emotion, of tenderness, and, after all, of harmony that can still remain.

10 December

This stagnation poisons me. I stifle in calm waters. Like the trout, I enjoy swimming upstream.

11 December

Several articles about my *Morceaux choisis,* or rather about Massis's article. Much more is said about that article than about my book itself. And the little that is said of it is moreover so stupid that I am reassured to see it directed against me.

15 December

"M. Gide does not even represent a literary school, not even the review in which he writes. His work is the most flagrantly unpunished intellectual and moral scandal of the century," I read in *La Revue française* that the Argus clipping-service sends me this morning. It is signed René Johannet.

This is the two hundred and eighth clipping (I paid the bill six weeks ago). In addition to advertisements, I receive nothing but savage attacks.

Paris, Lutétia, 16 December

Yesterday, Thursday, began my day calmly in this sixth-floor room where I am really comfortable. Wrote to Em. and to the good little René Michelet, from whom I had finally just received a letter. Then went to the *N.R.F.* to talk with Prunières, Allard, Gallimard, and Jean Schlumberger. The atmosphere is now very pleasant there and the disorder has ended, almost. Lunched at the Allégrets'. I had hoped to take M. with me, but we didn't lunch until one o'clock and furthermore it was the little girl's birthday. Exasperating waste of time. Before lunch I had managed to have a rather long conversation with André about his engagement; it seems to me that he is making a mistake and I tried to open his eyes. Nothing is more dangerous than the role I played in this case . . . and without any result, besides.

Went to pay a bill at Foinet's, the picture-framer's. Excellent call on Paul Laurens. Then rue Vaneau, to the hospital where Nicole has just had her appendix removed. Valentine was with her. Nicole glowing with grace and beauty.

Back to the hotel, where Mme Mayrisch and M. are to meet me. Wrote to Alibert while waiting for them. Took tea with them; then all three set out on errands. I return alone to the Lutétia; dined in my room on the slice of pâté and hard-boiled eggs that Em. had put into my bag. Then at eight o'clock to Roger Martin du Gard's, where I stay until one in the morning, reading him the beginning of my novel, commenting on it and criticizing it, and talking to him of Browning.

Why should I note all this? . . . As a specimen of the way I spend a day in Paris; and to teach me to waste less time today.

26 December

The effort toward a new state of affairs always seems anarchy at first in the eyes of the conservative. What could be more revolutionary than the Gospel?

It has been said that I am chasing after my youth. This is true. And not only after my own. Even more than beauty, youth attracts me, and with an irresistible appeal. I believe the truth lies in youth; I believe it is always right against us. I believe that, far from trying to teach it, it is in youth that we, the elders, must seek our lessons. And I am well aware that youth is capable of errors; I know that our role is to forewarn youth as best we can; but I believe that often, when trying to protect youth, we impede it. I believe that each new generation arrives bearing a message that it must deliver; our role is to help that delivery. I believe that what is called "experience" is often but an unavowed fatigue, resignation, blighted hope. I believe to be true, tragically true, this remark of Alfred de Vigny, often quoted, which seems simple only to those who quote it without understanding it: "A fine life is a thought conceived in youth and realized in maturity." It matters little to me, besides, that Vigny himself perhaps did not see all the meaning I put into it; I make that remark mine.

There are very few of my contemporaries who have remained faithful to their youth. They have almost all compromised. That is what they call "learning from life." They have denied the truth that was in them. The borrowed truths are the ones to which one clings most tenaciously, and all the more so since they remain foreign to our intimate self. It takes much more precaution to deliver one's own message, much more boldness and prudence, than to sign up with and add one's voice to an already existing party. Whence that accusation of indecision and uncertainty that some hurl at me, precisely because I believed that it is above all to oneself that it is important to remain faithful.

DETACHED PAGES

CONVERSATION WITH RATHENAU

X. claims that the Germans' lack of tact is a French invention. So I show him the letter I receive from Franz Blei, with whom I had rather good literary relations before the war (it is the first letter to have come to me from Germany since the war): "Why don't you come to Munich?" he asks. "You would be received with open arms and would certainly experience, on getting away from France for a moment, the same relief that we Germans feel when, in Switzerland for example, we escape the terrible oppression weighing on our country. . . ." What can I reply to that? Nothing, of course. I did not reply.

On the other hand, after having read M. Raphaël's book,[11] I felt a desire to talk with Rathenau, whom I did not yet know, and, taking advantage of a stay with my friends the Mayrisches, in Luxemburg, had them write

[11] *Walter Rathenau, ses projets et ses idées d'organisation économique* (*Walter Rathenau: His Plans and Ideas for Economic Organization*), by Gaston Raphaël, appeared in 1919.

him and suggest his coming to meet me at their house. This was in 1920, when Rathenau no longer occupied any governmental position and had for a time withdrawn from politics.

The two full days I spent at Colpach with Rathenau left me a clear enough memory so that, a year later, I can note down fragments of his conversation as readily as I could have done at the time.

I was somewhat embarrassed at first by the extreme affability of that enormous man, who immediately took me by the arm and led me along the paths of the estate. He revealed great emotion. "It is the first time since the war," he told me, "that I have left Germany—at least for pleasure, for anything other than business—the first time, it seems to me, that I can breathe freely." He expressed himself in French with hardly a mistake and, it can really be said, with no accent whatever.

"I attach to our meeting," he went on, "the greatest importance and consider it as significant as all the political arrangements between our two countries." I found no reply available at first and tried to put into my silence the distance he did not allow me to respect materially. I had thought that we should converse seriously without ceasing to feel between us the frightful gap the war had just left. But at the very first instant, as I say, he had seized my arm, my body, with as much cordiality and warmth as an old friend would have shown upon meeting me after a long voyage.

In spite of myself I thought, before the mysticism of some of his remarks, of what Groethuysen used to say to us at Charles Du Bos's. In the book he was writing before the war on the German character, he was trying to show that the German—composed of two extremes: a soul and an automaton—almost never succeeds in filling up the intermediate space, in being commonly and simply *human*. *From "Parsifal" to the Goose-Step* was to be the title of the study. It was Parsifal speaking now.

I remember particularly what he said to me of America, which, he claimed, "has no soul," has not deserved to have one, for she has not yet "deigned *to plunge into the abyss of suffering and sin.*"

That same day he outlined to me at length the financial

state of Germany, whose wealth, he said, was not mone-
tary but entirely in her productive power and in the hard-
working qualities of her people, so that she would not
begin to get back on her feet, he was sure of it, until the
value of the mark should be reduced to zero, thus forcing
her to begin anew, on a real rather than a conventional
basis.

Some of his theories, and the very ones with which I
was most inclined to agree, seemed to me so contrary to
the spirit of the Jewish race that I could not resist showing my amazement. He did not reply directly, but, approaching the question from the reverse and by a long
detour: "Have you noticed," he asked, "that when certain
qualities are too profusely" (this is not the word he used)
"distributed among a people, in a race, that people, that
race, does not succeed in producing an individual in
whom those qualities are very particularly concentrated.
In Italy, for instance, if there is no great musician, it is
because everybody is a musician. Germany, on the other
hand, in the time of Bach, was not at all generally musical.
And that is what permitted Bach—" And suddenly he
stopped, leaving me to conclude. Certainly he wanted to
imply that certain qualities were no less specifically
Jewish just because they were not distributed among all
the representatives of his race; and that those qualities
just happened to be the ones that I was wrongly surprised
to find in him.

The reasons that make those stars wane are perhaps
the very ones that linked them, according to Bourget, to
the generation preceding mine.[12] For the moral dispositions of one generation are not at all the same as those
of the following generation. Bourget extolled them as
apostles of pessimism. And it is toward the constellation
of the Lion that we feel impelled today. Nothing can be
done about this: what we seek in our masters is not discouragement. If Stendhal and Baudelaire still hold a very

[12] In the two volumes of his *Essais de psychologie contemporaine*
(*Studies in Contemporary Psychology*), which appeared in 1883 and
1885, Paul Bourget examined the literary idols of the youth of that
day: Baudelaire, Renan, Flaubert, Taine, Stendhal, A. Dumas *fils*,
Leconte de Lisle, E. and J. de Goncourt, Turgenyev, and H.-F. Amiel.

high place in our firmament today, this is because the
rays emanating from their work have still other virtues
from those Bourget recognized in them. To tell the truth,
it is because, of the whole pleiad cited in the *Essais de
psychologie contemporaine,* they alone are perfect artists,
and only perfect art is proof against aging.

✳

I am rereading Volume III of Flaubert's *Correspondance* and, whether it be latent or loudly stated, the blasphemy against life, that permanent blasphemy on the part
of a writer I love, causes me great pain. I feel the *duty*
to be happy, higher and more imperious than the factitious duties of the artist. I pray, I cry from the depths
of my soul's distress: My God, give me the faculty to be
happy—not with that tragic and fierce happiness of
Nietzsche, which I nevertheless admire too, but with that
of St. Francis, with that adorable, beaming happiness.

✳

Take care not to confuse art and manner. The manner
of the Goncourts, which made them seem so "artistic" in
their time, is the cause of their ruin today. They had
delicate senses; but an insufficient intelligence made them
go into ecstasies over the delicacy of their sensations and
give importance to what should be subordinated. It is
impossible to read a page by them where that good opinion they have of themselves does not burst out from
between the lines; they yield infallibly to that self-satisfaction which makes them think: "Ah, what artists we are!
Ah, how crude other writers are!" Manner is always the
indication, and it soon becomes the penalty, of a self-
satisfaction. The most subtle, the strongest and deepest
art—supreme art—is the one that does not at first allow
itself to be recognized. And just as "real eloquence doesn't
give a rap for eloquence," so true art doesn't give a rap
for manner, which is but its caricature.

✳

I hold that the composition of a book is of the first
importance and that it is by a lack of composition that
most works of art sin today. Certain ultra-modern schools

protest against this, but the effort at composition that they reveal was often unable to mask a somewhat artificial resolve. I am going to reveal to you my whole thought on this subject: the best thing is to let the work compose itself and give itself its order, and above all not to *force* it. And I use this word likewise in the sense that horticulturists give it: forced cultivation is a cultivation that makes a plant blossom prematurely.

I believe that the major shortcoming of writers and artists today is impatience: if they knew how to wait, their subject would automatically compose itself slowly in their mind; by itself it would cast off the useless matter and everything that impedes it; it would grow like a tree whose leading branches are developed at the expense of . . .

It would grow *naturally*.

It is through composition that a painter gives depth to his canvas. Without composition a work of art can offer only a superficial beauty.

It is necessary and it suffices. The work of art . . . in which whatever serves no purpose is harmful.

Fear that sort of balancing of the sentence (indulgence toward which I am only too inclined), that fatal number —which has nothing to do with rhythm and the natural expression of the movement of thought.

I have always had more understanding, more memory, and more taste for natural history than for history. The fortuitous has always interested me less than the necessary, and it has always seemed to me that one could learn more from what is repeated every day than from what occurs but once. (External inevitability—intimate inevitability.)

H. C. accused me one day of coquetry in the arrangement of my sentences; nothing could be more false. I like only the strict and bare necessity. When I began to write my *Nourritures*, I realized that the very subject of

my book *was* to banish all metaphor from it. There is
not a movement of my style that does not correspond to
a need of my mind; most often it is but a need of order.
The writer's eloquence must be that of the soul itself, of
the thought; artificial elegance is a burden to me; likewise all added poetry.

The wise Sainte-Beuve denounces, I do not remember
where, that frequent intellectual failing of urging oneself
by preference, and seeking invitations, in the direction in
which one is already most inclined by nature. And this is
what makes me so often deplore the fact that parents
should be given the care of children who already naïvely
resemble them and find in them the example and encour-
agement of their secret dispositions; so that, to tell the
truth, family education rarely straightens them up but
simply helps them to bend in one way or another, and
the sons of set parents are even more set themselves, bent
over to the right or the left and often unable to recover
the vertical position without a revolt that is full of risks.
If I were not a lover of brevity, I should write a whole
book on this subject, but one that would make people
cry shame; for after all, out of some forty families I have
been able to observe, I know hardly four in which the
parents do not act in such a way that nothing would be
more desirable for the child than to escape their influence. Some people are indignant at the alcoholic teaching his son to drink; but they, according to their lights, do
not act differently.

The man subject to afterthoughts buys a vase for the
pleasure of giving it to a friend who desires it. Between
the buying and the giving he has time to reflect; complicated scruples convince him that it is *indelicate* to give
this too expensive vase (ostentation of his wealth, putting
his friend in a false position, etc.). He takes it home.

Meanwhile the friend goes to the shop to buy the vase
and, not finding it there, thinks the other bought it to
keep it from him.

This judgment forms and becomes fixed in his mind.

When the man with the vase comes to give it to him, it is too late; he conflicts with the other's conviction that, if he is giving it away, it is because he has ceased to like the vase and that it has a flaw. He doesn't have to look long for it; it is a defect that completely depreciates the vase in his eyes. The man with the vase swears that he had not seen it. The conversation becomes bitter—and the vase is broken at the same time as their friendship.

And the worst of it is that the man with the vase becomes what the other claims him to be, makes him be. Useless to insist thereon.

I call "journalism" everything that will be less interesting tomorrow than today. How many great artists win their cases only on appeal!

1922

Yesterday Roger Martin du Gard came to read me the part of *Les Thibault* that I did not yet know. Martin du Gard incarnates in my eyes one of the highest and noblest forms of ambition: that which is accompanied by a constant effort to perfect oneself and to obtain, to demand of oneself, the most possible. I don't know whether I do not admire, even more than the finest gifts, an obstinate patience.

3 January

I planned to devote my morning yesterday and the best part of the day to work; a *pneumatique*[1] from Rathenau, expressing his desire not to leave Paris without having seen me, made me rush to the Crillon, where he was still staying one day more. I wanted neither to take the first step nor to leave his call unanswered. He received me in his private drawing-room and, for an hour, we talked in a rather serious way. It is very hard for me not to be embarrassed by his overcordial manner of seizing hold of one; his hand hardly left my arm once during the whole conversation, of which the refrain was "all Europe is rushing toward the abyss." Haguenin came to interrupt us and I yielded my place to him.

Lunched at Martin du Gard's and, right after lunch, launched into a criticism of his novel, or, more generally, of his manner—which carried us very far. He shows himself to be extraordinarily anxious and desirous of acquiring certain qualities that are quite opposed to his nature: mystery, shadow, strangeness—all things that the artist derives from certain dealings with the Devil. And for more than an hour we talked of the *indirect presentation* of events. I planned to note this all down this morning, but M. came and rang at my door rather early; and, besides, I feel as if doped by a dreadful night. Last evening I had

---

[1] The Paris post offices provide a special-delivery service connecting all the offices by pneumatic tube; letters so sent are called *pneumatiques* or *petits bleus* (because of the small blue form on which they are frequently written).

thought at length of *Les Faux-Monnayeurs;* tremendous effort to vivify my characters and *relate* them among themselves; after which, impossible to find sleep.

Em. writes me: "I am greatly worried by the campaign of vilification opened up against you. Of course it is the force of your thought and its authority that has instigated this. Oh! if only you were invulnerable, I should not tremble. But you are vulnerable, and you know it; and I know it."

Vulnerable . . . I am so, I was so, only through her. Since, it is all the same to me and I have ceased fearing anything. . . . What have I to lose that is still dear to me?

5 January

My good days of work are those I begin by reading an ancient author, one of those that are called "classics." A page is enough; a half-page, if only I read it in the proper state of mind. It is not so much a lesson one must seek in them as the *tone,* and that sort of being out of one's element which sets the present effort in proper proportion, without divesting the moment of any of its urgency. And this is the way I like to end my day too.

This morning I copy out La Bruyère's passage on true and false greatness. (II, 42.)[2]

8 January

Working this morning in front of the triple window of the drawing-room, I observe the strange gardening operation that the birds, warblers as well as sparrows, practice on the sallow-thorn bushes in my little garden. They peck

---

[2] The passage, which Gide does not include in the *Journal,* is:

"False greatness is cold and inaccessible; aware of its weakness, it hides itself or at least does not reveal itself boldly, letting only enough of it be seen as is necessary to impress and to keep from appearing what it really is: simply pettiness. True greatness is free, easy, and familiar, letting itself be touched and handled. It loses nothing from being seen at close range; the more it is known, the more it is admired; through kindness it stoops to the level of inferiors and effortlessly returns to its original position. At times it yields, neglects itself, gives up its advantages, always able to pick them up again and make the most of them. It can laugh, joke, and play, but always without loss of dignity. It is approached with freedom and restraint together; its character is noble and open, inspires respect and confidence, and makes princes appear to us as great and even very great without making us feel that we are small."

at and pinch off the nascent buds from each branch; but the branches, too flexible, provide a perch only at their base, so that the birds can reach with ease only the first buds, the lowest ones, those nearest the trunk. Those on the end of each tigella are consequently preserved; and it is precisely toward those that the sap rushes naturally; so that the shrub opens up and stretches out and widens as much as possible. The terminal buds always develop at the expense of the others, even to the point of completely atrophying them. Yet those sacrificed buds are, or would have been, quite capable of development too, but their possibilities remain latent; were it not for pruning which, protesting against the too great lateral extension of the shrub, drives life back to them; but this can be done only at the sacrifice of the terminal buds.

16 January

Charlie Du Bos sends me *The Marriage of Heaven and Hell,* which I had told him I wanted to read, sure as I was of finding in it a revelation and a confirmation of certain thoughts that have long been stirring within me. My meeting with Blake is of the greatest importance to me. Already I had glimpsed him, during the first year of the war, in a book of *Selections* from Élisabeth Van Rysselberghe's library, rue Laugier, where I was then living with the Théos. Like an astronomer calculating the existence of a star whose rays he does not yet perceive directly, I foresaw Blake, but did not yet suspect that he formed a constellation with Nietzsche, Browning, and Dostoyevsky. The most brilliant star, perhaps, of the group; certainly the strangest and the most distant.

4 February

Every day, and all day long, I ask myself this question —or rather this question asks itself of me: Shall I find it hard to die?

I do not think that death is particularly hard for those who most loved life. On the contrary.

Freud. Freudianism. . . . For the last ten years, or fifteen, I have been indulging in it without knowing it. Many an idea of mine, taken singly and set forth or developed at length in a thick book, would have made a great hit—if only it were the only child of my brain. I cannot supply the initial outlay and the upkeep for each one of them, nor even for any one in particular.

"Here is something that, I fear, will bring grist to your mill," Rivière said to me the other day, speaking of Freud's little book on sexual development. I should say! It is high time to publish *Corydon*.

22 March

Constant dizziness; fatigue. Return of winter; we are shivering. Everything takes on a frightful taste of ashes.

I do not understand very well what they call "my influence." Where do they see it? I don't recognize myself anywhere. It is what differs most from me that I prefer and I have never tried to push anyone save in his own path, in his own joy.

A good teacher is constantly concerned with teaching his disciples to get along without him. But because I say to Nathanaël, at the end of my book: "And now throw this book away; leave me," they get angry.[3]

Sadness is almost never anything but a form of fatigue in my case. But I must confess that there are moments, of late, when I feel mortally sad.

28 March

Gave, last Saturday, my last lecture on Dostoyevsky. In view of my great fatigue, and fearing that I might lack presence of mind, I had written down almost all of it.

I now have ahead of me an article on Valéry I promised for the special number of *Le Divan;* a brief notice on Vannicola, which the mayor of Capri requests for a publication that will make it possible to give poor Vannicola a decent tomb; an important article for the *Revue de Genève* (on the present state of Europe). And finally, this evening, Rivière asks me to do a note on Morand's charming book.[4] All this distracts me dreadfully from my novel. I cannot get back to it, moreover, until after the presentation of *Saül,* of which the rehearsals are soon to

[3] In the Envoi of *Les Nourritures terrestres* (*The Fruits of the Earth*).

[4] Gide's article appeared in *La Revue de Genève* for January 1923 in a symposium on "The Future of Europe" to which Keyserling, Middleton Murry, Pareto, Merezhkovski, and Unamuno also contributed. The book by Paul Morand is probably *Ouvert la nuit* (*Open All Night*), but Gide did not review anything by Morand at this time.

begin.[5] During them I shall scarcely be able to do more, probably, than dictate my lectures to the stenographer I have engaged for the month of April.

I have felt somewhat better for two days. I should like to work only in joy; that joyful activity of the mind which I knew last autumn and which took the place of happiness.

This afternoon heard Honegger's music for *Saül*. I fear that it may stand out too much and that the whole demoniac part may be enlarged out of all proportion.

Finished reading *Othello*, swooning with admiration.

8 May

One completely overcomes only what one assimilates.

It is in order to leave the skim milk for the weak that the healthy stomach takes the cream.

OSSIA:[6] If the vigorous man did not take the cream, the weak man would not have the skim milk.

Eleven o'clock [*Hyères, 11 July*]

I have already been in the water twice today; the second time, naked, followed by a long sun-bath on the sand.

12 July

What I should like to write now is *Les Nouvelles Nourritures*.[7] And I can write it properly only in spite of myself. It must be as unconcerted as anything can be.

This pine grove would be charming, which stretches out along the beach, which is broken up by dunes, and where cistus, lentiscuses, briers, and sallow-thorns form the underbrush. I never meet anyone here, but no god inhabits it either, since the trace of man has so profaned, disenchanted, soiled it. Everywhere old tin cans, rags, eggshells, nameless rubbish, greasy papers, turds, toilet-paper, broken bottles. Everywhere the image of selfishness, of overfamiliarity, and of gluttony.

[5] Gide's drama *Saul*, though published in 1903, was never produced in France until Copeau put it on at the Vieux-Colombier on 16 June 1922 for nine performances.

[6] *Ossia*, the Italian for "or else," a musical term to indicate an easier reading.

[7] *New Fruits of the Earth* did not appear until 1935.

14 July

I finish translating, this morning, the first act of *Hamlet* and give up proceeding further. I have spent three weeks on these few pages, at the rate of four to six hours a day. The result does not satisfy me. The difficulty is never completely overcome, and in order to write good French, one has to get too far away from Shakespeare. (It seems to me that this is peculiar to *Hamlet,* that the text of *Antony and Cleopatra* was much less thorny and allowed one to follow it better. And even though the very subject of *Hamlet* is stranger, richer, more subtle, and touches us more deeply right now, I did not for a moment experience those swoons of rapture that shook me all through the reading of *Othello.*) Marcel Schwob's translation, exact though it be, is obscure, almost incomprehensible in spots, amorphous, arhythmical, and as if unbreathable. Is it really this text that we heard at Sarah Bernhardt's?— without changes, without cuts? How it must have embarrassed the actors! Certain of Shakespeare's sentences are as wily as the devil, full of redundancies . . . I should like an Englishman to explain their beauty to me. Faced with Schwob's sentences, which strive to sacrifice neither a repetition nor a turning, you think: it must be very beautiful in English. But *Hamlet* has long been a sacred text and we admire without questioning.[8]

15 July

I have scarcely known, throughout my "career," anything but flops; and I can even say that the flatness of the flop was in direct ratio to the importance and originality of the work, so that it was to *Paludes, Les Nourritures,* and *Les Caves du Vatican* that I owed the worst ones. Of all my books the one that on the contrary brought me the warmest, most substantial, and promptest praises is the one that (not the least well turned out perhaps) remains the most outside my work, that *interests* me the least (I am using the word in its most subtle sense), and that, all things considered, I should be most willing to see

---

[8] André Gide's translation of the first act of *Hamlet* was published in the Paris bilingual review *Échanges* in December 1929. His entire translation of the tragedy, completed many years later, was first published in New York in 1945 by Pantheon Books.

disappear. After this, how could I be surprised that *Saül* should have been so coldly received by the critics? They saw nothing but declamation in it, as they saw nothing but words in my *Nourritures*. Are you then unable to recognize a sob unless it has the same sound as yours?

La Bastide, Saturday, 22 July

It seems to me that each of my books was not so much the product of a new state of mind as its cause, on the contrary, and the original provocation of that mental and spiritual disposition in which I had to keep myself in order properly to elaborate the book. I should like to express this more simply: that the book, as soon as it is conceived, disposes of me wholly, and that, for its sake, everything in me to my very depths tunes up. I no longer have any other personality than the one that is suitable to that work—objective; subjective? These words lose all meaning here; for if it happens that I use myself as a model (and sometimes it seems to me that there can be no other exact way of painting), this is because I first began by becoming the very one I wanted to portray.

I am rereading aloud with Mme Théo and Elisabeth Van Rysselberghe the seventh book of *The Ring and the Book* (Pompilia). Abnegation can go no further.

4 August

It is not a fear of being wrong, it is a need of sympathy that makes me seek with passionate anxiety the stimulus or the recall of my own thought in others; that made me, in my article on Germany, support my opinion by quotations from Thibaudet and Curtius; that, finally, made me translate Blake and present my own ethic under cover of Dostoyevsky's. If those in whom I recognize my thought had not been there, I doubt whether it would have been much hampered—but its expression would perhaps have been different. It is useless to go back over what has been well said by others.—Nothing is so absurd as that accusation of *influence* (in which certain critics excel every time they note a resemblance).—How many things, on the contrary, I *have not said* because I later discovered them in others! Nietzsche's influence on me? . . . I was already writing *L'Immoraliste* when I discovered him. Who could say how much he got in my way . . . ? how my book was shorn of all I disliked to *repeat*.

Brussels, 5 September

Read at Colpach a number of the short studies by Lytton Strachey collected in his latest volume.[9] The one on Racine, remarkable on the part of an Englishman, does not satisfy me however. He does not clearly establish Racine's starting-point and, admiring him very much, does not perhaps admire him just as one should. Seen through him, Racine appears, despite him, gray, timid, cramped. The quotations he makes could be better chosen, more typical. If one does not bring out Racine's perfection, the smallness of his orchestra, just like Mozart's, might seem poverty.

I prefer Lytton when he speaks of Shakespeare's last plays. Everything he says here is penetrating and persuasive. He also speaks excellently of Beddoes and of Blake. . . .

Reread Mérimée's *La Chambre bleue* and *Il Viccolo di Madama Lucrezia* with interest but without admiration.[10] Each problem of style and presentation is solved in the most elegant fashion, but the elements he plans to put into his tale and into his sentences are always of the same nature and cohabit too easily. One exhausts all the mystery at once, and the first astonishment awakens no secret echo in us.

But with what admiration I read aloud with Élisabeth Defoe's *Colonel Jack!* It is as beautiful as life itself; the art that presents and covers life could not be more discreet or more transparent.

[Cuverville] 10 October

It is necessarily easier to work, as Ghéon does, for a public that is already formed and to provide it exactly the product it demands than to anticipate the demand of a still unformed public.

Rivière's novel (*Aimée*), which I am reading in proof, exhausts me, flabbergasts me. I understand now why he likes Marivaux so much.

As I finish that reading, I am almost on the point of making a resolution never again to write in the imperfect.

[9] *Books and Characters.*
[10] *The Blue Room* and *Madame Lucrezia's Alleyway* are two short stories.

11 October

Em. reminds me of this remark of Rivière ("reminds me" is a mere convention, since I had completely forgotten it) which he made to us at Cuverville: "I was born to write very beautiful things, which will bore everyone and which no one will read."

28 October

As a result of the column in *Le Temps* (fiftieth annivary of Gautier's death), I write to Paul Souday:

"I am astonished and somewhat saddened, I confess, to encounter in your column that imputation of 'puritanism' that Eugène Montfort invented some time ago with the obvious intention of discrediting my judgment and doing me harm. Do you really think one must be a puritan not to enjoy Gautier's art, or do you think that in Gautier's art there is nothing shocking save for a puritan?"

Wasted two hours on this—and, naturally, I do not send it.

A straight path never leads anywhere except to the objective.

Back at Cuverville, 26 November

Never take advantage, for any new work, of the impetus from the preceding one.

Likewise, win over for each new work a new public.

30 November

From that moment (when she had burned T.'s letters) she felt released, at the same time, from all her duties toward him.

3 December

Jacques Rivière constantly seeks to caress himself in others. His extraordinary pursuit of affinities and his predilection for what resembles him. His admirations always have an element of flattery and self-indulgence.

7 December

Art is prudence. When you have nothing to say, or to hide, there is no need to be prudent. The timorous are not prudent, but cowardly.

15 December

Three hours at the piano;

An hour of correcting proofs (*Si le grain ne meurt . . .*);

An hour of Shakespeare (*Cymbeline*);

An hour of Sainte-Beuve's *Port-Royal*
—this is my daily menu.

Ordinarily my correspondence takes about two hours more—and I often give six hours to the novel.—A half-hour or an hour's exercise—and, with the wasted time, my too short day is filled.

I do not succeed, despite my ardent desire, in devoting much more to work.

From 16 to 17 December

Visit from Maurois, who reads me what he has done with Shelley.[11] It does not seem to me that he has sufficiently re-created his character, and, besides, it is hard to see what connection with him, Maurois, made him choose this subject. He does not take sides with Shelley and does not seem to confess himself through him, as Pater would have done at once, for example. But it is a very workmanlike job.

For three days now I have had such tense and vibrant nerves that I don't know whether or not I shall be able to keep on much longer—I mean: pursue my work much farther.

"It is a region," said Maurois of the neighborhood of Elbeuf, and quoting the remark of an old peasant, "it is a region in which, if you want to see people at the windows, it is better to shout 'fire' than 'help'!"

21 December

In Christianity, and each time that I plunge into it again, it is always she that I am pursuing. She feels this perhaps; but what she feels above all is that I do so to tear her away from it.

Wednesday

I am leaving for Paris—whence I hope to bring back Martin du Gard on the 4th or 5th. For a week now nothing has worked right. I am a fish of the rapids and stifle in these too calm waters.

Stopped at the Terminus. With M. and his mistress, B., spent one of the dullest evenings, at the Casino de Paris, where everything seemed to me frightful. Silliness, vulgarity, bad taste, idiotic and hideous display of costumes.

[11] This is Maurois's *Ariel*.

[*29 December ?*]

Yesterday, Thursday, at the Vieux-Colombier with the Martin du Gards. The new play by Vildrac, *Michel Auclair*, was being played. The first act seemed to me rather bad; but the second, almost excellent in spots. The third reflects excessively the indigent philosophy of the school.

30 December

Almost empty day. At ten o'clock Sichel, whom I had met two days before at Martin du Gard's, came to read me (in my room at the Lutétia) his article on *Paludes*, which he declares to be the book of mine he prefers. Lunched at the Allégrets'; Élie, suffering from paludism and an excess of fatigue, received me for a moment at his bedside. He is taking advantage of this rest to read. When I was a child, I admired his faculty of devouring in two hours a book that would have kept me two weeks. But today I am suspicious of people who read quickly. . . . Élie Allégret has just dashed through in this manner *La Chartreuse de Parme*, which he vaguely remembered having already read in his youth.[12] His judgments on the book are childish. He questions me, asking me to explain what sort of influence Stendhal has had. . . . Etc. . . .

Nothing could be more demoralizing than the shoddy waste of hours at the Allégrets', on a holiday. I left rather soon after the meal.

Went back to the hotel to sleep an hour.

Went to see Copeau, whom I find harassed and very low. He complains of the solitude for which he has worked so obstinately. He thrust aside all advice and behaved so that his best friends withdrew from him. "I'll hang on to the end; but don't talk to me." Now he could accept having people talk to him. . . . He feels utterly abandoned. One cannot but abandon a mystic.

Met Paul Valéry at Adrienne Monnier's. Walked back with him at length. He claims to be embarrassed, even exasperated, by the false situation he owes to his success.

"People expect me to represent French poetry. They take me for a poet! But I don't give a damn about poetry. It interests me only by a fluke. It is quite accidental that I wrote poetry. I should be exactly the same if I hadn't

[12] Stendhal's novel, *The Charterhouse of Parma*.

written any. That is to say that, in my own eyes, I should
have the same value. That has no importance to me.
What does matter to me I should like to say. I believe I
might have said it, that I could still say it if I had leisure
and tranquillity . . . but I have ceased to belong to myself. The life I am leading suppresses me."

Dined at the Martin du Gards'—delightful all three of
them. Spent the evening chatting with Roger.

1923

2 January

Dined at the Valérys'. Paul tells me (as I already suspected) that *La Pythie* issued entirely from one line:

Pâle, profondément mordue.[1]

He sought the rhyme, then the rhymes. They dictated the form of the stanza, and the whole poem developed without his knowing at first how it would be nor what he was going to say in it.

He is more and more incapable of listening to others and of taking into consideration what would interrupt his thought. His speech is more and more rapid and indistinct. I often have great trouble understanding him and have to ask him to repeat one out of every four sentences.

He talks again of his *"tædium vitæ,"* which at moments becomes a physical suffering, an unbearable nervous and muscular anguish. What am I saying?—at moments? . . . This is a state in which he finds himself, he says, nine days out of ten. He grants that this anguish had completely left him when traveling, particularly in England. He exclaims:

"Oh, if only I had enough money not to have to bother with writing at all! . . ."

10 January

Francis Jammes sends me his volume *Choix de poèmes.*[2] Some of them, at the beginning, remain exquisite. But the dominating note, alas! is silliness, false naïveté, self-satisfaction. There is nothing prouder than his modesty; whence his refusal to learn anything, his belief in the divinity of his inspiration, his self-indulgence. Infatuation is always accompanied by stupidity.

"Bookish" is a reproach that is often directed at me; I lay myself open to it by my habit of always quoting those

[1] "Pale, and most deeply stung," is the fifth line of *The Pythian Priestess,* one of Valéry's most characteristic poems.
[2] *Selected Poems.*

to whom my thought seems related. People think I took that thought from them; this is false; that thought came to me of itself; but I enjoy, and the more so the bolder the thought is, thinking that it has already inhabited other minds. When, reading them later on, I recognize my thoughts in them, as it happened with Blake, I go crying their name everywhere and publishing my discovery. I am told that I am wrong. I don't care. I take pleasure in quoting and persuade myself, like Montaigne, that only in the eyes of fools do I appear any less personal for it.

Those on the contrary who gather the ideas of others take great care to hide their "sources."—There are examples of this among us.

11 January

I say a few words to Em. of the "drama" that calls me to the side of E.

I have no reason to hope, or even to wish, that Em. should ever be able to consider what she glimpses and imagines of that story otherwise than as a most lamentable catastrophe. And yet I have the greatest difficulty keeping from protesting when she concludes, from the little I dare tell her: "I have always thought it was unfortunate that El. had been raised without religion."

(For it goes without saying that El. is not happy, cannot be happy, has not the right to be happy—and here I cannot rectify without imprudence; but I suffer intolerably from these false ideas that I know to derive from those false premises whereby falsehood finds support in what should on the contrary overcome it.) Thus it is that all the events of life, as the events of the war did likewise, serve only to push each person farther in his own direction, so that nothing is more empty and illusory than what is commonly called "experience."—An experience teaches only the good observer; but far from seeking a lesson in it, everyone looks for an argument in experience, and everyone interprets the conclusion in his own way.

If my head were not so tired, I should write much longer on this subject. And this must be the subject of several pages of *Le Journal d'Édouard*:[3] "Concerning the

[3] Édouard is one of the principal characters of *The Counterfeiters*, and his *Journal* has an important role in the book.

interpretation of events." This exclamation: "A religious upbringing would have kept her from doing that," can be said in a tone of regret, of blame, as well as of approbation, and imply either: "What luck! How fortunate that . . . !" or "What a shame!"

I am reading some of Alain's *Propos* with very great admiration.[4] I prefer him, and even by far, to Maurras and do not see where Maurras could be said to be superior to him—unless in his deafness. Maurras is a deaf man, as England is an island; whence his strength.

Si le grain ne meurt . . . Supplement:

I used to provide my aquarium with diving-beetles, with boat-flies, with dragonfly larvæ, and became passionately interested in observing their combats at length. But what charmed me even more was the unknown race that awakened and crawled teeming in the clump of mud surrounding the roots of the water plants I used to tear up from a pond and bring back dripping in the bottom of my botanizer's box.

Sunday, 14 January

Leaving for Roquebrune, for Genoa, for the unknown. —I never leave Cuverville without a sort of heartbreak.

Paris, 16 January

Went yesterday to the Vieux-Colombier, where Dullin's company was giving *Antigone*, or "Sophocles's lady," by Cocteau.[5] Suffered unbearably from the ultra-modern sauce in which was served up that wonderful play, which remains beautiful more in spite of Cocteau than because of him. One can understand moreover what tempted him here, and he has cooked it up with consummate cleverness; but those who applaud him are those who to begin with considered Sophocles as a great bore and who have never drunk of "the true, the blushful Hippocrene."[6]

Cocteau's play is not at all *blushful*. It reflects the same

---

[4] The philosopher Émile Chartier always wrote in the form of informal, brief *propos* (remarks) on literature and philosophy, war, society, religion, art, etc. For many years he had a few such pages in nearly every issue of the *Nouvelle Revue Française*.

[5] With Louis Jouvet, the actor Charles Dullin was one of Copeau's chief associates in his new theater. In 1921 Dullin founded his own group, known as *L'Atelier*.

[6] The quotation from Keats appears in English.

feeling that made Stravinsky say he would gladly collaborate on *Antony and Cleopatra*, but only if Antony were given the uniform of an Italian *"Bersagliere."*

Patina is the reward of masterpieces.

23 February

Leaving Rapallo for Annecy.

The day before my departure I had a wonderful climb into the mountains.

A week at Annecy with E. Charming little Savoie hotel, of which, given the season, we are the only guests. Read aloud Shakespeare's *Merry Wives* and *The Vicar of Wakefield*, which delights us. I finish at Annecy Keats's wonderful *Endymion*, which I did not yet know and which kept me intoxicated for days on end.

The exactingness of my ear, until the last few years, was such that I should have warped the meaning of a sentence for its rhythm.

Back in Paris 21 April, at Cuverville the evening of the 26th.

Violent attack (in *Les Nouvelles littéraires*[7]) by Henri Béraud, the author of *Le Triomphe de l'obèse*[8]—who cannot forgive me my thinness. Very diverting.—All the same, Massis's articles were of a very different type; this fellow gives every impression of being an idiot.

2 May

This morning, in *L'Action Française*, I have the great surprise of seeing Léon Daudet take up my defense against Béraud—very nicely, I declare—and speak of me as a "terrible and penetrating" writer. . . .

On the other hand, a little paragraph in the next column informs me that for the last fortnight Béraud has been fulminating against *L'Action Française*.[9]

But already I wonder that they do not make it up at my expense.

Under their blows and by the violence of their attacks, I become aware of my *ruggedness*.

[7] *Les Nouvelles littéraires* (*The Literary News*) is a weekly founded in 1922.
[8] *The Triumph of Obesity*.
[9] And the N.R.F. has just published a book by Charles Maurras.
[A.]

17 May

I have taken M. to spend four days at Annecy-Talloires.

This morning, solitary walk, climbing up to the break in the rocks (on the right as one turns one's back on the lake) through which falls a very beautiful cascade.

A long, wide ribbon of azured, silvered coolness that loses itself suddenly in a black, bottomless gulf.

Water? Not exactly; but foam, or at least water so divided, so aerated, and become so light that it falls quite slowly. The rather vertiginous path I am following overhangs the gulf and is itself overhung by immense rocks that half close over, forming a vault, but a broken vault like that of Agrippa's Pantheon, which allows a glimpse of the sky.

Odd: I do not like mountain-climbing, but—explain it as you will—every path that climbs draws me, and I rise as naturally as water descends.

In the train, yesterday, heard this charming sentence: "At the price matches have reached today, it really counts when they don't burn."

18 May

Read in the train Jean Cocteau's *Le Grand Écart*,[10] with a great effort toward approbation and praise; during the first quarter of the book I managed, through goodwill, to deceive myself, amused as I was by the extreme ingenuity of the images and the burlesque brusqueness of certain presentations. But soon irritation dominates before so constant and so avaricious an anxiety to lose nothing, such a wary turning to account. In this book art is constantly degenerating into artifice. If Cocteau let himself go, he would write light comedies.

Mme Van Rysselberghe pointed out yesterday (and very judiciously) how the richness of vocabulary of contemporary writers discouraged the effort of syntax. The syntax remains banal and lifeless when the labor of depicting and animating is entrusted to the choice of words. But no one notices this, and when a Boulenger gets alarmed at the corruption of the language, it is always useless and inoffensive neologisms that he condemns, words borrowed

---

[10] *The Splits,* a novel of adolescent life in Paris. Published in the United States as *The Grand Écart* (1925).

from abroad—and very rarely errors in syntax. Thus I have never seen anyone pick up the *"pour ne pas que"* which is becoming commoner and beginning to be accepted to such a point that I give up deploring it.[11]

29 May

The triumph of objectivity is allowing the novelist to borrow the "I" of others. I have misled by succeeding too well in this; some have taken my books for a series of successive confessions. That abnegation, that poetic depersonalization that makes me feel the joys and sorrows of others more keenly than my own, no one has described so well as Keats (*Letters*).[12]

31 June [*sic*]

I am rereading *The Merchant of Venice* in English. It is one of Shakespeare's plays that I prefer. Something winged, fluttering, from one end to the other of its texture, makes one forget its flagrant shortcomings. No relation (or else one that is so subtle as to be imperceptible) between the story of the "bond" and that of Portia's three coffers; in the fourth act the complication of the rings is grafted on as an extra, without any relation to the rest.

[11] "In order not that . . ." as in *Pour ne pas qu'il le fasse* for *Pour qu'il ne le fasse pas.*

[12] Gide was doubtless thinking of the following passage from a letter to R. Woodhouse dated 27 October 1818: "As to the poetical Character itself (I mean that sort of which, if I am any thing, I am a Member; that sort distinguished from the wordsworthian or egotistical sublime; which is a thing per se and stands alone) it is not itself —it has no self—it is every thing and nothing— It has no character— it enjoys light and shade; it lives in gusto, be it foul or fair, high or low, rich or poor, mean or elevated— It has as much delight in conceiving an Iago as an Imogen. What shocks the virtuous philosopher, delights the chameleon Poet. It does no harm from its relish of the dark side of things any more than from its taste for the bright one; because they both end in speculation. A Poet is the most unpoetical of any thing in existence; because he has no Identity—he is continually in for and filling some other Body— The Sun, the Moon, the Sea and Men and Women who are creatures of impulse are poetical and have about them an unchangeable attribute—the poet has none; no identity —he is certainly the most unpoetical of all God's Creatures. If then he has no self, and if I am a Poet, where is the Wonder that I should say I would write no more? Might I not at that very instant have been cogitating on the Characters of Saturn and Ops? It is a wretched thing to confess; but is a very fact that not one word I ever utter can be taken for granted as an opinion growing out of my identical nature—how can it, when I have no nature?" (*The Letters of John Keats*, edited by M. B. Forman, I, 245.)

One almost gets to the point of forgetting Shylock; he is no longer involved and thus one accepts the frightful injustice that is smilingly imposed on him. If Shakespeare were animated by Christian sentiments, what a fine occasion to show them here! But no, Portia's clemency does not for a moment become that of the Gospels, and it is by no means in the name of Christ that the Duke sets up a doctrine of forgiveness in opposition to the Jew's legitimate and fierce intransigence. His daughter and his fortune are taken from him; never for an instant is it admitted that the feeling of his legitimate right is confused with his desire for revenge. He is ruined, deserted, flouted; and they want to force him to become a Christian!—to recognize the superiority of a religion that has tricked him! But there is no question of religion (and very fortunately) in this play; simply of an easy ethic that allows laughter, friendship, and love, and it is to sheer cupidty that these fine sentiments are opposed. One would like Antonio's generosity not to stop with Shylock, and, since everyone's desires are satisfied at the end, that the Jew should at least recover his money.

1 July

Nothing irritates certain Catholics more than to see us attain naturally to a renunciation that they, with all their religion, have such difficulty achieving. They almost accuse you of cheating; virtue must remain their monopoly, and whatever you achieve without saying your beads doesn't count. Likewise, they do not forgive us our happiness; it is impious; they alone have the right to be happy. It is, moreover, a right they rarely indulge.

Saint-Martin-Vésubie, 3 July

First evening of work (continuation of the *Journal d'Édouard*); obtained with great difficulty; demanded of myself. But, afterward, frightful night; choking and my body shaken with nervous trembling. I can really not get ahead until I have rested more. Incomprehensible torpor, at any hour of the day, makes sleep more attractive than reading, than work, than life. I sink into abysses of indolence, of thoughtlessness, of emptiness.

This morning, despite the heat, hoisted myself, first through meadows and thickets, then from rock to rock, and finally going up the bed of a mountain torrent, to a waterfall under which I rushed as soon as I could undress. The icy water, falling from a height, stung like hail.

My more or less happiness, today, depends solely on the more or less perfect functioning of my body. This torpor is often unbearable. But I believe that nothing has done more to make me understand people of modest intelligence than these depressions, these weaknesses. Valéry is missing something because he has never waked up almost idiotic on certain mornings.

18 July

Yesterday set out at six thirty; went back up the valley of the Boréon; went through the pass of Les Ladres; came back down to Saint-Martin by way of the valley of the Madone. Got back at three thirty.

Took off my sandals for the fun of walking barefoot across a stretch of snow; thought I could not endure the bite of the cold to the end. Showered under a waterfall. Lunched at the refuge of the Madone. Glad to feel still up to the mark.

Finished rereading for the third time from cover to cover the collection of Shakespeare's *Sonnets*. And I read each sonnet twice in succession. Many among them are exasperating; but there are many whose suavity appears only on rereading. To be sure, I admire them; but I also admire myself considerably for having got to the point of admiring them. (There are numerous ones that I have certainly reread twelve times.)

21 July

Spent last night at Nice; arrived at Hyères-Plage yesterday. Swim yesterday; swim today, after which an extraordinary well-being. I breathe better than at Saint-Martin; here I find the air lighter and the temperature less overwhelming. The sea is indescribably beautiful. And no flies!

At Nice spent the morning playing with a wonderful child of four, brown as a nut, laughing and saucy, and talking with his eighteen-year-old sister, as dark as he, gay and visibly naked under her loose black dress. She lets me take the little fellow to the Galeries Lafayette, where I buy him a pistol with darts. For love of them I should have been glad to stay in Nice and almost missed my train.

Finished *The Tempest*.

25 July

When desire subsides so does my whole being.

When beauty no longer excites in us any need of approach, of contact, and of embracing, the state of calm that you were fool enough to long for at a time when an excess of desires tormented you, that state no longer seems to you anything but apathy and deserves to be praised only because, perhaps, it makes the idea of death less atrocious, by taming you to it.

(A Henri Béraud would probably consider "tame to" as an error; I doubt that the expression is correct, but doubt that any other one is so good.)

21 November

Went to see Bernard Faÿ, who talks to me at length of his brother Emmanuel, M.'s friend. He has just died in New York. He did not kill himself, but it's the same thing: he let himself die; he made himself die. He said to his brother, one of the last days:

"One has no heart in playing, in a world in which everyone is cheating."

Mme Simon Bussy accuses me of cheating with the devil.

4 December

Interview with Rivière.

Points to bring up in mine, if it is ever to appear:

What Rivière means by "globalism";

Never paint from nature;

Make one's preparations from nature; but do not inform the reader of one's preparations;

Analysis must always precede synthesis; but from analysis to the work of art there is all the difference that there is between an anatomical drawing and a statue. All the preparatory work must be reabsorbed; it must become invisible although always there.

Just as "it is impossible to write well without skipping over intermediary ideas" (as Montesquieu said), there is no work of art without short cuts.

14 December

"How is Souday with you?"

"He has been successively cold and boiling, according to whether he thought me to be a royalist or a republican. Since he has grasped the fact that I am neither one nor the other, he has become tepid; he grants me a certain value as an artist, but 'as a thinker' considers that I am worth nothing."

21 December

Jacques Maritain came then Friday morning, 14 December, to the Villa on the stroke of ten, as it had been agreed. I had prepared a few sentences, but none of them was of any use, for I understood at once that I did not have to play a character in his presence, but on the contrary simply reveal myself, and that this was my best defense. His curved, bent way of carrying his head and his whole body displeased me, and a certain clerical unction in his voice and gesture; but I overlooked this, and pretense seemed unworthy of us two. He tackled the question at once and declared straight out the purpose of his visit, which I knew and which was to beg me to suspend the publication of a certain book that François Le Grix had described to him as imminent and of which he begged me to recognize with him the danger.

I told him that I had no intention of defending myself but that he must be aware that everything he could think of saying to me about this book I had already said to myself, and that a project that resists the trial of the war, of personal losses, and of all the meditations that ensue runs the risk of being too deeply anchored in the heart and mind for an intervention like his to hope to change it. I protested that, moreover, there had been no obstinacy in my case and that even, after a first reading to a friend (Marcel Drouin) ten years ago, of the first two chapters of this book, on the advice of that friend I had interrupted my work; that I had almost given it up despite the profound upset that renunciation caused me; that if, on the other hand, at the end of the second year of the war, I had picked it up again and completed it, this was because it appeared clear to me that this book had to be written, that I was uniquely qualified to write it, and that I could not without a sort of bankruptcy release myself from what I considered my duty.

We both spoke with extreme slowness, anxious to say nothing that might misconstrue or go beyond our thought. He transmitted to me Henri Massis's fear of having, by the provocation of his articles, hastened that publication. I begged him to leave Massis all his fears and regrets and remorse and spoke of the wonderful letter Claudel had written me, about my *Dostoïevsky* likewise, in which I felt at least the impulse of a truly Christian thought, which I in nowise recognized in Massis's articles. Maritain then told me that Massis might have made a mistake, and as I pointed out to him certain points in those articles that obviously revealed a desire to falsify my thought: "He may not have understood it properly. . . ." I protested that he was too intelligent on other points not to force me to consider that falsification as conscious and voluntary.

"I have," I told him, "a horror of falsehood. That is perhaps just where my Protestantism lurks. Catholics cannot understand that. I have known many; and indeed, with the single exception of Jean Schlumberger, I have nothing but Catholics as friends. Catholics do not like truth."

"Catholicism teaches the love of truth," he said.

"No, do not protest, Maritain. I have too often seen, and with too many examples, what compromises were possible. And even (for I have that intellectual failing, which Ghéon used to reproach me with, of too easily putting words into my adversary's mouth and of inventing arguments for him) I see what you might reply to me: that the Protestant often confuses truth with God, that he adores Truth, not understanding that Truth is but one of the attributes of God. . . ."

"But don't you think that that truth, which your book claims to make manifest, can be dangerous? . . ."

"If I thought so, I should not have written the book, or at least I should not publish it. However dangerous that truth may be, I hold that the falsehood that covers it is even more dangerous."

"And don't you think that it is dangerous for you to say it?"

"That is a question that I refuse to ask myself."

He then spoke to me of the salvation of my soul and told me that he often prayed for it, as did several of his friends who were convinced like him that I was marked out by God for higher ends, which I sought in vain to evade.

"I am inclined to believe," I said to him smiling, "that you are much more concerned with the salvation of my soul than I am myself."

We spoke at length, on this subject and likewise of the Greek equilibrium and the Christian lack of equilibrium. As the hour was advancing, he made as if to rise.

"I should not like to leave you before— Will you allow me to ask you something?"

"Go ahead and ask," I said with a gesture indicating that I did not guarantee a reply.

"I should like to ask you a promise."

"? . . ."

"Promise me that when I have gone you will put yourself in a state of prayer and ask Christ to let you know, directly, whether you are right or wrong to publish this book. Can you promise me that?"

I looked at him at length and said:

"No."

There was a long silence. I continued:

"Understand me, Maritain. I have lived too long and too intimately, and you know it, in the thought of Christ to agree to call on him today as one rings someone up on the telephone. Indeed, it would seem to me unworthy to call on him without having first put myself in a state to hear him. Oh! I do not doubt that I can succeed in doing so. I know, moreover, just how that state is achieved; I have the recipe. But on my part there would be, today, a certain element of pretense; I am loath to do it. And moreover, may I tell you this: never, even at the time of my greatest fervor, even at the time when I used to pray —I do not say only every day, but at every hour, at every moment of the day—never was my prayer anything but an act of adoration, a thanksgiving, a surrender. Perhaps I am very Protestant in this. . . . And yet no, I do not know why I say this. It is, on the contrary, very Protestant to ask advice about anything. There are some who

would consult Christ to know how to lace a pair of shoes;
I cannot; I will not. It has always seemed to me unworthy
to ask anything of God. I have always accepted everything from him, with gratitude. No, do not ask that of
me."

"I shall then be obliged to leave you disappointed?" he
asked sadly as he held out his hand.

"*At first,*" I replied, putting into these words all the
hidden meaning that I could, without moreover knowing
just what meaning. And thereupon we separated.

I am writing this immediately upon my return to Cuverville and while my memory of it is still fresh.

DETACHED PAGES

(Recovered Pages)

I

"Have you noted," said Édouard, "the sort of moral
anchylosis produced in M. by his assumption of never
being in the wrong? It is an assumption that many people
make; I made it too in my youth, and if now I am so
sensitive to it in others, it is because I myself had the
greatest difficulty getting rid of it. My parents had accustomed me to act, not according to my inner urge, but
according to an ethical rule outside of me, which they
considered applicable to all men, so that, in the same
circumstances, any creature whatever, no matter how
different from me, would have seen the same moral postulate rise up before him, which he could not escape without flinching and without incurring the blame of others
(which would still be bearable), but also some self-repro-
bation or other that my upbringing in fact had striven to
make unbearable to me. Not to have acted, in whatever
combination of circumstances, precisely as I was expected
to act seemed to me abominable to such a point that all
inner peace was immediately compromised, that peace
without which I believed that I could not live—while on
the contrary . . . but at that time could I admit, could
I suspect even, that whatever is newest in each creature

and most peculiar to him is perhaps not the most detestable?

A great error is revealed here: minds accustomed to live according to the rule cease to recognize, as soon as someone escapes the rule, any other domination than that of one's own sweet will; a person seems to them a slave as soon as he is a slave to his passions, and, as he escapes the passions when he lives according to duty, he ceases to seem to them a slave and it seems to them that he is free the moment the slavery to which he submits is a moral, banal, and commonly accepted slavery. They cry out: "O Lord, deliver us from ourselves," and their way of delivering themselves is to bend their thought, their will, their whole being until they desire nothing to which their moral being cannot give complete assent, so that they have an illusion of acting freely while already their choice has ceased to be free, and that constraint to which they submit and the very difficulty they experience in submitting to it are at once a pledge of the error into which their nature hurled them and of the truth of that rule which forces and counterfeits their most sincere impulses.

But the rigorous puritan upbringing by which my parents had fashioned my childhood, but the habit and need of a discipline, allowed me to glimpse, once escaped from the common rule, something quite different from a mere surrender; and this allowed me to shrug my shoulders when I heard myself accused of listening henceforth only to the invitation of pleasure. To rediscover, underneath the factitious creature, the unspoiled self was not, or so it seemed to me, so easy a task; and that new rule of life which was becoming mine: to act according to the greatest sincerity, implied a resolution, a perspicacity, an effort that strained my whole will, so that I never seemed more moral to myself than at the time when I had decided to cease being moral; I mean: to be moral henceforth only in my own way. And I came to understand that perfect sincerity, the kind that, in my opinion, leads to the most valor and greatest dignity, sincerity not only of the act itself but of the motive, can be achieved only through the most constant, but also the least bitter, effort, only with the clearest vision (I mean: the least suspect of self-satisfaction), and the most irony.

It soon became apparent to me that I had gained almost nothing; that I was still acting only according to the best motive, so long as I made my acts measure up to that approbation which implied, before acting, a sort of deliberation and weighing in imagination, whence the action was delayed and blocked. The promptest, the most sudden action henceforth seemed to me preferable; it seemed to me that my act was all the more sincere since I had swept away before it all those preambles by which I used to attempt to justify it to myself. Henceforth, acting in any way whatever and not giving myself time to reflect, my least acts seemed to me more significant since they were no longer reasoned out. At the same time I delivered myself from anxiety, perplexity, and remorse. And perhaps that intimate gymnastic to which I had first submitted had not been altogether useless and helped me to achieve that state of joy which made me recognize my act to be good solely from the pleasure I took in doing it.

The Greeks, who, not only in the multitude of their statues but also in themselves, left us such a beautiful image of humanity, recognized as many gods as there are instincts, and the problem for them was to keep the inner Olympus in equilibrium, not to subjugate and subdue any of the gods.

It is not so much by his acts that a lover of humanity makes himself useful as by his example. I mean: by his very figure, by the image he offers and leaves behind, and by the happiness and serenity it radiates.[13]

II

T. explains:

. . . There is a certain indulgence by which every sentiment we experience is exaggerated; and often one does not suffer so much as one imagines oneself to be suffering.

I have never been able to renounce anything; and protecting in me both the best and the worst, I have lived as

[13] "A cheerful intelligent face is the end of culture, and success enough," says Emerson. "For it indicates the purpose of nature and wisdom attained." [A.] This passage, which Gide quotes in French, is found in Emerson's Conduct of Life (1860) in the chapter entitled "Culture."

a man torn asunder. But how can it be explained that this cohabitation of extremes in me led not so much to restlessness and suffering as to a pathetic intensification of the sentiment of existence, of life? The most opposite tendencies never succeeded in making me a tormented person; but rather perplexed—for torment accompanies a state one longs to get away from, and I did not long to escape what brought into operation all the potentialities of my being. That *state of dialogue* which, for so many others, is almost intolerable became necessary to me. This is also because, for those others, it can only be injurious to action, whereas for me, far from leading to sterility, it invited me to the work of art and immediately preceded creation, led to equilibrium and harmony.

It must, however, be recognized that, for a number of souls, which I consider among the best tempered, happiness lies not in comfort and quietude, but in ardor. A sort of magnificent using up is all the more desirable to them since they are constantly being renewed by it and do not so much suffer from the wearing away as they rejoice in their perpetual re-creation. As for me, I can tell you that I have never so keenly felt myself growing old as in that very quietude to which your rule of conduct invites one, but which you are less likely to achieve the more earnestly and nostalgically you strive to attain it. Your belief in the survival of souls is nourished by the need of that quietude and your *lack of hope* of enjoying it in life.

Shall I tell you what keeps me from believing in eternal life? It is that almost perfect satisfaction I enjoy in effort itself and in the immediate realization of happiness and harmony.

III

I was like the prodigal son who goes squandering his possessions. And that imponderable treasure which the slow virtue of my fathers, from generation to generation, had patiently accumulated on my head, no, I was not unaware of its value; but the unknown I could hope for by renouncing it seemed to me even more precious. The words of Christ rose up luminously before me like the column of fire that guided the chosen people in the night, and in the heavy darkness in which I decided to adventure I kept repeating to myself: "Sell all your goods and give them to the poor." My heart was filled with apprehension and joy, or more exactly: with the apprehension of my joy. For, thought I, it is not a question of interpreting the divine words to attain complete happiness; it is a question of accepting them without reservations, of understanding them "in spirit and in truth"; and then at last, and then above all, to put them into practice, for, as it is said in the Gospel, "every one that heareth these sayings of mine and doeth them not . . ."

I began then to seek out which, among the thoughts, opinions, and tendencies of my soul and mind that were most familiar to me, were the ones that I most certainly derived from my ancestors, from my upbringing and puritan formation, which at first had constituted my strength, from that sort of moral atmosphere in which I was beginning to stifle. And doubtless, pushing that relinquishment to the extreme, to the absurd, I should have ended up in complete impoverishment—for "what have you that you have not received?"—but yet it was complete impoverishment that I coveted as the truest possession. Resolved to give up in this manner every personal possession and convinced that I could not hope to dispose of everything except on condition that I possessed nothing in my own right, I repudiated every personal opinion, every habit, every modesty, my very virtue, as one throws off a tunic in order to offer an unveiled body to the contact of the wave, to the passing winds, to the sun. Strengthened by these abnegations, I soon felt my soul only as a loving will (yes, this is the way I defined it to myself), palpitating, open to all comers, like unto everything, impersonal, a naïve confusion of appetites, greeds, desires. And if perhaps I had been frightened by the disorder into which their anarchy led me, was I not able to reassure myself at once by recalling these words of Christ: "Why should you be troubled?" I surrendered then to this provisional disorder, trusting in a more sincere and natural order that would organize itself, I thought, and believing moreover that the disorder itself was less dangerous for my soul than an arbitrary and necessarily artificial order, since I had not invented it. Divine ray! I exclaimed, isn't what is opposed to you above all that false wisdom of men, made up of fear, lack of confidence, and presumption? I resign everything to you. I surrender myself. Drive out all shadow from me. Inspire me.

Considering later on that nothing separates one more from God than pride and that nothing made me prouder than my virtue, I began to detest that very virtue and everything on which I could pride myself, everything that allowed me to say: I am not like you, common run of men! And I am well aware that this excess of renunciation, this repudiation of virtue through the love of virtue itself, would appear, as merely an abominable sophistry to the pious soul who reads me. Paradox or sophistry that thenceforth bent my life, whether or not the devil prompted it I shall examine later on. It is enough for me to say for the moment that I advanced boldly on this path that was so new. What am I saying: path? Every step I took forward was a venture into the unknown.

1924

4 *January*

I am reading for the first time in English Stevenson's *Dr. Jekyll and Mr. Hyde*—with an admiration, alas, that is somewhat diminished. Too ingenious, too organized; it lacks grandeur. Wonderful subject; but I wonder if it is not a mistake to have made Jekyll "at peace" precisely after having got rid of Hyde—"his face seemed to open and brighten."—*It ought to be just the contrary.*

It is thanks to Hyde that Jekyll should be able to find tranquillity.

5 *January*

Finished the Stevenson. Jekyll's confession is wonderful and what I wrote yesterday is absurd.

If I do not tear out this page, it is for the mortification of rereading it some day.

I have gone back to William James's *Psychology*, but drop it after reading two chapters (among which the one on instinct) and assuring myself of its mediocrity.

14 *February*

Because I publish little, it is thought that I write slowly. The truth is that I go for rather long periods without writing. As soon as my brain is in good form, my pen or pencil cannot go fast enough. I wrote the whole last act of *Saül* in one day (at Arco). I am apt to write in the train, in the métro, on a bench along the quay or along the boulevards, on road embankments, and those are my best pages, the most truly inspired. One sentence follows another, is born of the other, and I feel as I see it being born and growing within me an almost physical rapture. I believe that this artesian welling up is the result of a long subconscious preparation. I am apt subsequently to make a few changes in this first sketch, but very few.

Only the work of joining is often very painful and demands a great intellectual concentration.

It happens that my rough drafts have many sentences

written between the lines, but this comes from the profusion of thoughts and the difficulty of putting them in order and fitting them together.

30 May

Good work yesterday evening, after a rather empty afternoon at Longchamp, then at the fair on the quay between the Invalides and the garden of the Tour Eiffel. I believe I have satisfactorily sketched out the important visit to La Pérouse after his unsuccessful suicide.[1] Unfortunately I left in Cuverville (?) some papers I shall need to finish it.

I am rereading Goethe's *Elegies,* and here is something that touches me more than the Béraud attacks: I discover that I have until now been guilty of a misinterpretation in the first line of the second Elegy:

Nun bin ich endlich geborgen.

Until now I have been reading *geboren* and once translated it (in my lecture on Influence): "at last I am *born,*" instead of "I am safe, escaped, under shelter.". . .

31 May

This notebook will not be the confidant of my sorrows. My whole being calls out all its strength and stiffens under pain. I even find a sort of salutary exaltation in it, and my horror of those adulterated pleasures that are taking M. away from me leads me back to work.

3 June

I intend to give to those who read me strength, joy, courage, defiance, and perspicacity—but I am above all careful not to give them directions, judging that they can and must find them only by themselves (I was about to say: "in themselves"). Develop at one and the same time the critical faculty and energy, those two contraries. Generally we find among intelligent people nothing but the stiff-jointed, and among men of action nothing but fools.

19 June

Off for Cuverville. In the train I read various articles in the special number of the *Disque vert* devoted to Freud.

---

[1] In *Les Faux-Monnayeurs (The Counterfeiters).*

Ah, how embarrassing Freud is! And how easily it seems to me we should have discovered his America without him! It seems to me that the thing I should be most grateful to him for is having accustomed readers to hearing certain subjects treated without having to protest or blush. What he especially brings us is daring; or, more exactly, he spares us a certain false and embarrassing modesty.

But how many absurd things in that imbecile of genius!

If it were as thwarted as the sexual appetite, mere hunger would be the great provider of Freudianism (just as we see thirst prompt the dreams of those without water in the desert). In other words: certain forces owe their violence to the lack of an outlet. It is true that the sexual desire, when not directly satisfied, is liable to multiple hypocrisies—I mean: of assuming the most varied forms— as the other hunger can never do. The point on which my assiduous investigations (if I were a doctor) would bear is this: what happens when, for social, moral, etc. reasons, the sexual function is forced, in order to find satisfaction, to leave the object of its desire; when the satisfaction of the flesh involves no assent, no participation of the rest of the person, when it is thus divided with a part of itself remaining behind? . . . What remains subsequently from that division? What traces? What secret forms of revenge are then prepared by that part which had no share in the feast?

21 June

On the advice of Bernard Faÿ, I am reading *Les Pléiades* by Gobineau. Impossible indeed not to take into account the tales of the three Calenders when judging *Le Bal du Comte d'Orgel.*[2] Gobineau's influence on Radiguet is undeniable (*Les Pléiades* was his favorite reading-matter), and it can even be said that the passage from one book to the other is almost imperceptible. But the publisher's ballyhoo will result in Radiguet's being read much more than Gobineau has ever been read, so that this imitation will go unnoticed.

[2] *The Pleiades* by Gobineau appeared in 1874; *The Count's Ball*, a novel by Raymond Radiguet, appeared in 1924 after the death of its author at the age of twenty.

24 June

It is not enough for the Dadas that I have written a book they like (*Les Caves*).[3] In addition, I should not write, or have written, anything but that. They do not rise to the point of realizing that it might be amusing for us too to displease, and to displease just such as they! Each of my books turns against those who were enthusiastic for the preceding one. That will teach them to applaud me only for the right reason and to take each of my books simply for what it is: a work of art.

26 July

What proves that his appetite was not very lively is that he claimed to prefer "nothing" as soon as he couldn't get the exquisite. Montaigne blames this concern for choice in the young; he prefers to see them a bit greedy rather than epicures.

27 July

Whoever acts like everyone else necessarily gets annoyed with whoever does not act like him.

I read in the Introduction to *The Scarlet Letter* by Hawthorne these two sentences to be put into the Barrès file: "Human nature will not flourish, any more than a potato, if it be planted and replanted, for too long a series of generations in the same worn-out soil. My children have had other birthplaces, and, so far as their fortunes may be within my control, shall strike their roots into unaccustomed earth."

Paris, 17 August

My fatigue can be recognized by these musical obsessions which, on certain days, never leave me for hours on end and wind their way through every thought I manage to have.

Despite my resistance, I have to recognize and name each note; in spite of myself I pursue the motif from tone to tone until my exasperation is pluperfect.

I left Cuverville early this morning. Marcel had not understood that I was leaving today. Yesterday evening he seemed very sorry about it and to have put off from

[3] The Dada movement, founded by Tristan Tzara in 1916, was a negative revision of literary values and a challenge to rational thought. After 1924 it was absorbed in Surrealism.

day to day the conversation he had promised me about my book. "I'll talk to you about it when I have reread it," he had told me.

I *knew* that he would get to it too late, as he always does.

But I doubt if, after a rereading, he would have talked any better about it than he did when caught short, somewhat embarrassed to have let himself be taken by surprise.

His remarks are most intelligent (as always) and there is not one of them that I am not anxious to take into account. I shall note them down in the notebook I have devoted to the novel.

He always takes the same care not to pay me any compliment; but now at least I know enough not to let myself become gloomy over it. There was a time when his silence in regard to praise flattened me out. I told him so and I am grateful to him for not changing his manner on that account. Moreover, he could not.

I do not know anyone more intelligent than Marcel Drouin save Valéry . . . and even then.

His weaknesses are all due to his temperament, and almost of a physiological sort. They are none the less intolerable to anyone who knows him well.

"To be right" . . . Who still wants to be? . . . A few fools.

Chartres, 6 September

Unadulterated awe; and not only in front of the cathedral. This warm morning of soft azure I wander in the old quarter of the lower town, on the edge of a charming, grassy, shady canal and of a stream of which I don't know the name. A bit worried at the thought that perhaps Roger Fry, who is with me, is waiting for me in the hall of the hotel. But *there is a spell upon me*,[4] and I need solitude. I persuade myself that he does too. How young I should still feel if I did not know that I am not!

Some people work over themselves to obtain the unity of their person. I let myself go.

[4] The words in italics appear in English.

INDEX

ANDRÉ GIDE *was born in Paris in 1869 and died there in 1951. He was awarded the Nobel Prize for Literature in 1947. Besides his* Journals *(1939, 1944, 1950), his major works include* The Immoralist *(1902),* The Counterfeiters *(1926),* Strait Is the Gate *(1909), and* Lafcadio's Adventures *(1914). He also wrote plays, essays, short stories, and books of travel.*